Retail Accounting and Financial Control

Retail Accounting and Financial Control

Fifth Edition

Robert M. Zimmerman
Robert M. Kaufman
Gregory S. Finerty
James O. Egan

WILEY

John Wiley & Sons

New York • Chichester • Brisbane • Toronto • Singapore

Library of Congress Cataloging in Publication Data:

Retail accounting and financial control.—5th ed. / Robert M.
    Zimmerman . . . [et al]
        p. cm.
    Rev. ed. of: Retail accounting and financial control / Louis C.
    Moscarello, Francis C. Grau, Roy C. Chapman.
    Includes bibliographical references.
    ISBN 0-471-63218-X
    1. Retail trade—Accounting.   2. Retail trade—Management.
    3. Retail trade—Finance.   I. Zimmerman, Robert M.   II. Moscarello,
    Louis C.   Retail accounting and financial control.
    HF5635.B417   1989
    657'.839—dc20   89-22664
                                                                CIP

Printed in the United States of America

10 9 8 7 6

About the Authors

Robert M. Zimmerman is a partner in Coopers & Lybrand, National Director of Retail Consulting and Chairman of the firm's National Retail Industry Program. He has over 20 years' experience as a retail executive and consultant.

Mr. Zimmerman has managed consulting engagements at Coopers & Lybrand that include: strategic planning, designing merchandise and financial information systems, reviewing organization structure, and evaluating the operating effectiveness of a wide variety of business functions. He is the co-author of the National Retail Merchants Association *Directory of Retail Software.*

For seven years prior to joining Coopers & Lybrand, he was president of his own consulting and systems development firm that specialized in retailing. Prior to that, Mr. Zimmerman was with Associated Merchandising Corporation. He began his retail career at Bloomingdale's Division of Federated Department Stores.

Robert Zimmerman is a Certified Public Accountant and has earned B.S. and M.B.A. degrees at New York University.

Robert M. Kaufman is a partner in the Boston office of Coopers & Lybrand. He serves as chairman of the firm's Northeast Group of Offices Retail Industry Group and associate chairman of the National Retail Industry Group. Mr. Kaufman has been an active member and speaker on behalf of the Financial Executives Committee of the National Retail Federation, including serving as the chairman of that group's FASB subcommittee for two years. He has extensive auditing and consulting service with virtually all segments of the retail industry, as well as with retail mergers, acquisitions, and divestitures of all sizes. Robert Kaufman received his M.B.A. from Cornell University and his B.A. from Colby College.

Gregory S. Finerty, Certified Public Accountant, is partner-in-charge of Coopers & Lybrand's Pittsburgh office retail practice. He has over 20 years of diversified experience in the retail industry and is a key member of the firm's National Retail Advisory Committee. Mr. Finerty is a graduate of the University of Steubenville. He is a member of the *International Mass Retailers Association* and frequently authors articles on various aspects of the retail industry for local and regional publications.

James O. Egan is a partner in Coopers & Lybrand's New York office, serving as a business advisor to numerous retail clients in such areas as business investigations, cost reduction, and cash generation programs as well as operational and financial audits. He has consulted extensively with executives of different types of retail companies in a variety of formats and sizes on financial and business planning, profit improvement, and mergers and acquisitions.

Mr. Egan has given talks and published several articles on current business issues impacting retailers. He was a member of the committee that prepared the *Retail Accounting Manual—Book Two* published by the National Retail Federation. Mr. Egan has also co-authored and instructed training courses on retail accounting methods and procedures and related management controls over the merchandising, store operations, distribution, and inventory control functions.

Mr. Egan is a member of the American Institute of Certified Public Accountants, New York State Society of Certified Public Accountants, National Retail Federation, and New York Metropolitan Retail Financial Executives Association.

Acknowledgments

This is the fifth edition of a book that was originally issued under the authorship of Herman F. Bell, in 1936, with subsequent revisions in 1956 and 1961. The fourth edition was substantially rewritten by Louis C. Moscarello, Francis C. Grau, and Roy C. Chapman and was published in 1976.

This edition, while changed in content and structure, relies on principles described by Mr. Moscarello to whom we are indebted. We are also especially grateful to the following Coopers & Lybrand partners and professionals for their contribution of important chapters: Clark L. Bernard, Joel B. Brandt, Charles W. Breckenridge, Joyce D. Brown, Stephen H. Epstein, Wendy L. Foss, John F. Gabranski, William W. Greer, Edwin Horne, Kathy McKeon, Michael M. Morrow, Thomas F. Reeve, Jr., Cynthia B. Satterwhite, Robert J. Spear, and William Stephan.

Special recognition and thanks needs to be given to Sharon A. Lockhart who coordinated and shepherded this book from initial concept through to its completion.

Contents

Introduction

This fifth edition of *Retail Accounting and Financial Control* has been designed for business people in the accounting and operating divisions of retail companies and their outside accounting professionals. It assumes that the reader has some understanding of accounting and of retail processes.

The business operations discussed in Part One are primarily those of Specialty, Discount, and Department Stores. Other retail formats are considered where it is necessary to describe different techniques or contrast alternative approaches.

CONCEPT OF THE BOOK

This book covers accounting, financial, operating, and control issues from both a theoretical and practical perspective. Although most business functions are interconnected, it is necessary to separate them for presentation purposes. The structure of this book is as follows:

- *Merchandise Management* follows the flow of merchandise from planning, to receipt, through to disposition and identifies the information necessary to manage these processes.

- *Operations* describes transaction processing and the control objectives for merchandise, cash receipts and disbursements, and information.

- *Accounting* presents unique considerations affecting retailing including the Retail Inventory Method (RIM), other valuation techniques and Retail LIFO.

- *Financing* covers activities typically part of the Treasury function for retailers.

- *Financial Analysis* describes how retail financial information is presented and how key performance indicators should be analyzed.

Specific terms and references are defined within the text; however, Chapter 7 also lists and defines terminology specific to the retail area.

Although there are no special regulatory or licensing requirements in this industry, nor is the activity performed by retailers complicated or arcane, each segment of retailing is unique (e.g., high fashion boutiques versus fast food restaurants). In addition, each company within a retail segment must establish a unique identity with its customers. This identity is generally based on some combination of location, assortment, service, and price. This customization usually has a direct bearing on business operations and, therefore, on accounting and financial controls.

Retailing, as an industry, has many characteristics that differentiate it from other forms of commercial activity. Three of these characteristics are of overriding importance:

1. High volume of low-value transactions.

2. Broad exposure of merchandise to theft or damage by employees, customers, and suppliers.

3. Constantly changing product offerings.

These conditions, in turn, impact other aspects of the business such as personnel, space utilization, pricing, organization structure, and technology. Many of these issues will be considered in Part Two of this book.

TYPES OF RETAIL FORMATS

Retailing is an intensely competitive industry that constantly changes the products being offered to its customers and the ways in which these products are offered. One-stop shopping competes with niche specialization; full service competes with low price. Traditional forms of organization are consolidating while new concepts keep bubbling up and succeeding.

Retail formats can be generally defined according to three primary dimensions: structure, merchandise, and size. Structure and merchandise may be used concurrently or separately. For example, retail formats can be broadly differentiated as Food and General Merchandise; however, in-store retailing is different from shop-at-home businesses, regardless of merchandise. The third dimension, size, is important according to degree. That is, once a retailer grows beyond a certain size, in one location or many, business operations and controls will change. This cannot be calculated by formula, but should be recognized in practice.

The following categorization establishes an order; however, as just discussed, reality may not be as straightforward. Retailers are constantly evolving in response to the needs of customers. New combinations of products and display are critical to survival.

I. Food
    A. Grocery
        1. Supermarket
        2. Convenience Stores
    B. Dining
        1. Fast Food
        2. Fine Dining
        3. Food Service

II. General Merchandise
    A. Department, Discount, and Chain Stores
    B. Specialty Stores
        1. Apparel
        2. Hard Goods

The classification of any specific retailer into one of these categories may be difficult, and more importantly, of little value, for example:

- Very few department stores carry the full line of merchandise that was originally carried while many specialty stores are truly multidepartmental.

- Everyday low pricing or heavy promotional activity exists across all retail formats.

- Area registers can be found in discounters and front-end checkout lanes can be found in nondiscounters.

- Chain store distribution techniques are being used by most multilocation retailers.

What is important is the implementation of systems and controls that provide accurate, timely information at the lowest possible cost. Historically, it was not economically feasible for retailers to manage or control at the item level. Because of their high volume of low-value transactions it was sufficient to develop groupings of merchandise (departments, class, subclass) and manage them through average gross margin and open-to-buy calculations. Item level activity is important since it is at this level that stores and their customers actually buy, but it was not usually the level of control. Advances in automation are changing this scenario.

Technological changes in retailing have been pursued in order to improve merchandising and operations (the right reasons). The development of SKU-level (Stock Keeping Unit) databases that can accurately reflect order, receipt, sales, and on-hand information, in units and dollars, is changing merchandising and operating techniques. These developments, discussed in Part Three, are just beginning to be felt in the accounting areas, but it is reasonable to expect that the Retail Inventory Method may be replaced or augmented with more specific, cost accounting-like techniques such as Direct Product Profitability (DPP). Electronic Data Interchange (EDI) is resulting in imaginative new linkages between businesses up and down the distribution and financial chain. Accounting and control systems must keep pace with these changes. It is unlikely that new developments will render existing accounting concepts obsolete, but it is certain that accounting techniques must evolve in order to take advantage of new opportunities and to satisfy new requirements.

PART ONE

Merchandise Management and Control

Prior editions of this book did not deal with merchandise information issues. There are still significant differences in levels of detail, accuracy, and control between merchandise and financial information; however, it is now recognized that one set of books, for merchants and accountants, is achievable and desirable.

CHAPTER ONE

Merchandise Planning

All business activities start with planning. The planning differs only in the formality of the effort and the level of detail. Merchandise planning is a retail function in which one encounters a wide spectrum of techniques. The reasons for the variation found revolve around two major issues: (1) Information is not available and/or (2) no value is perceived from the exercise.

Automation has been the key to clarifying the first issue. Information is now available at whatever level of detail is needed. Indeed, the problem in many organizations is how to make effective use of all the detail that is available.

Indirectly, automation has helped resolve the second issue as well. With full recognition of the uncertainty of customer behavior, complexities of competition, and intuitive aspects of merchandise decision making, companies who have better information tend to make better decisions. Furthermore, companies with superior plans can better react to changes that occur during the year.

As these factors are recognized and acted upon, retailers develop comprehensive merchandise information systems, integrated with financial information systems, and both based on a hierarchy of plans that are in conformity.

PURPOSE OF THE PLANS

Merchandise planning is a multidimensional process encompassing:

- Measurement—units or dollars.
- Merchandise—division, department, class, item, stock-keeping-unit (SKU).
- Location—company, region, store, warehouse.
- Time—year, season, month, week.
- Elements—sales, inventory, gross margin, and so on.

The following chapter will describe in detail the operation of the various planning processes. However, in general all plans share certain purposes:

- To help ensure that all merchandise activities are consistent with the company's objectives.
- To establish a basis for measuring subsequent performance and for modifying subsequent decisions.
- To ensure that corporate resources are adequate to handle merchandise requirements, and/or that merchandise plans do not exceed corporate capabilities.

"The right merchandise, in the right place, at the right time" is a retailing cliche. However, the underlying reason for merchandise planning, and for the increasing emphasis on automated planning systems, is to make that cliche a reality. Of course, there is one additional consideration, not included in the cliche, but of critical importance to every retailer: at a profit. Planning systems provide management the ability to establish guidelines at whatever level of detail is appropriate for a particular business to help achieve that profit. For example, planning gross margin is generally not sufficient; it is preferable to plan the elements of gross margin from initial markon through to maintained margin. Conversely, planning sales by class and location may be more detail than is necessary.

Automation has reduced the arguments regarding the benefits of planning by making needed information available at an affordable price and without great clerical effort. New information systems techniques permit sophisticated modeling, simulation, and the linkage of the initial plans with all subsequent merchandising activities. Merchandising planning is a base for effective business management and its importance will grow as the retailer's information systems capability develops. This is not to say, however, that lack of sophistication is justification for not planning. This approach suggests that other great cliche: If you don't know where you're going, any road will take you. The traditional retail approach to nonplanning is to measure this year's results against last year's. While this is better than no comparison, the underlying assumption is that there have been no changes in merchandise assortment, price points, competition, customers, financial requirements, and so on. Even a high level plan will provide better guidance in many areas.

Special Situations

Theoretically, the merchandise plan should reflect the corporate plan. This is not always so. Not all retailers choose to maintain a "single set of books." Some retailers choose to maintain two levels of plans—a more conservative financial plan and a merchant's plan.

Differences in time measurement may lead to two sets of books. If the merchant's seasons and months do not conform to the financial year, two sets of plans may be kept. Despite timing differences, these plans may be made to "match," but not all retailers choose to do this.

THE PLANNING PROCESS

Corporate

In a retail company, the planning process usually begins several months before the beginning of the new year, with senior management's establishment of annual corporate objectives. These objectives include sales, margins, overall expense levels, profit, and possibly an inventory turnover goal.

Many factors are considered during the creation of the annual sales budget. The overall state of the economy and competition in the marketplace are two determinants. Another key factor is the number of new stores that the retailer plans to add in the upcoming year. It is generally agreed in retailing that mature stores perform differently than newer stores. For this reason, the sales plan is created in two pieces. The "comparable store" or "comp" sales plan for stores that have been open more than a year is usually expressed as a percentage trend over last year's sales. The "non-comp" plan, for stores that have been open less than one year, and new stores that will be opened, is usually created on a store-by-store basis (a store not yet opened is generally modeled on an existing store that is considered similar). The two plans are then added together to form the corporate sales plan.

Gross margin, expense, and profit plans are based upon last year's history and tempered with senior management's knowledge of factors that will cause major changes in these numbers—a major cost cutting campaign, for example, or movement into a private label program that would increase gross margin.

The corporate plan thus established becomes the framework for three additional planning processes. These take place in different departments of the company and are expressed at a more detailed level than the corporate plan:

- Financial plan
- Merchandise plan
- Store plan

Although they will be presented in a sequence, the planning processes themselves are not necessarily sequential, and may take place concurrently. Moreover, results from any of these plans may be used to re-evaluate and revise the corporate plan (Exhibit 1.1).

Financial

The corporate plan for sales, margins, expenses, and the resultant profit or loss must be translated into pro forma financial statements and detailed expense budgets for each company cost center.

General ledger expense categories are used as the basis of expense planning. Typically, expenses are classified as overhead—pertaining to the central office—or direct—pertaining to the stores. Expenses are generally controlled as a percent of sales, and monthly variances correspond to variances in the sales plan.

Merchandise

Buyers support the company's overall corporate objectives through the creation of a merchandise plan. The planning process imposes a structure over the "creative" art of buying and requires merchants to calculate and quantify how they will achieve the corporate goals for sales and margins; while keeping the inventory investment in line with the inventory turnover goal. The latter point is critical: the merchandise plan is the company's primary tool for controlling the level of inventory—a retailer's major investment.

The merchandise plan is created at a level that conforms to the way that merchandise is organized. Typically, the plan is at class or department level, in dollars, total company rather than by store. Occasionally the merchandise plan is created from the top down—subdividing the corporate sales plan by department and class. More typically, it is built from the bottom up and results are compared with the corporate plan.

EXHIBIT 1.1 Corporate Plan

COOPBRAND CLOTHING STORES

CORPORATE PLAN ($000)

CREATE DATE: 09/15/ XX

ITEM	SPRING			FALL			TOTAL		
	NEXT YEAR	THIS YEAR	% DIFF	NEXT YEAR	THIS YEAR	% DIFF	NEXT YEAR	THIS YEAR	% DIFF
SALES	$18,360	$17,000	8.0	$21,640	$20,000	8.2	$40,000	$37,000	8.1
GROSS MARGIN	42.0%	42.0%	0.0	42.0%	42.0%	0.0	42.0%	42.0%	0.0
MARKDOWNS	24.0%	25.0%	(4.0)	24.0%	25.0%	(4.0)	24.0%	25.0%	(4.0)
SHRINK	2.0%	2.6%	(23.1)	2.0%	2.6%	(23.1)	2.0%	2.6%	(23.1)
AVG MONTHLY INV	$9,180	$9,154	0.3	$10,820	$10,769	0.5	$10,000	$9,962	0.4
WKS SUPPLY	13	14	(7.1)	13	14	(7.1)	13	14	(7.1)
INV TURN	2X	1.85X	8.1	2X	1.85X	8.1	4X	3.7X	8.1
GROSS PROFIT	$7,711	$7,140	8.0	$9,089	$8,400	8.2	$16,800	$15,540	8.1
STORE OP EXPENSES	$5,400	$5,200	3.8	$6,000	$5,500	9.1	$11,400	$10,700	6.5
STORE CONTRIBUTION	$2,311	$1,940	19.1	$3,089	$2,900	6.5	$5,400	$4,840	11.6
CORPORATE EXPENSES	$1,850	$1,700	8.8	$1,900	$1,850	2.7	$3,750	$3,550	5.6
NET PROFIT	$461	$240	92.2	$1,189	$1,050	13.2	$1,650	$1,290	27.9
(BEFORE TAXES)									

The merchandise planning horizon is different from the corporate planning horizon. Typically, the merchandise plan is made for a six-month season. If an entire year is planned, it is expressed as two six-month seasons. (Some retailers have moved beyond the traditional planning seasons, to divide the year into three, four, or more selling seasons.)

Factors that would influence the merchandise plan include trends in the marketplace, vendor information, competitive factors, and the company's own advertising and promotion plans. Prior years' history by class and department is also analyzed by buyers, to reveal sales trends.

Merchandise planning at department or class level begins with the creation of a sales plan, which is broken down by month. Once the sales plan has been established, the other plan elements follow. Gross margin and individual gross margin elements—initial markup, markdowns (ad and clearance), employee discounts, and inventory shrinkage—are planned as a percent of sales.

An inventory turn objective (which may or may not match the corporate plan) is established for the class. By converting this turn into weeks' supply of inventory (for example, inventory turn of four times equals 13 weeks' sales on hand at any time), the weeks' supply target can be applied to the sales plan. Beginning of month inventory (BOM) can be calculated from this formula.

BOM and the sales plan are then used to calculate the monthly purchases budget as follows.

Next month BOM inventory			$500
This month's BOM		$400	
This month's Planned Sales	$100		
This month's Reductions	50	150	
Less: Remaining inventory			250
Required purchases			$250

Merchandise plans once made are used for weekly and monthly monitoring of performance. Comparison of actual results to a plan provides merchants with information that they can translate into action. For example, if sales are down, orders can be canceled, markdowns accelerated, and so on. Certain plan elements—sales, markdowns, inventory, and purchases—are also used by the open-to-buy system (discussed next).

The merchandise plan in dollars is the "official" company plan used to evaluate merchandise performance. However, an even lower level of planning may be undertaken by buyers. These detailed plans are called unit plans, assortment plans, or ladder plans. Assortment plans are concerned only with sales and inventory. They are expressed in units rather than dollars (although if multiplied by an average price they should roughly equal the merchandise plan).

The assortment plan is built up from specific items. The buyer prepares such a plan to ensure that the company is adequately covered within a given class or subclass and that all key attributes or price points are represented in the proper quantities. The plan period may be by month but it is generally made by week (Exhibit 1.2).

Store

As with merchandise plans, store plans are often built from the bottom up. Store managers are asked to estimate the sales growth that they can achieve for the upcoming year. Once these plans are totaled and reviewed, they may be revised based upon the corporate plan. Store sales plans are always broken down by month and may be further subdivided by week and by day to tie into store incentive programs.

The store planning process may also include the creation of an operating budget by store. This budget includes all of the direct expenses that are within the store's control. The planned sales, less the corporate gross margin plan (this rarely varies by store), less planned store direct expenses, equals a contribution by store. "Contribution" is the amount that the store contributes to corporate overhead. (Payroll is usually the most significant component of store direct expense.)

Both merchandise and assortment plans, once made at corporate level, may also be further subdivided into store level sales and inventory plans. These plans would be used by systems such as store space planning (planogramming), distribution, and replenishment. In a multichain environment, merchandise plans may be made for groups of stores rather than for each individual store. Stores are often grouped by their sales within a department or class into A, B, and C volume groups. A single sales and inventory plan is made for each volume group (Exhibit 1.3). Automated systems track these volume group plans and use them to assist in allocating merchandise among stores.

EXHIBIT 1.2   Merchandise Plan

COOPBRAND CLOTHING STORES

CREATE DATE: 09/15/ XX

MERCHANDISE PLAN ($000)
SPRING SEASON ENDING 07/31/ XX

DEPT: 321   WOMEN'S DRESSES

ITEM	FEB	MAR	APR	MAY	JUN	JUL	SEASON
SALES	$1,600	$1,905	$2,050	$2,050	$1,865	$1,894	$11,364
GROSS MARGIN	44.4%	43.1%	41.8%	39.6%	41.8%	41.8%	42.0%
IMU	55.0%	55.0%	54.0%	53.0%	54.0%	54.0%	54.2%
MARKDOWNS	21.1%	24.0%	24.0%	26.0%	24.0%	24.0%	24.0%
EMPLOYEE DISCOUNTS	0.5%	0.5%	0.5%	0.5%	0.5%	0.5%	0.5%
SHRINK	2.0%	2.0%	2.0%	2.0%	2.0%	2.0%	2.0%
BOM INVENTORY	$5,500	$5,950	$6,200	$5,900	$5,350	$5,200	$5,683
MARKDOWNS	$338	$457	$492	$533	$448	$455	$2,723
DISC/SHRINK	$40	$48	$51	$51	$47	$47	$284
RECEIPTS	$2,428	$2,660	$2,293	$2,084	$2,209	$2,711	$14,385
WKS SUPPLY	12.0	12.0	13.0	12.6	13.0	13.5	13.0
MERCHANDISE MARGIN	$710	$821	$857	$812	$780	$792	$4,771

EXHIBIT 1.3 Store Plan

COOPBRAND CLOTHING STORES

CREATE DATE: 09/15/XX

STORE CONTRIBUTION PLAN ($000)
SPRING SEASON ENDING 07/31/XX

STORE: #1 - 6TH AVENUE

ITEM	FEB	MARCH	APRIL	MAY	JUNE	JULY	SEASON
SALES	$110	$131	$141	$141	$128	$130	$781
GROSS MARGIN	44.4%	43.1%	41.8%	39.6%	41.6%	41.8%	41.8%
IMU	55.0%	55.0%	54.0%	53.0%	54.0%	54.0%	54.2%
MARKDOWNS	21.0%	24.0%	24.0%	26.0%	24.5%	24.0%	23.9%
EMPLOYEE DISCOUNTS	0.5%	0.5%	0.5%	0.5%	0.5%	0.5%	0.5%
SHRINK	2.0%	2.0%	2.0%	2.0%	2.0%	2.0%	2.0%
BOM INVENTORY	$382	$413	$430	$412	$365	$350	$392
MARKDOWNS	$23	$31	$34	$37	$31	$31	$187
DISC/SHRINK	$3	$3	$4	$4	$3	$3	$20
RECEIPTS	$167	$183	$160	$134	$148	$184	$976
WKS SUPPLY	12.0	12.0	13.0	12.6	13.0	13.5	13.0
MERCHANDISE MARGIN	$49	$56	$59	$56	$53	$54	$327
STORE OP EXPENSES	$41	$40	$39	$37	$37	$39	$234
STORE CONTRIBUTION	$8	$16	$20	$19	$16	$15	$94

CHAPTER TWO

Open to Buy

Open-to-buy is a management tool whose purpose is to calculate whether inventory levels will be sufficient to meet sales projections. Open-to-buy identifies when purchase orders should be placed, when merchandise should be received and when goods are expected to be sold. Although it starts as a plan, it is a dynamic calculation that is continuously revised to reflect actual sales, purchase orders and receipts. Open-to-buy reflects not only expectations but how plans have been modified by reality.

BENEFITS AND PROBLEMS

The open-to-buy report (see Exhibit 2.1) provides important information to merchandise personnel, financial management and senior management. These include:

- Knowledge of exactly when merchandise orders should be placed and when inventory must arrive in order to satisfy sales plans.

- Identification of capital required to maintain projected inventory levels; this alerts management to know to obtain more capital, increase sales, or decrease purchases.

- Determination of actual sales, purchase orders and the impact of receipts on projected inventory levels; this alerts management to increase or decrease purchase order levels.

EXHIBIT 2.1   Open to Buy

COOPBRAND CLOTHING STORES

CREATE DATE: 04/03/ XX

OPEN TO BUY REPORT ($000)
MONTH END 3/31

DEPT: 321 WOMEN'S DRESSES

ITEM	MAR ACTUAL	MAR PLAN	APR FCST	APR PLAN	MAY FCST	MAY PLAN	JUN FCST	JUN PLAN
BOM INVENTORY	6,010	5,950	6,360	6,200	5,957	5,900	5,123	5,350
SALES	1,850	1,905	2,050	2,050	2,050	2,050	1,865	1,865
ADJUSTMENTS	510	505	543	543	584	584	495	495
RECEIPTS/ON ORDER	2,710	2,660	2,190	2,293	1,800	2,084	1,600	2,209
EOM INVENTORY	6,360	6,200	5,957	5,900	5,123	5,350	4,363	5,200
OPEN TO BUY/(OVERBOUGHT)	(160)	0	(57)	0	227	0	837	0

FORECAST (FCST) ASSUMES PLAN NUMBERS WILL BE MET.
RECEIPTS/ON ORDER ARE MONTH END RECEIPTS AND COMMITTED FUTURE ORDERS.

Some retailers question the value of open-to-buy controls. Sometimes cited are:

- The purchase order that inevitably gets refused because of an overbought condition is for basic merchandise that *must* be bought. However, if open-to-buy controls are eliminated for this reason, the retailer can find inventory levels constantly building as some items are reordered while others stagnate. It would be beneficial, in this situation, to establish a separate open-to-buy category for basic stock merchandise thus ensuring adequate inventory levels.

- Opportunistic buys, or close-outs, provide another excuse to eliminate open-to-buy. This reasoning reflects the presumption that the purpose of open-to-buy is to restrict purchasing. It should be made clear that this is a purpose only when it needs to be. More likely, with unplanned purchases the importance of open-to-buy is in insuring that all segments of the business (warehouse, stores, merchandise, and finance) can handle the inventory levels anticipated.

SPECIAL SITUATIONS

An open-to-buy (OTB) calculation can be done at cost or at retail. The decision should be based entirely on what makes most sense. Those companies on the retail method of accounting for inventory will, in general, find it more convenient to follow the retail method for OTB. Under the retail method, merchandise purchases at retail are offset by sales, markdowns, and shortage reserve. In calculating OTB many retailers do not deduct the shortage reserve. By not "buying back shortage," they somewhat reduce the risk of excess inventory.

Some companies operate more than one line of business, each selling the same type of inventory. The inventory may be supporting both mail order and store customers, or own store's and wholesale customers. It is particularly important in this arrangement that accurate sales projections are supported by tight controls over orders, receipts, and distributions. An OTB system cannot resolve the inevitable conflict that will arise when different channels of distribution both lay claim to the same, remaining item of merchandise, but it is especially important that there is a constant awareness of projected inventory levels.

In a multichain environment, OTB is used to determine when purchase orders should be placed for the company. Open-to-ship is another technique used to determine where the merchandise should be sent to after it has been received. Open-to-ship looks at planned inventory levels by store as part of an allocation decision. This is covered in more detail in Chapter 4.

OTB SYSTEMS

The OTB system provides information to measure actual sales and inventory levels against the merchandise plan. OTB is a tool for monitoring and controlling purchases in order to meet the planned ending inventory and stock turn objectives. The OTB system is provided with information from feeder systems such as:

- Merchandise planning.
- Open orders.
- Sales (by SKU or department/class).
- Accounts payable.
- Price management.
- Stock ledger

Various elements of the OTB system are typically updated interactively (Plan and Open Orders), daily (Sales), and monthly (BOM Inventory). The data are used to provide screens and/or reports at the following levels:

- Consolidated (all) stores.
- Individual warehouse.
- Department or class.
- Retail dollars.
- Weekly or monthly (weekly requires a weekly sales and inventory plan).

OTB Data Elements

PLAN DATA. Plan data on the OTB system consists of the following elements for consolidated stores, by department, in retail dollars, by month for a twelve-month planning horizon.

- Beginning and ending inventory.
  —Consolidated (all) stores.
  —Warehouse inventory—individual warehouse inventory.
- Purchase order receipts—All merchandise planned to be received against an open purchase order for that month.
- Direct receipts—All merchandise planned to be received in the stores such as those from rack jobbers and other vendor serviced items.

- Sales—Total retail dollar sales for the month.

- Adjustments—Elements such as markdowns and returns to vendors would be reductions which, like sales, would create additional open-to-buy.

Warehouse plan data elements are the same as the all store data elements and consist of:

- Beginning and ending inventories.

- Receipts.

- Shipments to stores.

- Adjustments.

The system can calculate an annualized stock turn based upon the monthly beginning and ending inventories and planned sales or shipments. The planning elements follow the basic OTB calculation of:

- Beginning inventory.

- Plus receipts (central and direct).

- Less sales (shipments).

- Less adjustments (markdowns and RTVs).

- Equals ending inventory.

The source of the planning data will initially come from the merchandise planning system. Once in season, plans are typically maintained and adjusted. The revised or latest plan will be used by the OTB system.

ACTUAL DATA ELEMENTS. Actual sales and inventory information are used by the OTB system to show progress against plan, to project an ending inventory position, and to calculate a resulting OTB amount. Data elements are:

Beginning Inventory All Stores. Includes on-hand, received merchandise in stores and warehouses. By definition, this equals the ending inventory from the previous month. This number is corrected to the book inventory amount after book inventory is adjusted for a physical inventory count.

On Order. Retail dollar amount of open orders for the OTB month. This number is updated as orders are approved or canceled. If not otherwise stated, the delivery date on the purchase order is used to determine which OTB month should be charged for the purchases. This number will also be updated as merchandise is received and orders canceled from the system.

Past Due.   The sum of the open orders with an OTB month prior to the current one.

Received.   Amount of merchandise received this month against an open order.

Direct Receipts.   Includes receipts entered (often through accounts payable) for store direct vendors.

Month-to-Date Sales.   Month-to-date (MTD) retail dollar net sales processed through the end of week.

Actual Plan Sales.   The amount of actual sales needed to make the monthly sales plan. This is calculated by subtracting the actual MTD sales from the planned sales.

Percent Plan.   Actual sales divided by plan sales.

Adjustments.   Includes all price changes, returns to vendor, accounts payable chargebacks, and shrinkage reserve.

End-of-Month Inventory—Projected and Actual.   During the month, the ending inventory amount will be projected based upon the following calculation:

Actual beginning inventory

Plus:	Actual on order
	Orders past due
	Receipts

Less:	Planned sales
	Planned adjustments

Equals:	Projected ending inventory (end-of-month inventory)

Once the month is completed, the ending inventory is calculated using actual data:

Actual beginning inventory

Plus:	Actual receipts
Less:	Actual sales and adjustments
Equals:	Actual ending inventory

Open-to-Buy.   The difference between planned ending inventory and projected ending inventory for the current and future months. Prior period overbought/underbought conditions roll forward because the prior period actual ending inventory is equal to the next period beginning inventory.

Warehouse data elements and calculations are defined the same as the store's elements with the exception that shipments to the stores and other warehouses replace the sales data.

CHAPTER THREE

Purchase Order Management

Purchase order management (POM), for purposes of this text, will be considered as the automated systems that support merchandise processing activities from the writing of a purchase order through the receipt and processing of the merchandise. A properly designed POM system should provide the following advantages:

- Improved efficiency of all merchandise handling.
- Simpler and faster purchase order preparation.
- More accurate and current open-to-buy and on-order information.
- Fewer errors in receiving and marking.
- Improved accuracy and timeliness of unit and dollar merchandise systems.
- Reduced invoice processing costs and accounts payable problems.

This chapter will describe two POM functions: purchase order processing and receiving and marking. It will also cover special issues that arise in a POM environment. Other functions, such as open-to-buy, merchandise distribution, invoice matching, and accounts payable are discussed in subsequent chapters.

PURCHASE ORDER PROCESSING

An automated POM system can receive an order in several ways, but the three most common are:

- Handwritten with subsequent entry.
- Worksheets completed on the system.
- Computer generated.

Each approach has its own substructure and its own validity for a specific retailer. It is normal to expect that most retailers will need to support all three methods.

Establishing appropriate master files can be the key to minimizing purchase order (PO) entry time and trauma, while providing greater control over the entire process. The files that will be accessed most frequently in PO entry are department, vendor, and item masters. These files should display the data elements that will most likely be required for the PO entry activity; generally providing the user the ability to override fields on any specific order. Permission to override and the audit trail that are subsequently generated start the POM control process. Master files can also be linked so that, for example, vendors may be valid only for certain departments. Special purpose files may also be created that will provide such tools as pre-established size scales and quantities within size.

It is here, at the beginning of the POM system, that the basis is established to expedite merchandise movement, minimize paper handling, reduce costs, and improve controls. Some additional points that should be considered for the PO entry process include:

HEADER LEVEL. This refers to the various identifiers and instructions that precede the detailed entry of styles, quantities, and dollars. Much of the header level information is retrieved from the master files discussed previously. However, there are innumerable special conditions that must be conveyed to a vendor, but which may not be easy to accommodate within a POM system. These include: special handling, routing, allowances, volume discounts, advertising allowances, and so on. Careful decisions must be made here to avoid automating features for which the costs to capture will far outweigh their value to the company.

STYLE ENTRY. Specific requirements will vary considerably; systems design must determine the extent to which functionality is required that allows for the following:

- Displaying a style listing for entry of quantities.

- Entry of a style number against an item master file.

- Entry of style number and information at the time of order entry.

- Bulk order with style data to be determined after receipt.

The style entry function should also provide support in converting differing units of measure (e.g., purchased as dozens, sold as each), extending at cost and retail and flagging gross margins that exceed predetermined tolerances. This gross margin check is certainly needed at the end of the order entry process and, in fact, it is generally only at the end that margins are checked against standards by department or class.

ALLOCATION OF QUANTITIES.   In a multistore company, vendors may be asked to ship merchandise in at least three standard ways:

- Drop ship—pack and ship separately to each location.

- Pack separately but ship centrally.

- Pack and ship centrally.

The PO entry process may support any, or all, of the above techniques; or, it may create an order with shipping instructions to follow. Chapter 4 covers distribution techniques. Of significance for POM systems, however, is the time at which the merchandise allocation decision is being made:

- Predistribution is decided when the PO is created. It is therefore, integral to the POM system.

- Postdistribution is decided after the merchandise is received. It is not, generally, part of the POM process.

- Single order with distribution to follow is sometimes called "pre-post." The distribution module is not part of the POM system, although they are linked.

PURCHASE ORDER WRITING.   The completed purchase order (see Exhibit 3.1) needs to be available to the vendor and to several functional areas within the retail company. However, none of this can be done until the PO is approved.

The approval process should start with the OTB system. If this is automated, then validation can occur as part of the order entry processing. If OTB is not integrated, or if the order is of a size that requires specific

EXHIBIT 3.1 Purchase Order

COOPBRAND STORES PURCHASE ORDER

COOPBRAND
DEPARTMENT # : 321
ORDER # : 1234567
VENDOR DUNS # : 987654321

VENDOR NAME : USA CORP.
STREET : MAIN STREET
CITY : NEW YORK
STATE: NEW YORK

SHIP TO INFORMATION:
STORE NAME : COOPBRAND STORE #1
STREET : 1200 6th AVE
CITY: NEW YORK
STATE: NEW YORK
ZIP CODE: 10020

ORDER DATE	CANCELLATION DATE	TERMS	WHO PAYS FREIGHT	F.O.B. POINT
7 1151 XX	9 1151 88	30 DAYS NET	STORE	L.A., CA.

IN STORE DELIVERY DATES					RECEIVING AND MARKING INSTRUCTIONS
8 1151 XX 100%	/ / %	/ / %	USE HANG TICKETS		

LINE	CL	STYLE	SIZE	COLOR	ITEM DESC.	QTY	COST U/M	UNIT COST	TOTAL COST	RETAIL U/M	UNIT RETAIL	TOTAL RETAIL
1	10	23456	6	BL	DRESS	12	EA	$29.25	$351.00	EA	$45.99	$551.88
2	10	23456	8	BL	DRESS	16	EA	$29.25	$468.00	EA	$45.99	$735.84
3	10	23456	10	BL	DRESS	24	EA	$29.25	$702.00	EA	$45.99	$1103.76
4	10	23456	12	BL	DRESS	24	EA	$29.25	$702.00	EA	$45.99	$1103.76
5	10	23456	14	BL	DRESS	12	EA	$29.15	$351.00	EA	$45.99	$551.88
6											
7											
8											
9											
10											
11											
12											
13											
14											
15											
16											
17											
18											
19											
20											

PAGE 1 OF 1

BUYER SIGNITURE T. Jones

TOTAL COST = $2574.00

DMM SIGNITURE Henry James

TOTAL RETAIL = $4047.12

MAIL ALL INVOICES TO : COOPBRAND STORES; PO BOX 567; NEW YORK, N.Y. 10020

approval, design decisions must be made to clarify how orders pending approval are to be handled. They can be entered into the system and released with a security code or kept outside the system until the necessary approvals have been obtained.

Many purchase orders will be transmitted directly to vendors through some electronic data interchange (EDI) process. Most of the technical requirements of this process will use established industry standards and third-party software; however, there is a need here to insure the adequacy of internal controls.

RECEIVING AND MARKING

PRE-RECEIPT. The existence of an automated purchase order file with information as to what is expected, when, and from whom, represents an opportunity to establish excellent controls over the receiving dock. If desirable, carriers can be required to call for appointments. This gives the receiving department valuable knowledge of anticipated workloads, identifies shipments that may require expedited handling and identifies "no order" shipments before they arrive. This advance notice also allows the retailer to have all necessary paperwork ready to move the merchandise. (Many trucking companies and consolidators have automated systems that will connect to the retailer's and handle some or all of the functions from scheduling through ticketing.)

DETAIL RECEIPT. All retail receiving systems should start with some form of prenumbered, controlled, receiving documents. These can range from a pad of dock receipt forms to an on-line terminal at the receiving dock. What is most important is that there is effective control over receipt of a shipment. The basic information required at this time includes: date, vendor, carrier, number of cartons, weight, pro number, PO number, and value (if available).

If on-line, someone in the receiving area would access the PO file. If not, the subsequent entry of the dock receipt would start the POM process.

Most retailers now print a listing of the merchandise still open on the PO for the detailed checking of the shipment (see Exhibit 3.2). There is some debate over the desirability of printing expected quantities on this checking document. Some believe that checkers may accept the preprinted quantities without verifying them. Others feel that unaided counts will contain excessive errors. This is a fine point, but one that can have a profound affect on the accuracy of subsequent systems. To some extent, this dilemma can be resolved if vendors are source marking with machine readable symbols (UPC). This technology permits the retailer to scan the merchandise received and have an accurate record at the style/color/size (SKU) level.

The recording of quantities, and their subsequent entry into the POM system, provides the data that will now drive and update many critical merchandise and accounting functions:

- On-Order.

- Postdistribution.

- Unit controls.

EXHIBIT 3.2   Receiving Document

COOPBRAND STORES RECEIVING DOCUMENT						

DOCUMENT NUMBER	STORE NUMBER	RECEIPT DATE	DEPT. NUMBER	ORDER NUMBER	ORDER NUMBER	ORDER NUMBER
123456	2	08/25 / XX	321	123456	234567	

VENDOR NAME		CARRIER NAME		INVOICE NUMBER	INVOICE NUMBER	INVOICE NUMBER
USA CORP.		APACHE TRUCKING		789107	565646	

NUMBER OF CARTONS/PACKAGES	CONDITION OF SHIPMENT	PRO NUMBER		INVOICE AMOUNT	INVOICE AMOUNT	INVOICE AMOUNT
166	OK	12345678		$2,574.00	$2,925.00	$

WEIGHT OF SHIPMENT	FREIGHT CHARGES	CITY	POINT OF ORIGIN STATE		COUNTRY	
124 LBS.	$375.00	L.A.	CA.		USA	

LINE	CL	STYLE	SIZE	COLOR	ITEM DESC.	COST U/M	UNIT COST	RETAIL U/M	UNIT RETAIL	QUANTITY EXPECTED	RECEIVED
P.O. NUMBER 123456											
1	10	23456	6	BL	WOMEN'S DRESS	EA	$29.25	EA	$45.99	12	12
2	10	23456	8	BL	WOMEN'S DRESS	EA	$29.25	EA	$45.99	16	16
3	10	23456	10	BL	WOMEN'S DRESS	EA	$29.25	EA	$45.99	24	24
4	10	23456	12	BL	WOMEN'S DRESS	EA	$29.25	EA	$45.99	24	24
5	10	23456	14	BL	WOMEN'S DRESS	EA	$29.25	EA	$45.99	12	12
P.O. NUMBER 234567											
6	14	55678	8	RD	WOMEN'S DRESS	EA	$37.50	EA	$57.99	18	18
7	14	55678	10	RD	WOMEN'S DRESS	EA	$37.50	EA	$57.99	24	30
8	14	55678	12	RD	WOMEN'S DRESS	EA	$37.50	EA	$57.99	36	30

CHECKER'S SIGNITURE	*John Doe*	MANAGER'S SIGNITURE	*Jim Smith*	PAGE 1 OF 1

- Open-to-buy.

- Monthly accounts payable accrual.

- Ticketing.

TICKETING.   More and more merchandise is being vendor source marked, but it is unlikely that store marking will be completely eliminated. At the present time, many companies prefer to show their own department and class code, a season code indicating date of receipt and, of course, the price. Whether the retailer is producing a complete ticket, in UPC format, or additional data to add to a vendor tag, the POM system should be able to generate the complete document as a result of the receiving process.

Ticketing itself can be done in the distribution center, warehouse, or store. The decision is generally made based on where the merchandise arrives, how it is handled, available labor, and cost. The question of where and when the tickets are produced must be considered separately. Computer-produced tickets can be generated at the warehouse for attachment there or at stores, however it may be prudent to defer ticketing merchandise that is to be warehoused for a period of time if the price is liable to change.

If merchandise is to be shipped direct to stores, tickets may be centrally produced and sent out in advance of receipt. However, while central ticketing from a POM system is very effective, it is important to remember that stores will still need local ticket-making capability.

CHAPTER FOUR

Merchandise Distribution

In a multistore environment, the distribution function can turn a company from marginally profitable to extremely successful. It encompasses the process of having the right goods at the right time and avoids costly activities after the fact such as transfers and markdowns.

Merchandise distribution is the process of allocating quantities purchased among stores. Distribution techniques are typically used for new or nonbasic merchandise such as seasonal products or advertised merchandise. Distribution systems may be contrasted with replenishment systems, which are used to reorder staple or basic items with a sales history of 6 to 12 months. Replenishment systems are discussed in Chapter Six. Three major distribution techniques are discussed next.

PREDISTRIBUTION

In predistribution, buyers allocate merchandise between stores at the time that they are writing purchase orders. The breakdown by store is included as part of the purchase order information. The merchandise is packed by store, to be drop shipped to stores or received by stores from a central warehouse.

Benefits of predistributed orders are that vendors can pack the merchandise by store; if shipped to a central warehouse location, goods do not have to be detail received and repacked. Savings in time and handling costs can be realized. Drawbacks are that the distribution decision is made weeks before the merchandise is actually received; conditions may have changed so that the merchandise is not allocated in the right quantities to the stores that need it the most.

POSTDISTRIBUTION

Postdistribution means that a bulk order is placed to the vendor. The merchandise is received at a distribution center, counted and checked, after which the distribution decision is made. Merchandise is transferred to stores from the distribution center. Postdistribution provides a major benefit by allowing merchants to allocate merchandise based upon current store sales and stock levels. If vendors tend to ship less than quantities ordered, postdistribution permits optimal allocation of the actual quantity received.

Another benefit of postdistribution relates to invoice matching. Vendors will send a single invoice for merchandise shipped in bulk. Predistributed orders, even if shipped to a central facility, may result in one invoice per store.

The major drawbacks of postdistribution are the added expense of sorting the merchandise and the time required to process the goods.

PRE/POST—A HYBRID

In a hybrid approach which has characteristics of both pre- and postdistribution, a bulk order is placed. One to two weeks before the order is ready to be shipped, a store-by-store breakdown is sent to the vendor. This system is useful in situations where commitments have to be placed with vendors far in advance, or when buyers have the chance to make an opportunistic purchase and there is no time to first work out store-by-store allocations.

DISTRIBUTION SYSTEMS

Automated allocation systems are a boon to large retail chains. Such systems make use of sales and inventory plans by store, usually at class level. These plans may be updated frequently to reflect actual sales trends. Merchandise receipts are then allocated among stores based upon a comparison of their sales and stock plans to actual sales, on-hand inventory, and merchandise in transit. Factors such as vendor pack sizes, multiple colors, and sizes per style are handled by such systems. Other features of distribution systems include the ability to tailor allocations to specific store types (i.e., urban vs. rural, warm vs. cold climate), and the production of exception reports that indicate high or low sales performance.

Distribution systems interface with:

- Purchase order management systems.
- Warehouse systems such as pick list generation, ticketing, and truck routing.
- Planning systems (particularly store plans).
- Store billing systems.
- Invoice matching.

CHAPTER FIVE

Sales

All businesses must know what merchandise their customers are buying. Retailing is unique only in the high volume of low-value transactions that are typically handled. It is this unique characteristic, however, that is responsible for so much of the development that has occurred at the retail point-of-sale (POS).

Knowledge of sales activity can be gained by being on the sales floor, or it can be obtained from highly automated information systems. Most large retailers now use electronic point-of-sale (EPOS) systems in some way; this chapter focuses on that process. It should be recognized however, that there are other ways to obtain item or stockkeeping-unit (SKU) level sales information that, for some retailers, may be preferable. Two of the most common are:

- *Stock Counts.* Recording receipts and then subtracting on-hand inventory provides some measure of what has sold. This approach lacks accuracy for several reasons: Returns and transfers must also be accounted for in the calculation, and stock counts are notoriously inaccurate and cut-off controls are generally inadequate.

- *Stubbing.* Multipart price tickets permit one part (the stub) to be removed at the time of sale. Subsequent processing of the stub will depend on whether merchandise information on the ticket is machine readable or not. While stubbing, in its various forms, has been in use for some time, its major weaknesses are the number of stubs that are never captured and the cost of the entire process.

EPOS terminals have given retailers the ability to capture information, accurately, by style, color, and size, as a by-product of handling the sales transaction. This, in turn, has been the trigger for the development of highly complex merchandise information systems. These systems are now causing fundamental changes in the way that retail businesses are managed. Most significant is the ability to take advantage of specific information (such as direct product profitability) rather than relying on class level averages. Retailers no longer depend on manufacturers for product movement data; retail point-of-sale systems provide superior information.

EPOS systems also help in two other areas: cost and customer service. Retailers and their suppliers of automated systems are constantly improving both of these areas. Further enhancement will probably come from those activities that increase the use of automation throughout the chain of distribution. For example, vendor source marking and Universal Product Coding (UPC) should improve customer processing at the point-of-sale. New hardware and innovative processing techniques will further speed customer handling time. The expansion of in-store automation should increase the productivity of store processors and communication lines.

REGISTER FUNCTIONS AND CONTROLS

Before considering the sales capture activity, it may be helpful to briefly outline the basic features that can be found in standard point-of-sale systems. Electronic cash registers (ECR) are generally stand-alone devices that do not have the full range of functions found in electronic point-of-sale terminals; however, the line between these two devices is rapidly blurring. Point-of-sale terminal configurations can be broadly classified as front-end checkout, area registers, or stand-alone. Within each of these groupings, highly specialized functions will be developed for different retailers (e.g., layaway systems). Front-end checkout systems also have special characteristics to provide the rapid transaction processing that is typically required in that environment. Otherwise, the basic transaction set will include most of the following activities:

- Cashier accountability.
- Entry of sales and returns.
- Transaction extensions and additions.
- Validation of appropriate fields.
- Calculation of taxes and allowances.

- Payment media accepting and accounting.
- Credit authorization (in-house and third-party) and debit card processing.
- Transaction logging and control, including voids.
- Printing as required (register receipt, on sales check, transaction tape).
- Supervisor access to current activity reports.
- Procedure and controls closing.

SALES CAPTURE

Levels of Detail

All retailers do not record sales at the same level of detail. The range of possibilities starts with the proverbial cigar box and moves through such levels as: division, department, class, and style down to SKU. The reason for this wide variance is usually pragmatic, that is, the economics of the business do not justify the cost that would be incurred to capture more detailed data. Frequently, this situation occurs where the merchandise is not reorderable, or where other techniques provide management with adequate knowledge of what is selling.

The level of detail to be captured at the register should support the financial stock ledger as well as merchandising requirements. If there is no breakdown of sales, merchandise and financial controls cannot be exercised below the total store level.

If information is desired by department or class, those numbers will usually have to be entered at the register for each item sold. Therefore, it is important to have the merchandise properly ticketed with the correct codes. Sales clerks should not enter department numbers based on memory. Sales by department/class are very useful for long-term analysis of store merchandising, as well as in the daily monitoring of activity by store managers. Some point-of-sale systems, even though transactions are captured at the SKU level, are unable to provide daily interim and flash sales results by department. The solution to this shortcoming is often to enter department numbers in addition to the SKU code.

Entering Sales by SKU

SKU describes the lowest level of information for an item of inventory. In general merchandise retailing, this can include: department, class, vendor, style, size, and color. The numerical codes that identify each of these elements can be 25 digits long, much too lengthy for key entry at the point-of-sale. Several techniques are employed to resolve this problem:

- A short SKU number is a reference code, generally six digits in length, that can substitute for the longer number at the point-of-sale. The short SKU is established by the computer so that, whenever necessary, full details about the item can be obtained. The short SKU can be key entered at the register in a reasonable amount of time.

- Interactive terminals as sales registers can, through a series of questions, identify the product without entry of any numbers. Touch-screen technology has been used effectively with this approach.

- Scanning at the point-of-sale is considered, at the present time, to be the most effective procedure to accurately capture SKU-level sales in a high transaction retail environment. Several marking techniques and technologies have been used for this purpose. The UPC bar code symbols, originally developed for the grocery industry, are now the standard for the general merchandise industry as well. Since so many items now have the UPC code printed on the tag or label by the manufacturer, this approach provides great benefit to retailers and their suppliers.

PRICE LOOK-UP AT POINT-OF-SALE

The increased sophistication and capacity of EPOS terminals, coupled with widespread item identification (primarily UPC), makes price look-up (PLU) advantageous. The PLU process is one in which the point-of-sale terminal will "look up" an SKU number at the time of entry. The retail price is retrieved from an item file, displayed on the register, and becomes the amount charged to the customer. This technique has several significant benefits:

- SKU numbers are verified at the time of entry.

- Accuracy of pricing to customers is very high.

- Promotional markdowns can be captured as a by-product of the sales transaction, thereby eliminating stock counts before and after promotions.

- Item ticketing and/or reticketing can be eliminated where desirable (and legal).

- Customer service can be enhanced through speedier and more accurate processing.

The success of PLU systems is primarily dependent on two aspects of the operation: the accuracy with which items are coded and the completeness and accuracy of the in-store PLU file. The first element, item coding, is best solved through vendor source marking. Because UPC coding has become a common feature on tags and labels, the retailer must only place SKU identification on a small percent of the items carried in stock.

However, the second issue, the accuracy of in-store PLU files, is highly dependent on the systems and controls at the retail level. An average supermarket can have as many as 25,000 items in stock; a large department store can have almost one million SKUs in inventory. Both represent challenging efforts in assuring that:

- All items sold in the store are on the PLU file.

- Prices on the PLU file are correct and match prices on the shelves or items.

- Files are updated for price changes on the correct date.

POINT-OF-SALE MARKDOWNS

EPOS terminals can replace price change forms as a technique for recording markdowns in the store. The traditional method of counting stock on hand and recording its new price would still be preferable when permanent price changes are being made. However, for temporary situations, such as promotions, or for other discounts and allowances granted at the point-of-sale (employees, institutions), the EPOS terminal provides a superior way of capturing the price change.

If a PLU file is being used, then promotional prices, and the number of sales made at those prices, can easily be determined. Through central programs that accumulate information from the EPOS system, promotional markdowns can be recorded in the retail stock ledger with greater accuracy than under the before-and-after count method. If there is no in-store PLU file, point-of-sale markdowns can still be determined if SKU number and price are entered. These transactions can be compared against item master files at the central computer and price change records generated where this is indicated. (As a matter of internal discipline, store management should follow up on price discrepancies that are not expected or properly authorized.)

CHAPTER SIX

Monitoring and Replenishment

Merchandising activities have as their primary objective: fulfilling customer demand to the highest possible degree while maintaining inventory levels and operating costs at the lowest possible level and while realizing gross margins sufficient to provide an acceptable net profit. The merchandise information capture discussed previously is a means to help realize these objectives. Recognition of the different merchandise characteristics to be managed will allow a reasoned decision to promote, markdown, transfer, reorder, and so on.

The segmentation of merchandise presented in this section, into fashion and basic, are broad generalizations. In practice, there are many items that exhibit characteristics of each segment. There are also other attributes, such as source of supply, that will affect the way the merchandise should be managed. Increasingly, retailers are focusing their inventory management techniques so that each unique segment can be handled in ways that consider the realities of its purchase and sales environment. Automated information systems support this focused analysis and operation while enhancing merchandise productivity.

FASHION MERCHANDISE

Fashion merchandise is generally characterized by high product volatility in a very short selling season. Managing fashion merchandise requires that fast decisions be made based on minimal data. (While fashion is considered synonymous with apparel, more hard goods merchandise now exhibits fashion characteristics.) Most of the critical decisions for fashion merchandise are made in the planning and procurement stages. At that time, it is necessary to understand overall trends at the store and in the industry so that initial orders, placed months in advance of the actual selling season, will have a high probability of being successful. Although sales of individual fashion items may be difficult to forecast, retailers with historical data can use it to develop customer size profiles as well as color and classification preferences.

Once the selling begins, it is important to quickly identify positive and negative trends in fabric, color, look, style, and price point. While the time frame for action is short, substantial sales and gross margin dollars can be gained through prompt action. Although specific styles may not be reorderable, comparable merchandise may be available. Merchandise that is not selling early in the season should be quickly moved to another location or marked down to sell.

STAPLE/BASIC MERCHANDISE

Hard goods seem to be the predominant type of staple merchandise; however, certain apparel items, even with size and color dimensions, exhibit the continuity of demand that define basic goods. The designation "staple" may not always be clear cut; it can change for certain items of merchandise because of the type of retail store in which they are found; aspects of fashion exist in more and more categories; and, even within staple categories, some items will sell better than others.

In managing this category of merchandise, the retailer strives to maintain the highest level of in-stock position with the lowest level of inventory. Many techniques and refinements are employed to achieve ever higher levels of inventory turn; for it is in this area especially that both elements of the Gross Margin Return on Inventory Investment (GMROI) formula (gross margin and inventory investment) can be maximized. Improvements, such as the following, are continually being developed throughout the processing chain:

- Shelf space allocation and location optimization.
- Electronic Data Interchange (EDI) and other programs with suppliers and shippers.
- Effective utilization of warehouse, distribution center and direct store delivery.

- Improving the merchandise flow throughout the retailer's facilities.
- Forecasting demand at warehouse and store locations.

AUTOMATIC REPLENISHMENT

Replenishment systems are a major technique used to manage staple merchandise. They generally function by forecasting item demand then, based on other criteria, calculating inventory required to satisfy that demand and, finally, comparing inventory required to that available to determine the order quantity.

The actual calculation of replenishment quantities considers factors such as the following:

- *Review Time.* The number of days between review of an item for replenishment. Certain automated systems can review all items each day. Most systems cycle through the inventory over one week or more.

- *Lead Time.* The number of days between replenishment review and availability of merchandise for sale.

- *Forecasting Demand.* Generally accomplished by comparing actual sales to forecasts that were based on historical data and seasonal patterns. Demand for the coming period is calculated based on the relationship between these current and historical demands.

- *Level of Service.* Statistically it is not possible to satisfy every customer's merchandise request 100 percent of the time. The extent to which demand is satisfied is called level of service. Different merchandise classifications or items should be targeted for different levels of service. Generally these levels will run between 70 to 90 percent. Replenishment systems can increase level of service by increasing safety stock.

- *Safety Stock.* Forecasts of demand may be higher or lower than actual results but, on average, should be accurate. Safety stock represents additional inventory required to protect against forecasts that may be too low. The amount of safety stock necessary will be calculated based on forecast accuracy and desired level of service.

- *Order Quantity.* The automatic replenishment process concludes with the generation of an order quantity. This is a result of the calculations outlined above plus other limiting factors such as economic order quantities, pack sizes, or vendor minimums. Every one of these variables can be changed through different arrangements with the vendor or at the retailer; there are many opportunities within the replenishment process to minimize inventory investment while increasing customer service levels.

TRANSFERS

As noted, one of the cliches of retailing is "the right merchandise, in the right place, at the right time." This statement explicitly recognizes that "the right merchandise" may not sell in the wrong place. The objective of all merchandise systems is to place goods properly in the first place; however, some merchandise will always end up at the wrong place at the wrong time. Disposition of that merchandise should be made a high priority. The retailer cannot allow unsold merchandise to accumulate. It is unlikely that future revenue will be greater than at present or will justify the increased carrying costs. Once it is determined that merchandise is not selling, there are several alternatives that should be considered for its disposal; the most frequently used techniques being markdowns and transfers.

Interstore transfer is a controversial technique because it frequently seems that the costs incurred are greater than the markdown that would have been required to dispose of the merchandise at the original store. Certainly, there are many situations where merchandise must be transferred because it cannot be sold, even if marked down, at its current location, or because it is in critical demand elsewhere. What is clear is that retailers should understand the costs of transferring merchandise so that merchandise actually moves only when it is economically justifiable.

The transfer process increases opportunities for physical loss of merchandise and for inaccurate recording of the transfer. Techniques available to control interstore transfers are:

- *Transfer Control.* Using the natural checks and balances between the sending and receiving stores or departments is a basic and effective way of controlling the movement of transferred merchandise. This is typically accomplished by having the sending store initiate transfer paperwork (see Exhibit 6.1); the receiving store confirms receipt of the merchandise sent and a central merchandise control office follows up on discrepancies. The use of numerically controlled transfer forms allows the merchandise control office to locate and reconcile missing document sets or parts. They, with support from the receiving store, will also assure that quantities sent and received agree.

- *Transfer Pricing.* Under the retail method of inventory control, net transfers to or from a location should be reported in the stock ledger as

EXHIBIT 6.1   Transfer Document

COOPBRAND STORES TRANSFER DOCUMENT						DOCUMENT #		987654	
						DEPARTMENT		321	

	STORE NUMBER	STORE LOCATION		
SENDING STORE	1	6TH AVENUE	DATE SHIPPED	9/15/ XX
RECEIVING STORE	2	PARK AVENUE	DATE RECEIVED	/ /

# OF CARTONS/PACKAGES SHIPPED	24	FILLED BY EMPLOYEE #	504720
# OF CARTONS/PACKAGES RECVD		RECEIVED BY EMPLOYEE #	

LINE	DEPT	CL	HSE	STYLE	SIZE	COLOR	ITEM DESC.	QTY	RETAIL	EXT. RETAIL	RECVD COMPLETE
1	321	10	201	23456	8	BL	WOMEN'S DRESS	2	$65.00	$130.00	
2	321	10	201	23467	8	RD	WOMEN'S DRESS	2	$65.00	$130.00	
3	321	10	245	45678	12	PK	WOMEN'S DRESS	4	$65.00	$260.00	
4	321	11	201	34567	10	BL	WOMEN'S DRESS	2	$85.00	$170.00	
5	321	11	201	34578	12	BK	WOMEN'S DRESS	2	$85.00	$170.00	
6	321	12	201	67890	8	WH	WOMEN'S DRESS	4	$79.00	$316.00	
7	321	12	201	67901	8	GR	WOMEN'S DRESS	4	$79.00	$316.00	
8	321	12	245	67913	10	BL	WOMEN'S DRESS	4	$79.00	$316.00	
9	321	12	245	67934	12	RD	WOMEN'S DRESS	2	$79.00	$158.00	
10	321	14	201	76432	8	PK	WOMEN'S DRESS	2	$99.00	$198.00	
11	321	14	201	55678	10	BL	WOMEN'S DRESS	4	$99.00	$396.00	
12	321	14	245	43674	12	GR	WOMEN'S DRESS	2	$99.00	$198.00	
13										$0.00	
14										$0.00	
15										$0.00	
16										$0.00	
17										$0.00	
18										$0.00	
19										$0.00	
20										$0.00	
PAGE 1 OF 1							DOCUMENT TOTALS	34		$2,758.00	

an adjustment of total merchandise handled. The merchandise should be transferred out at its last retail; cost will be assumed to be the departmental cost compliment. If merchandise is being moved to a new location, where it will be sold at a further marked-down price, many retailers will first record the markdown at the sending location and then transfer the merchandise at the new, low retail value. This assigns the diminution in value to the location where it occurred rather than penalizing the receiving store.

CHAPTER SEVEN

Merchandise Terms—Definition, Application, Calculation

Consistent with other specialized branches of accounting, retail accounting (especially within the merchandise cycle) uses terms or expressions that require definition and some discussion of their practical application. This chapter includes only the most commonly used terms relating to merchandise cycle accounting. Terms relating specifically to the last-in, first-out (LIFO) method of inventory determination are discussed in Chapter Twenty-One.

RETAIL INVENTORY METHOD— KEY TERMS

The retail inventory method (RIM) is a method of controlling merchandise by using retail price amounts. Determination of end-of-period inventory at "cost" under the retail method is achieved by applying the cost-multiplier percentages of the respective departments to the departmental inventory dollar amounts at retail prices. This method is discussed and illustrated in detail in Chapter Twenty.

COST. The term *cost* is used to refer to the known cost of purchases and the estimated cost of ending inventory calculated using the retail method. The cost of purchases refers not only to the invoice cost for merchandise but other capitalization costs as well. The most common additional item is the cost of freight in to the store or distribution center. Other costs that may be included are buying costs, warehouse and distribution costs, occupancy costs, insurance, and so on. To be included, the costs must "add value" to the inventory, that is, be a cost of bringing inventory to its saleable condition and location. These costs depend on the specific facts and circumstances of each particular retailer.

RETAIL.   Retail refers to the selling price that is marked on merchandise (either for a specific item or in aggregate). Original retail, or alternatively, purchases at retail, represents the selling price established when the merchandise is initially marked for sale. This price may be subsequently revised either upward or downward by markups and markdowns and cancellations of markdowns and markups.

MARKUPS.   Markups are upward revisions to the original retail price established for an item or a group of merchandise. If a marked retail price of $500 is subsequently revised upward to $515, the increase of $15 is a markup.

MARKUP CANCELLATIONS.   When an error occurs in creating markups to the original marked retail prices, a correction is necessary to reduce or eliminate the markup, thereby obtaining either a lower retail or the original marked retail price. Such changes are known as markup cancellations. Although in a technical sense they may be viewed as markdowns, they are applied to reduce the amount of markups previously taken. However, the fact that a reduction in retail price follows an increase through a markup does not necessarily justify treating the reduction as a markup cancellation rather than a markdown. A markup cancellation is generally used to correct an unintentional error in pricing. Markup cancellations may also be used where the original markup is of a special nature and understood to be temporary at the time it was made and subject to reversal at a later date.

Generally speaking, price reductions are to be treated as markdowns and not as markup cancellations. To do otherwise, except in very rare and clear cases, is to open the door to abuse and permit the concealment of markdowns. This potential abuse is so troublesome that some controllers deem it desirable not to recognize markup cancellations at all.

Markup cancellations are to be taken *only* to correct markups on purchases of a *current* season. They should not be applied as corrections of cumulative markon in inventory as at the beginning of a season. Any corrections of such cumulative markon should be recorded as markdowns.

MARKDOWNS.   These are amounts deducted from original or current marked retail prices to arrive at new reduced retail prices.

Assume purchases that cost $100 were marked to sell for $150. If this retail price is reduced to $140, the $10 reduction is the markdown. There may be further markdowns; for example, the retail price may be reduced to $130 and then to $120. The additional $10 reductions in each instance are also markdowns.

MARKDOWN CANCELLATIONS. After merchandise has been reduced in retail price by markdowns, it may be found desirable to restore the original selling price or increase the retail to some intermediate price. This most frequently occurs when merchandise has been marked down temporarily, as for a special sales event, and the original price is restored on any unsold merchandise. It also may be done to correct other previous markdowns. These price changes, although upward revisions, are treated as markdown cancellations, to be offset against markdowns previously taken.

Goods originally marked to sell for $150 were marked down by $30 for a special sale. At the conclusion of the sale, the remaining merchandise was restored to its original selling price by processing a price change of $10. This $10 is not considered as a markup in the usual sense but as a partial offset to the markdown of $30. In this illustration, the markdown would not be considered to be $30, but $30 less the markdown cancellation of $10, or a net of $20.

Markdown cancellations are applicable only when they offset markdowns taken within a season. Restorations of retail prices on merchandise marked down prior to the beginning of the season are considered as markups, rather than as markdown cancellations.

CORRECTIONS OF RETAIL. The original retail established for purchases is sometimes revised downward, either to correct unintentional errors in original pricing or to reflect the retail of rebates granted by vendors directly related to the amount of markdowns incurred by the retailer.

Such corrections are recorded as reductions of purchases at retail rather than as markdowns.

Care should be exercised in classifying price changes as corrections of retail, so that retailers can guard against the manipulation of markons by the treatment of markdowns as corrections of original retail.

Corrections of retail that arise where markdowns are offset by related rebates from vendors should be limited to the proportionate amount of the markdown covered by the rebate, based upon the departmental markon percentage. For example, if the markdown is $2500 where the rebate is $1000, in a department with a markon of 50 percent, purchases at cost would be reduced $1000 and purchases at retail would be reduced by $2000. The difference of $500 ($2500 less the rebate at retail of $2000) would be recorded as a markdown.

INITIAL MARKON. This is the excess of the original retail value recorded for an item (or a group of goods) over the related recorded cost.

Purchases with a recorded cost of $200 are originally marked at a retail of $400. The difference between the recorded retail of $400 and the related cost of $200 represents the initial markon of $200.

MARKON. This is the difference between original marked retail (selling) price, plus any markups, and the purchase cost.

Purchases that cost $100 are marked originally to sell for $150. The $50 added to cost is the markon. If, however, the retail price of $150 is revised upward to $155, the markon increases to $55.

The term markon may refer to markon on specific purchases, or to total markon on purchases for a month, season, year, or other period and should not be confused with cumulative markon.

CUMULATIVE MARKON. Cumulative markon represents purchases at retail for a period *plus* markups for this period *plus* the beginning inventory at retail *less* the cost of purchases for the period and the cost of beginning inventory. This concept is represented by the formula:

Cumulative Markon Calculation

Purchases at Retail	$350
+ Beginning Inventory at Retail	225
+ Markups	10
− Purchases at Cost	200
− Beginning Inventory at Cost	100
= Cumulative Markon	$285

Inventory at the beginning of a period is $100 at cost and $225 at retail. Subsequent purchases cost $200 and are first marked to retail at $350 then revised upward to $360. Markdowns amounting to $30 are taken, none of which specifically cancels any part of the markup of $10. Cumulative markon is the markon of $125 in the opening inventory plus the markon of $160 on purchases, a total of $285.

MARKON PERCENTAGE. Markon percentage is computed as the percentage of markon to originally marked retail, or in cases where the original retail price has been revised upwards, markon as a percentage of original retail plus markups.

CUMULATIVE MARKON PERCENTAGE. This term is the cumulative markon as a percentage of the sum of beginning inventory at retail and purchases at retail plus markups. This percentage is applied to an ending inventory at retail to calculate the amount to be subtracted from ending inventory at retail to reduce such inventory to an estimated cost.

The difference between revised retail of $515 (originally retail of $500) and $300 (the cost of opening inventory plus the cost of purchases) represents cumulative markon in the amount of $215. The percentage of cumulative markon in this case is the ratio of $215 to $515, or 41.75 percent, or alternately, 0.4175.

NET MARKON. This term refers to cumulative markon *less* markdowns. Net markon is not to be confused with gross margin. There is some similarity between the two, but gross margin includes purchase discounts and is calculated after all retail reductions. Net markon is a more limited term. It does not enter into computations under the retail method, except as required when the LIFO method of inventory determination is used (see Chapter Twenty-One).

MAINTAINED MARKON. Since markdowns, sales discounts, and shrinkages intervene between the original marking of merchandise and its ultimate sale, it is necessary to distinguish between the original (or revised) merchandise retail and sales retail. The retail placed upon merchandise is not the price expected to be realized on all goods sold, and there may be sales discounts and stock shrinkages. These factors are taken into consideration in setting the original retail price, so that sales retail (that is, after markdowns, sales discounts, and shrinkages) will produce the desired maintained or realized markon.

Original retail is usually higher than sales retail just as cumulative markon is usually higher than maintained markon. Therefore, in deriving cost from original retail, it is necessary to reduce retail by cumulative, rather than by maintained, markon. In comparing markon on purchases and stock with maintained markon sales, it should be recognized that they are not percentages of the same base, although both are expressed as percentages of retail.

PRICE LINES AND MARKON. Initial markons are usually established with the expectation that the resulting maintained markon will be sufficient to absorb operating expenses, as well as to allow some margin of merchandising profit. However, the establishment of departmental markons is not solely a mathematical process; it must take into consideration all competitive and other pertinent factors. Examples include the desirability of maintaining a complete line of certain products or promoting special sales events. With the goal markon in mind, the actual pricing is adjusted to meet existing market conditions. In all likelihood, the same markon cannot be placed upon every purchase of merchandise in a given department.

For a considerable number of merchandise classifications, "price points" are established on the basis of a store's experience with the desires of its customers, as well as to buttress the image the store is attempting to project in its trading area. Merchandise is then "brought in" at these price points, with resultant variations in markons of specific purchases above and below the desired average markon for the department.

SALES DISCOUNTS.   Retail accounts receivable are not commonly subject to trade discounts or cash discounts on remittances, as may be true with the accounts receivable of wholesalers or manufacturers. However, in limited circumstances, sales discounts are made available, most commonly to employees of the store. These discounts are generally deducted from the sale price of the merchandise as the sale is recorded. Just as with markdowns, sales discounts are not considered in determining markon or cumulative markon.

SHRINKAGES AND OVERAGES.   This term refers to differences between actual inventory on hand and the corresponding amounts reflected in the stock records, where the latter amounts are greater than the actual stocks on hand. This difference is also called stock shortage. Excesses of actual stocks on hand over the amounts shown in the stock records are referred to as *stock overages*. Stock overages may result from inaccurate physical inventories or recording errors in the records. A shrinkage ordinarily represents an aggregate of stock recordkeeping errors and actual physical losses of merchandise through such factors as theft, breakage, and spoilage. Shrinkages have no effect on markon, cumulative markon, or the cost multiplier but are recorded in the same manner as markdowns.

DISCOUNTS EARNED.   Recognition of cash discounts on purchases earned varies among retailers. Some retailers recognize these discounts when received, while others defer recognition until the related merchandise is sold. Additionally, some retailers record purchases net of these discounts, others record purchases gross of discounts and record any unearned portion as a reduction of inventory. In addition to different theoretical beliefs, practice varies with the complexity of the retailers' systems and experience.

The argument for deferring recognition of cash discount income until the merchandise is sold, regardless of when discounts accrue or are received, rests upon the belief that income is generated by the sale, not the purchase, of merchandise. Discounts on purchases under this method represent the discounts applicable to the purchases of the period, without regard to when payment for these purchases is made. The discounts are recognized only to the extent the related merchandise is sold and the unearned remainder is reflected as a deduction in the end of period inventory balance.

Other retailers argue that cash discounts are earned as a function of cash management decisions rather than the sale of merchandise. They maintain that the timing of invoice payments is generally not related to the sale of merchandise. Additionally, early payment of invoices to obtain discounts generally increases the burden of financing inventory by increasing short-term interest expensed in the current period. Given these circumstances, the second group argues that recognition on a "when-received" basis results in a better matching of revenue and expense.

After establishing a policy specifying when the discount is to be recognized, the retailer must also determine how to record the discount. Purchases can be recorded either net of purchase discounts or gross. When purchases are recorded net of discount, no account is set up for discounts earned; there is only an expense account for discounts lost. This method has the benefit of automatically resulting in an inventory valuation appropriately stated net-of-discounts, since the cost multiplier will be derived from net-of-discounts purchases. When purchases are recorded gross of discounts, the unearned portion of discounts received must be applied as a reduction of inventory.

EXPRESSING INVENTORY AMOUNTS. Explanations of the retail inventory method usually state that the merchandise records are kept at retail and also at cost, that is, "cost" as computed under the retail method. This resultant inventory valuation has been variously described as inventory at cost, inventory at the lower of cost or market, inventory as computed under the retail method, and inventory on the basis of the lower of cost or market as determined by the retail inventory method.

The retail method can be described as an attempt to estimate the cost of ending inventory by applying the relationship noted between total cost and total retail of goods available for sale for a period to the end of period retail amount. How nearly the estimated cost approximates the actual cost depends upon a number of factors, most notably the range of cost multipliers within the department and the inventory mix at the end of the period. The limitations of the retail inventory method will be more fully discussed in Chapter Twenty.

The end of period cost estimated using the retail inventory method differs from the actual or theoretical cost (which could only be known if each item in ending inventory could be identified and matched with its invoice cost); however, the estimated cost is usually referred to as *inventory at cost.* Some retailers use an alternative term *inventory at mercantile.*

The following list summarizes some of the common methods of describing and estimating inventories of retailers:

- Inventories at original retail prices (before giving effect to any reductions).

- Inventories at retail (at marked retail prices).

- Inventories at actual cost.

- Inventories at mercantile (estimated cost under the retail inventory method).

- Inventories at the lower of cost or market.

MERCHANDISE TURN.   Merchandise turn represents the rate of merchandise movement. This rate is derived by dividing sales for the designated period by the average inventory, at retail, for that period.

INVENTORY-TO-SALES RATIO.   The inventory-to-sales ratio reflects the relation between current inventory levels and current sales. The ratio may be stated in terms of either units or dollars. If ratios are determined based on dollar amounts, retail figures should be used for inventory (and for sales).

Inventory-to-sales ratios are an important aid to management in ascertaining whether a sound relating of inventory to sales is being maintained on a current basis.

Using retail figures, the inventory-to-sales ratio is derived by dividing the inventory at the beginning of a period by the actual (or projected) sales for the period. The period commonly used is a month or four- or five-week period. For example, if inventory, at retail, on April 1, is $10,000, and sales for the month of April are $2500, the inventory-to-sales ratio is 4.

For practical use in monitoring and planning stock and sales, the buyer or department manager in this example may not wish to wait until the end of April to derive the inventory-to-sales ratio. At the beginning of the month, or at any time during the month, it may be useful to develop this ratio utilizing estimated sales or actual sales to date and estimated sales for the balance of the month. Since the purpose of deriving the ratio is to be able to plan operations more knowledgeably on a day-to-day basis, an estimate can be made sometime during the month of April of the probable inventory level at the end of the month. Then, on the basis of planned sales for May, the estimated inventory-to-sales ratio for May can be developed. If unsatisfactory, it may be possible to revise departmental plans to achieve more desirable results.

The inventory-to-sales ratio is a tool of day-to-day departmental management derived from actual results or estimated partially or wholly upon projections. Monthly departmental tabulations of this ratio over past periods, together with comparisons with estimated and goal ratios, should be an informative, useful aid to merchandise control.

CHAPTER EIGHT

Gross Margin Return on Inventory Investment (GMROI)

Retailers utilize a number of different performance measurement indicators when evaluating their operations. One of these performance indicators is referred to as the Gross Margin Return on Investment (GMROI) rate. A GMROI rate combines the effect of profit margin and inventory turnover in one performance measurement indicator and thus facilitates equitable comparisons of the profit contributions from different merchandise investments.

The GMROI rate for a merchandise item with an annual sales volume of 1000 units, an average inventory investment of 125 units, a cost per unit of $.75 and a selling price per unit of $1.00 would be calculated as follows:

Example 8.1   GMROI Calculation

$$\frac{\text{Annual Sales}}{\text{1,000 Units}} \div \frac{\text{Average Inventory}}{\text{125 Units}} = \frac{\text{Annual Inventory Turn}}{8.0}$$

$$\frac{\text{Annual Inventory Turn}}{8.0} \times \frac{\text{Cost Markon}}{33\%} = \frac{\text{GMROI}}{2.7}$$

The Cost Markon rate is the percentage rate by which the cost of the item must be increased to reach its selling price. In this example, the item's cost is $.75 which must be increased by $.25 or 33.33 percent to reach the $1.00 selling price. The Cost Markon rate, rather than the gross margin, is used in the GMROI rate calculation because it represents the rate earned based on the item's cost.

The same result is also achieved by dividing average inventory at cost (125 units × $.75 = $93.75) into gross margin dollars ($250). This method is used by the National Retail Federation for their calculations.

GMROI RATE COMPARISONS

GMROI rate calculations and comparisons can be made for individual merchandise items as well as for entire departments or stores and can serve as a catalyst for the development of strategies for improvements in the rate of return realized on the retailer's inventory investment. For example, GMROI rate calculations for three different merchandise items might show the following:

Example 8.2   GMROI Rate Calculations and Comparisons

Item	Gross Margin	Cost Markon		Annual Inv. Turn		GMROI
A	40.0%	66.67%	×	2.0	=	1.33
B	30.0%	42.86%	×	4.0	=	1.71
C	25.0%	33.33%	×	10.0	=	3.33

A comparison of these GMROI rates indicates that investments in item C would yield a return of $3.33 on each dollar invested in this item, whereas items A and B would only return $1.33 and $1.71, respectively, even though their margin rates are higher. This is because item C has a higher turnover rate and provides a greater rate of return relative to the cost amount of the inventory investment.

This example also shows that there is more than one way in which GMROI rates can be increased. They can be increased by reductions in the average inventory level, thus improving the turnover rate or by changes in selling price, which if increased might improve the margin rate, or if decreased might stimulate sales and thus improve the turnover rate. Retailers can use GMROI rates as a guide for the development of strategies that will improve the rate of return from their inventory investment. Based on the preceding example the following strategies might evolve:

- *Reduce the Average Inventory Investment in Item A by 10 percent.* If this could be accomplished without a corresponding decline in sales, the GMROI would become 1.48 rather than 1.33. This means that an additional $.15 would be earned for each dollar invested in item A.

- *Decrease the Selling Price of Item B to Stimulate Turnover.* If the selling price was reduced so that the margin rate could be cut from 30 to 28 and if as a result the turn rate would improve from 4.00 to 5.00, the GMROI rate would increase from 1.71 to 1.94. This would mean a return improvement of $.23 for every dollar invested in item B.

- *Increase the Selling Price of Item C.* If the selling price could be increased so that the margin rate would go from 25 to 26 without a corresponding slowdown in the turn rate, the GMROI rate would become 3.51 rather than 3.33. This would mean a return improvement of $.18 for every dollar invested in item C.

The point is that the profit contribution from a retailer's merchandise investment can be improved by increasing margin rates or turn rates or by any combination of the two. GMROI rates quantify the relationship of these factors when considered together rather than as individual components of a retailer's strategy. GMROI rate comparisons for different merchandise items, departments, or even entire stores can be an effective tool for the identification of earnings improvement opportunities.

Retailers should recognize, however, that no specific GMROI rate should be considered as either acceptable or unacceptable. GMROI rates are a relative performance measurement indicator that can be used for the identification of merchandise investments. These investments can produce better than average or less than average returns relative to the retailer's other merchandise investments. Comparisons of GMROI rates and evaluations of those merchandise investments that produce less than average returns can facilitate the development of merchandising strategies that provide more margin dollars for the retailer without an increase in the retailer's inventory investment.

EFFECT OF VENDOR PAYMENT TERMS

GMROI rates are a useful tool for analysis of the rate of return on selected merchandise investments. GMROI rates are somewhat misleading, however, due to the use of inventory turn rates rather than the flow of funds as a component of the GMROI calculation. This results in a return rate that reflects the physical possession of goods rather than the actual financial commitment which exists in terms of the funding requirement between the time of payment to the vendor and the receipt of funds from customers.

A refinement to the GMROI rate calculation, referred to as a cost-of-money adjustment, reflects the funding requirement as a result of the difference in time between payment to a vendor and the sale of the merchandise.

The performance measurement indicator which results is referred to as the cash-flow adjusted GMROI rate.

This rate considers the cost of the financial commitment which arises as a result of differences in time between payments to vendors and the removal of the merchandise from a retailer's inventory; it does not reflect the effect of credit sales. Although in certain situations it may be appropriate to consider the effect of credit sales, it is not generally necessary. Retailers customarily establish trade receivable service charge policies providing a return on credit sales which is considered separate and apart from the return on their merchandise investments. Retailers also must sometimes offer credit without a related service charge because of competitive conditions. On the other hand, vendor payment terms are a fundamental part of the overall agreement between a retailer and a vendor and should be considered in conjunction with merchandise investment decisions.

Cash-flow adjusted GMROI rates are computed by increasing or decreasing the GMROI rate by the cost of money adjustment. An example of how this would be done for the three merchandise items used in the preceding example follows:

Example 8.3   Cost of Cash Flow

Item	GMROI		Money Adjustment		Adjusted GMROI
A	133.34	×	(.22)	=	133.12
B	171.44	×	(8.88)	=	162.56
C	333.30	×	(1.92)	=	331.38

These cash-flow adjusted GMROI rates show that the profit contribution from a retailer's merchandise investment changes to some extent when the cost of funds utilized as a consequence of differences in time between the date of vendor payment and the date of sale for the merchandise is considered. The degree of change depends, of course, on the magnitude of the time differential and the retailer's current cost of funds. Cash-flow adjusted GMROI rates provide a more equitable basis for the comparison of merchandise profit contributions in situations where differences between a vendor's payment terms and the retailer's inventory holding period are a significant factor.

The additional data required for the calculation of the cost-of-money adjustment includes the payment terms for the vendors involved and the retailer's current interest rate on short-term borrowings (although a retailer may choose a different interest rate if it is more representative of the retailer's current cost of funds).

This data has been used to compute the cost-of-money adjustment for the three merchandise items just discussed. Cash-flow adjusted GMROI rate

Example 8.4   Cost of Money Adjustment

Step 1. Compute days on-hand.

Item	Days in Year		Annual Turn Rate		Days On-Hand
A	365	÷	2	=	184
B	365	÷	4	=	91
C	365	÷	10	=	37

Step 2. Compute number of days requiring vendor funding.

Item	Days On-Hand		Assumed Vendor Payment Terms		Days in Turn Cycle Requiring Funding
A	184	−	180 days	=	4
B	91	−	10 days	=	81
C	37	−	30 days	=	7

Step 3. Annualize funding days.

Item	Funded Days		Annual Turn Rate		Annualized Funded Days
A	4	×	2.0	=	8
B	81	×	4.0	=	324
C	7	×	10.0	=	70

Step 4. Compute cost of money adjustment.

Item	$\dfrac{\text{Funded Days}}{\text{Days in Year}}$		Proration Factor		Current Short Term Interest Rate		Cost of Money Adjustment
A	$\dfrac{8}{365}$	=	.0219	×	10.0%	=	.22%
B	$\dfrac{324}{365}$	=	.8877	×	10.0%	=	8.88%
C	$\dfrac{70}{365}$	=	.1918	×	10.0%	=	1.92%

calculations would generally be appropriate for specific merchandise items or relatively narrow lines of merchandise only. Calculations of cash-flow adjusted GMROI rates for broader classifications of merchandise would usually be impractical due to variations in vendor terms and turnover rates within such classifications. The cash-flow adjusted GMROI rate analysis technique is useful, however, for comparisons of the return on merchandise investments where differences between vendor payment terms and inventory holding periods vary significantly from one merchandise item to another. In such situations, the cash-flow adjusted GMROI rate calculation can be used as an augmentation to the GMROI rate analysis so that the effect of favorable or unfavorable vendor payment terms is considered in conjunction with the merchandise investment decision.

RELATIONSHIP BETWEEN SALES SPACE UTILIZATION AND GMROI RATES

When making merchandise investment decisions, retailers must consider the economic use of sales space as well as the return that will be realized from their inventory investment. The GMROI rate considers only the investment in inventory and *does not* reflect the effect of sales space utilization. The calculation of gross margin dollars per square foot provides an effective comparison.

The following illustration shows how gross margin per square foot would be calculated for the three previously discussed merchandise items.

SAR rates may also be calculated by multiplying sales by the applicable margin rate and then dividing the result by the square feet of sales area used. Using this approach, the SAR rate amount for item C above would be calculated as follows:

Example 8.5   Gross Margin Dollars Per Square Foot Calculation

Assumed Sales	Gross Margin	Margin Dollars	Square Feet of Sales Area	GM $/Sq. Ft.
$1,000,000 ×	25% =	$250,000 ÷	3,000 =	$83.33

A comparison of these rates indicates that item A provides a margin dollar return of $200.01 for each square foot of sales space used, whereas items B and C provide only $120.01 and $83.33, respectively. This is a dramatic difference when compared to the GMROI rate, which reflects only the return from the inventory investment. This comparison shows the following:

Example 8.6   Productivity Comparison

Item	Return on Each $100 of Inventory Investment	Return on Each Square Foot of Sales Space Used
A	$133.34	$200.01
B	$171.44	$120.01
C	$333.30	$ 83.33

By comparing the margin dollar return in this way a retailer can readily see the profit producing relationship of inventory investment and sales space utilization. This can aid retailers in the development of strategies for overall earnings improvement in terms of space utilization as well as merchandise investment productivity. In the preceding example, a retailer might implement the following profit improvement strategies:

- *Reduce the Floor Space Allocated to Item B.* If a 20 percent reduction in floor space could be achieved without a corresponding decline in inventory investment or sales, the gross margin rate would become $150.01 rather than $120.01. This would mean a margin dollar return improvement of $30.00 for each square foot of sales space allocated to item B, in addition to making 500 square feet of sales space available for other profitable use.

- *Increase the Inventory Investment for Item C.* If the inventory investment could be increased by 10 percent without a decline in the GMROI rate or the use of more floor space, the gross margin rate return would improve from $83.33 to $91.66. This would mean a margin dollar return improvement of $8.33 for each square foot of sales space allocated to item C.

Retailers should strive to optimize the return from their inventory investment as well as to utilize sales space efficiently. The gross margin rate and GMROI rate performance measurement analysis techniques, when used together, are useful tools for assisting retailers in the accomplishment of these dual objectives.

SUMMARY

Today's sophisticated retail information systems make data available to assist retailers in the development of profit improvement strategies. One way to accomplish this is through the use of this data for analysis of the profit contributions from specific merchandise investments. To this end, the GMROI rate, cash-flow adjusted GMROI rate, and gross margin per square foot performance measurement analysis techniques are useful tools for comparative analysis of the margin dollar return from specific merchandise investments. It should be recognized, however, that there are other performance measurement techniques that also may be appropriate for the retailers use, such as Direct Product Profitability (DPP) analysis that measures the net profitability of each merchandise item after the allocation of all associated costs. The selection of the performance measurement techniques a retailer might use depends upon the retailer's specific circumstances, the related costs, and the expected benefits.

PART TWO

Operations and Control

CHAPTER NINE

Warehouse Control

In this chapter, the term warehousing is being used very broadly to represent all the techniques a retailer might employ to centrally receive merchandise prior to its delivery to stores. This would include distribution centers that are flow-through facilities, warehouses that stock goods for subsequent shipment, and all the variations in between. The objective is to maintain effective control over the merchandise moving through this channel.

The question of *effective control* is one that must be considered in every aspect of a retail business. However, it is especially important at the warehouse or distribution center, because of the concentrated nature of this function—a very high percentage of merchandise will funnel through this one location. From a security standpoint, truckloads of merchandise are at risk. For merchants, it is vital to get products to the stores in time for promotions or season openings. Finance managers must have accurate information as to the quantity and quality of the inventory investment. This is where merchandise first reaches the retailer and, therefore, a most important place to ensure the establishment of effective control.

RECEIVING DOCK

A dock receipt form must be prepared for every shipment that arrives at the warehouse. This need not be a complex procedure and can be accomplished through a computer terminal if that is desired. The essential requirement is

EXHIBIT 9.1 Dock Receipt

COOPBRAND STORES DOCK RECEIPT						
DOCUMENT NUMBER	STORE NUMBER	RECEIPT DATE	DEPT. NUMBER	ORDER NUMBER	ORDER NUMBER	ORDER NUMBER
123456	2	08 /25 / XX	321	723156	234567	
VENDOR NAME		CARRIER NAME		INVOICE NUMBER	INVOICE NUMBER	INVOICE NUMBER
USA CORP.		APACHE TRUCKING		789107	565646	
NUMBER OF CARTONS/PACKAGES	CONDITION OF SHIPMENT	PRO NUMBER		INVOICE AMOUNT	INVOICE AMOUNT	INVOICE AMOUNT
16	OK	12345678		$ 2,574.00	$ 2925.00	$
WEIGHT OF SHIPMENT	FREIGHT CHARGES	POINT OF ORIGIN				
		CITY	STATE		COUNTRY	
124 LBS.	$ 375.00	L.A.	CA.		USA	

that there be a receiving procedure that creates a prenumbered record of what has been accepted into the building, from whom and when. The information that should be recorded at this point includes: date, carrier, PRO number (carrier's invoice), vendor, number of cartons, weight, shipment condition, and purchase order number. If the dock receipt is created at a computer terminal, the purchase order could be validated at that time. Frequently, however, the dock receipt is prepared manually and entered into the computer system (if any) afterwards. This may be done because of physical problems of having computer terminals at the dock or because many retailers will accept a shipment even if there is no order on file.

Dock receipts are created by the receiving department. However, the numbering sequence and their subsequent disposition should be the responsibility of the accounts payable department. This is because the dock receipt becomes the control mechanism to ensure that the shipment is physically processed, that financial records are updated for the receipt of merchandise, and that vendor and carrier's invoices are processed for payment (see Exhibit 9.1).

DETAIL RECEIVING

For most retailers, the next step is a detailed count of the merchandise received. This count will be the basis for three important processes: warehouse storage, merchandise distribution, and vendor payment. Accuracy is extremely important. In a few cases, merchandise is stored, unopened, until its selling season. This would generally be feasible with vendors where adjustments could be made at the time that detail counting is finally done, since the vendor's invoice would have already been paid (an alternative is to check these cartons on a random sample basis only).

Chapter Three, dealing with purchase order management discusses various techniques used to detail merchandise received. Briefly, these can include receiving against: the purchase order, a computer-produced checking document, the vendor's packing slip, or on a blank piece of paper. In addition, each of these approaches (except the last) can show expected quantities or require "blind" entry. Whichever technique is used, it must be supported by a system that encourages accuracy throughout the process. This is usually accomplished through a quality control program that establishes individual and group objectives, measures individual performance, and strives for a proper balance between accuracy and productivity. An effective warehouse quality control program will include *all* the activities that precede and follow detail receiving.

WAREHOUSE STORAGE

Unless the facility is entirely flow-through, merchandise will be kept at the warehouse prior to shipment to the stores. This creates a new set of functions whose control implications must be considered. The levels of control will depend on the complexity of the operation, but they may include:

- Pallet control to the storage area.
- Locator systems for bulk storage and picking areas. These can be based on preassigned slots, random storage, or a combination.
- Merchandise retrieval (picking).

Too often retailers do not have sufficient information about what is in their warehouse and where the merchandise is located. As a result, new orders can be written for goods that are already owned, or merchandise that is owned may not be moved to the stores on a timely basis. To preclude these costly errors, it is helpful to continually monitor the accuracy of the warehouse locator systems. Cycle counting of warehouse merchandise against stock records, and from the records to the merchandise, should help to maintain a high level of quality. At the least, such procedures will identify inaccuracies as they occur. It is still management's responsibility to review the results of these efforts and ensure that corrective action is taken if errors become excessive.

DISTRIBUTION AND SHIPPING

In order for merchandise to move from warehouse to store, the first step that is required is determination of the quantity to be shipped. This can either be done in advance of receipt on the purchase order (predistribution), after receipt of merchandise (postdistribution), or from merchandise already being held in the warehouse (replenishment). (More details on Distribution are discussed in Chapter Four.)

When specific items of merchandise are being allocated to individual stores, as part of the distribution function, it is not uncommon to discover that the original count (detail receipt) was incorrect. If this problem exists to any great extent, an attempt should be made to improve the accuracy of the detail receiving operation and delaying the update of financial records until after the second count may be necessary.

After merchandise is picked for distribution, it will be packed, in some fashion, for the store, placed on a truck, and sent out. Each of these steps offers opportunity for inadvertent as well as intentional mistakes. It is necessary to have procedures in place that will ensure that the correct merchandise is placed in a carton, that the carton is addressed to the correct store, and that the carton is placed on the correct truck. Of course, in order to close the loop, it would be helpful to know that the merchandise was received, intact, at the designated store. The basic warehouse control system should provide a high degree of accuracy in all steps involved in processing merchandise. These systems should be validated by a continuous quality control program. While quality control is vital to the success of a warehouse operation, it can only be valuable in combination with the proper systems. In other words, quality control must be built into each of the basic processes.

CHAPTER TEN

Merchandise
Accounts Payable

A retail accounts payable department is the culmination of a process that starts (usually) with the buyer writing a purchase order, goes through the vendor's shipping and billing activities, and, finally, the retailer's receiving department. Accounts payable departments must process the documents resulting from these events in a way that will support good relations with vendors, while maintaining the highest possible levels of control at the lowest possible cost. Many accounts payable departments have had difficulty satisfying all these objectives.

The accounts payable department's basic control responsibilities are:

- To accurately record the value of all merchandise belonging to the company on a timely basis.

- To ensure that all vendor invoices are for shipments received.

- To ensure that payment is made in the correct amount, at the correct time, only to those properly entitled.

VENDOR MASTER FILES

Vendor name and address files become a major element in the control of disbursements; especially in automated systems, the establishment of a well-controlled vendor master file (VMF) is a first priority. Even if the file contains expanded merchandise and performance information, its initiation and change should be solely the responsibility of the controller's office or of the Accounts Payable department. Furthermore, all additions and changes to the file should generate a printed audit trail which is reviewed and retained. If the VMF is being used to collect other, noncritical information, that portion of the file should be accessible for inquiry and change to whatever extent is necessary without compromising control over the disbursement name and address.

INVOICE PROCESSING

Purchase order management, presented in Chapter Three, describes the purchase order and receiving functions; the accounts payable department puts these documents together with the vendor's invoice to complete the transaction.

Invoices can arrive in a number of ways: through electronic data transmission (EDI), with the merchandise shipment, through the mail, to the receiving location, or to a centralized Accounts Payable department. Invoices might be a statement-type, covering more than one shipment. Finally, a vendor might send multiple copies of an invoice. All these variations suggest that, insofar as possible, a retailer should not base the merchandise control system on invoices, but should assure tight control over receipts. If this is done, the invoice can be processed against the receiving/purchase-order record, not vice versa.

The activities involved in the invoice processing function are mostly affected by the degree to which the process is automated:

- In a fully automated, EDI environment, there may be no manual intervention.

- In an automated purchase order management system, the entry of invoice header and total data may be sufficient to complete the process.

Whether automated or manual, the controls and procedures which should be established over invoice processing are as follows:

INVOICE MATCHING.   One-for-one checking of the items and quantities between the vendor invoice and the detailed receiving record.

ORDER CHECKING. A comparison of items, costs, and terms between the vendor invoice and the purchase order.

BILL FIGURING. Verification of extensions and additions on the vendor's invoice, based on cost and retail prices from the purchase order or from an authorized price list. Some invoices only reflect unit prices at retail and then deduct an agreed upon "trade discount" from the total.

JOURNALIZING TRANSACTIONS. The purchase journal is an accounting record that supports the debit to purchases (in the general ledger and the retail stock ledger) and the credit to accounts payable established as the result of invoices successfully matched and processed during the period. In addition, those individuals who are held responsible for inventory levels, buyers and/or store managers, carefully review their sections of the purchase journal to insure its accuracy, because it is the report that reflects merchandise charged in to their department at cost and retail (see Exhibit 10.1).

PURCHASE ACCRUALS. At the end of each accounting period, merchandise receipts not processed through to the purchase journal should be accrued. One of the controls strongly recommended for all retailers is the creation of a sequentially numbered receiving record, created for every shipment at the time of receipt (see Chapter 3). The accounts payable department should maintain control over the number sequences outstanding and receive a copy of each receiving record after it is issued. The accounts payable copy should be cleared when the vendor invoice is processed; remaining copies will be the basis for the purchase accrual.

Retailers generally do not accrue invoices for which merchandise has not yet been received (merchandise-in-transit) except at year-end closing. At that time, invoices processed in the new accounting period are usually reviewed to identify transactions belonging to the prior period.

DISBURSEMENT. This chapter started by identifying one of the accounts payable department's basic responsibilities to be insuring the correctness of the payment. It is at the time of disbursement that controls must be strongest. The techniques used may rely on automated controls, manual reviews, or combinations of techniques, but their objectives should be to insure that:

- Payment is made only for merchandise received.
- Payee name and address agree with invoice.
- All discounts and allowances have been deducted.
- Duplicate payments are not made.

EXHIBIT 10.1 Purchase Journal

COOPBRAND CLOTHING STORES

CREATE DATE: 09/03/ XX

PURCHASE JOURNAL
MONTH ENDING 07/31/ XX

DEPT: 321 WOMEN'S DRESSES

DATE	TRANSACTION TYPE	INVOICE NUMBER	VENDOR NAME	VENDOR DUNS NUMBER	COST	RETAIL	GROSS MARGIN
07/06/XX	INVOICE	1234567	KRUGER CLOTHING	543579343	$3,427.00	$5,218.00	52.26%
07/06/XX	INVOICE	2345678	BROADLOOM INC.	895738745	$4,839.00	$7,488.00	54.74%
07/06/XX	CREDIT MEMO	3456789	RESALE ASSC.	472347934	($535.00)	($830.00)	55.14%
07/09/XX	INVOICE	4567890	CUTS ARE US	347374438	$5,655.00	$8,708.00	53.99%
07/09/XX	INVOICE	5678901	PROFIT PROFILES	327475589	$434.00	$668.00	53.92%
07/11/XX	INVOICE	6789012	HEMLINE USA	498954985	$45.00	$69.00	53.33%
07/11/XX	INVOICE	7890123	PANTS PLUS	894894894	$5,345.00	$7,953.00	48.79%
07/14/XX	INVOICE	8901234	GARMENTS GALOUR	478743784	$565.00	$880.00	55.75%
07/15/XX	INVOICE	9012345	NY FASHION	347847843	$3,455.00	$5,363.00	55.22%
07/15/XX	DEBIT MEMO	2345678	BROADLOOM INC.	895738745	$68.00	$105.00	54.41%
07/21/XX	INVOICE	1357924	VENDOR DELUXE	487347478	$4,366.00	$6,782.00	55.34%
07/21/XX	INVOICE	2468013	HEMLINE USA	278778893	$4,355.00	$6,753.00	55.06%
07/25/XX	INVOICE	3579246	KRUGER CLOTHING	474778344	$676.00	$1,054.00	55.92%
07/28/XX	INVOICE	4680235	PROFIT PROFILES	437849898	$234.00	$360.00	53.85%
					$32,929.00	$50,571.00	53.58%

TOTAL ENTRIES: 14

- All outstanding claims have been deducted.
- Payment is made by the due date.

PREPAYMENTS. Occasionally, certain vendors offer cash discounts for payment within a time period that the retailer cannot normally achieve. If these discount terms are not negotiable, and if the vendor is a well-established, financially sound and reputable company, the retailer may elect to prepay these invoices in order not to lose the cash discount.

These invoices are usually received directly in the accounts payable department where they are processed for payment prior to matching and order checking. The prepaid invoice is then routed back through the system to complete the normal processing steps. At the time of prepayment, the debit should be to accounts payable or to a prepayment account, not to merchandise purchases. When the completed transaction comes through the normal accounts payable cycle, merchandise purchases is debited and the prepayment account credited.

Obviously, prepayments should be kept to an absolute minimum and, if possible, avoided altogether. In addition to adding unnecessary processing costs to each transaction, additional controls must be instituted to insure that these invoices are not paid twice and that all prepayments are properly cleared in a timely manner.

RETURNS TO VENDORS. Goods to be returned to vendors (RTV's) are entered on prenumbered "chargeback" or "claim" forms after proper approval (which frequently includes vendor authorization), and are shipped out through the vendor return goods room. This room operates along the lines of the delivery room wherein nothing is permitted to leave the store unless entered on a chargeback (some goods, of course, may go out on memo charges). Quantities and prices are verified before goods are passed for shipment. The completed chargebacks are forwarded to the accounts payable office, which maintains a numerical control over, and accountability for, all chargeback numbers.

The chargeback forms are prepared at least in duplicate, with one copy for the vendor and one copy retained by the store. There may be a third copy for inclusion with the package to facilitate handling by the vendor, and additional store copies for distribution to the statistical area, marking area files, and accounts payable. On the store's copy, the retail value is shown. The retail value should be the same as the amount charged into stock when the merchandise was purchased. (If there have been any retail price changes, they should be canceled.) The chargebacks are entered on the purchase journal as negative amounts so as to reduce the purchases to net figures.

If the goods being returned have already been paid for, accounts payable should obtain assurance, from the buying organization, of collectibility or the retailer's ability to apply a credit toward future purchases, preventing a debit balance from the RTV.

Given the clerical cost of processing vendor chargebacks and claims, it may be desirable to institute a policy pursuant to which claims under a specified minimum dollar amount are not processed.

ALLOWANCES AND ADJUSTMENTS

Allowances from vendors can be obtained for a variety of reasons and, based on the justification, will usually be treated either as a reduction of expense or of merchandise cost.

ADVERTISING ALLOWANCES. These transactions can have two treatments. Generally, when these allowances are given to support specific ads, they represent a reduction of advertising expense. Frequently, the retailer may not deduct these chargebacks against merchandise purchases but must wait for reimbursement, sometimes from third parties such as the Advertising Checking Bureau.

In some instances, deductions against merchandise cost are allowed by the vendor but are identified as an advertising allowance. In these cases, it might be appropriate to treat the deduction as a credit against purchases.

MERCHANDISE ALLOWANCES OR PRICE REBATES. Whether quantity discounts or not, these allowances may affect retail prices. When retail prices are reduced as a consequence of an allowance, purchase at retail should be credited with a reduction proportionate to the cumulative or specific purchase markon percentage of the allowance received. In other words, these reductions are not markdowns but are adjustments to the retail price of purchases. However, when the amount of retail reduction is in excess of the retail equivalent of the allowance, the excess is treated as a markdown. When no retail reduction follows a vendor's price allowance, the allowance is credited against purchases at cost with no adjustment of purchases at retail. This has the obvious effect of increasing the markon percentage.

When a considerable period of time intervenes between the specific dates merchandise was purchased and the receipt of material amounts of vendor credits, a special problem arises. This would ordinarily be the case with regard to seasonal or annual quantity or other allowances. A seasonal allowance distorts the purchase markon of the month in which it is entered, but for the season as a whole the markon may be only slightly affected, provided the markon is determined on the seasonal basis. An allowance on purchases of an entire year not only distorts the purchase markon of the month in which the allowance is entered but also affects the seasonal markon average. In this connection, it is necessary to consider whether the effect upon markon is great enough to warrant special procedures in handling an allowance of this type. It is desirable that markons not be unduly distorted, but allowances from vendors are proper departmental purchase adjustments and should enter into the determination of gross margin.

Two courses of action are open where the distorting effect of purchase allowances is sufficient to call for special treatment. That part of the allowance not applicable to the current season may be treated as a special item of departmental gross margin, similar to discounts earned, and kept out of tabulations of purchases. In fact, the entire allowance may be so treated, including that part applicable to the current season; but this tends to keep the markon slightly lower than it otherwise would be, with a consequent tendency toward a corresponding inflation of inventory. Practically, however, the effect upon inventory may be so slight as not to require adjustment. Theoretically, assuming that there is no issue as to collectibility, it would be appropriate to estimate, at the close of each season, any allowances not yet received but accruable, and to appropriately adjust that season's purchases. The difference between the estimates already applied and the totals received will then fall into the purchase accumulations of the season of receipt.

DISCOUNTS IN INVENTORIES AND DISCOUNTS EARNED

Cash discounts comprise an important element of gross margin. A distinction should be made between cash discounts, which are part of the invoice terms and are contingent upon payment of the invoice in accordance with such terms, and trade discounts, which effectively represent an adjustment of the invoice price whether deducted directly on the face of the invoice, or whether already deducted in determining invoice amounts.

Cash discounts generally are greater than ordinarily would be allowed solely for the use of funds. Practically speaking, they represent a mixture of pure cash discounts and the outgrowth of trade practices and customs.

Accounting for Discount Income

The accounting for discount income and for the related valuation of inventory is directly dependent upon the recordkeeping for purchases. In effect, purchases can be recorded net of cash discount or gross of cash discount, and the related discount income and inventory valuation treatments will coincide with whichever of these two recordkeeping practices is followed.

Many retailers will deduct all cash discounts from invoice totals, effectively recording purchases net of discounts. The practical effect of this practice is the derivation of higher markon percentages (in the retail ledger) as opposed to entering invoices at gross amounts. This, of course, results because the discounts effectively reduce the cost of merchandise purchased. When a retailer records gross purchases based on gross invoice amounts, without deduction of discounts, certain questions must be considered with respect to the subsequent valuation of inventories (whether or not the retail method is used) and to the determination of earned discount income.

The theoretical argument is sometimes made that discounts need not be deducted from inventories and that there is no objection to carrying merchandise at gross invoice cost. Proponents of this theory assert that discount earnings are not dependent upon the sale of merchandise but represent financial income arising from prompt payment of invoices. Accordingly, such discounts should be taken into income on a cash basis, as deducted at settlements, and not on an accrual basis. This theory may be appropriate under circumstances involving discount rates which are so low as to represent only reasonable interest for prompt payment. However, the average discount rates of a retailer frequently are much higher than those that can be reasonably be considered as interest, and vendor discount rates have never borne any particular relationship to the fluctuating costs in the use of funds. Moreover, vendors who offer retailers cash discounts effectively adjust for such discounts in the establishment of the selling prices of merchandise items.

Where discount rates are relatively nominal, or where discount deductions are not almost always taken, the discount earnings may be looked upon as "other income," a form of nonmerchandising income attributable to financial management. However, discount income normally is a significant factor entering into the determination of gross margin. Purchase discounts are *not* normally treated as other income, but as a component of cost of goods sold. Since gross margin can only result from sales, any discount on unsold merchandise should not be included in gross margin.

As hereinafter discussed, this desired result is achieved by eliminating unearned discounts from merchandise inventories when such inventories are reduced to "cost." This, of course, presupposes that invoices are included in purchases on a gross-of-discount basis. However, a comparable adjustment in the valuation of merchandise inventories is automatically made when purchases are recorded net of purchase discounts.

In accounting for discounts, it is necessary to differentiate among the following:

- Discounts accrued (on all purchases).

- Discounts received (on a cash basis as vendor settlements are made).

- Discounts earned (on merchandise sold).

The following explanations of accounts pertaining to discounts outline the problems involved.

DISCOUNTS ON PURCHASES

This account would include discounts applicable to all purchases made during the accounting period. It is usually equal to the discounts applicable to invoices paid during the period, plus the discounts to be received upon payment of accounts payable outstanding at the close of the period, minus the discounts received on accounts payable at the beginning of the period. In effect, it represents purchase discounts on an accrual basis directly related to purchases. A common recordkeeping procedure in this regard would be to enter purchases gross of discounts and accounts payable net of discounts, as follows:

Purchase (gross)	$45,000	
Discounts on purchases		$ 2,200
Accounts payable (net)		42,800

DISCOUNTS RECEIVED. This account would include the discounts received on the cash basis, discounts deducted from invoices when payments are made to vendors within the period. The amounts of the discounts on accounts payable at both ends of the period and also any discounts lost during the period represent the difference from "discounts on purchases" of the period.

When discounts are accumulated and reflected in the records on a cash basis, it is necessary at the close of each accounting period to adjust the figures for discounts deductible from open accounts payable. Adjustment may be made directly against accounts payable or via a "discount receivable" account which is offset against accounts payable. The offset to either of these two balance sheet accounts, that is, accounts payable or discounts receivable, is the income account used to recognize discounts received.

As a practical matter, only a net adjustment is normally made at the end of each accounting period for the net increase (or decrease) necessary to reflect the amount of discounts inherent in accounts payable at the end of the period.

DISCOUNTS EARNED. This account would include the discounts on merchandise sold during the period. The amount would be equal to the discounts on purchases of the period, plus discounts applicable to opening inventory-not previously taken into income because the merchandise was not sold, minus discounts applicable to closing inventory-not taken into income because the merchandise is still on hand.

DISCOUNTS UNEARNED. Discounts are unearned when the merchandise on hand is unsold. Effectively, this account represents the adjustment applicable to closing inventories necessary to state such inventory on a net-of-discount basis.

Stated differently, this adjustment is necessary to state inventories at cost since, regardless of the method of inventory valuation, the actual cost of merchandise is invoice price less discount. When cost of sales is charged with the invoice price of purchases, it also is credited with the discounts allowed on such purchases. Therefore, inventories should not be priced at more than the net cost of purchases. The end of each accounting period it is necessary to determine the amounts of "unearned discounts" remaining in inventories and to deduct such amounts from the inventories. Adjustments (debits or credits) of the unearned discount account from period to period are reflected in discounts earned.

PURCHASES ENTERED NET OF DISCOUNTS. When purchases are entered net of discounts, accounts payable are automatically stated on a net basis and there is no separate accountability for discounts. Under this procedure the inventory valuation per books would be stated net of discounts. If the cost method is used, a physical inventory should be priced at net (of discount) costs; if only gross invoice costs are available, the discounts should be computed and deducted from inventory to arrive at the appropriate cost valuation.

If the retail method is used with purchases entered in the retail ledger net of discounts, the departmental cost multiplier derived from the retail ledger will automatically result in a departmental inventory valuation appropriately stated net of discounts.

In summary, when purchases and accounts payable are entered net of discounts, there are no discount problems and discount adjustments are not ordinarily required. If information is desired with respect to discount totals, statistical tabulations can be made as to discounts on purchases, discounts deducted at settlements, or discounts earned.

LOADED DISCOUNTS FOR IMPORT MERCHANDISE. Costs of imported merchandise are regularly charged with commissions paid to foreign buying agents. Some retailers also charge foreign purchases with a proportionate share of the expenses of foreign buying offices and with expenses of foreign travel. Ostensibly, such loading is designed to record purchases at an aggregate cost comparable to that which would have been incurred if the goods were purchased from importers in this country and to recover from higher selling prices the "extra" costs associated with the acquisition of imported merchandise. While these may be sound economic objectives, from an accounting standpoint there is a question as to whether these expenditures comprise merchandising costs or expenses of doing business that should be charged off as incurred.

In this regard, the authors concur with the long-established and predominant accounting practice which excludes foreign buying and foreign travel costs in the derivation of inventories where such items have been loaded in purchases basically to encourage improved markons. For this purpose, a valuation reserve is frequently set up against inventory of imported goods equal to the average percentage of loading included in such purchases.

CHAPTER ELEVEN

Sales Audit Function

A retailer's daily sales and cash collection totals usually consist of a large volume of relatively small individual transactions. A broad diversity of transaction types are often involved, including cash sales, layaways, CODs, charge account (house) sales, and third-party or bank card sales, as well as credits and refunds for merchandise returns. The paperwork supporting these transactions includes register tapes and readings; sales invoices or sales checks; layaway and COD documents; merchandise credit and refund documents; and payment vehicles such as currency, customer checks, gift certificates, vendor coupons, and charge card slips.

Because of the volume of transactions and quantity of paperwork involved, there is considerable risk that errors might occur. This risk is increased by the large number of sales personnel with varying levels of experience, training, and capability who have responsibility for processing and recording transactions.

To minimize the risk of error, retailers frequently establish a formal *sales audit function* with day-to-day responsibility for the compilation of sales information and verification of its accuracy, prior to its being recorded in the retailer's books.

RESPONSIBILITIES OF THE SALES AUDIT FUNCTION

Specific responsibilities of the sales audit function vary from one retailer to another based on the retailer's needs and circumstances. Major responsibilities may include:

- Daily compilation of gross and net sales totals, and other sales and refund statistics such as gross and net sales on a departmental basis.

- Daily reconciliation of sales and receipt totals to supporting documentation. Each cash register is usually reconciled individually so that errors or improperly processed transactions by specific sales personnel can be identified and addressed.

- Reconciliation of cash receipts and documents accepted in lieu of cash, such as gift certificates, vendor coupons, third-party charge card slips, debit card slips, and the retailer's own charge account documents to recorded amounts. The counting and depositing of cash receipts should be performed by someone other than sales audit personnel to reduce the risk of theft of cash by personnel, who could fraudulently change sales and receipt totals.

- Review and test documentation in support of transactions, such as sales invoices, refund documents, credit memos, and layaway documents to determine their accuracy, content, and authenticity. Documents in support of transaction cancellations and corrections—"overrings," void transactions, and employee or senior citizen discount documentation—should also be reviewed for required "approval signatures" since they can conceal theft of cash.

- Compilation, reconciliation, and verification of revenues and cash collections that are attributable to sources other than sales, such as alteration charges, delivery charges, and handling charges.

- Verification of data such as sales commissions, sales tax collections, and cash register overage and shortage amounts.

- Establishment of charge account and layaway sales and cash collection control totals.

- Determination of lease department sales and refund totals, and reconciliation and verification of lease department transactions.

TRANSACTION CONTROL AND VERIFICATION

Specific sales audit transaction control and verification techniques vary. The following practices have been found to be effective for most retailers:

- Control procedures that assure all transactions are processed and recorded on a timely basis such as:

  Current listings of all active and inactive cash registers, checked daily to see that the transactions from all registers have been reported. (This can be done manually or on an automated basis as with computerized transaction processing systems.)

  Comparisons of beginning register readings to the prior day's ending register readings; checking of beginning transaction numbers to the prior day's ending transaction numbers; reviews to determine that no transaction numbers are missing from the numerical sequence; and the reconciliation of recorded amounts to supporting documentation.

  Daily issuance of sequentially numbered sales books to personnel where manual sales checks are used. Unused documents are returned at the end of the shift and all documents are numerically accounted for by sales audit personnel.

  Use of transaction exception reports. Sales transactions rung on point-of-sale terminals, tied to a computer system, should have certain transaction editing and verification features to identify missing transaction numbers, incomplete transactions, invalid transaction dates, invalid stock keeping unit (SKU) numbers, insufficient deposit or down payment amounts on layaway or charge sales, and listings of void and "no sale" transactions. In situations where certain types of transactions are restricted to specified registers, such as employee purchases, refunds, or layaway sales and collections, invalid transaction types may also be reported as an exception.

  Use of transmittal envelopes, called tally envelopes, to record the amount and numerical sequence of all sales checks issued during the day. The type of sales transaction, such as charge, COD, or cash will also be listed on the face of the envelope. At the end of the day, sales personnel tally the data shown on the envelopes, which can serve as the basis for a departmental flash sales report, and send the envelopes, along with the day's transaction documentation, to the sales audit department for review and verification. As a general rule, tally envelopes should only be used when cash sales make up a small percentage of total sales or in situations where a day's sales consists of a relatively small number of individual transactions.

- Control procedures that check the accuracy and authenticity of transactions:

Selective verification of the mathematical accuracy of sales checks and invoices.

Review of supporting documentation for completeness, legibility, and appropriate authorization. Sales audit personnel should maintain a listing of the authorized approvers for the various transaction types. In computerized transaction processing systems, authorizations can be controlled by assigning restricted identification numbers to authorized approvers.

Testing of documentation for transaction types where a relatively high degree of risk is involved, such as overring corrections, transaction cancellations, credit memos, refunds, and employee discounts. Many retailers have adopted the practice of selectively confirming credit memo and refund transactions with customers by phone or mail to check their authenticity.

Prompt follow-up concerning cash register overages and shortages, missing transaction numbers, and missing or incomplete transaction documentation.

Maintaining physical security over transaction records and supporting documentation to reduce the risk of unauthorized access.

ORGANIZATIONAL STRUCTURE

The organizational structure of a retail sales audit function varies with no particular structure or approach considered typical. The most significant differences center around two areas: the *timing* of sales audit activities and *store level versus corporate level* sales audit activities.

- *Timing of Sales Audit Activities.* To facilitate timely posting and recording of transactions, retailers often record transactions prior to the sales audit process. This is referred to as a *postaudit* approach. Although preauditing is desirable to minimize the need for adjustments after the initial recording of transactions, many retailers are willing to accept some degree of error in their accounts to facilitate timely preparation of sales reports and customer accounts receivable information.

A postaudit approach is frequently used by retailers with point-of-sale terminals and electronic communication techniques that facilitate rapid information gathering. When a retailer uses a postaudit approach, the systemic transaction processing controls should be sufficiently developed to minimize the risk of material errors or omissions in the reported information.

- *Store Level versus Corporate Level Sales Audit Activities.* Many retail organizations, particularly those with many store locations, have both a store level and a corporate level sales audit function. In this situation, the stores have a local sales audit function with responsibility for control and verification of transactions for a particular store or group of stores. In contrast, the corporate level sales audit function compiles corporate-wide sales information and test transaction information that has been submitted to the corporate office by individual stores. Division of responsibilities will vary, however; common corporate level practices would include:

Control procedures to assure that all stores have reported their daily transactions on a timely basis

Reconciling deposits and other banking activities reported by stores to independently provided bank statements and corporate general ledger accounts

Reconciling customer accounts receivable totals provided by the stores to the detailed subsidiary ledgers

Reviewing individual store's sales and collection reports and other supporting information to assure that established store level sales audit procedures have been followed

Investigating and correcting errors or other discrepancies in store level reports

Compiling selected corporate statistics from store level reports and preparing comparable performance reports for individual stores or groups of stores.

SUMMARY

In nearly all retail organizations, it is essential that someone who is independent of the initial sales transaction processing effort have day-to-day responsibility for the compilation, verification, and checking of the retailer's sales and cash collection transactions. These responsibilities are frequently assigned to a formally organized sales audit function that may include store level as well as corporate level sales audit activities.

CHAPTER TWELVE

Internal Audit Function

The Institute of Internal Auditors' Statement of Standards for the Professional Practice of Internal Auditing defines internal auditing as an independent appraisal function established within an organization to examine and evaluate its activities as a service to the organization.

In small retail organizations, this function is often performed by the company's owners as they continually check every facet of the company's operations to see that things are being done properly and to find ways to improve the company's operations. However, as a business grows larger and becomes more complex, the owners usually find that it is no longer possible for them to conduct effective informal self-audits. As a result, a formal internal audit function is frequently established. The specific responsibilities of this function will depend on factors such as the size and geographic diversity of the company's operations, the company's organizational structure, and management philosophies concerning the role of internal audit.

In some retail environments, the primary responsibility of the internal audit department is to examine the performance of work at stores, confirming compliance by store management and employees with established company policies and procedures. In other situations, the internal audit department is responsible for periodic appraisals of virtually every aspect of the company's operations—matters such as buying, advertising, distribution, inventory control, warehousing, cash management, electronic data processing, and financial planning and reporting. In some instances, this results in the internal audit function having two components—one focusing primarily on audits of the company's stores, and another auditing corporate level activities. These two components are generally referred to as *store auditing* and *corporate or operational auditing,* respectively. In either case, there is a fundamental obligation on the part of the internal audit department to provide independent appraisal services that meet the needs of the sponsoring organization's management.

The Institute of Internal Auditors has issued a Statement of Standards for the Professional Practice of Internal Auditing, which retail internal auditors should adhere to in the performance of their work. The five general standards set forth in this statement are:

- Internal auditors should be independent of the activities they audit.

- Internal audits should be performed with proficiency and due professional care.

- The scope of the internal audit should encompass the examination and evaluation of the effectiveness of the organization's system of internal control and the quality of performance in carrying out assigned responsibilities.

- Audit work should include planning the audit, examining and evaluating information, communicating results, and following up.

- The Director of Internal Auditing should properly manage the Internal Auditing Department.

INTERNAL AUDIT MANAGEMENT PRACTICES

The preceding general standards establish important conceptual guidelines for the internal audit effort, which must be supported by the company's top management if the internal audit department is to function effectively. Typical practices that promote this support are:

- *Establishment of a Formal Charter for the Internal Audit Department.* A common practice is the establishment of a written statement that sets forth the purpose, mission, authority, and responsibilities of the internal audit department. This document is generally referred to as the internal audit charter and should be approved by both the company's board of directors and the company's top executive officer. The internal audit charter communicates to other company management how executive management sees the role of internal auditing within the organization and establishes a framework for the scope of the company's internal audit activities.

- *Providing Board-Level Support for the Internal Audit Function.* If the company has formed a board-level audit committee, the management of the internal audit department should periodically report to this committee the plans and activities of the department. Additionally, the director of internal audit should be authorized to communicate with the chairman of the committee directly, in situations where executive management fraud or other irregularities exist. If an audit committee has not been formed, the director of internal audit should report internal audit plans and activities periodically to either the chairman of the board or the entire board of directors.

- *Communication with Executive Management.* Executive management should be informed regularly of audit findings and the status of corrective actions to initiate appropriate executive management follow-up. This can be accomplished by sending only audit reports that meet certain pre-established criteria.

- *Affirming the Status of the Internal Audit Function.* The internal audit function should report to a person with sufficient stature in the organization to assure that the objectives of the function can be achieved. Most often this is the chief financial officer, but it is not uncommon for the internal audit function to report directly to the chief executive officer. It is important that this individual exhibit positive and continuing support for the activities of the internal audit function. If others in the organization perceive that the support for internal auditing is not genuine and sincere, the effectiveness of the function will be eroded.

- *Conducting All Internal Audit Activities in a Professional Manner.* No degree of management support can assure the effectiveness of the internal audit function if the function itself is not conducted in a professional manner. Therefore, it is important for the management of the internal audit function to adhere to the standards of professional practice and to the Institute of Internal Auditor's code of ethics. A summary of the code of ethics follows:

Internal auditors shall have an obligation to exercise honesty, objectivity, and diligence in the performance of their duties and responsibilities.

Internal auditors, holding the trust of their employers, shall exhibit loyalty in all matters pertaining to the affairs of the employer or to whomever they may be rendering a service. Members shall not knowingly be a party to any illegal or improper activity.

Internal auditors shall refrain from entering into any activity that may be in conflict with the interest of their employers or that would prejudice their ability to carry out objectively their duties and responsibilities.

Internal auditors shall not accept a fee or a gift from an employee, a client, a customer, or a business associate of their employer without the knowledge and consent of their senior management.

Internal auditors shall be prudent in the use of information acquired in the course of their duties. They shall not use confidential information for any personal gain nor in a manner that would be detrimental to the welfare of their employer.

- Internal auditors, in expressing an opinion, shall use all reasonable care to obtain sufficient factual evidence to warrant such expression. In their reporting, internal auditors shall reveal such material facts known to them, which, if not revealed, could either distort the report of the results of operations under review or conceal unlawful practice.

- Internal auditors shall continually strive for improvement in the proficiency and effectiveness of their service.

- Internal auditors shall be ever mindful of their obligation to maintain high standards of competence, morality, and dignity.

DIFFERENCES IN THE RESPONSIBILITIES OF INTERNAL AND EXTERNAL AUDITORS

The primary responsibility of a retailer's independent outside or external auditors is the expression of an opinion on the fairness of the presentation of the company's financial position, results of operations, and changes in financial position; and on whether the presentation is in conformity with generally accepted accounting principles consistently applied in relation to those of the preceding year.

External auditors perform tests of the company's accounting records and other procedures they consider necessary to permit the expression of this opinion. Often these tests and procedures disclose weaknesses or potential areas for improvement in a retailer's operations that the external auditors will bring to management's attention. However, this is usually a byproduct of their work, not its primary purpose.

The identification of weakness and the furnishing of recommendations for improvement is the fundamental purpose of the internal audit function. Typical internal audit departmental responsibilities that differentiate it from the external audit function include performing audits that are for the specific purpose of:

- Confirming compliance with established company policies and procedures.

- Analyzing the profitability of the audited activities and determining whether resources committed to the activity are used economically.

- Identifying opportunities for improvements in nonfinancial areas.

- Assessing the quality of management's performance.

Although external auditors may comment on these matters, it is not their primary focus, except in instances where they have been specifically engaged to perform work of this nature.

COORDINATING INTERNAL AND EXTERNAL AUDIT ACTIVITIES

Although the basic responsibilities of the internal and external audit functions are different, the two groups are often involved with similar matters. Their activities should be coordinated to assure that all of the company's audit needs are fulfilled in the most efficient and cost-effective manner possible. This would typically include:

- Development of a joint annual audit plan that identifies the areas and locations audited by both groups and the areas and locations where the external auditors will be able to rely on the work of the internal auditors.

- Distribution of internal audit reports or summaries to the external auditors for use in planning their audit scope.

- Follow-up by internal audit personnel concerning weaknesses in controls as well as other problems identified by the external auditors.

- Direct participation by internal audit personnel in the examination of the company's financial statements.

COORDINATING INTERNAL AUDITS AND LOSS PREVENTION ACTIVITIES

The scope of internal auditing should include reviews of the means by which a company safeguards its assets. In many retail environments, a formal loss prevention function will also focus on these matters. The responsibilities of these two groups are different: the internal audit function's purpose is to independently audit and report upon methods and procedures while the loss prevention function is directly involved in the day-to-day management and administration of these programs. There is a need for a coordinated effort by these two groups to enhance the overall effectiveness of the loss prevention effort. Typical ways in which the efforts of these two groups might be coordinated include:

- Periodic internal audits of the activities of the loss prevention function.

- Periodic audits of the company's loss prevention practices.

- Distribution of copies of audit reports to loss prevention management in situations where weaknesses or potential improvements in loss prevention practices have been observed.

- Reviews of loss prevention reports by internal audit personnel to identify areas or locations which should be considered for audit.

- Periodic audits of specific areas where shrinkage is likely to occur, with loss prevention personnel being assigned as a part of the audit team.

- Joint reviews of store or warehouse locations that have abnormal shrinkage results. Internal audit would generally review recordkeeping practices while loss prevention personnel would review surveillance and physical security practices.

- Joint reviews of contemplated changes in systems or newly developed systems to evaluate them from an internal control and security viewpoint.

AUDITING RETAIL ELECTRONIC DATA PROCESSING SYSTEMS

The use of point-of-sale terminals, which capture detailed sales information for entry to the retailer's accounting and operating records, and the use of electronic communications techniques is now common in many retail organizations. These technological developments have spurred the implementation of fully integrated retail information systems. Adequate internal audit coverage of a retailer's electronic data processing (EDP) activities is a priority matter in many retail organizations. Internal audit should cover the following EDP systems activities:

- *Pre-Implementation Audits.* The auditing of new electronic data processing applications or revisions to existing applications prior to the actual operational use of these applications. This requires audit involvement at various stages in the systems implementation process, such as systems planning, design, development, and pre-implementation testing.

Audit activities include:

Reviews of the systems plan to see that user needs have been appropriately identified and provided for and that the development plans are realistic and achievable.

Evaluation of the system's design for control features that will assure the reliability and completeness of the system's output.

Testing of the system's control features prior to the system's actual use.

Review of the system's supporting documentation for adequacy.

- *Existing Application Audits.* This is the periodic auditing of selected EDP applications, or systems that are currently being used in the retailer's operations. These audits confirm that the systems are functioning as intended, that control features and supporting documentation are adequate and that changes in the retailer's circumstances or to the system itself have not resulted in control breakdowns or weaknesses.

- *Electronic Data Processing Facility Audits.* These are audits of the retailer's overall EDP environment to assure that the company's EDP activities are subjected to adequate control procedures on a day-to-day basis. These audits encompass data center management and administration, data security and access, systems development, maintenance standards, and the overall quality of the company's EDP operations.

Internal audit efforts in a retail organization that uses EDP methods should encompass all of the preceding audit approaches. Additionally, the internal audit personnel who perform this work should have appropriate EDP audit skills.

FOREIGN CORRUPT PRACTICES ACT

In 1977, the U.S. Congress enacted the Foreign Corrupt Practices Act, which imposes certain recordkeeping and internal accounting control requirements on all companies, including retailers who have securities registered pursuant to Section 12 of the Securities Exchange Act of 1934. These are summarized as, issuers of securities to which the Act applies shall:

- Make and keep books, records, and accounts which, in reasonable detail, accurately and fairly reflect the transactions and dispositions of the assets of the issuer, and

- Devise and maintain a system of internal accounting controls sufficient to provide reasonable assurances that:

Transactions are executed in accordance with management's general or specific authorization.

Transactions are recorded as necessary to permit the preparation of financial statements in conformity with generally accepted accounting principles or any other criteria applicable to such statements, and to maintain accountability for assets.

Access to assets is permitted only in accordance with management's general or specific authorization.

The recorded accountability for assets is compared with the existing assets as reasonable intervals and appropriate action is taken with respect to any differences.

The enactment of this law has resulted in a greater degree of concern on the part of top management of many companies with respect to the adequacy of the company's internal accounting controls and recordkeeping practices.

RETAIL INTERNAL AUDIT FUNCTION

Retail organizations frequently structure their internal audit function so that it consists of two components—one that focuses primarily on audits of corporate level activities (the corporate audit function) and another that audits those activities which take place at the retailer's store locations (the store audit function). The nature of the audits that these two groups perform are often quite different. The corporate audit function will generally address activities that are conducted on a centralized basis and effect the entire company. The store audit function generally performs audits that are designed to determine that personnel at specific store locations are adhering to the company's established store policies and procedures and are using the company's systems in the intended manner. It is important that the audit activities of these two groups be effectively coordinated. Deficiencies disclosed by store audits often indicate weaknesses in the company's corporate level policies, procedures, and systems that should receive corporate level attention.

The audit approach of both groups should address matters that are unique to the retail operating environment as well as the elements of internal accounting control that are common to all businesses. An overview of some of the matters that should be addressed by the retail internal audit function follows:

- *Merchandise Buying Systems and Procedures.* Internal audits of merchandise buying activities should evaluate the effectiveness and efficiency of the retailers' controls in regard to merchandise procurement, including:

Vendor selection compilation of financial history, information merchandise quality, comparative prices, buying history, returns, discounts, advertising allowances, rebates, and other allowances related to the vendors' products.

Establishing reorder points and quantities.

Monitoring of "open-to-buy" allowances.

Placement, approval, and recording of purchase commitments.

Recording and processing of returns as well as the collection of vendor debit balances.

Establishing merchandise selling prices and the initiation and implementation of selling price changes.

Compliance with governmental customs regulations, labeling and warranty requirements for imported merchandise.

- *Corporate Inventory Management.* Corporate internal audit activities should cover the following inventory management functions.

Determining the planned inventory levels for each store location.

Determining actual inventory levels relative to planned levels.

Correction of inventory levels, which are not in accordance with those which the retailer intends to maintain.

Coordination of the inventory planning and control function with the retailers buying and sales activities.

- *Invoice Processing Systems (Accounts Payable).* The objectives of the audit includes evaluations to determine that the invoice processing system is structured so that it:

Provides adequate recognition of liabilities incurred in the proper accounting period and in the correct amounts.

Provides adequate distribution of charges to the proper accounts and locations.

Facilitates effective cash management as to the timing of payments, collection of debt memos, and planning of cash needs.

Minimizes the possibility of erroneous codings of vendor numbers, invoice numbers, amounts due, discounts, terms, and other key data.

Facilitates the answering of inquiries on specific vendor charges and amounts.

Minimizes the possibility of errors and duplications of effort and provides for the efficient and effective use of the retailer's resources.

Provides a proper degree of coordination between the retailer's buying and invoice processing activities.

- *Warehousing and Distribution Center Operations.* The internal audit of warehousing and distribution center operations should be designed to evaluate the retailer's systems and procedures for:

Selection of merchandise for warehousing.

Establishing order and shipping quantities.

Controlling the merchandise receipts and accounting for the receipt of merchandise.

Handling receiving exceptions, that is, damages, shortages, overages, and incorrect items.

Matching invoice costs and quantities with purchase orders and the receipt of merchandise.

Locating merchandise and controlling its physical movement while in the facility.

Physical safeguarding of merchandise.

Establishing and monitoring perpetual inventory records as to receipts, quantities on hand, and shipments.

Reconciliation and the identification of reasons for differences between perpetual records and physical counts.

Pricing of warehouse and distribution center inventories, including allocations of labor, overhead, and freight costs.

Planning for labor needs relative to volume fluctuations.

Coordination of shipping volumes and needs with the retailer's traffic management activities.

Controlling merchandise shipment and accounting for the shipment of merchandise to stores.

Handling shipping exceptions, that is, damages, shortages, overages, and incorrect items.

Processing of merchandise that passes through the facility, including activities such as labeling, marking, ticketing, carton packaging and repacking, and merchandise inspection.

Monitoring and control of the productivity levels of warehouse and distribution center personnel.

- *Traffic Management.* The objectives of the internal audit with respect to the retailer's traffic management function should include evaluation of the systems and procedures for:

Selection of freight carriers.

Route selection.

Freight rates and routing compliance verification.

Recording, control, and collection of freight claims.

The compilation of information relative to freight costs and the allocation of freight costs to merchandise inventories and cost of sales.

Monitoring of costs and compliance with respect to contract freight carriers.

Processing of freight bills.

- *Advertising and Sales Promotion.* The internal audit of a retailer's advertising and sales promotion activities should cover:

  Cooperative advertising recording, billing, and collection, and the resolution of disputes.

  Selection and control of advertising costs (i.e., bids, contracts, selection of the types of media used, and the selection of modeling and advertising agencies).

  Contractual arrangements with advertising agencies, modeling agencies, and outside printing and mailing services.

  Control of merchandise and supplies that are used in the production of the retailers' advertising material.

  Coordination of the advertising of specific merchandise with buying activities in regard to such merchandise.

  Determination of the effectiveness of advertising and sales promotion efforts.

  Compliance with federal and local advertising laws.

- *Store Planning.* The internal audit of store planning activities should include the evaluation of:

  The selection process for the locations of new stores.

  Planning and implementation of store floor layouts, merchandise display methods, and departmental square footage allocations.

  The selection process for contractors and others services providers.

  Preparation and control of blueprints, construction permits, and the monitoring of construction contracts.

  Coordinating plans stores with other management groups such as merchandise buying and store operations.

- *Real Estate Management.* Internal audit of real estate management activities should encompass:

Lease negotiation and renewal.

Common area assessments and other operating costs that may be passed on to the retailer by landlords.

Monitoring compliance with lease terms.

Maintenance services contracts.

- *Human Resources Management Activities.* The internal audit effort, which may be coordinated with the audit of the retailers' payroll systems should encompass:

Personnel selection and recruitment.

Personnel records management.

Personnel development and training programs.

Employee performance evaluation programs.

Personnel planning activities.

Salary and wage administration.

Fringe benefit administration.

Procedures to minimize the potential for violation of legal requirements personnel practices.

- *Cash Management Activities.* Internal audit activities should encompass the systems and procedures used by the retailer in regard to:

Mobilization and concentration of cash.

Monitoring of cash balances and the forecasting of cash requirements.

Investment of surplus funds.

Minimization of borrowing.

- *Matters for Review by the Store Audit Function.* Some of the more significant activities that effect most retailers' store level operations on a day-to-day basis include:

Sales of merchandise and the collection of customer payments.

Receipt and checking of merchandise and the processing of information concerning these receipts.

Employment and supervision of store employees.

Monitoring and control of the store's inventories.

Utilization and maintenance of the store facilities.

The store audit function must develop an audit approach that focuses on the store's compliance with the companies' established policies and procedures.

The broad objectives of the store audit function generally include evaluation of the following:

- *Operating Environment*

   Overall control structure in regard to organizational responsibilities, supervisory approvals, and the adequacy of staffing.

   Comprehension and understanding of established company policies and procedures.

   Effectiveness of key supervisory functions such as sales floor, stock room, store office, and merchandise management supervision.

   The effectiveness, accuracy, and timeliness of the preparation of reports and information by store personnel for submission to corporate management.

- *Sales and Payment Collection Activities.* Audit objectives should include evaluations to determine that:

   All cash sales are recorded for the correct amount at the time the sale is made.

   All noncash sales are appropriately authorized and recorded.

   All refunds and customer credit memos are appropriately authorized and recorded.

   All changes to the retailer's established selling prices are appropriately authorized and recorded on a timely basis.

   All sales correction transactions such as voided transactions and over-rings are authorized at the time when they occur.

   All sales and sales related transactions are reconciled to supporting documentation on a timely basis.

   All cash receipts are safeguarded from theft or loss.

   All collections of cash and cash equivalents are deposited promptly and intact.

   All sales to the Company's employees are made in the authorized manner.

   All sales personnel and store office personnel have been adequately trained in the procedures for processing sales and collection transactions.

   There is an appropriate segregation of duties in the selling, transaction recording, reconciliation, and control functions.

   In situations where retailers permit customers to buy on a direct credit basis, the internal audit objectives should also include evaluations to determine that:

All credit sales and adjustments to customer accounts are properly authorized and recorded.

The issuance of charge cards is adequately controlled.

Finance charges, if any, are calculated correctly and properly recorded.

Customer inquiries are responded to on a timely and satisfactory basis.

Detailed records of customer's accounts are maintained and reconciled at regular intervals to appropriate control totals.

Statements of accounts are furnished to customers at regular intervals and undelivered statements are adequately controlled and researched.

Customer credit limits are effectively communicated and monitored.

Adequate procedures are used for monitoring and collection of delinquent accounts.

All write-offs of uncollectible accounts are properly authorized and recorded.

There is an appropriate segregation of duties in the credit authorization, payment collection, and accounts receivable control functions.

- *Merchandise Receiving and Checking Activities.* Audit objectives should include evaluations to determine that:

All merchandise receipts are appropriately checked and verified as to the quantity received.

All merchandise receipts are for merchandise that has been ordered and authorized.

Adequate information is maintained to support claims for receiving exceptions (i.e., shortages, overages, damaged or defective merchandise and incorrect items).

Discrepancies in receiving information are resolved in a timely and proper manner.

All merchandise receipt transactions are accounted for and recorded on a timely basis.

All receiving and store office personnel are adequately trained in the procedures for the processing merchandise receipts and related documentation.

Receiving activities are conducted in an environment that is conducive to accurate checking and counting of merchandise.

All merchandise receipts are adequately safeguarded from theft or loss.

There is an appropriate segregation of duties with respect to the receiving of merchandise and the control and processing of receiving information.

If merchandise tagging and marking activities are performed within the store, the audit objectives should also include these activities.

- *Store Personnel Functions.* Audit objectives for the in-store personnel function should include evaluations to determine that:

  Payments are made only to currently employed personnel and that they are compensated at the authorized rate of pay.

  All changes to payroll (additions, terminations, and compensation rate adjustments) are properly authorized.

  Adequate and up-to-date documentation is maintained on the status of each store employee.

  Payroll amounts are calculated accurately.

  Store personnel are adequately informed of the company's policies.

  Store-level training and performance review programs are conducted in the intended manner.

  Procedures for scheduling sales floor personnel are adequately coordinated with the store's peak and slow selling periods.

  There is an appropriate segregation of duties in the payroll preparation and administration functions.

- *Inventory Control Activities.* Audit objectives in regard to the store's inventory control activities should include evaluations to determine that:

  Adequate physical safeguards are used to protect the inventory from theft or loss.

  Transfers of merchandise between store locations are properly controlled and accounted for.

  Store-level retail price changes are adequately controlled and executed.

  Layaway and leased department merchandise is appropriately identified and/or segregated.

  Store-level inventory control responsibilities are coordinated with corporate level inventory control functions.

  Merchandise displays are maintained in accordance with the company's established policies.

- *Utilization and Maintenance of Store Facilities.* Audit objectives should include evaluations to determine that:

  The physical condition and appearance of the store is maintained in a manner that is consistent with corporate policy and that is conducive to the retailer's sales promotion efforts.

Store maintenance activities are coordinated with corporate-level maintenance responsibilities.

Control is exercised in facility related costs such as heating, air conditioning, communications, store supplies, and other similar matters.

Store facilities are adequately safeguarded from unauthorized entrances or use resulting in increased risks of loss due to fire or other hazards.

SUMMARY

As retail organizations grow larger and more complex, the need for an independent appraisal function within the organization often results in the establishment of a formal internal audit function.

The internal audit function's efforts should be coordinated with those of both the company's external auditors and the company's loss prevention function and should encompass all of the company's significant financial and operating activities.

CHAPTER THIRTEEN

In-Store Cash Control

Comprehensive, consistent controls must be established over cash in stores because the retailer's exposure and vulnerability are substantial.

OPENING CONTROLS

Before opening the store for start of regular business, cash in the registers should be counted and recorded. The amount should also be matched with the close-out figure from the previous day for each register. This procedure will not be needed in environments where all cash is removed from registers every night. Procedures should be established, and disbursements made at the start of day, to make sure that there is enough cash in the registers for change.

Some stores may assign separate tills for each cashier for better control. However, it is not unusual to see stores with a common till for more than one cashier. After the first cashier's shift is over, he or she does a closeout and clears the contents of the till as if it were the end of the day closeout and also clears the register for the next cashier. Control may be lost if a cashier starts on a register before it has been balanced. Use of separate tills is more frequent in a front end checkout environment such as a grocery or discount store.

VOIDS

Standard procedures should be installed to handle voids and returns. Controls should be established at three levels: (1) the register should record all voids on magnetic medium, (2) the register should record voids on the paper audit trail or journal tape, and (3) the cashier should record the void on the original sales receipt. Separation of responsibility calls for the supervisor to ring the void into the register and also write it onto the register journal tape, if possible. At the end of the day, the transaction number of each void should be matched with both the register paper trail and the cashier's end of day report.

RETURNS

Returns can be handled either at a central area that handles returns for all departments or customers can return merchandise to the department where it was purchased. Better control is achieved with all returns coming in at a central site. However, improved service results if merchandise is returned directly to the department, because merchandise can be moved immediately onto the floor. The second option potentially relieves long lines at a central return counter. In a front end checkout environment, it is more convenient to handle all returns through a central return counter.

CLOSE-OUT CONTROLS

Detailed procedures should be outlined for balancing the registers at close-out. It is customary to balance registers at the end of a business day or at the end of a cashier's shift. Random balancing is sometimes used, especially in a front end checkout environment. In this process, registers are not balanced every day, but a cashier may be asked by the supervisor to "balance" the register at random.

Close-out procedures usually vary based on the type of point-of-sale (POS) terminal being used. Most terminals have capabilities to track all types of media, namely, cash, credit cards, charge cards, gift certificates, discounts, and so on. At the end of the day, the POS terminal should print out totals for each category. This will help with balancing cash in the register with the printed totals and provide an audit trail if there is a shortage. In most cases, the POS register will develop a "Daily Cash Report" summarizing the detail transactions in the various categories specified, such as net credit card charges, gift certificates tendered, layaway payments made, and so on. This report develops a net cash accountability amount as well as a cash deposit requirement figure. As a further aid to auditing, the system should also provide a sales report that lists every transaction in detail. Normally this report is only produced when a balancing problem occurs. Some POS terminals can print out a bank deposit slip at the time of closeout, which facilitates transferring funds from the store to the bank. This option works well in a single register environment but is not favored in a multiregister store, where it is necessary to produce a single deposit slip after consolidating sales from all registers. (See Exhibit 13.1.)

Printouts from the POS terminal should provide a net total of all sales for the day. This total must be reconciled with two other numbers before the register is declared "balanced." The *merchandise total,* which takes into account taxes, fees and discounts, should match with the POS total. And the *total sales figure,* provided by the cashier, should also match the POS total.

There are two ways of handling cash collection at the end of the day: First, all cash can be removed at closeout and transferred to a central store safe. Second, a fixed amount of cash (in small bills and change) can be left in the register and the remaining cash can be transferred to a central safe. Both options have their advantages, the first offers better control and is preferred in a front end checkout environment. However, the second option is more practical. Leaving, say $200, in the register eliminates the need to dispense cash for change when the store opens next day and registers can be made ready to operate in only a few minutes. Physical control of cash involves transferring funds by the cashiers to a central counting area after closeout. This is usually done in bags, boxes or wallets and it is the responsibility of the cashier to make sure that the money gets safely transferred.

Deposits to the bank should normally be made at least once a day and the store manager is responsible for the safe transfer of cash from the store. Arrangements should be made for night depository privileges. All deposits should be made into an account which is subject to withdrawal *only by the home office.* The bank should also be instructed not to cash other checks or money orders drawn to the order of the company from these special accounts. Some retailers may establish a second account for discretionary use by the store's management. This account would typically be funded by corporate and be used for items such as freight payments.

Frequently, the store manager will write out a bank deposit slip and a withdrawal slip at the same time. The withdrawal slip is sent to the main office and facilitates collection of funds from the local bank. If the withdrawal slip is sent to the central office by mail, there is usually a two to three day delay before the central office can have the funds as "available." Retailers usually reduce this delay by either wire transfer of funds or making special arrangements with local banks to expedite check processing.

EXHIBIT 13.1 Daily Register Report

Date: __8-11-XX__ Fountain: _____
Store: __24__ Resale: ___✓___

Register #: __1__ Opening Bank $: __49.50__
Bank #: __1__ Over/Short $ (+/−): __−.50__
  Manager's Signature: __Store Manager__

Cashier's Name: __John Doe__
Cashier's Signature: __john doe__

Time: In   Out   In   Out   In   Out
   9:30 12:00 1:00 4:00

Closing Reading $:	9857.12		
Beginning Reading $:	8746.01		
TOTAL SALES:			1111.11
Cash in register at close of shift			
Currency:			
Bills	120.00		
Half	2.50		
Quarters	8.25		
Dimes	6.10		
Nickels	3.05		
Pennies	.33		
TOTAL CURRENCY	140.23		
Subtract Closing Bank	−		
Cash Pick-ups	50.00	90.23	

	Cashier	Supervsr		
1st Pickup	g. Doe	supervsr	400.00	
2nd Pickup	g. Doe	supervsr	350.00	
3rd Pickup				
4th Pickup				
5th Pickup				
6th Pickup				
TOTAL CASH		840.23		
Personal Checks	27.27		
Travelers Checks	50.00		
TOTAL CASH AND CHECKS		917.50	

Media in Register:			
Vendor Coupons	1.30		
Voids & Adjustments	17.50		
Visa	25.00		
Master Card	35.35		
AmEx	10.15		
Discover	30.04		
Employee Discount (disc. amount only)	21.82		
Refunds	51.34		
TOTAL MEDIA:		192.50	
TOTAL CASH, CHECKS + MEDIA:			1110.00
OVER/SHORT +/−			1.11
MEMO: SALES TAX			83.69
MEMO: NET SALES			1027.42

REASON FOR OVER/SHORT: __.50 Due to Open Bank Short__
MANAGER'S SIGNATURE: __Store Manager__

CASH SHORTAGE

Tracking and follow-up of register shortage is a very important issue. If there is a shortage pattern, it must be noted and investigated. Reporting techniques which detect patterns in shortages such as; registers with a regular shortage, or cashiers who report a regular shortage, or register-cashier combinations that produce a regular shortage, may help in investigating shortages.

Most POS terminals keep track of totals at three levels. X-Reading is the running total for the day and can be obtained at any time. Z-Reading is the end of the day total and can be reset to zero, usually with a key, after the register has been balanced. The third is an accumulating total that cannot be reset to zero and keeps track of a total from the time the register was first installed. Each of these totals help in monitoring and tracking sales and shortages.

Petty cash funds and the register fund should be kept separate. This will increase control over cash from registers. Withdrawals from the register cash fund should be avoided as much as possible, not only because control is compromised but also because it erodes discipline. Generally, disbursements for all merchandise and all branch expenses are made centrally, therefore there is no need to maintain a general checking account at the branch. A separate account should be maintained to make withdrawals for purposes like supper money, certain freight charges, local travel and entertainment expenses. This fund should be reimbursed by the central office at regular intervals, based upon approved vouchers submitted by the branch.

CHAPTER FOURTEEN

Credit Sales
Accounts Receivable

Charge sales continue to grow as a percentage of total sales. Recent studies of department store and specialty store operations show that credit sales represent approximately 60 to 65 percent of total sales.

TYPES OF CREDIT SALES

HOUSE OR PROPRIETARY CREDIT.   Credit granted and program administered by the retailer, receivables are owned by retailer, and can only be used at the retailer's stores.

PRIVATE LABEL CREDIT. Credit cards bear the retailer's name but the program is managed by and receivables are owned by a third party, usually a bank or credit company. Card can only be used at the retailer's stores.

THIRD PARTY OR BANK CARDS.   Credit granted and receivables owned by a bank or financial institution, cards bear the credit institution's name.

Examples include VISA, MC, Diners Club, American Express, and so on. Card can be used in many locations.

Private label cards, and proprietary credit are the two most common forms of in-store credit. Third-party credit sales represent typically between 5 to 15 percent of sales where in-house credit is available.

The three most typical types of proprietary credit plans are the 30-day account, the time payment (installment) account and the revolving credit arrangement. By far, the revolving credit account is the largest contributor to charge sales.

Third-party cards shift the majority of the maintenance of the system (credit, billing and collection) to the third party. Retailers are usually charged a fee for this service which is generally negotiable depending on volumes and nature of the credit.

PROPRIETARY CREDIT

The pros and cons of proprietary credit have been debated for many years. Proprietary credit is considered to be very costly, especially when compared to third-party credit; however, many retailers have opted not to abandon their house credit operations. Retailers' attribute customer loyalty and status to their house credit operations. Also significant are the customer credit card lists. These lists are a lucrative and advantageous means of increasing sales since charge customers tend to spend more than cash sale customers. Additionally, the lists may be considered an asset since many retailers sell them.

Industry studies continue to evaluate the cost of maintaining a revolving credit card. Principal costs of furnishing credit include payroll costs associated with the administration of credit, collection of bad debts and interest costs. The retailer does generate revenue by billing the customer a finance charge for providing the credit program; however, finance charges do not normally offset the costs of credit.

Types of Proprietary Credit

Various forms of proprietary credit have found their place in the retailer's business depending upon the customers' needs.

Regular or 30-day accounts represent the simplest form of credit in that this credit facility requires full payment on a 30-day basis. No service charge is assessed. A very limited number of retailers offer such credit.

Revolving credit plans are the most popular form of house credit. When a customer's credit is approved the revolving credit arrangement represents a personal line of credit. Terms of the credit require a minimum monthly payment based upon the unpaid balance. A finance charge is added monthly based upon the outstanding balance. Many revolving arrangements allow a grace period whereby payment in full for purchases can be made without any finance charge. Normally, the grace period is 30 days. Statistics show that approximately 30 percent of customers using a credit card qualify as such convenience customers. Customers not using the grace period are assessed a finance charge which is calculated by applying a monthly periodic interest rate to the outstanding balance of the customer's account. The periodic rate is called the Annual Percentage Rate (APR) and is limited by state law. Federal laws require extensive disclosure of the facts of a credit arrangement as well as the APR used.

The third type of proprietary credit is the installment account, more commonly called a time payment account or TPA. These are custom-designed credit programs that are used for certain large dollar (big ticket) purchases. There are two forms of TPAs: Closed-end installment contracts which are strictly controlled by federal regulations and open-end installment contracts which are less stringent.

Under the closed-end contract each sale must have a new credit application and contract. Therefore, a customer cannot add new purchases to the account. Most often in these arrangements the retailer will take a security interest in the property purchased.

An open-end installment contract allows the customer to add new purchases to the account. Purchases are not secured under this arrangement. Most retailers offer open-end contracts. TPA terms are normally longer than the revolving credit terms and specify a fixed installment amount covering the total selling price and finance charges which will be billed monthly similar to an auto loan.

A special accounting problem connected with this class of sales is the repossession of merchandise when accounts become uncollectible. If at all possible, retailers desire to avoid repossession. Repossessed merchandise is difficult to resell, and the handling of such merchandise is likely to conflict with store policies. Moreover, the expense of repossession and reconditioning often consumes all profit on the transaction. Nevertheless, repossession is often necessary as a matter of principle to uphold the credit policy of the store.

A preferred method of accounting is to place a selling price on the repossessed goods and take them into stock at this selling price "as is"; that is, without inclusion of retail of the reconditioning expense. The cost can be obtained by deducting the average departmental markon percentage. "As is" selling price, as determined, is credited to the customer's account. If the account balance exceeds the credit, the difference is charged to bad debts. If, as may happen occasionally, the account is less than the credit, the difference is treated as a bad debt recovery or as miscellaneous income, unless by agreement the customer is allowed a specified amount, or any credit balance standing open is refunded.

The finance charge that is added to the merchandise price on an installment sale is normally not recorded as part of sales. Rather, it should be treated as interest earned or other income. Customers' TPA accounts are usually charged with the full carrying charges at the time the sales are recorded and other income is credited. At fiscal closing, a computation is made of the amount of carrying charges included in the outstanding installment accounts receivable, and that amount of other income is deferred to future periods. In effect, the carrying charges are taken into income ratably as the installments are collected, rather than in full as the sale is recorded.

CREDIT GRANTING

A customer applies for credit by completing an application. The application is forwarded to the credit department for review and approval. In reviewing the customer's credit-worthiness, a credit point-scoring system is usually employed. In some limited cases, credit granting is done solely on a subjective basis. Point scoring systems have become the most popular method of evaluating credit-worthiness. The system removes subjectivity by using various computerized statistical analysis techniques. In the case of proprietary credit accounts, the retailer establishes his own criteria (number of other credit cards, monthly earnings, age, etc.) indicating whether or not the individual would be a good credit risk. Numerical values are assigned to each criteria and if the aggregate points are in excess of the established minimum, then credit is granted. Credit criteria is normally established according to the economic markets in which the retailer operates. For example, the numerical values assigned to criteria applicable to a rural community certainly would not be the same as those assigned to the New York City area. Because of the ever-increasing number of economic markets, point-scoring systems are normally parameter driven. That is, a system should be able to adjust numeric point values to the criteria as desired.

Credit-scoring systems also can be used to assign the level of credit a customer can reasonably carry based upon the level of points accumulated. Further, scoring systems can be adjusted periodically depending on the retailer's need to extend credit or conversely, to improve the quality of the customer accounts receivable. The use of a point-scoring system reduces the cost of bad debts for the retailer.

By their nature, point-scoring systems have lessened the importance of obtaining credit bureau reports in order to approve a customer's credit. However, credit bureau reports are still important in that if a credit application does not attain sufficient points in the point-scoring system, the retailer will secure a credit report to determine whether additional information will cause the customer to qualify. Under a judgmental credit system, the credit bureau report remains a necessity to granting credit.

Current industry practice blends the objectivity of a point-scoring system with the ability to subjectively override its results.

Behavioral systems are starting to be integrated into point scoring systems. Although expensive, behavioral systems provide the modeling capability to predict when an account will become delinquent. At the same time, these systems can be used for modeling positive customer behavior, which would lead to issuing more credit. Normally, point-scoring systems are overridden anywhere from 5 to 15 percent of the time.

CREDIT AUTHORIZATION

Many forms of credit authorization are used for charge sales. As the retailer continues to increase proprietary credit to improve sales levels, the problems associated with credit management have been solved by new forms of technology which directly benefit credit authorization. Many POS systems are linked to a central credit system that now have the decision-making ability available to approve credit purchases. Furthermore, such systems have controls to alert the cashier to a number of credit matters including things such as the customer's purchases being over the established credit limit, the account being past due, or a restriction having been placed on the account which requires the cashier to notify the credit department before the sale can be completed. The controls in POS systems are normally linked to a parameter driven system, meaning that the retailer can customize the protections and controls that are deemed necessary. Such systems are much faster than other forms of credit authorization and speed the check-out function during peak selling periods.

Terminal authorization systems are widely used for both Private Label and Bank Card authorization. Such systems use touch-tone devices connected to computerized account number files. Printed account lists denoting unaccepted credit risks (negative lists) are also frequently used. Phone authorizations to the credit department prior to sale, and floor limits in which the store or credit company establishes selling amounts over which a sale must be authorized are other means used in authorizing credit when a POS system is not utilized. Any means used raises the question of customer inconvenience. The methods employed should not cause delays at the register.

BILLING AND COLLECTION OF CUSTOMER ACCOUNTS

As a result of the tremendous volume of credit cards and credit sales, the use of cycle billing has become widespread. Under this system, computer systems designate groupings of customers' accounts called *cycles,* and each cycle is billed on the same predetermined date (generally other than month end) each month. This procedure of billing the various cycles monthly on the same dates is known as *cycle billing.*

For many years, the customers' accounts were grouped alphabetically for purposes of billing; however, technology has allowed the retailer to make the customer groupings according to many varied criteria. Retailers now group accounts according to criteria such as numeric account sequence or geographic regions. Such alternatives to alphabetical grouping can produce expense reductions.

In those retail organizations where separate controls are maintained for each individual cycle, generally called *multiple cycle controls,* sales and other credit information, such as remittance advices, is accumulated each day and sorted by cycles, with the respective totals by cycle recorded in cycle controls. The source data is also used to update the customer account until the next billing date for the respective cycles. The source data is not normally mailed with the customer's monthly statement as is done by many travel and entertainment cards (e.g., American Express). Alternatively, the monthly statements are descriptive and contain all pertinent transaction information including merchandise description, transaction date, store location, and so on.

The use of multiple cycle controls makes it possible to compare cycle controls with the sum of customers' account balances rendered each billing date, and any differences can be readily determined. In addition to this comparison, a reconciliation of all the cycle control totals with the general ledger balance at the end of the month (or four- or five-week period) is usually made. Exhibit 14.1 illustrates a reconciliation of cycle control totals with the general ledger control account as of a month end or period end.

Frequently, only a single overall control mechanism is maintained, rather than the multiple cycle controls previously described. Under this method, customer billing, the comparison of the general ledger control and the supporting detail of customers' accounts is done only at the end of the month or period.

Typically, all unbilled transaction data is summarized. This data, together with totals of billed amounts at the last respective billing date, is compared with the month-end (or period-end) general ledger control. The tabulation of unbilled data under this method is also usually done at the balance sheet date. This method offers limited internal control benefits, especially when there is a large number of accounts. Except for smaller stores, this method is normally impractical.

According to federal law, the customer's statement, under either cycle method, must be mailed no later than 14 days prior to the due date.

Both cycles offer unique cash flow considerations. The nature of multiple cycle billing, that is, daily or weekly billing, results in some consistency in cash remittances, whereas the single cycle would have an initial surge of cash after the monthly billing which would then diminish throughout the remainder of the month (see Exhibit 14.2).

EXHIBIT 14.1

ABC Department Store
Analysis of Accounts Receivable Control
January 28, 19XX

Totals of Transactions Since Billing Date,
Per Individual Cycle Controls

Letter Cycle	Latest Cycle Billing Date	Billed Balance at Billing Date	Add Credit Sales	Deduct Cash Remittances	Deduct Credits	Add/(Deduct) Journal Entries	Add Finance Charge	Balance at End of Period 1/28/XX
A	1/1	318,701	109,263	97,572	27,133	(4,145)	4,655	305,769
B	1/2	922,413	399,952	237,866	83,086	(15,390)	14,937	1,000,960
C	1/5	700,201	217,359	99,056	37,479	(9,500)	11,030	782,555
D	1/7	468,299	127,110	31,946	21,588	(5,202)	7,543	544,216
W-Z	11/28	762,498	300,034	270,956	73,139	(12,570)	11,050	716,917
		10,777,160	5,138,624	4,004,981	1,212,159	(125,086)	161,330	10,734,888

EXHIBIT 14.2   Cash Flow Patterns

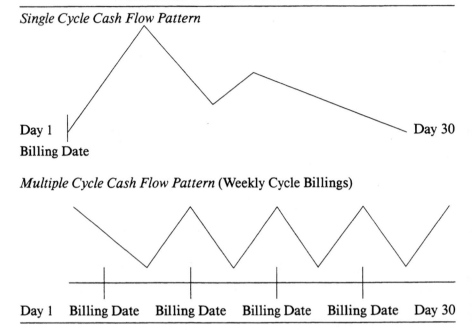

Single Cycle Cash Flow Pattern

Day 1
Billing Date
Day 30

Multiple Cycle Cash Flow Pattern (Weekly Cycle Billings)

Day 1   Billing Date   Billing Date   Billing Date   Billing Date   Day 30

Advocates of the single cycle coincide the monthly billing with the predominant payroll dates of the major industries in the area as well as anticipated receipt of the customers' pension checks, social security, and/or welfare checks. They also argue that certain multiple cycle billing dates are ineffective since the billing is received at a time when the customer has little cash for payment of bills and, accordingly, cash flows are slowed.

There are various other advantages and disadvantages to consider in selecting a single control or multiple cycle controls over customer accounts receivable. While the use of multiple cycle controls is believed to achieve the greatest measure of control, in the interests of economy and simplicity, many retailers have adopted the single control approach. In making a decision, many factors, including number of customer accounts, experience with receivable shortages, personnel, and so on are normally considered.

FINANCE CHARGES

Revolving credit agreements contain provisions for the retailer to charge interest on the unpaid balance, typically referred to as a finance charge. To avoid a finance charge, the entire balance on the account must be paid before the next closing date. Thus customers have a grace period when they can pay for their purchases in full and avoid any finance charge. The finance charge is calculated on the average daily balance. To determine the average daily balance, a daily balance is determined by taking the beginning balance of the customer account each day, adding new purchases and charges and subtracting any payments or credits and unpaid finance charges. All the daily balances are totaled and averaged by dividing the total of the daily balances by the total number of days in the billing period. The resulting average daily balance is used to apply the monthly periodic rate. The monthly periodic rate is 1/12th of the Annual Percentage Rate (APR). Generally, the APR is computed once each month and is the lower of a state-mandated maximum rate or a rate based upon various government security rates (e.g., Treasury bills).

Finance charges are normally recorded as income when earned. Classification of finance charge income in the Statement of Income varies. Most classify it as a reduction of selling, general and administrative expenses while others include it in net sales. The amount of finance charges included in income must be disclosed for all income statements presented if the company is publicly held.

Numerous studies have shown that the retailer loses money on credit card operations even though millions of dollars are collected in finance charges. The retailer must incur many costs (e.g., postage, credit department payroll costs, financing costs, and bad debts) to maintain an in-store credit program.

The costs of providing a proprietary credit program and the resulting collection efforts are largely dependent upon the store's sales and credit policies and in part upon the effectiveness of the collection procedures employed. By tightening access to credit, a retailer can control bad debts and minimize administrative costs but will also reduce credit sales. Conversely, a liberal credit policy will increase costs by producing more overdue and uncollectible accounts but will also increase credit sales. However, liberal credit policies can be more desirable when effective and consistent collection policies are employed to reduce bad debts.

RECEIVABLES MANAGEMENT

There are several ways to determine if, and to what extent, an account is delinquent. Basically, delinquency occurs two ways: (1) when the payment is less than the minimum due, or (2) when payment is not received by the due date. A basic example of delinquency follows: Assume a billing date of August 7, a minimum payment due of $10 and a due date of September 7. If payment is not received by September 7, the account becomes delinquent. From September 8 to October 7, the account ages from 1 day past due to 29 days and so on, until the balance is collected. The due date is the date the delinquency starts if payment is not received. Likewise, aging of the account begins with the due date, not the billing date.

A delinquency condition is more difficult to determine when the payment received is less than the minimum due. Normally, in this case, a payment that is less than the minimum due does not constitute a delinquency until the payment shortage accumulates to one full minimum payment. For example, assume the billed balance is $500 and the minimum payment due is $50. Further assume that only $45 is collected on the account, thus $5 of the minimum is not collected. Since the past due amount ($5) is less than one full minimum payment, this account would not be delinquent. Only when the shortage exceeds the minimum would the account be delinquent. This method has obvious shortcomings in promoting prompt collection. Timely follow-up may discourage the customer from continuing to pay less than the full minimum payment. Many retailers do not accumulate shortages as described above. Rather, any shortage is immediately considered a delinquency, and more intensive follow-up procedures are applied.

Aging of the accounts receivable is the most important tool for measuring the efficiency of a retailer's credit policies. Two methods are employed, most often simultaneously, to determine the aging of accounts receivable. The installment method ages the minimum payment due that has become delinquent. If the minimum is not paid, only the amount of the delinquent installment is aged, not the full amount of the customer's account. Exhibit 14.3 demonstrates the installment method of aging. If and when a minimum payment is received, the oldest amount past due is cured first.

The installment method is not a good tool to calculate the total amount of receivable which is likely to become uncollectible. Again referring to Exhibit 14.3, the installment method of aging would reflect only $50 past due. However, the account balance is $100. Under this method, the remaining $50 (comprised of the current minimum balance due ($10) plus the portion

EXHIBIT 14.3 Installment Method of Aging Accounts Receivable

Assume the customers account balance is $100 and the minimum monthly payment due was $10. Further assume the account has not been paid for 5 months.

Aging Categories	Days Past the Due Date						
	0–29	30–59	60–89	90–119	120–149	150–179	180 & Older
	$10	$10	$10	$10	$10	$10	$10

Account Balance	$100
Installments Past Due (Delinquent installments 30 days & older)	50
Current Minimum Balance Due	10
Total Amount Due	$ 60

of the account not yet billed ($40)) is not considered to be past due and therefore would not be considered delinquent under this method. Because of this shortcoming in measuring the potential extent of bad debts, many retailers supplement the installment method, with the contractual method of aging to better analyze delinquency.

Under the contractual method, when the minimum payment is not collected within 30 days of the first due date, the *whole* account balance is considered delinquent. As a point of fact, most revolving credit agreements contain certain default provisions that allow the retailer to demand immediate payment of the entire unpaid balance if the minimum monthly payment is not paid on time. Retailers rarely exercise this provision; however, the contractual method of aging is based on this theory. Therefore, referring to the example in Exhibit 14.3, the same account would have the whole $100 considered past due 30 days after the initial minimum payment of $10 was not received.

The contractual method is an excellent supplemental tool for the credit manager to analyze the total dollars that are delinquent and is a better indicator of problem accounts which need to be monitored. However, it does not have the benefit of predicting cash flows as does the installment method.

The collection of delinquent accounts becomes correspondingly more difficult and expensive as the receivables become increasingly older. Therefore, effective control of collection costs must be predicated on prudent credit policies and on early and active collection procedures once delinquency is determined. Another consideration that is less determinable but equally important, is the reduction in future sales to delinquent accounts. Statistical evidence indicates that purchases drop sharply with the increasing age of delinquent accounts. While delinquent balances are undesirable, the retention of the customers may be desirable. As a practical matter, many credit managers make special efforts to retain those customers with delinquent balances as long as such balances are being paid. When the aggregate of credit costs becomes excessive, these costs will reduce and may eliminate the profitability of sales. Every reduction in the cost of carrying customers' accounts or in collection expense will obviously be reflected in the overall profitability of the business.

Supplementary techniques used in measuring the effectiveness of receivable management include the use of ratios and statistical data such as the number of days of credit sales represented by the balances of accounts receivable, monthly collection percentages in absolute terms and in terms of a trend (i.e., cash collections of a month or four- or five-week period related to the balance of accounts receivable at the beginning of the month or period), bad debt loss ratio, delinquency ratio, and collections of past due accounts.

Given the tremendous growth of credit sales, the billing and receivable management computer applications have become increasingly sophisticated. The effectiveness of aging as a primary tool of credit management is undeniable. Aging provides a list of delinquent customers who will become the target of more vigorous collection procedures, although admittedly, the essence of good collection practice is the consistency of efforts applied across the board. In targeting the potential problem accounts, aging provides the basis for a concentrated analysis of the quality of a retailer's accounts receivable. It constitutes an effective measurement of the efficiency of credit department policies and procedures and provides the credit manager with an opportunity to control the cost of credit operations by indicating what steps should be taken to tighten credit policies and emphasize collection procedures.

CHAPTER FIFTEEN

Accounting for Miscellaneous Transactions

COD SALES

There are three general methods of handling COD sales.

1. CODs are not recorded as sales until collected. The delivery department or outside carrier employed may require perhaps three days to effect delivery, and during this time uncollected CODs are open items on the records of the sales audit office. As collections are made, the related amounts are credited to sales and the items are cleared from the control account. Undelivered items are cleared upon return to stock, but no credit slips are issued. Under this plan, there are no COD accounts receivable, and a minimum of COD returned sales (those

returned by customers subsequent to acceptance and settlement). Uncollected items as of any given date are considered part of stock, rather than merchandise sold.

2. COD sales checks are audited daily and charged to COD accounts receivable. Credits to COD accounts receivable comprise cash collections or returns to stock. For the latter, shipping copies of sales checks which have been utilized as address labels will be employed as credit slips once the merchandise is signed back into stock. Under this plan, CODs are treated like charge sales and carried as accounts receivable until collected.

3. COD sales, other than parcel post, freight, and express CODs, are "sold" to the outside delivery carrier. Remittance is made to the store by the carrier on the basis of receipt of sales data properly validated by the store's delivery department. Remittances received from the carrier, representing the aggregate amount of COD sales turned over to the carrier, are credited directly to sales. Sales are subsequently reduced for undelivered items, with the amount of returns being offset against subsequent carrier remittances.

Under the first method there will be a number of checks carried over from day-to-day, thereby resulting in differences between daily audited sales figures and the corresponding departmental reported totals. The second method is likely to ensure that all COD sales checks clear through the sales audit daily, but credits for nondeliverable items may be numerous. The third method may require some checking to ensure that all COD sales checks written in the selling departments are accounted for, either as cash receipts or customer cancellations.

DEPOSIT SALES

Similar to CODs are sales where deposits are accepted on account. Such deposits are received as partial payment against goods on hand or goods on order, the balance to be paid by additional deposits or upon delivery of the merchandise. There are two usual methods for recording these sales.

Under the first method, these transactions are treated as incomplete until delivery of the goods, or at least until the goods are ready for delivery, if full payment has been made in the interim.

Under this method, the deposits as received are recorded as liabilities, with such liabilities canceled upon completion of the sales transactions. This method is also applicable where deposits are received on orders for merchandise not in stock. A deposit is entered on a deposit check, a portion of which is given to the customer as a receipt. When the merchandise is ready for delivery, a regular sales check is written for the full amount and notation is made thereon of the deposit number and amount and of the net balance due. The sales checks are audited for the gross amounts, with appropriate transfers being made to offset and cancel the related deposit liabilities. Details of the deposits are usually kept on records maintained by the sales audit office. A control account in the general ledger reflects the total amount of outstanding deposits.

Under the second method, the transaction is regarded as a completed sale at the time the deposit is received. A sales check is written at this time for the full amount, and the deposit is deducted on the face of the check. The deposits are recorded as cash sales and the balances due on the transactions are recorded as COD sales. The CODs arising in this manner are included with the regular COD receivables and are closed out in the usual manner when collected. When this method is used, care should be exercised to prevent inclusion in physical inventory of goods already sold under the deposit plan. This is best done by actual segregation of the goods.

If this second method is used, great care should be exercised in recognizing as sales any orders for goods not in stock. Generally speaking, such orders should not be treated as sales.

LAYAWAY SALES

Layaway plans are not normally offered in department stores except for "big ticket" items such as jewelry or furs. Layaways in discount and specialty stores are very popular, and the program may apply to all types of merchandise. These sales are treated as a type of deposit sale, and are similar to installment sales except that merchandise is not released to the customer until the full amount is paid. Generally, the procedure is to physically set aside the merchandise for a stipulated period of time during which payments are made which will aggregate to the total sales price of the merchandise by the close of the "layaway" period. If the article is not taken by the customer at the close of the period, it may be returned to stock.

It is important that the customer is informed about the existing cancellation and refund policies. Not only does this improve customer relations, it also protects the company from state escheat tax implications. There are various refund policies that can be offered. Some retailers give full or partial refunds if the layaway transaction is not completed, while others offer credit toward future purchases. If anything less than full credit is given, the charges for the incomplete layaway should be stipulated. The amount a retailer can charge in this case is governed by state law. If the layaway terms do not disclose the cancellation and refund policies, many states consider payments received on an incomplete layaway transaction to be escheatable.

As in the case of other deposit sales, the sale is considered complete either when the full sales price is paid (a cash sale), or at the time of the first payment (a charge sale). In the latter case, the charge sale is recorded at the full amount of the sale, the initial payment being treated as a collection on an open account with the excess of selling price over the first payment as an account receivable. Under the first method, where recognition of the sale is delayed, deposits are recorded as liabilities to customers. Under the second method, the merchandise should be definitely segregated so that it will not be confused with departmental inventories.

The file of active layaway accounts should be reviewed frequently to ascertain delinquent accounts. Missed payments should be followed up promptly and the merchandise returned to stock as soon as possible.

MERCHANDISE AND GIFT CERTIFICATES

These certificates are issued either in exchange for cash or as charges to accounts of customers, with all such amounts reflected as liabilities on the books of account. From time to time the certificates are used by holders to apply in whole or in part on purchases made from the store. If used in its entirety, a certificate is surrendered to the store cashier in lieu of cash, and the transaction is recorded as a cash sale. If the customer wishes to use only part of a certificate, a voucher is obtained for the amount desired, and an entry of such amount is made on the face of the certificate. Such vouchers are accepted by cashiers in lieu of cash, and the transactions are entered as cash sales. The sales audit office receives the used certificates and vouchers to verify the cash sales totals and advises the accounting department as to the amounts to be transferred from the certificate liability account to cash sales. The general ledger account reflecting the amount of unused certificates outstanding should be supported by a detailed record of all certificate numbers and corresponding amounts outstanding.

DISCOUNT SALES

Included under this heading may be sales to institutions, clergy, businesses, interior decorators, and special customers. Many stores still allow discounts to all or some of these classes of customers even though it is a generally waning practice.

When discount customers purchase for cash, the discount is deducted from the sales checks and accounted for in the sales audit office. Discounts on charge sales may be deducted from sales checks, or they may be subtracted from monthly statements either as rendered or as settled. The first method renders departmental analysis easier and also eliminates the need for providing for allowable discounts at the close of accounting periods. The second method does not initially require as much time as the first, but it does not meet all requirements without supplementary work.

These discounts represent a loss in retail value, similar to markdowns, and accordingly, they must be reflected in the departmental stock accounts. When discounts are deducted from sales checks, the discounts are tabulated and entered in the stock records as credits to stock in the same manner as sales. Where sales checks are audited gross and the discounts are deducted from customers' bills, the stock records do not require credit entries for such discounts in order to reflect the proper closing stock status. However, sales will be overstated and discounts understated unless adjustments are made to the respective totals for the aggregates of discounts deducted from customers' accounts. The usual practice is to deduct the amount of discounts from sales and enter that total as a discount credit to stock.

Sales to employees are also considered discount sales. The most common practice is to write a sales check for all employees' sales, whether cash or charge, deducting the discount at the point of sale. Thereafter, the audit office tabulates departmentally the employees' discount amounts listed on all such sales checks. The nature of employee sales normally suggests the retailer centralize procedures. Some more common methods include requiring all such sales to run through charge accounts thereby providing a check over employees' cumulative purchases, requiring the use of a discount key at the register for all sales, or requiring some form of written documentation for all employee purchases.

SPECIAL ORDERS

Although not large in dollar volume, "special order" transactions cannot be ignored in a discussion of retail sales. The related problems are sometimes perplexing and involve accounts receivable, book inventories, and detailed stock records, as well as periodic gross margin statements. The concern is with the practical accounting problems involved, including such questions as at what times and under what conditions sales orders should be taken up into the sales account, how the inventory recordkeeping is affected, and in what periods gross profits on such transactions should be reflected in the accounts, either in whole or in part. The problems are more significant in some lines or departments than in others. Retail furniture companies, for example, are definitely concerned with such questions.

In retail environments where sales are normally delivered to an address supplied by the customer, the basic problem is when may a sale be considered as legally complete before delivery (as, for example, when held at the store pursuant to customer's instructions). Admittedly, there are many legal ramifications to be considered in determining when a sale is complete.

However, a practical test to determine whether this is a sale is whether the customer may be billed for the merchandise at once, regardless of delivery date; there should at least be constructive delivery by segregation of the goods from regular stock. Unless merchandise can be billed, the transaction can scarcely be considered a complete sale. Only when the charge becomes a real account receivable is it proper to exclude the merchandise from inventory. In retailing, even after delivery, there is a large percentage of returned sales. There is even greater likelihood of cancellations where delivery of merchandise has not been completed.

From an accounting viewpoint, the FASB has addressed these questions in FAS #48, "Revenue Recognition when Right of Return Exists."

There are different problems with respect to special orders, that is, orders for merchandise not in stock or to be made up from goods in stock, as, for example, draperies, curtains, and upholstery. Before delivery can even constructively be made, there are materials to be purchased or labor and production costs to be incurred. It would be incorrect to enter this type of order as a sale until all related costs have been charged into purchases. Ordinarily, no sale should be recognized until delivery is made, but in any event, such recognition should definitely by delayed until all costs have been incurred and the merchandise is ready for delivery. Any other course will erroneously inflate profits and misstate the book inventory figures. In some cases, departmental stock records can be kept current by transfers to workrooms of goods to be used toward the filling of orders. Such merchandise will then be in workroom stocks while the orders are in process of being completed.

WILL CALL TRANSACTIONS

With respect to furniture and similar household merchandise, it is a common practice for customers to place orders well in advance of desired delivery dates. This may be done to take advantage of special prices being offered temporarily or seasonally, or to allow for time required to obtain merchandise similar to that in stock, but different in details such as shades of fabric, size, or finish, or to assemble and prepare goods for delivery. In many instances, a store is requested to hold the goods until notification by the customer as to time and place for delivery.

Many furniture stores withhold recording of such sales until actual delivery, meanwhile including held merchandise as part of stock and carrying any deposits received as liabilities.

STORAGE CHARGES

Questions of accounting procedure arise where storage charges, such as for fur storage, are made to customers. It is common practice for storage charges to cover the period from the date goods are received until the close of the calendar year. While charges may be made on various bases, a common basis is a charge related to declared or appraised value, with no regard to the length of the storage period, provided it is within the calendar year. If storage is continued into the new year, the customer ordinarily becomes liable for a storage fee for the second year. Some goods are received early in the season and remain in storage until near the end of the year. Other articles may come in late and be taken out early, without, however, affecting the amount charged.

The full storage charge should not be recorded as income upon receipt of goods. In many cases, no amount of storage income is recorded until the goods are taken from storage. In operations of the latter kind, practically all the storage sales as recorded are realized in the months well toward the end of the storage year. The result is that a disproportionate amount of the storage revenue is realized in those months in which the bulk of items is withdrawn, regardless of the fact that storage expense continues throughout the year and is exceptionally heavy at the time that garments are first placed in the vaults. A widely used alternative accounting practice is to defer all expenses of storage until such time as the garments are withdrawn, recognizing at such time both the storage expenses and the storage revenue. This is preferable to charging off all expenses as incurred but deferring the revenue pending withdrawal of the garments. However, it has the disadvantage of excluding storage operations from the accounts throughout most of the year, and then suddenly recognizing all storage activity in a relatively brief period.

A more appropriate procedure is to absorb the storage expenses as they arise and to allocate storage revenue on a pro rata basis over the period in which the garments remain in the vaults. Under this plan, the full charge for the year is made against the customer when the goods are received, with the offsetting credit being to a deferred storage sales account. Since it is rarely the practice to bill the customer for storage charges before the articles are withdrawn from storage, or at the end of the storage year if not withdrawn, the sales checks as written are retained in house. As garments are withdrawn from storage or at the end of the storage year if not withdrawn, the sales checks are removed from file and the customers are billed.

Transfers from the deferred storage sales account to sales are made monthly (or for each four- or five-week period) on a pro rata basis. Any remaining balances in the deferred sales account related to goods taken from storage may be transferred to sales in the respective months or periods of removal. Sometimes these procedures will be applied only in the fall months, when there are large withdrawals from storage.

REPAIR CHARGES

Charges for repairs to customers' own goods or for cleaning, where the goods are delivered when finished or are held for customers to call, should present no problem in accounting for sales. Charge customers may be billed and amounts recorded as sales when the work has been completed. For cash customers, amounts will be treated as cash sales when customers call for their goods and pay the charges. If payments have been made when goods are left for repair, the amounts paid can be recorded as deposit liabilities that are later transferred to revenue when the repair work is completed.

Where repair or cleaning is done on customers' goods placed in storage, it is the usual practice not to bill the charges until the articles are withdrawn from storage or until the end of the storage year. This is done as a practical matter since the customer normally would not make payment until there has been an inspection, by the customer, of the repair work. The problem remains, however, of getting such charges into sales when the work is completed, because cost and expense are incurred long before the items are withdrawn or before the close of the storage period.

Two extreme practices appear to be followed by some retailers: (1) to record the charge at once as a sale, regardless of when the costs are incurred, and (2) to record the sale only when the charge is billed. Under the first practice, the charge against the customer is included as an additional item on the sales check written to cover storage charges. However, it is not billed to the customer until the articles are withdrawn from storage or until the end of the storage year. The method is to be criticized for recording a sale before related costs are incurred and recorded. It is customary to spread the work of repairing and cleaning of stored goods throughout the less active months of the storage period. Operating results are inaccurately stated where sales income is recorded in advance of the entry of cost of sales. The inaccuracy may be material if large amounts of repair and cleaning charges are involved.

Under the second practice, there is also inaccuracy because costs are recorded, but sales income is deferred. A modification is to defer the costs along with the revenue until the charges are billed, and at that time to recognize both costs incurred and related revenues for accounting purposes.

CUSTOMER CREDITS

Customers returning merchandise personally are issued either cash credit or credit against credit purchases (charge credit). With this type of credit transaction, the merchandise is received and the credit is issued in the selling department, or alternatively at service desks if the latter are maintained. A countersignature by the manager is recommended. Cash credits can be surrendered by customers in exchange for cash or applied on new purchases.

Charge credits are summarized and forwarded, together with control totals, to the accounts receivable department for application against the individual charge accounts affected. Cash credits are summarized, with control totals being forwarded either to the accounts receivable or the accounting department.

In addition to the credits representing the return of merchandise, there are credits that represent special allowances to customers. These credits are written essentially by the bill and merchandise adjustment departments, although floor authorities also are often permitted to write this type of credit. These customer adjustments are often discretionary in nature. Credits that represent purely policy adjustments should be charged off to expenses. Credits representing a true merchandise allowance should serve to reduce departmental gross margins.

ITEMS NOT RECORDED AS SALES

There are some items charged to customers or collected from them that for obvious reasons are not classified as sales. For example, excise taxes or local sales taxes payable by customers are not sales. A store is simply the collecting agent. The amounts of such taxes, whether collected in cash at the time of sale or entered together with the merchandise item on a customer's charge account, should not be recorded as sales but as a liability to the taxing authority. Parcel post, express, and freight charges to customers should be credited to expense accounts (or supply inventory accounts if maintained) or sundry income, and not to sales.

These items differ from alteration and workroom charges to customers. Charges by workrooms classified as service workrooms are, in fact, sales. However, although entered on sales checks, so that the amounts may be collected from customers, such charges are usually credited to alteration or workroom cost accounts rather than to sales. They are thus applied to reduce alteration and workroom costs that are included net in total merchandise costs. This procedure is normally followed in the accounts and merchandise statements so that there will be shown the ratio of gross margin to sales of merchandise only and also the ratio of service workroom net costs in relation to merchandise sales.

CHAPTER SIXTEEN

Sales Staff and Payroll Issues

Payroll costs are often the single largest nonmerchandise cost of a retailer. Controlling these costs is essential to a profitable retail operation. This section will focus on payroll and manpower scheduling considerations unique to retailing.

The payroll system, like all systems, should be designed to enhance the company's strategic goals. Management determines the strategic direction of the company, and then operational goals are designed to promote and complement these strategies. An effective payroll system will be designed to achieve the maximum amount of sales within the company's defined strategy, and to avoid any costs that do not provide an adequate return on investment. When considering payroll costs, management must consider not only compensation expense, but also the costs of hiring and training employees. The major difference between the payroll system of retailers and that of other industries is the large salesforce maintained by retailers. This chapter focuses primarily on the salesforce.

Before designing or modifying a payroll system, it is important to be aware of the operational goals that will impact this system. First, management must determine the customer service orientation of the firm. Customer service is crucial to all retailers, because retailers do not go to their customers, rather their customers come to them. Thus, if customer service is inadequate, they may lose customers and not have the opportunity to win them back. In the end, the retailer must keep the customer happy. The two obvious methods of doing this are through offering the customer (1) low prices and (2) excellent service. There will be a trade-off between sales volumes and customer service.

Management must determine whether their firm will spend more or less time making a sale than is the industry average. If they choose to spend more time, they should be able to charge the customer for the additional service provided. This tactic should be taken only if the increase in price will more than cover the additional payroll costs, that is, only if there will be an increase in gross margin. It is recognized that the increase in price will result in some loss of volume. What is lost in volume, however, should be made up in gross profit. Conversely, if less time is spent with each customer, the opposite should hold true and what is lost in gross margin should be made up in volume. Once management has determined the customer service orientation that will best enhance their market strategy, the payroll system should be designed, managed, and controlled to promote the desired level of service. As this chapter will show, this can be done with effective scheduling, incentive compensation schemes, evaluations, and training programs.

A second, and often less recognized, goal related to the payroll system is that of increasing employee morale. This is important because as morale increases so does productivity and more productive employees should increase profitability. Additionally, as employee morale increases, so should customer service. Whatever the customer service orientation of the company, sales are bound to increase if sales personnel are pleasant, courteous and enthusiastic. Finally, the increase in employee morale can reduce the rate of employee turnover. The traditionally high turnover rate in the retailing industry is very costly to the retailer in terms of hiring and training new employees. A reduction in this rate will increase profitability.

SCHEDULING AND STAFFING

The scheduling of employees is particularly important to a retail organization. Because payroll is one of the largest expenses of a retail establishment, overstaffing will result in large excess costs. However, understaffing will result in lost sales. The retail manager's challenge is to find a balance between these two. When scheduling employees, the following variables must be considered:

- Service goals of the establishment.
- Shopping hours of customers.
- Length of contact made with customers.
- Expense constraints.

The service goals of the establishment will be set in conjunction with the company's market strategy. The length of contact made with customers will depend in part on the type of product sold, and in part on the company's customer service orientation. Expense constraints will be determined based on cash flow, investment opportunities and case management strategies. Customer shopping hours will be determined by a variety of factors, none of which are truly predictable or controllable. This, then, becomes the most difficult piece of scheduling. Retail managers must use all available data in order to predict this flow, including:

- Past history of peak shopping times.
- Knowledge of customer reaction to sales and promotions.
- Weather conditions, and seasonal shopping trends.
- The state of the local economy.

Each retail establishment will have its own list of factors that will aid in predicting customer flow. This flow, coupled with the amount of time spent with each customer, will determine the ideal staffing requirements.

To predict customer shopping hours, the retail manager should not only rely on common sense, but periodically should perform a formal study through a point-of-sale computer system, or through a manual headcount. While a computer system can easily provide very accurate data, it has some limitations. It cannot analyze the number of customers that enter the store without making a purchase. These customers also require service. Nor can it analyze the amount of time spent with a customer. Therefore, it is recommended that when a point-of-sale system is used to analyze customer flow, that actual headcounts also be taken periodically. The retailer must keep in mind that any formal study, whether it is done with a point-of-sale system or through headcounts, is only an analysis of *past* data. This information must be used in conjunction with other data (such as weekly sales forecasts, weather conditions and the state of the local economy), to predict *future* customer flow. Predicting customer flow is an art, not a science. Finally, each store and possibly even each department, will have its own traffic patterns and must be analyzed individually.

Due to the inability to hire people for only one or two hours a day, a manager can rarely staff a store with the ideal number of sales personnel. Therefore, once the ideal staffing requirements, are determined the retail manager must develop *practical* staffing requirements.

In a very simple example, a manager of a small retail store has determined that peak shopping hours are from 11:00 A.M. until 1:00 P.M. and again from 6:00 P.M. until 8:00 P.M. Given this, and his analysis of other variables, he has decided that in his store he ideally needs the following staff:

9:00 A.M.–11:00 A.M.	8 salespersons
11:00 A.M.–1:00 P.M.	9 salespersons
1:00 P.M.–6:00 P.M.	5 salespersons
6:00 P.M.–8:00 P.M.	9 salespersons
8:00 P.M.–9:00 P.M.	5 salespersons

Having determined the ideal staffing requirements, the store manager must determine the practical staffing requirements that most closely match the ideal. In the above example, it will be impractical to hire four employees to work a two hour shift from 11:00 A.M. to 1:00 P.M. To work around this, the manager may hire five employees to begin work at 9:00 A.M., and spend some of their time stocking or arranging shelves. Four more employees will begin work at 11:00 A.M. There are now the necessary 9 employees from 11:00 A.M. until 1:00 P.M. Two of the employees who begin work at 9:00 A.M. are part-time employees and will leave at 1:00 P.M. However, the store will still be overstaffed from 1:00 P.M.–6:00 P.M. with seven employees when only five are needed. The manager must decide whether to be overstaffed during this period or understaffed during another period. The former will result in excess costs, the latter lost sales. The solution must depend on the goals of the organization and expense constraints. Computer software packages are available to help store managers with the decision making process (Exhibit 16.1).

INCENTIVE COMPENSATION

To motivate employees to work towards the goals of the organization, management often establishes one or more forms of incentive compensation. It is crucial that compensation plans are designed to reward the appropriate behaviors. A poorly designed plan may motivate the workforce to

EXHIBIT 16.1 Sales Floor Schedule

COOPBRAND CLOTHING STORES

CREATE DATE: 07/24/XX

SALES FLOOR SCHEDULE
WEEK OF 07/31/XX

STORE: #1 - 6TH AVENUE
DEPT : 321 - DRESSES

EMPLOYEE	MONDAY SCHED	HOURS	TUESDAY SCHED	HOURS	WEDNESDAY SCHED	HOURS	THURSDAY SCHED	HOURS	FRIDAY SCHED	HOURS	SATURDAY SCHED	HOURS	SUNDAY SCHED	HOURS	TOTAL HOURS
SMITH	9 TO 5	8	9 TO 5	8	9 TO 5	8	9 TO 5	8	9 TO 5	8	OFF	0	OFF	0	40
JONES	9 TO 5	8	9 TO 5	8	9 TO 5	8	9 TO 5	8	9 TO 5	8	OFF	0	OFF	0	40
HARRIS	10 TO 6	8	OFF	0	10 TO 6	8	10 TO 6	8	10 TO 6	8	10 TO 6	8	OFF	0	40
TORRES	OFF	0	11 TO 7	8	11 TO 7	8	OFF	0	1 TO 9	8	10 TO 6	8	10 TO 6	8	40
JAMES	OFF	0	OFF	0	3 TO 7	4	4 TO 9	5	4 TO 9	5	12 TO 6	6	1 TO 6	5	25
TAYLOR	3 TO 7	4	3 TO 7	4	OFF	0	OFF	0	4 TO 9	5	11 TO 3	4	10 TO 6	8	25
RAINES	3 TO 7	4	3 TO 7	4	OFF	0	4 TO 9	5	OFF	0	2 TO 6	4	10 TO 6	8	25
OPENING COVERAGE (9 TO 12)		8		7		9		8		8		5		6	51
MIDDAY COVERAGE (12-5)		19		19		22		17		21		21		19	138
CLOSING COVERAGE (5-9)		5		6		5		9		13		4		4	46
TOTAL COVERAGE		32		32		36		34		42		30		29	235

133

work against management's goals. Management will want to encourage assertive salesmanship, without causing overly aggressive selling that can lead to lost sales.

Store Manager

If a retailer awards bonuses, pay raises, or promotions to store managers based on sales volume alone, store management may overspend on staff rather than risk losing sales. Conversely, if rewards are based solely on reducing costs, the stores may be understaffed. It is important for management to establish the organization's goals and develop an incentive program that rewards store managers who effectively promote those goals. The best incentive/bonus plans reward store managers based on a store's overall profitability. The following is a discussion of various types of incentive compensation plans.

Commissions

Incentive compensation for retail sales staff is most often in the form of commissions. Commissions tie compensation directly to a salesperson's results and provide an objective measure of compensation, (as opposed to a subjective evaluation of performance). The relationship between performance and pay is, therefore, obvious to the employee making commissions a very effective method of motivating employees. The behavior that is encouraged will depend on how commissions are structured. Commissions may be based on dollar volume sold, number of units sold, gross margin, quotas, a combination of these, or on any of a number of other factors.

The factors on which a particular company bases commissions, will depend on the selling behavior that the company wishes to encourage. For example, if the company is seeking to increase revenue, they will want to base commissions, at least in part, on sales. If they, however, are seeking to increase the gross profit percentage, they will want to base commissions on gross margin. This will become an important distinction when small, lower priced items actually have a larger gross margin percentage than the big ticket items have. Before designing a commission system, management must clearly define what behaviors will best promote the company's market strategy, and lead to the attainment of the company's defined goals.

Although a salesman may be paid entirely on commissions, commissions are most often paid in combination with a base salary. The *commission-salary combination* can best be described as a trade-off between control and incentive. The more a person's salary depends on commission, the more incentive there is to sell and the less control management has over him. Conversely, if a person's salary is derived mainly from base pay, the incentive to sell aggressively is reduced and management's control over his activities are increased.

When *straight commissions* are paid, the salesperson has no income security, but also has no limits placed upon their earning potential. To counter the lack of security, many companies allow their salespeople to draw upon future commissions. That is, they can obtain a cash advance that will insure a minimum income during slow periods. The advantages to the retailer of straight commission plans are that payroll remains a fixed expense of sales and there are no payments for inefficient time. The disadvantages are the risk of overaggressive selling and the potential for poor customer service when sales staff ignores nonbuying and even slow buying customers.

A variation of commissions is called "Push Money." Push money is an additional payment for the sale of specific items. It may be vendor paid or company paid. This can be an effective tool when management or vendors wish to introduce a new product or change the product mix. Push money incentives must be used carefully, however, as they tend to encourage overly aggressive selling and, in some cases, misrepresentation due to the desire to sell the specific product. When using this type of incentive, it is important to fully educate the salesforce on the particular product to encourage effective selling.

Commissions, either straight or in combination with a salary, are not applicable to all retail establishments, nor to all employees. Commissions should not be used when productivity is difficult to measure or when salespeople are actually order takers or cashiers. (Sales commissions would not be appropriate in grocery stores.) Commissions are appropriate only when there is direct selling to customers.

Straight Salaries

At the opposite end of the spectrum from straight commissions are straight salaries. Employees who are paid a straight salary receive monetary rewards as raises. The problem with annual or semi-annual raises is the lack of direct correlation between selling ability and monetary reward. In many cases, pay raises represent cost-of-living allowances and seniority rather than merit pay. Straight salaries allow management to control salesforce activity and can be particularly effective when a retailer wants to encourage salespersons to be involved in other activities.

Bonuses

When commissions are not applicable or desirable, management may monetarily reward employees with bonuses. One advantage that bonus programs have over straight salaries is that they allow management to vary an individual's pay widely from period to period. An advantage over commission plans is that bonuses permit management to reward employees for activities other than sales, such as outstanding customer service, displays, or managerial skills. If employees are aware of what management expects of them, and bonuses are paid based upon these expectations, bonuses will serve as effective motivators. Bonuses do not provide the direct sales incentive of commissions, but they serve as effective rewards for desired behaviors and can increase employee morale.

Selling Cost

Under the selling cost method of compensation, the retailer establishes a standard percent of sales that selling costs should be. At each salary evaluation period, the employee's hourly salary is computed as the average sales per hour times the predetermined standard selling cost rate. Thus, the higher an employee's hourly sales are, the higher his salary will be. This holds an advantage over a straight salary, in that the employee knows that pay raises will be directly related to productivity. The advantages to the retailer are that unlike a straight commission structure that provides immediate compensation for increased productivity, these "commissions" (in the form of pay raises) are noted until the following evaluation period, and selling costs remain a relatively constant percent of revenue.

There are, however, several drawbacks to this method. It may be necessary to develop separate standards for different stores, different departments and, in some cases, different individuals. This is especially true if some employees have more nonselling duties than other employees, or if some work during peak shopping hours while others work during slower hours. Furthermore, this method does not provide a monetary reward system for outstanding nonselling activities.

Prizes and Contests

Prizes and contests may be used to supplement other forms of compensation. Prizes may be awarded for any number of behaviors that the company wishes to promote. Often the company will recognize the prize winner in a ceremony or newsletter. This peer recognition acts as a motivator and reward in addition to the prize itself. Prizes and contests should not be awarded based on the same factors as commissions or bonuses unless the retailer feels that public recognition, in addition to the monetary rewards of commissions, is necessary.

Group Compensation

The methods of compensation just discussed have focused on individuals. In some instances, the retailer will want to use a method of group compensation in addition to individual compensation. Group compensation encourages cooperation and teamwork among employees. Storewide or departmental bonuses or prizes may be paid based on sales, profitability, or any other factor.

These compensation programs are the most commonly used by retailers and they are often used in combination. When designing an incentive compensation program, each retailer must consider the strategic goals of his company. The compensation program put into place must encourage the type of behavior that will best promote company goals and objectives. In addition, employees must be made aware of how the company expects the compensation plan to help achieve these goals while providing employees with monetary rewards.

EVALUATION SYSTEMS

In addition to compensation, another effective method of motivating employees is through performance evaluations. Evaluations may serve as a method of determining base salary increases and promotions and of offering feedback to employees. Performance evaluations allow management to praise employees who are performing well and to correct performance deficiencies. There are several types of evaluations including rating scales, rankings, checklists, and essays. For any type of performance evaluation to be effective, the following conditions must be met:

- The evaluation system must reflect the goals of the organization.

- Employees must be aware of what is considered good performance.

- Rewards must be based on evaluations.

To be effective, an evaluation system must reflect the goals of the company. Performance objectives must be defined in terms of the company's strategic goals. Like compensation plans, if evaluations stress only the dollar volume of sales, while the company expects significant nonsales efforts, there will be conflict. The challenge of the retail manager is to determine the proper mix of rewards that will motivate employees to use the "right" amount of aggressiveness in their sales techniques. Employee evaluations should be structured so that they not only reward sales volume, but also reward customer service and any other traits such as product knowledge or creative merchandising, that management wishes to encourage in their sales personnel.

When evaluations are used as a method of determining employee promotions, they must reflect all the attributes needed for promotion (a good store manager will be more than a superstar salesman). Evaluations, will not necessarily motivate employees in the same way that incentive compensation does. The two systems should be designed to complement each other.

An effectively designed evaluation system will not only promote company goals, but will also increase employee morale. A well-designed evaluation and reward system will aid the company financially by improving morale, increasing sales, and helping the company retain their best and most effective employees.

EMPLOYEE TRAINING

The objectives of a training program are primarily to increase profitability. A training program can do this by increasing sales volume and decreasing costs. Sales volume will be increased by teaching employees various selling techniques, by training employees in the appropriate level of customer service and by increasing motivation and morale. Costs will be reduced by decreasing the required amount of supervision and decreasing the employee turnover rate. The continued training of experienced employees should not be ignored. Updating and improving sales and management skills can result in increased benefits to the company.

PAYROLL RECORDING AND PREPARATION

The recording and preparation of payroll for retailers differs from that of other industries primarily due to the emphasis on incentive compensation, particularly commission sales. Commissions must be paid and recorded in the proper periods to insure that sales personnel are paid correctly and on a timely basis, to achieve a proper matching of expense and revenue.

Accounting for and Recording Payroll

When salespeople are permitted to draw on future commissions, it must be recorded on the company's books and then deducted from the employees' paychecks in the appropriate period. Draws against commissions are considered expenses of the period in which they are actually earned. Until that time, they are considered prepayments and accordingly are recorded as assets.

There is an important exception to this accounting rule—when salespeople are guaranteed a minimum income. If their commissions are not adequate to reach this minimum, they make draws against future commissions. If a salesperson leaves the company, he would not be required to repay the company, as his draw actually represented a minimum salary. In this case, the draw is an expense of the period in which it is actually paid. Any draws over and above this "minimum salary," however, would still be considered prepaid assets.

When sales staff have large debit balances, that do not represent a minimum salary, a determination should be made as to collectibility. An allowance account should be set up for possible uncollectible accounts, and balances that cannot be collected should be written off.

One problem that arises is that of sales that are returned for a refund. Often the commission is paid and recorded before the sale is returned. Because the item is returned, there is actually no sale and no commission earned. A similar problem is encountered when credit sales are uncollectible. In the case of returns, retailers may try to reduce future commission paychecks for past overpayments. Retailers rarely reduce commissions for bad credit losses because the company, not the salesforce, sets credit policy. The expense, however, should be reduced in the period in which it had originally been recorded rather than in the period in which it was actually deducted from the individual's salary.

Payroll Preparation

When compensation is paid based upon sales volume or gross profit, additional records must be kept to monitor this data by individual employees. This information can be kept in the form of a subsidiary ledger that should be reconciled to the general ledger balance. Payroll checks will be prepared based on this information.

CONCLUSION

Throughout this chapter, we have discussed designing a retail payroll system that will complement and help to achieve the goals of the company. This is vital to the success of the retailer. The payroll system, like all systems, should be designed to enhance profitability, growth, or other primary goals, as determined by management.

CHAPTER SEVENTEEN

Merchandise Shortage

Retailers typically maintain book inventory controls that provide current information concerning inventory balances throughout the year. Merchandise shortage, or shrinkage, is the difference between the inventory balance according to the book controls and the inventory balance as determined by a physical count.

Merchandise shortages, or in some cases overages, are a perplexing and costly problem for most retailers. There is a diversity of factors that cause shortage including the retail operating environment itself that results in a high degree of exposure to merchandise shortage risks. It is not unusual for retail shrinkage rates to be in the range of 2 to 5 percent of sales.

MERCHANDISE SHORTAGE CAUSES

Merchandise shortages can result from theft by both internal and external sources, carelessness or negligence on the part of management and employees, and the intentional or unintentional override of established controls. Most retailers cannot accurately identify the specific causes of their merchandise shortage. As a result, it is often quite difficult to develop appropriate control measures.

Unique attributes of the retail operating environment that tend to increase the risks of merchandise shortage include:

- Openly displayed and readily accessible merchandise. Often this is in conjunction with self-service minimal sales floor coverage by store personnel, and liberal merchandise return policies. These practices are conducive to merchandise theft as well as vandalism, price tag changing, and abuses of the merchandise return policy. All may cause inventory shortage.

- Store-level inventory control responsibilities that are carried out by employees who often have very limited experience, training or educational backgrounds and who are being paid the minimum or near minimum wage. Frequently, these same employees are also responsible for the handling of sales and refund transactions. These conditions make effective controls difficult and are conducive to theft by employees. They also lead to breakdowns in established control procedures.

- Merchandise that is situated in broadly dispersed geographic locations. In the case of large chains, thousands of different locations may be involved. This creates a need for an effective communications network, entails more extensive recordkeeping and results in the delegation of control responsibilities to a broader number of personnel. In most cases, staff members have varying levels of leadership capability, experience, competency, and motivation. Additionally, broad geographic dispersion creates a need for an extensive merchandise distribution and transportation network. This often results in shrinkage during the merchandise distribution and transportation process.

- Large quantities of different types of merchandise that constantly change throughout the year does not necessarily increase the retailer's exposure to merchandise shortage risks, but due to the large volume of paperwork involved, does make accurate recordkeeping a more difficult and cumbersome task.

MERCHANDISE SHORTAGE STATISTICS

Both the International Mass Retail Association (IMRA) and the National Retail Federation (NRF) prepare annual publications that contain merchandise shortage statistics. These statistics are based on data provided by participating retailers.

In recent years, the overall shrinkage rate, based on the retail value of the merchandise, as reported by these publications, has been in the vicinity of 2 percent of sales for all participating store types. Department stores and mass merchants have been experiencing a somewhat higher rate than specialty stores. IMRA annual studies have stated that participating retailers generally attribute their shrinkage to the following causes, in descending order of significance: (1) employee theft, (2) customer shoplifting, (3) paperwork errors, and (4) vendor theft.

When evaluating shrinkage rates, it should be recognized that they can vary significantly from one retailer to another as well as between stores and merchandise departments within a retail organization. This results from variations in operating conditions, retail business types and shortage control practices. Consequently, retailers should not rely upon industry averages to determine whether or not their specific shrinkage rates are acceptable. Instead, they should evaluate their specific operating conditions and shrinkage experience relative to their shortage control costs and practices to determine the acceptability of their specific shrinkage rates.

CONTROLLING MERCHANDISE SHORTAGE

Shortage controls need to encompass operating conditions as well as inventory accounting and control practices. Putting shortage controls in place means focusing on prevention and detection as well as recordkeeping accuracy. To fulfill this need, retailers frequently maintain a formal loss prevention function having the overall responsibility for the prevention and detection of merchandise shortage. This approach recognizes that preplanned preventive action is critical to shortage control and it entails the involvement of the loss prevention function in a broad range of activities requiring a management perspective.

The Loss Prevention Function

Activities of the retail loss prevention function include:

- Involvement with merchants and store planning personnel in the design of store layouts and merchandise displays. Their objective is to help minimize shortages related to the accessibility of merchandise. They also try to prevent blind spots on the sales floor that make effective sales floor monitoring more difficult.

- The administration of loss prevention training programs. These programs focus on the loss prevention responsibilities of both management and employees and make store personnel aware of basic loss prevention techniques and practices. This type of training can be augmented by recognition awards to both management and employees of stores that achieve favorable shortage results.

- The selection and implementation of employment screening techniques that identify high-risk employment candidates prior to their employment. These include reference checks, credit checks, psychological testing, and interviews by loss prevention personnel. Some retailers have also started to use drug tests as a part of the pre-employment screening process.

- Communications throughout the year to both management and employees covering shortage control issues. These help sustain a relatively high level of concern among employees about shortage control during the course of the year. Most retailers only compute shrinkage at the end of their fiscal year and as a result, shortage control concern tends to diminish as the year progresses.

- The determination of surveillance needs relative to the number of operating locations, high-risk areas, hours of operation, and peak risk periods as well as the selection of surveillance methods, techniques, and equipment.

- Involvement in the development and implementation of company-wide policies, procedures, and practices that reduce the retailer's exposure to merchandise shortage risks. This can include store opening and closing procedures, merchandise return and refund procedures, employee purchase policies and procedures, codes of conduct, personnel evaluation policies that cover shortage control responsibilities, development and use of information systems providing data and controls that can be useful in the prevention and detection of shortage, and the selection and implementation of merchandise tagging and marking equipment and procedures.

- The day-to-day review and administration of company-wide security practices and procedures. It is important that the loss prevention function report to an individual with sufficient stature in the organization to assure management support.

- The investigations of all real or suspected instances of theft as well as violations of established shortage control policies.

The larger a company, the greater the need for a formal loss prevention function. A company's size and organizational structure will also have a significant influence on the specific role and responsibilities of the loss prevention function. In smaller companies, these responsibilities may be fulfilled by personnel who have duties other than loss prevention and, in some cases, loss prevention responsibilities may be spread among several positions.

The Internal Audit Function

Many retailers maintain a formal internal audit function that has certain merchandise shortage control responsibilities including:

- Periodic visits to stores and other operating locations with the objective of testing and evaluating adherence to established control policies and procedures. This is often done on a surprise basis.

- Periodic testing and evaluation of the retailer's inventory accounting controls and records, and advising management of identified deficiencies and recommended corrective actions. This includes recommendations for changes in existing policies and procedures that would result in improved control.

- Observation of physical inventory counts, checking of counts and the testing and evaluation of physical inventory compilation procedures and controls.

- Testing and evaluation of operating and financial reporting systems, both computerized and manual to assess the adequacy of control features. This should be done during the system's development and implementation phases as well as at periodic intervals once the system becomes operational.

- Performing periodic audits of specific areas where shortage is likely to occur.

Theft Control

The methods retailers use to prevent and detect theft are varied and often unique to a particular retailer's circumstances. A number of practices that retailers in general have found to be effective, including:

- Maintenance of an environment where shortage control is an everyday concern throughout the organization: top management, buyers, sales, store design and layout, receiving, distribution center, administrative personnel, construction, maintenance and delivery as well as loss prevention personnel. Nearly everyone in a retail organization must be involved in the shortage control effort in order for it to be effective.

- Utilization of information systems identifying the sources of shortage to the most precise degree possible and including built-in control features which can reduce a retailer's shortage risk exposure. Most retailers are now utilizing computers to maintain inventory records by a

Stock Keeping Unit (SKU) number. By accumulating such merchandise tracking information, specific departments and merchandise items that are the sources of shortage can be identified, thereby making the development of appropriate solutions easier. Also, these systems often contain built-in control features at point-of-sale including automated verification of selling prices, SKU numbers, validity checks, and register operator monitoring information that can reduce a retailer's shortage risk exposure.

- Structured training programs for both management and employees emphasizing their specific shortage control responsibilities along with basic loss prevention techniques and practices. These cover how to monitor sales floor areas, suspicious behavior patterns, shoplifting techniques, and what to do when someone is suspected of theft. They should also point out that one of the most effective loss prevention techniques is prompt and courteous customer service.

- Formation of shortage control committees including management and employees from various departments throughout the organization. These committees help promote shortage awareness within the organization and provide for interchange of ideas for improved shortage control.

- Utilization of physical security controls including uniformed and nonuniformed security personnel; electronic article surveillance tagging and monitoring devices; visible and concealed cameras; observation mirrors and concealed observation posts; merchandise display security devices such as locks, chains, cables, and showcases; secured vehicles for the transportation of merchandise; floor layouts limiting the accessibility to high value merchandise and making sales floor observations easier.

- Establishment of operating policies, practices, and procedures that deter theft. These include the following:

Store opening and closing procedures.

Restrictive merchandise return and refund procedures.

Pre-employment screening practices.

Restrictive employee purchase procedures.

Supervised and restricted employee entrance and exit areas.

Use of employee identification badges.

Spot checks of employee packages and purses.

Written codes of conduct.

Supervision and observation of restrooms, fitting rooms, stockrooms, and sales floor areas.

Supervision and monitoring of cash register operators.

Supervision of trash removal and maintenance activities.

Receiving, checking, and marking of merchandise in a secured and supervised environment.

Restrictions on the transfer of merchandise from one location to another without authorized approval.

All these approaches to theft control have in common the following: (1) emphasis on prevention rather than detection, (2) an ongoing top management commitment to theft control, (3) a high degree of concern about theft control on the part of both management and employees, and (4) the use of physical security controls and operating, practices that reduce both the temptation and the opportunity to steal.

Paperwork Control

Retail inventory recordkeeping requirements generally entail a large volume of input from diverse sources at broadly dispersed locations making accurate recordkeeping a very difficult and cumbersome task. As a result, retail inventory records usually contain some degree of error. Paperwork errors can mislead a retailer concerning merchandise shortages and often have an adverse effect on management's attitudes with respect to the need for, and importance of, a comprehensive shrinkage control effort.

Effective inventory records control requires the appropriate treatment of the retailer's transactions other than sales and purchases, including:

- *Price Changes.* Retailers using the retail inventory method record all inventory purchases at both initial selling value and cost. All subsequent selling price changes such as markups, markup cancellations, markdowns, or markdown cancellations must also be recorded.

- *Known Losses.* Inventory losses resulting from factors such as breakage, damage, spoilage, or identifiable theft are decreases in the retailer's inventory that should be recorded so that the known inventory shortage component can be segregated from the unknown shortage component. This also serves to improve the reliability of the inventory records for stock control and buying purposes.

- *Internal Use.* Retailers often take merchandise such as furniture, maintenance supplies, and office supplies from inventory for their own internal use. Transactions of this type should be recorded in the inventory records with a corresponding entry to the appropriate asset or expense account.

- *Merchandise Transfers.* Merchandise will frequently be transferred from one location to another for a variety of reasons. All transfer transactions, as well as any related selling price changes, should be recorded.

- *Returns to Vendors.* Retailers may return merchandise for a variety of reasons subsequent to its being recorded in the inventory records. All returns of merchandise previously recorded as an inventoriable receipt should be recorded.

- *Customer Returns.* Returned merchandise that is available for sale should be recorded in the retailer's inventory records. If the selling price has been changed as a result of the return, the selling price change should also be recorded.

- *Merchandise Exchanges.* Customers frequently exchange one merchandise item for another item with an identical selling price. In situations where the two items have different SKU numbers or are from different departments or subdepartments, the exchange transaction must be recorded to maintain the accuracy of the inventory records.

- *Discounts.* Retailers frequently make special discounts available to select groups such as employees, senior citizens, and charitable organizations. When these purchases take place, the amount recorded as sales in the retail inventory records should be the established selling price rather than the discounted price so that the amount removed from inventory equals the recorded inventory value of the merchandise.

- *Cancellation and Correction Transactions.* Cash register operators can make mistakes when ringing transactions resulting in incorrectly entered sales or refund amounts. Also, customers sometimes decide not to buy merchandise or decide to change what they want to buy while at the cash register. This necessitates the voiding or cancellation of transactions already entered into the cash register to prevent the recording of erroneous amounts in the retailer's sales and inventory accounts. These transactions should also be authorized.

Frequent Retail Inventory Recordkeeping Errors

- *Unrecorded or Incorrectly Calculated Price Changes.* This is a frequent error source since price changes are not generally an integral part of the retailer's accounting system. Additionally, there is often motivation on the part of both management and employees for the misstatement of selling price changes. For example, buyers may not want their markdowns recorded so that attention will not be drawn to their buying mistakes. In some cases, markdowns may even affect bonus amounts which a buyer might receive. On the other hand, an insider who is stealing merchandise may not want markups recorded so that sales of merchandise at higher than recorded prices will make shortage rates appear to be lower than what they actually are.

- *Register Operator Errors.* These may be in the form of overcharges, undercharges, or the misclassification of the type of merchandise sold.

Undercharging is sometimes done deliberately so that acquaintances will receive merchandise either at reduced prices or in some cases for free.

- *Mismarked Merchandise.* Many opportunities exist for merchandise to be marked at a selling price other than what is intended. This can be the result of illegible purchase orders, inadequate or incorrect communications, the improper use of marking equipment, or carelessness and neglect on the part of the people doing the marking. Merchandise may also reach the sales floor without being marked at all, sometimes leading to register operators guessing prices.

- *Invoice "Retailing" Mistakes.* A common practice, in non-automated systems, is to place the retail selling price of merchandise on a vendor's invoice when it is processed for payment. This serves to enter both the cost and selling value of the merchandise into the retailer's inventory records as purchases are recorded. However, like merchandise marking, this is often an error-prone process.

- *Merchandise Counting Mistakes.* The receiving and checking of merchandise sometimes is not given adequate priority. These responsibilities are carried out by inadequately trained and supervised personnel. In addition, these activities are often performed at unsecured locations like the sales floor. These conditions are conducive to counting mistakes and as a result are a frequent cause of recordkeeping errors.

- *Lost or Misplaced Documents.* Due to the widely dispersed nature of many retail organizations, there is generally a high risk that documents may be lost, misplaced, or not submitted to the proper processing location on a timely basis causing inventory recordkeeping errors.

- *Unrecorded or Incorrectly Recorded Transfers.* A frequent recordkeeping problem is the transfer of merchandise from one location to another without the timely recording of the transaction. Transferred merchandise is often not counted and checked with the same degree of care given to merchandise that is received directly from vendors. This can result in erroneously recorded transfer amounts as well as actual merchandise shortages.

- *Inventory Counting and Pricing Mistakes.* There are numerous opportunities for error in the taking of physical inventories as well as in the inventory pricing process. These potential sources of error should not be overlooked when investigating shrinkage causes.

ESTABLISHING AND MAINTAINING A CONTROL STRUCTURE

The components of an effective control structure generally include:

- *Transaction Processing Techniques.* Procedures must be established for the initial processing of every identifiable transaction type before any control of these transactions is possible. These procedures must cover how and when the transactions will be processed as well as who should do them. Cost considerations should also be kept in mind.

- *Transaction Verification and Completeness Controls.* These are checks and balances on the overall control structure that verify the validity, accuracy, and completeness of transactions. They include predetermined batch control totals; numerical control of documents; periodic reconciliation of recorded amounts to supporting documentation; transaction approvals by personnel knowledgeable as to the details of the transaction; use of corroborative transaction validation techniques, such as the matching of counts of items received per receiving documents to items ordered per purchase orders and items billed per invoices; and arrangements whereby the work of one person is checked by another person or by automated edit features.

  Without these checks and balances there is greater risk of transactions being omitted from processing, not being processed on a timely basis, or being erroneously recorded. To reduce these risks, a control structure should be evaluated keeping in mind the answers to these questions:

  Are all transactions recorded on a timely basis?

  Are all transactions recorded for the correct amount?

  Are all transactions supported by appropriate documentation?

  Have transaction authorizations and approvals taken place in the proper sequence?

  Have unauthorized transactions occurred?

  Will errors or exceptions be detected and corrected promptly?

If these questions cannot be answered easily there is usually a need for improvement in the retailer's transaction verification and completeness controls.

- *Supervisory or Disciplinary Controls.*   The following features of the control structure are generally considered to be supervisory or disciplinary controls:

Independent reviews of the work performed.

The separation of noncompatible responsibilities.

Records accessibility restrictions.

These are features of the overall control structure that minimize the risk of breakdowns in established practices as the result of carelessness, neglect, misunderstanding, and human error as well as from intentional circumvention or shortcut efforts.

When assessing the effectiveness of the supervisory or disciplinary controls over a retailer's transaction processing activities, the following questions should be asked:

Does someone independent of the actual processing and recording of the transactions have day-to-day responsibility for the supervision of these activities?

Is the supervisory review function performed on a timely basis and in sufficient depth to detect omitted or erroneous operations, procedures, or transactions?

Is the supervisory review documented, where appropriate, that is, initialling, dating, check-off, or other means to evidence that the necessary supervisory review has taken place?

Are either manual or automated techniques used to check the accuracy of the work performed?

Is access to files and supporting documentation as well as assets, such as cash or merchandise, restricted to the extent necessary to preclude the risk of unauthorized accessibility?

Does anyone have an inordinate degree of responsibility with respect to the processing and recording of transactions? If so, what are the risks in their having this responsibility?

- *The Control Environment.*   The control environment is perhaps the most important component of the overall control structure as it affects every transaction that occurs. The control environment is the specific

EXHIBIT 17.1   Negative Factors in the Control Environment

Environmental Circumstance	Effect on the Control Structure
Inadequate training and experience	People will not be knowledgeable concerning established practices; therefore, the probability of control breakdowns is relatively high.
Poorly organized work space or sloppy work habits	Documents might be lost, misplaced, incorrectly processed or not processed at all.
Inadequate records security	Records might be lost, altered, inadvertently mutilated or destroyed.
Inadequate communication between management and employees	Instructions may be misinterpreted, questions may not be asked and established practices may not be communicated.
Inadequate time allowed for the performance of recordkeeping work	Errors and mistakes may be made or shortcuts might be taken.
Utilization of forms or instructions that are overly complex or exceptionally difficult to understand	The probability of errors and misunderstandings increases.
A lack of written instructions explaining established transaction processing and control practices	Confusion, wrong interpretations and inconsistencies in the handling and recording of transactions are likely to occur. This can be a particular problem when personnel turnover takes place.
Infrequent or inadequate employee performance reviews or a lack of performance standards	Employees will not be aware of matters which need their attention in order to improve their efficiency and performance as well as to minimize errors.
Inadequate feedback concerning errors	The error is likely to be repeated.
Unclear responsibility assignments	Necessary functions may not be performed.
Attitudes on the part of management which indicate a lack of concern about accurate and reliable recordkeeping	Employees will be influenced by these attitudes, thus increasing the risk of control breakdown.

circumstance, at a particular location, or in regard to a particular person or group of people, that contributes to or detracts from the effective operation of the entire control structure.

The control environment comprises many factors. A few negative examples are shown in Exhibit 17.1.

Unfortunately, negative circumstances similar to those mentioned frequently exist in many organizations and can contribute to retail inventory recordkeeping errors resulting in shrinkage. These circumstances must be identified and corrected if effective control is to be maintained. This requires a top management commitment as well as an adequate appropriation of time and resources.

SUMMARY

Retailers generally attribute merchandise shortage to three underlying causes:

- Internal theft.
- External theft.
- Paperwork error.

It is usually not possible, to determine the specific effect of each of these three causes on a retailer's overall shortage rate. This makes the implementation of effective control programs difficult. Further, the fact that paperwork errors are one of the underlying causes of shortage often has an adverse effect on management attitudes with respect to the need for and the importance of a comprehensive shrinkage control effort. Effective paperwork control must be a fundamental component of any effective shrinkage control program so that shrinkage information will be viewed as reliable and, direct management's attention to the actual sources and causes of merchandise shortage.

An effective shrinkage control program should emphasize preplanned prevention rather than after-the-fact apprehension. It should include controls designed to prevent and deter theft as well as controls which serve to insure the reliability and accuracy of the retailer's paperwork.

CHAPTER EIGHTEEN

Physical Inventory

Retailers are relying more on sophisticated unit control merchandise systems to track inventories. However, the only way to validate this critical information is with periodic physical inventories. If performed properly, these inventories will allow retailers to verify, (or for retailers with less sophisticated systems to accumulate), a variety of information including:

1. The age of stock, using seasonal and other selected age groupings.

2. The different classifications of merchandise included in departmental stocks.

3. The different price lines and their relative importance.

4. The number of units, and respective dollar totals, of different stock groupings.

5. The amounts of consigned goods, materials, and supplies.

6. The distribution of merchandise into selling floor stock, backroom stock, and warehouse stock.

7. The identification of slow moving or damaged merchandise.

However, if these inventories are not performed properly they may have a disruptive impact on store operations and profitability. A concerted planning effort is necessary to prevent this from occuring.

RESPONSIBILITY FOR INVENTORY TAKING

Although, the primary responsibility for the physical inventory rests with the controller, the importance of cooperation by the merchandising and store operations departments cannot be overestimated. Frequently, an inventory office is established under a supervisor who takes full responsibility for planning and executing the physical inventories and coordinating the efforts of these departments. The responsibilities of such an inventory office are:

1. Arrangement of the schedule of inventories.

2. Preparation for inventory taking.

3. Supervision of inventory taking.

4. Tabulation, analysis, summarization, and reconciliation of inventories.

5. Analytic review of inventory results.

6. Investigation of inventory differences.

7. Review and critique of systems related to the movement and handling of merchandise and submission of suggestions for improvement.

The internal audit function should also be involved in the process. Its responsibilities include preinventory review of inventory plans and procedures and observation of the inventory-taking process. In some cases, the internal auditors are responsible for coordinating the entire physical inventory process, ensuring adequate segregation of duties.

INVENTORY COUNTING SERVICES

Many retailers use store personnel to count inventories, however, there are several national firms that provide independent individuals to count the inventory in accordance with the retailer's instructions. By using specialized portable computer equipment, they can summarize inventories by individual departments or even by item (SKU).

The advantages of using these services include accuracy and speed of the count by utilizing experienced, trained personnel with elaborate batch control procedures. The disadvantages include cost and possible problems because professional counters may not be familiar with the merchandise, nor the special nuances of individual chains.

The use of an outside service requires additional planning. A joint tour of the retail facilities prior to the inventory should be arranged to point out unique or unusual circumstances such as procedures for counting sealed cartons, leased department or consignment merchandise to be included or excluded from the count, or procedures for counting merchandise stored under display fixtures, display and backroom merchandise.

PLANNING FOR PHYSICAL INVENTORIES

The first step in the planning for physical inventories should be the drafting of general instructions for communication to merchandise managers, buyers and assistants, distribution center managers, and to the service department managers concerned with inventories (heads of receiving and marking, accounts payable, sales audit, accounts receivable, inspection, and adjustments). General instructions should cover the more important phases of inventory taking and highlight changes in circumstances or procedures since prior inventories along with those areas that have been particularly difficult or prone to error in the past.

Specific instructions relating to problems of various departments should be covered by conferences and consultations between the inventory office and department heads, and in meetings attended by department heads, salespeople, and others who do the actual listing and checking.

It is important that the responsibility for the various phases of inventory taking be clearly established and set forth definitively in the instructions. (Detailed treatment of instructions will be discussed later in this chapter.)

Many items must be covered in a plan for taking a complete and accurate inventory. The more important of these are discussed next.

Physical Layout of Departments

Department managers should be asked to submit sketches of the physical layout of their departments showing the location of the various sections and cases, drawers, and other fixtures used for storage and display of merchandise. This physical layout can be used to estimate the number of personnel required to take the physical inventory and the number that must be assigned to specific areas as well as the amount of forms and supplies needed. In addition a determination can be made as to the feasibility of precounting merchandise in reserve stock or other areas. Also, the progress of the physical inventory can then be monitored through the use of the physical layout or floor plan.

Methods of Counting and Listing, and Subsequent Checking Procedures

A variety of methods exist for counting, listing, and checking the merchandise. Listing may be made directly on the inventory-taking forms, usually by having one person count and call the items and another enter them on the forms. There are a number of variations of the direct listing procedure, depending upon the extent to which it seems desirable to double-check the results. For example, after the first listing, the caller and lister may change places and make a complete recount against the first listing; one person may do both the counting and entering and a second person cover the same ground with the two listings being compared; an independent checker may follow the inventory team and check its listings against the stock. Checking may be restricted to spot checks or tests but some measure of checking should be done, governed by the kind and value of the specific merchandise.

Assignment of Personnel

Since store or department managers are usually responsible for the accuracy of the physical counts in their store or departments, they should have sufficient time to select and instruct the employees who are to work on the inventory. If there is an adequate number of trained clerks available for the inventory taking, the work is more likely to be completed with accuracy and dispatch. In some instances, however, outside temporary employees will have to be hired to assist with the inventory. In such instances, care must be taken to provide time to acquaint them with the merchandise and to teach specific inventory instructions.

Arrangement of Stock

The counting and listing of merchandise is facilitated by good arrangement of stock as to merchandise department classification, season letter, and selling price.

Examination for Proper Ticketing

A preliminary review of the stock is desirable to verify that all merchandise items are properly ticketed and that all price changes have been made.

Identification and Arrangement of Merchandise

The following types of merchandise should be identified in advance and segregated or otherwise taken on separate listings:

- Merchandise on loan or consignment.
- Damaged, defective, soiled, or obsolete goods.
- Merchandise out for repair or refurbishment.
- Layaway merchandise.
- Merchandise sold but not delivered.
- Merchandise held by police or security department as evidence.

In addition, it is highly desirable that all goods received be processed and placed in inventoriable stock areas. Further, goods returned by customers should be returned to stock areas, and credits for such returns should be submitted to the accounts receivable department.

For large-unit merchandise such as furniture, preliminary counts may be made and entered on tags attached to the merchandise. Upon rechecking, the tags, or part of them, are removed and assembled either for listing on sheets or for summarization without individual listing. The tag method is also well adapted to yard goods and house furnishings.

Establishment of Cutoff Procedures

Prior to the physical inventory taking, every effort should be made to submit to the accounts payable office all invoices (or receiving reports for merchandise received without invoices) covering merchandise that has been opened and checked and placed in forward or reserve stock. Invoices covering merchandise not received or not placed in inventoriable stock should be stamped "Not Taken in Inventory." All unprocessed price change or merchandise transfer documents should be forwarded to the inventory control department for processing.

It is essential that, prior to the physical inventory taking, every effort be made to collect and submit all inventory-related paper work—invoices, receiving reports, merchandise transfers and credits, price changes, and sales checks—to the appropriate accounting department. This also involves the establishment of special procedures regarding the handling and movement of merchandise prior to and after inventory taking, focusing on such aspects as goods sold, transferred, returned to vendors, marked and remarked. The store can then focus on the important problem of fixing the point of "cutoff" between transactions prior to and after inventory taking.

At some particular point the records of sales and purchases are closed for the period, and it is important that inventory listings exclude goods for which sales, or purchase returns, have been recorded and include goods for which purchases, or sales returns, have been recorded. For the stock ledger, it is necessary to also use the same cutoff point for the recording of price changes and transfers so that book and physical inventories will be on the same basis.

INSTRUCTIONS

Physical inventory instructions are prepared for use by store and/or department managers, the personnel assigned to counting and listing, and the supervisory personnel who check the inventory team ("executive checkers"). It is also necessary to notify all accounting, control, and operations supervisors that inventories are to be taken and, therefore, that the appropriate cutoffs should be established.

Instructions to buyers and assistants and/or department managers consist of reminders or suggestions regarding essential preparations for the inventory. They are reminded to keep the receiving and marking rooms clear of merchandise (to the fullest extent feasible), to make returns and take markdowns in timely fashion, and to see that invoices, chargebacks, sales and credit checks, transfers, price changes, and so on, applicable up to the time of inventory, have been sent to the appropriate accounting offices. A resume of procedures for the distribution of inventory sheets, tags, or cards, and for listing and checking is usually included in these instructions, together with reminders of places where merchandise may be located and the requirements for separate listings of certain items of stock. There may also be suggestions regarding the arrangement of stock for the physical inventory, as well as guidance in reviewing, collecting, and arranging completed inventory sheets, tags, or cards and forwarding them to the inventory office.

Instructions to executive checkers cover their duties and procedures under the general inventory practices that have been adopted and the extent and manner of checking that is to be done. If original listings are completely rechecked by the inventory teams, or by another person, the executive checkers' duties will be largely supervisory. Where only test-checks are made, it is usual to assign such work to the executive checkers.

The following are illustrations of inventory instructions to store and/or department managers, executive checkers (in a situation where only test-checking is done), and to inventory-taking personnel. The specific inventory instructions to be adopted must follow the inventory procedure of the specific store or department.

INSTRUCTIONS TO STORE AND DEPARTMENT MANAGERS

The actual taking of the inventory will be conducted in your store (or department) on the assigned dates. In order to assure the accurate recording of the inventory, it is imperative that adequate and trained personnel be scheduled, that control be maintained over all inventory documents issued, and that there be individual management supervision throughout the entire inventory taking. The following outline of the procedures concerning the recording of the inventory must be reviewed very carefully prior to inventory date to assure an accurate inventory.

INVENTORY PERSONNEL. Inventory personnel consist of experienced employees and contingents. On inventory day, the following instructions must be adhered to:

1. All inventory personnel must report to work promptly.

2. All inventory personnel must be instructed on the proper method of taking the inventory.

3. Inventory teams must be established consisting of one experienced employee and one temporary (contingent) employee. These teams consist of a caller and a writer, respectively.

4. Inventory teams are assigned inventory sheets and the specific areas which they must inventory. Area supervisors must start off each team to be sure they are directed to start in the proper areas.

CONTROL/INVENTORY FORMS. Control over all inventory documents must be maintained to assure proper submission to the Home Office. To maintain this document control, the following instructions should be followed:

1. Numerically sequenced and controlled inventory sheets assigned to inventory teams and inventory assignment logs set up for each department. The following information must be recorded on the inventory assignment sheets:

   Starting sheet number.

   Department name and number.

   Signed out to: (Caller) and (Recorder).

2. All other inventory forms must be completed by their related department managers and returned to the inventory control desk. All unused forms which have been distributed must also be returned to the inventory control desk.

Special Note: Due to the importance of document control, it is required that a qualified employee be assigned the function of supervising the operation of the control desk. This entails the assigning of all inventory sheets and the control of all other inventory forms.

INVENTORYING MERCHANDISE. It is the responsibility of each inventory team to be sure to inventory all merchandise located within their assigned area or section. In the inventorying of merchandise the following must be adhered to:

1. Merchandise must be inventoried at the correct selling price, as shown on the ticket.

2. When merchandise is not ticketed, items are to be pulled off the shelf, gondola, or rack and placed in a cart for the department manager to price and inventory.

3. When merchandise is damaged, it is to be inventoried at the ticketed price, removed from the shelf, and placed in a cart labeled "Damaged Goods." The department manager inspects this merchandise to determine whether a markdown is to be taken and a new selling price

assigned. A separate listing of all such damaged goods must be prepared.

4. One inventory sheet for each shelf, bin or rack set forth in the floor plan must be used.

5. After each shelf fixture has been counted, a copy of the preprinted "INVENTORIED" tag must be attached.

INVENTORY SUPERVISION.   It is the direct responsibility of store management to personally supervise the taking of the physical inventory. It is extremely important that there be a check on all inventory teams, within one hour of beginning the inventory, to be sure they are following proper instructions and recording the inventories as prescribed. This enables corrective action to be taken before too large an area has been incorrectly inventoried. Continued supervision must be conducted by management throughout the inventory day. Only through close supervision of all inventorying areas will store managers be able to assure themselves that an accurate inventory has been taken and thereby properly reflects the store's inventory position.

COLLECTING INVENTORY SHEETS.   When an area of the store has been completely inventoried (as outlined on the floor plan) and checked, inventory sheets can be collected, returned to the control desk, and placed in numerical order. All sheets must be accounted for by comparison to the inventory assignment logs.

OBTAINING A FLASH TOTAL.   After the count has been completed but before the inventory reams have been released, if possible, a "flash" total dollar amount of inventory should be obtained. If this amount differs significantly from the stock ledger or from prior years, additional procedures such as expanded recounts and price testing, department "walk-thrus" to spot areas not inventoried, and so on should be considered.

INSTRUCTIONS TO EXECUTIVE CHECKERS

1. Make a detailed check of a fair sample of the work of each inventory team to assure yourself that the work is being done carefully and accurately.

2. The checker will look at the merchandise and carefully check the price ticket and compare it with the following entries on the inventory sheet: department number and price. The merchandise must be carefully counted to determine the quantity; the checking should be done both from the merchandise to the inventory sheet and from the

inventory sheet to the merchandise. Exercise special care on the more expensive and larger quantities of merchandise. You can detect errors quickly by scanning the columns. Watch for omissions.

3. If you feel that the inventory is not being taken correctly, contact your control supervisor.

4. No erasures should be made on the inventory sheet. If an error is found, call the control supervisor who will in turn consult the store or department, if this seems necessary. If the error is verified, then draw a pencil line through the error and write in the right price, etc., above the entry in a clear, legible manner and initial it.

5. Call on a representative in the department who is familiar with the stock for any information regarding items on the inventory sheets which you do not readily locate. In all cases you must verify the quantity and price. As each sheet is checked, the checker will sign his or her name in the space provided on the inventory sheet.

6. When the inventory has been completed and you are satisfied that the merchandise has been listed correctly, the sheets will be collected in the order in which they were issued and examined to see that all the necessary information is entered thereon. After accounting for all the sheets that were issued to the department, the sheets will be bound together in books by classifications. Thereafter, the completed inventory, together with all unused material, will be delivered to the Inventory Office.

Special instructions covering the more technical phases of procedure are issued to personnel assigned to accounting and listing. General procedures are usually outlined to the inventory personnel in meetings with department heads and these are followed up by supervision. An illustration of technical instructions to counters and listers follows:

INSTRUCTIONS TO INVENTORY PERSONNEL

1. Report to work promptly on inventory day.

2. Write legibly; use numerals (1, 2, 3, 4, 5, etc.), not strokes.

3. You will be assigned to a two-person "team." Each team will be responsible for the accurate counting and recording of all merchandise in a specific area.

4. Record department name and number on each inventory sheet.

5. The caller will count and call the quantity and selling price shown on the ticket. The other person will repeat and record the information.

6. Before inventory, be on the lookout for merchandise which is not properly priced. Where price tickets are missing, have them replaced by the buyer or assistant. All merchandise must bear a season letter.

7. It is strictly against the regulations to copy prices and quantities from stock books or scraps of paper. All listing must be done directly from the merchandise to the inventory sheets.

Never list more than one merchandise classification on a sheet.

Never list merchandise from two different shelves, bins, or drawers on the same sheet.

Never use dittos.

Season letters must be printed, not written.

Sheets must be signed in the space provided by the person who counts and by the lister.

8. All merchandise will be recorded on the inventory sheets at the unit retail price. This applies to all departments carrying packaged or multiple-price items. Examples include:

Packaged merchandise which sells for a package price (package of three for $1.98) to be recorded as one unit at $1.98. If a package is broken (or if single item), record the actual number of pieces at the unit retail price (in this example, one at $.66).

Multiple-price items (other than packaged) are recorded at the unit retail price, such as:

Items selling for three for $10.00 are recorded as "so many" units at $3.33 (unit price)

Two for $1.50 are recorded as "so many" units at $.75.

Two for $1.79 are recorded as "so many" units at $.90.

9. Use one inventory sheet for each shelf, bin, or rack.

10. **Do not erase.** If you make an error, void the error by drawing a line through the entry.

11. When your "team" has completed taking its assigned Department Inventory, return all inventory sheets to the person assigned to the Control Desk. Make certain that they correctly record the last number used by your team on the assignment sheet.

A specimen of detailed instructions for the taking of physical inventory by the store or department manager appears in Exhibit 18.1.

EXHIBIT 18.1 Instructions for Taking Inventory

Floor Plans	1. Using floor plan worksheet, draw a block layout of fixtures in stockrooms and selling areas.

2. On the floor plan, number fixtures consecutively starting at the main entrance of each area.

   a. When an understock section of a fixture is to be taken early and sealed, assign a separate fixture number to it.

   b. Mark a block "office" if merchandise is in an office.

   c. If a fixture is added before inventory, it can be added to the plan and the next fixture number assigned. If a fixture must be moved, it retains its original assigned number.

3. Using special peel labels, number each fixture.

Fixture List   4. List all numbers assigned to fixtures on fixture list sheet(s).

   a. With floor plan and list, review fixtures, decide on number of sheets per fixture, and post on fixture list.

   b. Post the number of shelves, bins, drawers, or sections in each fixture—an inventory sheet must be in each one.

   c. Check any fixture which will be difficult or take unusual time to count.

   d. Check any fixture which could be counted early and sealed.

   e. Check fixture which will require recounting due to high dollar value.

5. Add the number of inventory sheets you will need.

6. Post the number of inventory sheets needed on fixture list.

7. Make requisition for any extra personnel.

Team
Planning   8. Review your fixture plan and decide, based on the number of teams, the actual fixtures each team will count and in what order.

   a. Enter the name of an employee in the department assigned as one member of a team or just identify as Team 1, 2, etc. and decide on individuals later.

EXHIBIT 18.1   *(Continued)*

9. Plan on having the most difficult or time-consuming fixtures counted first. These should be marked on your fixture list.

Stockkeeping   10. As soon as you can, tell each salesperson the fixtures they are assigned for inventory. The second person can be assigned to the salesperson when inventory starts.

11. Begin checking stock as early as possible for soiled and damaged merchandise. Have any merchandise without price tickets pulled and tickets made.

Vendor
Return
Merchandise   12. As soon as list or information about merchandise to be returned to vendor is received from the buyer, pull and transfer to a designated location.

13. When merchandise is returned direct to a vendor from your store, make claim send to accounting department.

Customer
Returns   14. Be sure all call pick-ups and mail returns are being handled promptly and that they clear before inventory. Check credit and refund books and be sure all returns have cleared. If in doubt, check with sales audit.

Sales Books
& Registers   15. Check all salespeople's books and registers to be sure all work has cleared.

Transfers   16. Pull and transfer merchandise before cut-off dates.

Reports   17. Be sure all reports (sales, purchases, transfers, and distribution) are checked on a current basis and that corrections have been made.

Inventory
Sheets   18. During scheduled time on calendar, pick up inventory sheets from the office.

    a. Turn in approved yellow copy of fixture list when inventory sheets are issued.

    b. Sign inventory check sheet.

    c. Verify number of inventory sheets received.

19. Using fixture list, post the department number and fixture number on all inventory sheets before they are put on fixtures.

Price
Changes   20. Make all price changes as soon as possible, avoiding last minute changes.

21. Give the next unused price change report in each book to your general office to be sent as a group to the general

EXHIBIT 18.1   *(Continued)*

accounting office the day before the physical inventory is taken. Write "inventory cut-off" and the department number(s) across the face of the form and only send the yellow copy.

Laying
Inventory
Sheet

22. Approval must be given before any inventory sheets are put on fixtures before the store closes. If approved:

   a. Be sure good customer service is maintained.

   b. Lay sheets on fixtures as inconspicuously as possible.

23. A responsible person should be assigned to help lay inventory sheets.

24. Lay the sheets in numerical sequence according to the fixture list and floor plan.

To Start
Inventory

25. Assign the department closing to a responsible person so you are free to start the inventory.

26. Have a meeting and review inventory team instructions and then assign extra people to work with salespeople.

27. Check the weakest teams first and/or teams not familiar with your department. Observe all teams as soon as possible to be sure merchandise is being counted and listed accurately.

28. Review the following Do's and Don'ts with the inventory teams.

   a. Do check fixture no. on inventory sheet with number on fixture before starting.

   b. Do *not* erase on an inventory sheet. Draw a line through and enter on next line or block.

   c. Do quickly check merchandise on fixture and if not in order to count, arrange before starting.

   d. Do *not* take an inventory sheet away from the fixture it is assigned to.

   e. Do *not* destroy an inventory sheet.

   f. Do ask the supervisor when more sheets are needed.

   g. Do ask the supervisor when in doubt about anything.

   h. Do print legibly; remember, someone has to extend the inventory.

   i. Do *not* mix stroke count and actual number listing.

INVENTORY PROCEDURES ASSOCIATED WITH USE OF AN OUTSIDE SERVICE

As previously discussed, an outside service may be used to count the merchandise inventories. However, even in this case one individual, usually the store manager, should still be responsible for monitoring the progress of the inventory, resolving exceptions as they occur and insuring that chain policies have been followed. This person should also be responsible for contacting the inventory service on the day of the physical to ensure that they have adequate staff. In addition, prior to the inventory a procedure should be established to recount (on a test basis) selected inventory counts, concentrating on departments that represent high dollar values or difficult to count items. Finally, proper summarization procedures such as sheet/tag control, batching, and so on, should be established and this summarization process should be monitored and reviewed by store personnel.

INVENTORY CUTOFF AND RECONCILIATION

There have been several references thus far in this chapter to the "cutoff," or line of demarcation, between transactions before and after inventory, which must be recognized if there is to be a valid comparison between the accounting records and the physical inventory. For a correct cutoff, it is important that departmental purchases be charged with all invoices for goods included in inventory, or sold before inventory date, and be credited with chargebacks for goods returned to vendors or segregated from stock for such return. It is desirable that pending claims with vendors or other departments be cleared or be appropriately recorded before the inventory. Transfers between distribution centers and stores, between stores or between departments should be fully entered on the records.

Goods not charged to purchases, however, such as consignment or memorandum items, should be excluded from inventory; and goods not credited to purchases, such as stock out for repair, cleaning, or on loan or exhibition, should be included in inventory.

With respect to departmental sales, the cutoff procedure calls for exclusion from inventory of items recorded as sold but undelivered at inventory date, and items returned by customers for which return credits have not been recorded at inventory date. Goods should be included in inventory for which departments have received no credit as sales, such as items on loan or memorandum to customers and items for which sales checks are delayed and thus are "missing" to the sales audit office at time of inventory.

These various distinctions are the essence of cutoff procedures. For accuracy in book controls of stock, such as the retail inventory method, it is important also that price changes (markups and markdowns) given effect in the inventory or on goods sold be fully recorded.

To properly capture this cutoff information the following items should be recorded at the time of the physical inventory and forwarded to the inventory control office:

Sales Audit Office
Last cash register readings and sales reports
Missing sales checks
Missing sales returns

Receiving Department
Last receiving report number (drop shipments)
Last distribution center manifest number
Last store transfer number
Last vendor return number

Selling Departments
Last price change numbers
Last chargeback number for return of merchandise

"Reconciliation" of inventory refers to the process whereby book control inventory figures and physical inventory figures are adjusted to a comparable basis, so that the difference will, in fact, represent the true shortage or overage. The word "reconciliation" is sometimes applied to the process of "rolling forward" or "rolling back" the physical inventory to the fiscal closing date. Exhibit 18.2 shows the reconciliation process of adjusting the book inventory to the date of the physical inventory to determine the shortage or overage as of that date.

SHORTAGES OR OVERAGES

Differences between book inventory control figures and physical inventory figures, as disclosed by the reconciliation process, may be due to errors in deriving the book figures or to incorrect taking of the physical inventories. Errors in the book figures may be due to breakdowns in the operation of the store systems.

It is a duty of the inventory office to investigate and explain the differences. The first step is to recheck carefully the figures entering into the derivation of the book inventory. If a large unexplained shortage or overage remains after having established the reasonable correctness of the book inventory, consideration should be given to retaking the physical inventory.

EXHIBIT 18.2   Reconciliation of Book Inventory and Physical Inventory

Book balance (at retail) at (last closing of stock ledger)		$
Add: Debts from date of last book figure:		
Purchases	$	
Markups		
Transfers in		
Invoices in transit	————	————
Deduct: Credits from date of last book figure:		
Net sales	$	
Markdowns		
Discounts		
Allowances for shortages		
Open vendor chargebacks	————	————
Adjusted book stock		(a)————
Physical inventory per inventory count		
Add:		
Memo sales to customer		
Merchandise out for repair	————	————
Less:		
Consignment inventory counted in physical	$————	————
Adjusted physical		(b)————
Disclosed shortage (overage) ((a) − (b))		
Add: shortage already allowed for in book figure		————
Total actual shortage (overage)		$————

If a second inventory results in a comparably large difference, there is an implication of negligence in the handling and marking of merchandise or of actual theft or dishonesty on the part of employees or the public.

Where unit controls are in use, they supply a valuable check on both physical inventories and book controls. Reference should be made to such records in investigating inventory differences.

The causes of inventory shortages and errors in the accounting records are numerous (discussed at length in Chapter 17) and may arise in the operations of the following offices or departments:

Order and invoice office

Receiving room

Marking room

Reserve stock rooms

Selling departments

Delivery departments

Sales audit department

Accounts payable office

Statistical office

Inventory taking

INVENTORY SUMMARIZATION

A variety of useful information and analyses may be obtained from inventory listings, in addition to determining departmental shortage or overage and departmental and store-wide results of operations. In planning for the physical inventory, the extent of information required for these useful reports should be kept in mind so that adequate provision is made in the listing forms and related instructions. Among the more important departmental and storewide inventory reports prepared from physical listings are the following:

1. Age of merchandise by seasons, comparative with the preceding year.

2. Inventory shortages or overages.

3. Slow moving merchandise.

4. Excess stock.

5. Comparison of stock by classifications.

6. Imported merchandise on hand, subdivided as to classification and season letter.

7. Consignment merchandise on hand.

8. Inventory turnover, departmentally and by classifications, price lines, styles, and so on.

CYCLE INVENTORIES

Many retailers, especially those with a large number of stores, feel they can no longer wait for year-end inventory counting to obtain vital planning, financial and shrinkage information. Waiting until year-end for this information can allow shrinkage problems to develop for many months before they are discovered. Public companies, too, might release quarterly results only to be faced with year-end changes due to shrinkage.

As a solution to these problems, retailers have developed a way to inventory individual stores, in rotation, throughout the year—cycle inventories. In a cycle inventory program, all stores are still inventoried annually, but each store has its own assigned time period. Ideally, this system spreads the effort of the inventory process over the course of the year. More important, it provides a flow of inventory data—throughout the year—on which to base merchandising decisions.

Although year-end annual inventories have the advantage of taking place in January, the lowest month of the year for most retailers, the value of having year-round control over inventory and shrinkage levels has led many retailers to try the cycle inventory approach.

The Problems Involved

The problems associated with cycle inventories start with the obvious operational disruptions during busier sales months, and move into more complex issues, such as how to get accounting and internal auditing departments to maintain, year-round, the intense level of scrutiny that usually accompanies a year-end inventory.

When developing a cycle inventory program there are important merchandising implications that must be considered, including:

- Seasonal sales periods.
- Presales buildup of goods.
- When to take price changes.
- Whether Stockkeeping Unit (SKU) level counts should be taken in conjunction with cycle counts.

Clean cutoffs are perhaps the most important issue to consider in developing cycle inventories. Customer purchases and returns, store deliveries from distribution centers and vendors, inter-store transfers and returns to vendor must all be processed by the inventory cut-off date. Financial and retail systems must also be integrated to produce timely and accurate reporting for accounts payable, warehouse billing and retail price changes. The credibility of these cutoff controls must be absolute, ensuring that every item counted in an individual store has been entered into the stock ledger for that store, and that any goods that have been removed from the store have been removed from the stock ledger.

Retailers are likely to incur additional costs by adding EDP systems and staff needed to process cutoffs, summarize higher levels of inventory and calculate shrinkage by cycle periods throughout the year. And if management questions results there is always the chance of recounts at year-end, meaning that the store would have to be reinventoried during the traditional year-end period.

Finally, it may be necessary for external auditors to do more testing to validate controls throughout the year.

Advantages of Cycle Inventories

Considering the time, trouble and added expense involved in a cycle inventory program, why would any retailer want to make the change? There are several very good reasons.

Large or small, companies in periods of dynamic growth can often lose control of their business in a very short time frame. While a constantly increasing sales volume hides a multitude of sins, shortage and inventory levels that are out of control can have a devastating effect.

Also, a cycle inventory program gives retailers more time for detailed analysis of their inventory results. And the adjustment of shrinkage reserves throughout the year minimizes the possibility of a major shrinkage surprise at year-end, ensuring more accurate interim projections for external reporting purposes.

In a cycle inventory program, it is possible for internal auditors and regional managers to observe and assist during the inventory of every store if desired, and they can always be present when problem stores are inventoried. Further, external auditors have the ability to observe more store inventories. If the company uses any automated replenishment systems, updates to the data files can be made monthly rather than annually, provided that unit counts accompany the cycle counts.

Transitional Issues

Issues are raised during any transition from annual to cycle inventories which ultimately involve all levels of the organization, including merchandising, distribution and store operations. Top management's total commitment to the program is necessary to overcome the traditional skepticism that often greets new approaches. Adequate resources, including people and systems support, are key to the program's success.

In an attempt to head off some of the anticipated problems, the following list of sensitive issues should be considered.

- Explanation of how shrink levels are to be recorded in the retail ledger during the fiscal year is needed to avoid confusion.

- Store managers should anticipate more difficulty taking inventories in the summer months, due to increased store activity.

- Explanation is necessary, especially in the initial stages of the program, of how the detail ledger adjustments for shrink would affect bonus plans based on shrinkage levels.

Interpreting the Results

Interpreting the results of cycle inventories is difficult during the initial stages of a program, due to a lack of comparative history. In the case of predicting shrinkage levels, for example, a store assigned a cycle month of April will have a shrinkage level based on only three months' data during the first transitional year. This short period may not be representative of actual shrink. In the initial years of a cycle inventory program, stores often have to be recounted at year-end to validate that the system is actually working for financial reporting purposes.

Even after the program has been in effect for a longer period of time, recounts may be required for validation. Since any cycle inventory program requires significant objective judgments, external auditors should be involved from the outset.

SYSTEMS ARE THE KEY

Cycle inventories have always been a desirable approach for retailers. In the past, however, the problems involved in executing a successful cycle inventory program often outweighed the advantages. However, with today's automated Merchandise Information Systems, accurate and reliable cycle inventories are now possible. The key problem is clean, accurate cutoffs. The traditional lag between transaction (receipt of goods at the dock) and capture (batched and sent to Accounts Payable for data entry) has been the downfall of cycle inventory programs in the past. Today, automated "on-line" systems, especially in the receiving area, eliminate the lag time and provide the level of control needed for a reliable cycle inventory program.

CHAPTER NINETEEN

Key Operating Ratios

Analyzing a particular retailer's operations and financial status requires an understanding of the retail industry as a whole and the particular segment within which the retailer operates such as the supermarket department or specialty store segment. Ratio analysis assists in monitoring this dynamic industry and those who operate within it.

Ratio analysis provides a broader view of the retailer and the interrelationships and reasonableness of the financial and operating data, against the background of the company and the economics of the retail industry. The ratios should be consistent with each other and with known changes (either internally or externally) that are taking place.

An integral part of an analytical or "businessperson's" review is to relate known facts and occurrences about the company's operations to the financial statements. For example, if new stores were opened during the year, sales, inventory, and accounts receivable accounts should show appropriate increases. Increases in the number of new stores and inflationary increases in selling prices could mask the attrition in the number of individual sales transactions caused by a loss of share of the consumer market. Conversely, no analytical review can be performed perceptively unless the person performing the review can knowledgeably correlate financial data with corresponding company operations and related operating problems. For example, an increase in the average collection period for customer receivables could be related to a worsening of general economic conditions among a company's customers, producing slower collections, or related to a newly instituted liberalization of credit terms.

An analysis of the financial and operating results of a retailer should take into consideration the macroeconomic issues influencing the retail industry as a whole. Probably the most important issue is consumer spending since it drives retail sales. Various factors are used to predict consumer spending. The ratio of consumer debt to income can help predict the amount of funds the consumer has available to spend. An increase in the savings rate would indicate a decrease in consumer spending. An increase in the inflation rate as measured, for example, by the consumer price index, may cause a decrease in consumer spending for nonessentials as salaries and wages lag behind, thereby decreasing the amount of funds available for discretionary spending. Employment trends and wage-per-hour growth are also indicators of consumer spending. In specialized areas of retailing, such as home furnishings and electronics, housing turnover is a good indicator of consumer spending. The more new homes that are purchased, the greater the spending for items to furnish the home.

Changes in the economy impact different retailing segments in different ways and at different times. Those retailers selling essentials such as food are less affected by the factors just discussed than other retailers selling nonessentials where purchases can be delayed until better times.

In addition to the macroeconomic issues previously discussed, the analyst should also be familiar with the external forces that could affect the retail company's business and industry. Examples of such external elements include:

1. New competitors entering the marketplace.

2. Changes in merchandising philosophy of competitors.

3. Population shifts, as for example from downtown to suburbs.

4. Changing demographic patterns (e.g., baby boom or the aging phenomenon).

Ratio analysis provides a methodology for outsiders to measure a company and for management to evaluate internal performance. However, no one ratio can provide a complete picture of the retailer; each ratio needs to be evaluated in the context of other ratios.

For any type of business of a given size within the retail industry, there are expectations of relationships that would be considered normal and those that would call for further investigation and inquiry. For instance, it is normal to expect a higher inventory turnover in a high-volume, low-margin discount store than in a regular department store. Similarly, one would expect the ratio of delivery expenses to sales to be lower in the former than in the latter. An example is that home centers have traditionally maintained a gross margin percentage of about 32 percent of sales. However, the discount warehouse-type home centers are recording margins of 26 percent. If an analyst stopped at this point, he may not have a favorable impression of the discount warehouse-type home centers. However, the discount warehouse-type home centers realize faster inventory turns of about 6.2 versus 3.5 for traditional home centers because lower prices stimulate higher sales volume. This translates into a higher return on total assets.

It is therefore important to tailor an analysis to the retailer and its particular segment of the industry. Broader analytics should lead to more detailed specific analytics.

MEASUREMENT OF THE COMPANY

Outsiders, such as investors and creditors, are normally interested in the final results of the particular retailer and not in the day-to-day activity. They primarily want to evaluate the profit earned by the company and the market value of their investment. They need to analyze the risks associated with their investment as well as the per share performance.

Historically, creditors may not have been alerted to an increase in the risk factors until there was a change in the repayment habits of the company. However, they have come to realize this is too late. Creditors now are interested in sales trends as well as inventory trends which may indicate an inability to move merchandise. They are interested in cash flow and profitability.

In order to measure and assess the meaning of deviation from normal, yardsticks are needed. These can be obtained from two major sources:

1. Comparison with the company's experience over the years.

2. Comparison with external data, such as industry statistics.

Data regarding the company's experience over the years should ordinarily be found in the financial and operating reports from prior years. The retail industry publishes a large amount of industry data, much of which is available in local libraries. Standard & Poor, Dun and Bradstreet, and Robert Morris, among others, provide industry surveys which detail the financial ratios against which a company can be measured.

Possibly the most widely used reference source for department and specialty store retailers is *Merchandising and Operating Results of Department and Specialty Stores* (MOR) published annually by the National Retail Federation. It presents key statistical data classified according to the type and size of the retailers.

The Standard & Poor's *Industry Survey* discusses growth record, as measured by revenues and net income and the percentage change from year to year; management efficiency as measured by return on equity, return on assets, operating income as a percent of revenues, and net income as a percent of revenues; investment performance as measured by the dividend payout ratio, and the price earnings ratio, and a dividend yield percentage; and liquidity and leverage performance as measured by debt to capital, and debt as a percent of net working capital.

Dun and Bradstreet Credit Services *Industry Norms and Key Business Ratios* includes a condensed balance sheet, net sales, gross profit, net profit after tax and working capital. The ratios are segregated into those that relate to solvency such as the quick ratio; current ratio, current liabilities to net worth, and total liabilities to net worth; efficiency ratios which include accounts receivable collection period, inventory turnover; asset turnover, and sales to net working capital; and profitability ratios which include return on sales, return on assets and return on net worth.

Discussions in key business and industry publications emphasize certain operating ratios as well as financial ratios. These operating ratios include the percentage increase in sales, gross margin percent, sales per square foot, sales per labor hour, gross margin return on inventory, inventory turnover, expenses such as selling and promotional costs as a percent of sales and shrinkage as a percent of net sales.

Comparisons employing such techniques as ratios, indices, percentage relationships, correlation analyses, and so on represent the heart of the analytical activity; figures taken individually are relatively meaningless. Comparisons help establish the completeness and reasonableness of financial data and their validity and consistency in the light of all relevant factors. Additionally, they focus on the exceptions and on variations, thereby making it unnecessary to evaluate the normal and expected. However, lack of change does not necessarily indicate an ongoing normal situation. The data being compared must be understood against the background of changing conditions. (*Example*: An unchanged amount of allowance for doubtful accounts may be suspect if the volume of net charge sales activity and net write-offs have increased or decreased.) Adjustments must also be made for longer term trends.

Comparisons can be made in many different ways. For example, comparisons can be made by elements of a group (such as sales by department), or a per unit basis (such as sales per square foot), or period by period depending on the circumstances and objectives of the analysis.

In most cases, the primary objective with respect to the performance of analytical review procedures is to identify significant factors such as:

1. Changes over a number of period (e.g., change in bad debt write-off experience, change in gross margin ratios).

2. Variations from present standards (e.g., an increase in customer accounts receivable without a corresponding increase in net charge sales).

3. Inconsistencies with assumptions (e.g., a method of sales bonus payments that is inconsistent with management's assumption of how it is being pursued).

4. Unusual relationships (e.g., the relationship of bad debt expense to sales, inventories to sales and sales expense to sales).

Analytical review procedures are designed to highlight the abnormal, the changing and the unexpected variations in data. However, significant variations represent only symptoms of possible problem areas and other underlying conditions. These must be identified and thereafter interpreted and evaluated.

We will now discuss each of the ratios in more detail, including how they are calculated, problems they may indicate and ways of interpreting them.

FINANCIAL RATIOS RELATED TO SOLVENCY

QUICK RATIO. This ratio is calculated by adding cash and accounts receivable and dividing the sum by total current liabilities. The quick ratio establishes the liquidity of the retailer and indicates how quickly he can satisfy short-term needs. Creditors are particularly interested in this ratio since it is indicative of a company's ability to liquidate current obligations.

CURRENT RATIO. The current ratio consists of current assets divided by current liabilities. A current ratio in excess of two is normally a sign of a strong business. The larger the current ratio, the larger the safety margin for creditors. However, this does not necessarily indicate liquidity.

Other ratios that relate to solvency are current liabilities to net worth, current liabilities to inventory, and fixed assets to net worth. Each of these ratios assists a creditor in analyzing the risk associated with extending credit to the retailer.

EFFICIENCY INDICATORS

Various ratios indicate how efficiently the retailer is using assets.

SALES TO TOTAL ASSETS.   In this ratio, sales are related to the total investment required to generate those sales. An extremely low ratio may indicate financial problems, whereas an extremely high ratio may indicate a lack of effective utilization of the investment.

SALES TO NET WORKING CAPITAL.   This ratio indicates the net working capital required to generate sales (i.e., if a sales to net working capital ratio is six, then $1.00 of net working capital is required to generate $6.00 of sales).

ACCOUNTS PAYABLE TO NET SALES.   This ratio is calculated by dividing accounts payable by net sales. It relates sales volume to the ability of a retailer to pay its vendors. A high percentage may indicate the company is using suppliers to finance current operations. Vendors may become reluctant to deal with such retailers unless purchases are made on a COD basis or without the establishment of letters of credit which can be drawn upon based on proof of delivery by the vendor.

Other efficiency indicators such as inventory turnover and accounts receivable turnover are discussed later in this section.

PROFITABILITY INDICATORS AND INVESTMENT PERFORMANCE RATIOS

The following relationships are closely monitored by outside investors.

RETURN ON NET SALES.   This key financial ratio is calculated by dividing net income by net sales. It indicates the net income being generated by net sales. The proportion of each sales dollar flowing to the bottom line is reflected by this ratio.

EARNINGS BEFORE INTEREST AND TAXES TO SALES.   This ratio is calculated by dividing earnings before interest and taxes by sales. Since interest can be considered a fixed charge, and since income taxes are based on pretax income, many investment bankers consider this amount, and its relation to sales, provide a better picture of the earnings being generated by annual sales. It is an indication of the retailer's profitability from current operations without regard to charges resulting from the capital structure, but before income taxes.

RETURN ON NET WORTH.   This ratio is calculated by dividing net income by average net worth, which is defined as total assets less total liabilities averaged over the period. It indicates the return on capital investments or the profitability of the capital supplied by the investors.

RETURN ON TOTAL ASSETS.   Net income is divided by total assets to calculate this ratio which indicates the profitability of total assets. Since net income covers a period of time, average assets over that period should be used in the calculation.

EFFECTIVE TAX RATE.   The effective tax rate is calculated by dividing income tax expense by pretax income. This ratio may assist in the evaluation of return on net worth, since it indicates the impact of taxes on net income.

EARNINGS PER SHARE.   Earnings per share is one of the ratios most widely used to evaluate the profitability of any company. This ratio is calculated in accordance with APB Opinion No. 15. It is the only ratio that is required to be presented prominently in the financial statements due to the significance investors and others attach to such data. The extent of the data presented and the captions used vary with the complexity of the company's capital structure.

PRICE EARNINGS RATIO.   This ratio is calculated by dividing the average of high and low share prices by earnings per share. It indicates the relationship of market price to earnings per share. It is one of the key decision factors used in determining whether to invest in a particular company.

DIVIDEND PAYOUT RATIO.   Calculated as dividends as a percent of earnings, this ratio indicates the dividend pay rate which is currently achieved by the investor. Depending on the investor's personal goals relative to income versus growth, this ratio may be a key decision-making factor for the potential investor. If the company is in an expansion mode, it will need to retain capital instead of paying dividends.

LEVERAGE RATIOS

An analysis of the following ratios provides an indication of the debt capacity of the retailer.

DEBT TO TOTAL ASSETS.   Calculated by dividing debt by total assets, this ratio indicates the extent to which borrowed funds have been used to finance operations.

DEBT TO EQUITY (OR NET WORTH).   An indication of the extent of a company's leveraging, this ratio is calculated by dividing debt by total shareholders' equity. It indicates the balance between debt and equity, that is, the relationship of short-term and long-term debt to shareholders' equity. The higher the ratio, the higher fixed interest charges that will have to be covered by earnings.

TIMES INTEREST EARNED.   This ratio is calculated by dividing pretax earnings by interest charges. It indicates the extent to which earnings can decline without a company having difficulty in meeting its interest charges.

INTEREST EXPENSE AS A PERCENT OF SALES.   Similar to times interest earned, this ratio indicates the percentage of each sales dollar that is used to pay interest charges.

DEBT TO TANGIBLE NET WORTH.   This is calculated by dividing debt by net assets less intangible items such as trademarks and beneficial leaseholds. The ratio is frequently found in the covenants of debt agreements. Lenders believe that it is a better indicator of the extent of a company's leveraging. By removing intangible items, they are able to analyze the "hard" assets available.

DEBT AS A PERCENT OF NET WORKING CAPITAL.   This ratio indicates the availability of net working capital to cover outstanding indebtedness. Since the percentage of net current assets recovered in the distress sale of a company is frequently higher than the percentage of noncurrent assets recovered, lenders are also interested in this ratio.

INTERNAL PERFORMANCE MEASURES

Ratios assist the retailer in developing, implementing and monitoring its own internal strategic plan. A company can measure itself against its own preexisting goals as well as industry norms. A retailer establishes goals based on historical performance, taking into account strategy changes and expected environmental or economic changes. These goals are frequently formalized in the form of a budget. Some budgets, though, are set deliberately high to stimulate operating personnel; others may be set low to convey a feeling of mild comfort. Realistic and attainable budgets are useful for the evaluation of results. However, the analyst should have a "feel" for the integrity of the budgetary process.

The retailer may establish goals along industry norms such as those found in Standard & Poor's, Dun and Bradstreet, Robert Morris and National Retail Federation publications, as previously discussed.

Various other publications specific to a particular segment of the retail industry also provide industry statistics on an annual basis. These publications include *Chain Store Age Executive, Progressive Grocer,* and *Drug Store News.* Buying groups are sources of information that may be particularly helpful since stores of a similar size, industry segment and location frequently join a particular buying group.

As the volume of information available for management's decision-making becomes overwhelming, ratios can assist management in concentrating on major issues. Top-level management, in particular, finds ratio analysis useful in decision-making. Management can utilize sales and performance statistics in making key operating decisions, such as: (a) determination of selling zones, (b) determination of store layout, (c) level of advertising expenditures, (d) resolution of the merchandising plan and merchandise mix, (e) scheduling of the sale force, (f) identification of less productive departments and employees, and (g) determination of the adequacy of capital expenditures and other expansion programs. Other types of statistics, such as customer return data, aid in the identification of problems with vendors, stores, and employees, as well as in the evaluation of the retailer's policies.

In addition due to rising costs, erratic growth, and increased competition, retailers have begun to emphasize productivity and to monitor the operating ratios that measure productivity. Ratios assist them in identifying trends and enable them to be proactive. Space utilization, employee productivity, inventory control, vendor evaluations, and financing alternatives are all being monitored through ratio analysis. Productivity is the ratio of output to input; in the retail industry, common measures are sales per square foot, sales per employee hour, and gross margin per average dollar of inventory.

Segmenting productivity by department or by product line can provide new insights; increased productivity in a modern economy is often achieved by "working smarter, not necessarily harder."

EVALUATION OF STORE OPERATIONS

Ratios can be used to evaluate a department, a store, or the entire company. It is important to compare stores of similar size and volume in order to draw appropriate conclusions. The comparison should result in better performing stores sharing information with poor performing stores.

A device commonly used by retail financial executives to help control escalating expenses and also monitor store performance is a branch operating statement. Within this statement lies the key to evaluating a retailer's profitability; this analysis of individual store performance can reveal the existence or emergence of problems and trends.

The question of whether location performance versus individual (e.g., branch store management) performance should be measured has been a controversial topic for several years. In essence, the matter becomes one of including or excluding various categories of expenses in evaluating branch store performance.

With respect to location performance, expenses incurred as a result of the existence and/or operation of that location are taken into account. These expense items include, among others, selling payroll, branch store management, receiving and distribution costs, equipment depreciation, rents, and utilities.

However, in considering individual performance, a distinction is made between the so-called "controllable" and "noncontrollable" expenses, with only controllable expenses taken into account. Since individual branch managers have no control over costs such as rents, utilities, fringe benefit costs, and fixture and equipment costs and related depreciation, it is theorized that these factors should not be considered when evaluating their performances.

Whatever method is utilized to review individual store performance, it should measure both the store's contribution (however defined) and the performance of local store personnel. Thereafter, if warranted, measurements of operating income by location can be developed.

In developing these levels of measurement, expenses have to be identified as direct, assignable, or allocable. Direct expenses, commonly referred to as "four-wall expenses," are those that are incurred by, or within, a specific location, without regard to whether they are controllable. These expenses should be charged directly to each individual store location.

There are other items of expense that, despite being incurred outside the "four walls" of a specific location, can be identified with the operation of the location. Examples of these are centralized mailings, shuttle services, deliveries, and advertising.

If this degree of refinement is desirable, those expenses which can be identified with specific locations should be assigned based on work load, usage, benefit, or some other logical basis. These expenses are initially accumulated in the expense center where they are generated, and then assigned periodically depending upon the reporting practice of the organization. Here again, no distribution should be made between controllable and uncontrollable expenses. In presenting the operating statement, no distinction should be made between direct or assigned expenses.

In the third category are expenses which cannot be identified with any specific location but are incurred for the benefit of the total organization. These expenses, commonly referred to as "central organization expenses," include such items as company management, accounting, data processing, and public relations. To arrive at an operating income level, some stores may wish to allocate central organization expenses to all store locations. These expenses are initially accumulated in the central organization expense centers, and then allocated based on the proportion of the net sales of each location to total net sales.

At best, the problem of measuring performance and therefore the problem of assigning or allocating expenses is a difficult one. The role of the buyer or merchant has changed dramatically over the years. With most companies operating in multiple locations, the buyer is no longer directly responsible for selling activities or store operations. Furthermore, operating personnel are being measured by their performance. In this framework, the authors concur with the approach of limiting expense measurement for departmental results to those elements that are direct controllable expenses.

Once an organization has determined the level at which performance should be measured, the question of controllable and noncontrollable expenses can be addressed. Controllable expenses encompass both direct and assignable items of expense. By definition, central organization expense is noncontrollable by the stores. In making this distinction, the items of expense considered controllable vary with each organization. These variances are caused by the type of organization and by the degree of autonomy exercised by branch store managers.

Elements of revenue or expense shown below the operating income line for the total organization should not normally be allocated to individual store locations. These elements include such items as interest expense, interest income, and taxes based on income.

There are any number of specific problem areas that may be disclosed by an analysis of individual store performance. Flat or declining sales volume experienced by a store is, of course, the starting point. The analysis of stores with negative or marginal contributions should raise the question as to the short- and long-term viability of the store based on established criteria for closing stores. A closure decision entails the establishment of anticipated loss reserves, including such closing costs as future rental payments; severance pay; inventory markdowns; and write-off of property, plant, and equipment. The grouping of negative or marginal contribution units can reveal geographic and/or other types of store problems which could have capital expenditure implications. An analysis of very profitable stores by year of lease expiration could indicate that the future profitability of such stores may well be adversely affected by substantial future increases in rent expense.

An analysis of the performance of recently opened stores can lead to questions regarding the company's criteria for site selections and the opening of new stores. Comparisons of similar size or comparable volume stores should highlight the better and poorer performances, and should raise basic questions as to what operating practices and controls are in place at the more profitable units that should be adopted or more effectively implemented by the less efficient units. Operating expenses as a percentage of sales, markon percentages, markdowns, and gross margins realized by store may alert the analyst to increasingly unprofitable locations.

COMPARABLE SALES ANALYSIS

Changes in total company net sales are usually analyzed by reviewing comparative sales reports by individual store location and, in some instance, by regions. Comparative reports of departmental net sales data are also useful, as are reports by type of sale (e.g., cash, charge, and third-party charges). In order to perceptively analyze changes in sales between reporting periods, it is essential that the analyst be familiar with the scope and breadth of the company's operations and any related changes made between periods.

Increases in the number of new stores and the inflationary increases in selling prices of merchandise items can mask an attrition in the number of individual sales transactions. Sales data must first be summarized on a comparable basis in order to fully understand changes in sales volume. As a general rule, locations or departments which do not achieve sales gains in excess of the rate of inflation have probably had a decline in the number of sales transactions, effectively reflecting a loss of its share of the consumer market.

Increases and decreases in sales volume must also be related to such factors as the following:

- Number of new and old stores.
- The company's modernization program.
- Degrees of profitability among merchandising departments.
- Changes in pricing strategy, for instance, weekly specials or everyday low prices.
- Effective, ineffective, expanded or curtailed advertising programs.
- Capability level of branch store managers.
- Changes in store hours (e.g., evenings, Saturdays, and Sundays).
- Changes in sales conditions (e.g., warranties and returns).
- Meaningful or perfunctory training programs and sales techniques.

The following ratios can aid in analyzing store and individual department operations since they can be calculated by overall company, store location and department.

SALES PER SQUARE FOOT OF GROSS OR NET SELLING SPACE.   Sales per square foot indicates the effectiveness of space utilization. If sales per square foot are low relative to other stores or departments, a problem may exist with store or department location, personnel or customer base. Gross selling space includes nonsales floor space, such as any storage areas, while net selling space is only the actual selling space and, therefore, a better measure of sales performance.

NUMBER OF SALE TRANSACTIONS PER DAY OR PER HOUR.   The sales rate indicates the volume of transactions being handled and the level of personal selling. It may also assist in employee evaluation and the scheduling of employees. It is a key ratio when reviewed in conjunction with other ratios. For example, an increase in initial markon and gross margin may appear favorable until the decline in number of sales transactions in noted. Such circumstances may indicate a loss of share of the consumer market and/or excessive inventory levels. Inventory carrying values may need to be adjusted and merchandising efforts may need to be redirected.

AVERAGE DOLLAR VALUE OF EACH SALES TRANSACTION.   The average dollar value indicates what a customer is spending in a particular department or store on each transaction. This ratio varies based on the pricing level of the department's merchandise. The designer ready-to-wear department has a much higher average dollar value for each sale than a children's shoe department, for example. The average dollar value of each sales transaction should be consistent with the average dollar value of inventory (at retail) for the department.

PERCENTAGE OF DEPARTMENTAL (OR STORE) SALES TO TOTAL SALES.
This percentage indicates sales being contributed by a particular department (or store). It should bear a relationship to the retailer's strategy with respect to the particular department and the level of inventory maintained in that department. The location of the department as well as the nature and price points of the merchandise within the department will significantly impact this percentage. When the ratio is calculated on a store basis, only comparable store sales should be included.

A listing of the more important sales reports which may be available for analysis follows:

- Daily report of departmental sales, showing comparison of day's sales with the same day of the previous year, as well as cumulative monthly (or four- or five-week) totals to date, this year compared with last year.

- Weekly report of departmental sales compared with the same week of the previous year.

- Comparative monthly (or four- or five-week) report of departmental sales, including cumulative totals to date (comparative with corresponding periods of last year).

- Comparative reports of merchandise classifications (comparative with corresponding periods of last year).
- Report of sales analyzed by sales personnel.

For unit control purposes:

- Analysis by classification, number of units sold, and unit prices.
- Reports of shortages and overages (based on physical inventories).
- Unit stock control reports (e.g., rate of sale, on hand quantities).

CUSTOMER RETURNS AS A PERCENT OF GROSS SALES.   An increase in the percentage of returns may indicate a problem with the quality of the merchandise. If a significant problem is identified, the percentage could be traced back to a particular vendor. Concessions should be obtained from the vendor, or the merchandise should be returned. It is also important that this percentage be monitored frequently in order to avoid major problems with customer relations.

SHRINKAGE AS A PERCENT OF NET SALES.   The shrinkage is determined as a consequence of the taking of a physical inventory, and such shrinkage is related to net sales. An increase in the percentage is normally a combination of problems relating to paper flow (i.e., a lack of accuracy or completeness in recording all merchandise-related transactions), customer theft, and employee theft. A review of inventory shrinkage and overage statistics by department and by store may indicate that proper cutoffs were not achieved or an accurate "physical" was not taken.

SALES DISCOUNTS AS A PERCENT OF SALES.   This percentage consists primarily of employee discounts in relationship to sales. It is normally an insignificant percentage.

ALTERATION AND WORKROOM COSTS AS A PERCENT OF SALES.   This percentage indicates the cost of providing those services to the customers. It can assist in the decision-making process regarding the desirability of continuing to offer alteration and other customer services. A complete comparative operating report for each workroom, showing revenue, and operating costs such as wages, merchandise, supplies, and so on, should be reviewed in performing an in-depth analysis of these costs. Statistical information as to number of units of work and average costs per unit is also helpful.

EXPENSE FLUCTUATIONS.   Because expense behavior follows a relatively uniform pattern each year, balances in expense accounts can be compared for comparable periods, or expenses can be calculated as a percentage of sales for comparable periods. If expenses relate to fixed costs (e.g., rental costs, real estate taxes, insurance, depreciation), compare balances; if they have variable characteristics (e.g., payroll and advertising), the "percentage of sales" approach may be more appropriate.

Retailers generally have rather sophisticated budgetary controls over operating expenses. They budget their expenses by individual expense center (e.g., credit and accounts receivable), and further broken down by natural expense classifications (e.g., payroll, supplies, insurance). It may be advisable to compare actual amounts with budgeted amounts.

PAYROLL-RELATED RATIOS.   Generally, payroll expense represents one of the most significant operating costs of a retailer. Related ratios include total payroll as a percent of sales and sales force payroll as a percent of sales. They represent employee productivity and, when compared with other competing retailers, indicate whether payroll costs are excessive. Payroll-related ratios should be calculated by department and by store and then compared against other departments and other stores. The payroll costs should include fringe benefit costs as well as wages. If this is not the case, management should consider the need to redirect the sales effort, to change the commission structure and to more effectively control the productivity of sales personnel. If a particular store's costs are out of line, management may consider reducing the number of sales personnel or rescheduling them.

Reports helpful in payroll-related decision making are:

- Comparative monthly (or four- or five-week period) payroll reports with detail showing salary expense of each department and office, grouped and summarized either along expense account classification lines or according to responsible executive divisions.

- Weekly report showing number of persons and/or persons and/or hours, regular hours and overtime, and total weekly salaries for each department and office and compared with the previous year to show increases and decreases.

SALES COMMISSION EXPENSE.   A simple procedure for reviewing the reasonableness of this expense is to compute it as a percentage of sales and compare it with historical trends. However, caution should be maintained in a company with a varying commission rate structure, depending on such factors as length of service and location, rather than a fixed commission percentage varying only by department.

SALES PROMOTION COSTS AS A PERCENT OF NET SALES.   This percentage consists of advertising and other promotional costs in relation to the sales being generated. It is helpful in assessing the benefits derived from various promotions. In order to perform a meaningful evaluation, the costs must be separately identified along with the sales generated by the promotion.

RENT EXPENSE AS A PERCENT OF NET SALES. Since stores are frequently leased, rental costs must be carefully monitored. This ratio is helpful in assessing the profitability of store locations. In calculating this percentage, one should include the base rent, additional rent based on sales and common area maintenance charges. The ratio can assist in evaluating new store locations as well as assist in making decisions as to whether to continue in a current store location.

OVERHEAD OR FIXED COSTS AS A PERCENT OF NET SALES. Costs such as corporate expenses, interest and depreciation are among the fixed costs which are included in this calculation. Since these costs do not fluctuate based on sales, the percentage decreases when sales increase and increases when sales decline. Therefore, these costs should be monitored more in terms of historical patterns and budgeted amounts.

DELIVERY EXPENSE AS A PERCENT OF NET SALES. Delivery costs may be significant to certain types of retailers such as those selling home furnishings. A breakdown of delivery cost by department, a tabulation of the number of deliveries and the calculation of the average costs of deliveries may pinpoint problems including excess costs. A retailer may utilize such statistics in deciding whether to handle delivery internally or utilize external shipping services for deliveries.

TOTAL STORE OPERATING EXPENSES AS A PERCENT OF NET SALES. Store operating expenses include variable and fixed expenses associated with operating a store location. This ratio assists in monitoring the store profitability. When store operating expenses exceed expectations and industry norms, cost reduction programs and/or changes in merchandising strategy may well be in order. However, if the long-term viability of a particular store is highly suspect, the only alternative may be closure.

EVALUATION OF PERSONNEL

Ratios are particularly helpful in the evaluation of personnel. Goals should be established so that employees know what is expected of them. Ratios can be used in setting these goals and in determining salary increases and bonuses. All levels of personnel should be evaluated against pre-established standards, with particular attention paid to that most important store employee, namely, the store manager. A store manager is critical to the success or failure of a store, and much depends on the quality of this individual. The store manager must be motivated, preferably by base salary and incentive compensation arrangements which have the practical effect of associating the economic well being of the manager with the economic well being of the retail organization as a whole. In turn, the store manager must motivate all the other store employees, with appropriate goal setting for all subordinates.

Common ratios used to evaluate and establish goals for store personnel are sales—per hour worked, per dollar compensation, per sales employee, and per total store employees. These ratios indicate the effectiveness of employee utilization. Such ratios can also assist in employee scheduling. Poor employee productivity may indicate that additional training and/or improved hiring techniques are required.

However, constant supervision and frequent inspections are probably the most effective methods for maintaining high standards for employees. Many retailers use a rating system to assess the performance of salesforce employees. The evaluation is based on the supervisor's observations of the employee as he or she handles a customer.

EVALUATION OF ASSET MANAGEMENT

The effective utilization of a retailer's assets is important to maintaining continued profitability. Inventory typically represents a significant portion of a retail company's total assets and, in order to maintain liquidity, must be turned over rapidly. The retailer who does not follow astute merchandising practices and fails to move merchandise in the appropriate selling period is often vulnerable to seasonal, as well as fashion, changes.

In addition to the various methods and periodic merchandising reports (e.g., open-to-buy and slow-selling) used by retailers to minimize and control their investment in inventories, additional comparisons and statistics are helpful in assessing the inventory position as of a particular date. The need for the establishment of, or additions to, the reserve for future markdowns may result from a review of various merchandise statistics. Various reports are frequently available to assist in the analysis of inventory, including:

- Excess stock report (classified between domestic and foreign).
- Age of stock (i.e., by season letters) by classifications.
- Comparison of inventory for several seasons, showing inventory markon percentages.
- Merchandise in stock on memorandum.
- Merchandise out on loan to display and other departments.

- Merchandise out on memorandum for repairs and to customers and manufacturers.
- Division of stock between domestic and foreign merchandise, subdivided to show merchandise classifications and season letters.
- Reports of shortages and overages.
- Unit stock control reports.

In order to evaluate merchandise inventory management, statistics by merchandising division, department and store should be reviewed. Listed below are some examples of merchandise statistics which, in addition to the comparison of department and store inventory levels with comparable periods and planned levels, are valuable tools and techniques in measuring the existence of slow-moving or obsolete inventory.

INITIAL MARKON PERCENTAGE.   This represents the relationship of the excess of original marked retail (selling) price, plus markups, over cost to the retail price. A higher than average initial markon may indicate lower purchase costs obtained through special vendor discounts; certain imported goods frequently have higher initial markons. However, higher initial markon percentages may indicate a problem with the retailer's initial pricing strategy, particularly if a high markdown percentage exists.

It is helpful to perform a thorough analysis of purchases when reviewing inventory management. Key reports in the analysis of purchases are:

Departmental purchases showing markon percentages (daily, weekly, or monthly, and cumulative).

Purchases by classifications and manufacturers.

For unit control purposes: Analysis of purchases and returns by classification, unit price, quantity, and so on.

Orders outstanding.

Open-to-buy balances.

MAINTAINED MARKON PERCENTAGE.   This percentage is calculated as initial markon less markdowns, sales discounts, and shrinkage as a percent of retail. It effectively indicates the gross margin realized on the sale of merchandise, (before unknown costs and before taking into account purchase discounts). A wide discrepancy between initial and maintained markon percentage could indicate a variety of problems in merchandise buying, pricing or security. The maintained markon should be sufficient to absorb alteration and workroom costs and operating expenses as well as allow some margin of merchandise profit.

MARKDOWN PERCENTAGE OF NET SALES. This ratio is calculated by dividing markdowns taken by net sales and indicates the level of markdowns necessary to move the merchandise. An increase in the markdown percentage can be indicative of merchandising problems. In performing an in-depth analysis of markdowns, certain internally generated reports are frequently available, such as:

Analysis of markdowns by reasons.

Analysis by season letters.

Analysis by manufacturers of goods.

Comparison of markdowns for several seasons.

Percentages of markdowns to departmental sales.

GROSS MARGIN PERCENTAGE. This percentage of sales is probably the most important operating ratio, focused on by both management and outsiders. It represents the difference between sales and total cost of merchandise sold. The total cost of merchandise sold represents the sum of opening inventory, at cost plus, gross cost of merchandise received during the period, including freight costs plus alteration and workroom costs, if any, less closing inventory, at cost and cash discounts earned. The higher the gross margin, the more profit available to cover operating and other expenses.

Interpreting the Data

What does a reduction in gross profit tell you? It may reflect inventory obsolescence (thus necessitating additional markdowns), deterioration of store location, reduced sales levels, increased shrinkage due to spoilage or pilferage, a change in sales mix or a change in pricing strategy.

In order to identify the reasons for changes in gross margin percentages between reporting periods, preparation of an analysis of gross margin is required. (See Exhibit 19.1, Gross Margin Analysis.) This analysis highlights those factors which contributed to the change in gross margin. As seen in the exhibit, gross margin dollars increased $100,000. To determine the portion of the increase caused by sales volume increases, apply the prior year's gross margin percentage to the total sales increase. The example indicates that $82,500 of the $100,000 increase was due to sales volume increases leaving $17,500 which resulted from an increase in the gross margin percentage (increase in the gross margin percentage times total sales for current year). The causes of the increase in the gross margin percentage are analyzed in Section II of the exhibit.

As is evident, a variety of factors contributed to the increase in the gross margin, including a reduction in alteration costs and an increase in the

EXHIBIT 19.1   Gross Margin Analysis

Section I	19X1	19X0	Increase (Decrease)
Net Sales	$6,300,000	$6,000,000	$300,000
Cost of Sales	4,550,000	4,350,000	200,000
Gross Margin $	$1,750,000	$1,650,000	$100,000
Gross Margin %	27.78	27.50	
	27.50		
Increase in Gross Margin %	+.28		
Increase in Gross Margin % Attributed to:			
Increase in Sales Volume			
300,000 × 27.50 =	$ 82,500		
Increase in Gross Margin %			
6,300,000 × .28 =	17,500		
	$100,000		

Section II	19X1	19X0	Change Favorable (Unfavorable)
Gross Margin Change Attributed to:			
Initial markon	+40.70	+40.50	.20
Markdown[a]	− 7.90	− 7.50	(.40)
Shrinkage[a]	− 4.24	− 3.75	(.49)
Employee Discounts	− .28	− .28	—
Alteration Costs	− 1.50	− 2.26	.76
Discounts Earned	+ 1.00	+ .79	.21
	27.78	27.50	.28

[a]Represents markdown (or shrinkage) dollars at retail converted to cost by application of the departmental cost multiplier (complement of initial markon).

initial markon. These were offset by an increase in markdowns and shrinkage. The analyst may then explore further with the merchandising management the reasons for the increased markdown activity and increase in shrinkage.

Most of the data for the analysis comes directly from the retail stock ledger. If individual stock ledgers are not maintained by store and by department, the gross margin should be computed using the net sales of the retailer (all stores), by department, multiplied by the all-store gross margin percentage for that particular department. These departmental amounts should then be accumulated and the total for a store derived.

The use of a total all-store gross margin percentage, combining all departments within a store, should be avoided, as it may produce distorted results. The range of departmental markons can be so wide, and the mix of merchandise on hand at any one date can be so unrepresentative of purchases made during a period ending on that date, that an "average" all-store gross margin derived from such markon data could be meaningless and/or misleading.

The gross margin percentage should be reviewed in conjunction with other financial factors. An increase in sales accompanied by a lower gross margin percentage may indicate a change in sales mix resulting in low margin goods achieving a greater representation than desired. The lower gross margin may be indicative of a possible deterioration of the store location or of increased shrinkage due to spoilage or pilferage. There may be a need for additional inventory writedowns; management should also re-examine its sales promotion efforts. In addition, a change in the sales commissions structure may be required.

An increase in cost of goods sold with a reduction in gross margin may also indicate an unfavorable change in sales mix. An increase in the sales of unprofitable lines indicates a need to redirect sales efforts as well as merchandising efforts.

If cost of goods sold appears out-of-line with sales, the recordkeeping for sales should be reviewed, and/or a reassessment of the propriety of inventory carrying values may be in order.

GROSS MARGIN RETURN ON INVESTMENT.   This ratio is calculated by dividing gross margin dollars by average inventory at cost. It indicates the gross margin return for every dollar invested in inventory. A retailer achieves the most benefits when this calculation is done on departmental, classification and SKU levels.

GROSS MARGIN RETURN PER DOLLAR OF INVENTORY.   This ratio is calculated by dividing gross margin dollars by the average of total dollars in inventory. It indicates the return on the inventory investment.

INVENTORY TURNOVER.   The inventory turnover rate is derived by dividing sales for the designated period by the average inventory, at retail, for that period. It represents the rate of merchandise movement. A slowdown in the turnover frequently indicates merchandising problems. A decrease in sales not accompanied by reduced inventory levels or sales substantially under plan with inventory levels achieving plan may indicate excessive inventory levels and a deteriorating inventory aging. There may be a necessity to recognize markdowns on a more timely basis.

From an operational standpoint, a decline in the inventory turnover rate should raise a key management concern regarding excessive inventories. There may also be a corollary increase in handling costs and possibly the necessity for storage space expansion, with attendant additions to fixed costs. Too, the adverse effect on buyers' remaining open-to-buy also comes into play, with possibly adverse effect on future sales from buying limits imposed. Since inventories are the least liquid of current assets, a disproportionate investment in inventories may impair the company's ability to meet its current obligations. These multi-faceted adverse implications may well mandate the development by management of a course of action designed to dispose of the excessive inventories as quickly as possible.

However, the reverse situation may also indicate problems. A significant increase in sales without a corresponding increase in inventory levels (i.e., a significant increase in inventory turnover above industry norms) may indicate inadequate inventory levels. An inability to serve customers frequently occurs in this situation. Excessive out-of-stock conditions can lead to a poor customer perception of the retailer, as well as the incurrence of excess costs in connection with replenishment of merchandise in smaller than normal quantities.

Inventory turnover should be analyzed by department. For example, the turnover for the junior sportswear department is often three times that of the jewelry department due to the nature of the merchandise carried. In order to perform a meaningful analysis, only similar merchandise departments should be compared.

STOCK TO SALES RATIO.   Whereas the inventory turnover ratio is normally applied to company data on an annual basis, the stock to sales ratio is normally applied to individual departmental monthly data. This ratio reflects the relationship between current stock and current sales. It may be stated in either units or retail dollars. The stock to sales ratio is an important aid to management in ascertaining whether a sound relationship of stock to sales is being maintained on a current basis. It is a practical aid in monitoring and planning stock and sales and a tool for the buyer and departmental management in day-to-day merchandise control. If feasible, this ratio analysis should be performed weekly in order to maximize merchandise control.

PERCENT OF INVENTORY OVER SIX MONTHS OLD. As an indicator of aged merchandise, this percentage is calculated by dividing inventory dollars at retail in the over-six-month category by total retail inventory dollars, normally on a departmental basis. However, this statistic is even more valuable if it can be calculated on a merchandise classification basis. If the percentage increases, additional markdowns may be required to sell the old (out-of-season merchandise. The same analysis can be performed by assigning season codes to the inventory. All out-of-season inventory can then be monitored.

To facilitate the review of obsolescence in those situations where no accurate inventory agings exist, or reliance cannot be placed upon unit records, the analyst may wish to obtain and review a comparative schedule of fourth quarter merchandise receipts by department matched with year end inventory levels and corresponding sales for the period. A comparison of departmental promotional or clearance markdowns of current versus prior year fourth quarter periods may also be useful. It should be pointed out, however, that these procedures have inherent limitations and that analytic reviews of comparative inventory agings and the trend of sales (units and dollars) will provide more useful insights into identifying problem situations.

INVENTORY TO NET WORKING CAPITAL. The relationship of inventory to net working capital is a measure of the extent to which the retailer's working capital is tied up in inventory.

The relationship is a delicate balance between maintaining sufficient inventory to generate sales without having excessive funds invested in inventory.

A point to remember is that significant increases in inventory levels and/or low inventory turnover ratios do not always mean a slowdown of business, an over investment in inventory, inventory imbalances, inflated inventory values resulting from the inclusion of obsolete and unsalable merchandise or improper cut-offs. They can reflect the early receipt of the next season's merchandise, the effects of inflation on the cost of merchandise, or a change in merchandising philosophy. These conditions do not, in themselves, generally present inventory valuation problems.

CREDIT DEPARTMENT AND ACCOUNTS RECEIVABLE MANAGEMENT

While the most widely recognized tool for measuring the effectiveness of a company's collection procedures is the aging of accounts receivable, ratios can be utilized in a variety of ways to evaluate the performance of the credit department as well as outside collection agencies. Since receivables and inventory are frequently pledged as collateral in order to obtain financing, these ratios are also closely monitored by financial institutions. Key ratios in performing an analysis of accounts receivable follow.

DAYS' SALES OUTSTANDING. Days' sales outstanding (DSO) is calculated by dividing the gross accounts receivable balance by the average daily credit sales realized. It indicates the length of time cash is tied up in receivables, that is, the degree of liquidity of the accounts receivable. An increase in days' sales outstanding may arise from a liberalization of credit terms extended to customers. Alternatively, it may indicate a problem with the efficiency of the retailer's credit department and the effectiveness of its collection efforts, including those of collection agencies.

Retailers should also be alert for an abnormally large decrease in DSO caused by large declines in customers' accounts receivable balances. Such declines may be caused by significant returns of merchandise. Such returns may require inventory write-downs. Alternatively, if the merchandise is returned to vendors for credit, there is always the spectre of non-utilization of the vendors' credits if activity with these vendors is curtailed because of the quality or non-salability of their merchandise. This may require management to reassess certain vendor relations and selection procedures.

ACCOUNTS RECEIVABLE TURNOVER. This ratio represents credit sales divided by the average gross accounts receivable balance. It indicates how rapidly receivables are being collected and is similar to days' sales outstanding.

PERCENT OF RECEIVABLES CURRENT. Calculated by dividing the balance of current receivables by the total accounts receivable balance. This ratio is an indicator of the quality of receivables outstanding. It should represent the total accounts which are not deemed to be past due on installment type accounts or under the retailer's credit terms. A decline in the percentage indicates possible collection problems which may be caused by a too lenient credit policy, lack of adherence to the established credit policy, or a deterioration in the retailer's collection practices and policies.

CREDIT SALES AS A PERCENT OF TOTAL SALES. This percentage indicates the level of utilization of credit cards issued by the retailer. Since the use of a credit card frequently indicates customer loyalty, an increase in the percentage may indicate an increase in the customer base. Use of bank cards (e.g., VISA and Master Card) sales should also be monitored in relation to total sales to determine patterns of their use by customers. Management may consider eliminating a bank card if the fees are high and there is little utilization.

Other statistics relevant to an evaluation of the quality of accounts receivable include:

1. Collection percentage [cash collections on account for the month (or 4- to 5-week period) related to the balance of receivables at the beginning of the month (or 4- to 5-week period)].

2. Allowance for doubtful accounts as a percent of customer accounts receivable.

3. Net bad debt write-offs as a percent of own net charge sales.

4. Net bad debt write-offs as a percent of customer accounts receivable.

5. Bad debt provision as a percent of own net charge sales.

All of the statistics mentioned in this section become even more meaningful when compared to past trends.

FINANCE CHARGE INCOME AS A PERCENTAGE OF ACCOUNTS RECEIVABLE.   The reasonableness of finance charge income can generally be reviewed by computing such amount as a percentage of average accounts receivable balances and comparing this with historical trends. The analyst should also ascertain whether any changes have been made in the method of computing finance charges which might affect the comparability of the amounts shown.

Evaluation of Credit Department Personnel

Evaluation of credit department personnel can be accomplished through analysis of a variety of factors. The following statistics may assist in providing goals and analyzing the performance of the credit department:

1. Number of credit applications processed, approved, declined.

2. Number of collection calls per person per day.

3. Collected dollars per person, per call, per day.

The collection agencies employed can be evaluated by relating collections, net of agency fees, to the gross amounts of receivables turned over for collection.

PROPERTY AND EQUIPMENT MANAGEMENT

Besides inventory and accounts receivable, retailers often have significant funds invested in property and equipment. Management of this area is often neglected. This neglect shows up in lost sales due to customers not wanting to shop in stores in need of renovation. In analyzing property and equipment management, it is important to determine the retailer's renovation policy, the age of the individual stores, whether there has been adherence to the renovation policy, and the need for renovation. Capital budgeting is critical to maintaining quality stores.

In performing a property and equipment analysis, it is often beneficial to review the terms of the leases, including their expiration dates, in conjunction with the operating performance of stores and an awareness of the cost of renovating an existing store versus the cost of opening a new store. With this information more knowledgeable decisions can be made relative to the merits of renovating a store versus opening a new one. The capital investment would exclude any preopening costs and working capital requirements. This also should be a part of the capital budget.

ANALYSIS OF THE DISTRIBUTION CENTER

Many retailers own or lease distribution centers and it is important that the operations of these be evaluated on a regular basis. As a background to making any such valuation it is important to recognize that for any well run distribution center operation there should be some measurement of labor productivity, and that personnel should be scheduled based on projected workloads. Accordingly, the projection and tracking of carton/piece volumes is the key to productivity measurement in a warehouse type environment. Moreover, this type of data is essential to the knowledgeable budgeting of costs for such an environment, particularly bearing in mind the peaks and valleys of monthly and seasonal and promotional activity that characterizes a distribution center in the retailing business.

Any analysis of the operations of the distribution should commence with a determination of the percentage of merchandise being handled through the distribution center since some distribution centers may not handle all merchandise. This may be due to a conscious decision on the part of management to drop ship merchandise directly to the stores, or may be occasioned by the capacity of the distribution center.

The number of cartons or pieces being handled each day through the distribution center should be determined over a representative period of time with a view to judging efficiency and trends. Further, the number of days turnaround from receipt of merchandise from the vendors to shipment to the stores is critical to merchandise planning. Accordingly, number of days turnaround goals should be established and communicated to employees, and monitored on an ongoing basis. The costs incurred by the distribution center are normally measured in total as a percent of company sales, but, as earlier indicated, will probably be more meaningful on a per carton/piece handled basis, particularly if only a percentage of the company's merchandise is handled through the distribution center.

Distribution center personnel can be evaluated based on the number of cartons/pieces handled per person per day. Productivity studies, particularly in the food distribution area, have proven successful in increasing productivity without capital expenditures.

EVALUATION OF THE ACCOUNTS PAYABLE AND ACCOUNTING DEPARTMENTS

Productivity analyses of the accounts payable and accounting departments appear to be infrequently considered in evaluating the performance of these departments. However, there are a variety of statistics that may assist in their objective evaluation.

For the accounts payable department, the number of days from invoice receipt to processing for payment, the number of invoices processed per person, and the number of errors by person would be helpful in analyzing performance. In addition, since debit balances in accounts payable can tie up a retailer's resources, it is important that a listing of aged debit balances in accounts payable and of balances be provided to buying and management personnel on a recurring basis. Buyers should be required to project prospective utilization or collection or indicate the need for writeoff of such balances. The overriding responsibility for the utilization of debit balances in accounts payable belongs to the buyers, but the accounts payable department can play a key role in providing the necessary data on a regular recurring and prompt basis.

The accounting department can be evaluated based on the number of days required to complete the monthly closing process and prepare and distribute financial reports. Also, monitoring the number of errors by person has shown to be effective in reducing the number of errors.

The cost of operating the accounts payable and accounting departments as a percent of total company sales and in relation to budget should be monitored on a monthly basis. It should be recognized, however, that these two departments have fairly fixed costs. Accordingly, evaluating them as a percent of sales may not be meaningful since they have no control over the sales levels.

INDUSTRY SPECIFIC RATIOS

Certain ratios are only appropriate within certain retail industry segments. For example, important ratios for analyzing supermarket or grocery chains, in addition to the ones already discussed, are as follows:

SALES PER CHECKOUT. This ratio indicates the volume (units or dollars) being handled by each checkout register.

AVERAGE NUMBER OF ITEMS STOCKED. The inventory level and diversification are monitored through this statistic.

MANUFACTURERS' COUPONS REDEEMED EACH WEEK. This data is an indication of the level of coupon activity. It should be separately analyzed by store, by vendor coupon.

POUNDS MOVED PER MAN HOUR. For perishables, which require more man hours to rotate the stock and ensure freshness, hourly statistics are helpful.

In the chain drug industry, statistics are often shown for the average price of prescriptions, number of prescriptions filled, number of stores opened, and number of stores remodeled.

The particular services offered by a retailer may necessitate the periodic reporting of other ratios. For example, furniture and appliance stores should monitor finance charges as a percent of total revenues as well as maintenance contract revenues as a percent of total revenues since these types of income are more significant to them than to other types of retailers.

SUMMARY

Many retailers limit themselves to a few traditional and often simplistic measures, such as sales per man hour, sales per square foot and inventory turnover. These measurements are very broad, and more specific measurements will provide more meaningful information that will facilitate the more effective monitoring of performance. Each department or functional activity should be measured only with regard to those functions or those areas over which it can exercise control in areas that it has some control over. This is particularly true when developing reward systems related to measurement criteria since employees will not try to achieve goals where they have no control over the activities or functions being measured.

PART THREE

Accounting

CHAPTER TWENTY

Inventory
Dollar Control

Chapter Nineteen emphasized the necessity for adequate control over merchandise and outlined a number of the principal methods by which merchandise is controlled in the larger retail organizations. For smaller retailers the same principles apply, even if it is not feasible to carry out the control measures in detail. However, to some degree, in smaller companies control often requires reliance upon personal supervision without complete accounting control.

In any size retail business, the proper determination of inventory on hand at the close of a fiscal period is essential for the evaluation of the results of operations, as well as for control over merchandise stock.

METHODS OF INVENTORY MEASUREMENT

There are three principal methods of measuring merchandise on hand:

1. Physical inventories, whether taken on a cycle basis or at the end of the fiscal period.
2. Book inventory controls maintained on a cost basis.
3. Book inventory controls maintained on a retail basis.

The method of measurement by physical inventories represents the opposite extreme from methods whereby inventory is valued by means of book records or stock ledgers maintained on the basis of cost or retail.

The physical inventory approach minimizes use of accounting records as transactions occur and relies principally upon summaries, such as totals of sales or purchases. Operations are checked periodically by inventories of physical stock.

Under the book control methods, every transaction is accounted for and the book records reflect the inventories that should be currently on hand. Physical inventories are still necessary at intervals in order to compare the results of the inventories with the corresponding book figures. Differences may reflect actual loss of merchandise, errors in the processing of transactions, errors in the counting or summarization of the physical inventory, or combinations of any of these factors.

Measurement by Physical Inventories

In retail operations where inventory is comparatively small and can be readily counted and summarized, inventory can be taken with great frequency—monthly, weekly, or even daily. For such operations this procedure affords a satisfactory method for determining profits and monitoring the movement of merchandise stock. The stock on hand, when compared to purchases and sales, determines whether there has been a gain or a loss, and reveals any merchandise shortage.

The physical inventory method is a practical method for many small retail stores but in some cases may indicate a need for greater control. As with all physical inventories, the valuation of inventories must give appropriate consideration to any unrecognized impairment in the value of merchandise if profits are to be properly measured.

COST METHOD. Certain retailers value inventory utilizing the cost method, tracking sales at retail and by specific stock-keeping unit (SKU). Traditionally this method has been practical for retail operations that carry a limited number of SKUs, such as jewelry stores, furniture dealers, and automobile dealers. Some departments within a department store may be kept on the cost method, such as jewelry and fur departments. As computers and computer users have become more sophisticated, it has become increasingly practical for even retailers with many SKUs to use this method.

THE BOOK RECORD. The cost method requires recordkeeping for each SKU carried at cost. Traditionally cost has included purchase cost, including the cost of transportation. Merchandise available for sale includes inventory as of the beginning of the period plus cost of purchases. Cost of sales, determined on an item-by-item basis, plus markdowns (at cost) are deducted from goods available for sale to arrive at inventory on hand. If the retail operation normally experiences shrinkage, an estimate of this shrinkage should also be deducted from cost to arrive at inventory on hand. This inventory on hand would then be checked by periodic physical inventories.

While most retailers using the cost method include only invoice cost plus cost of transportation, others have included certain distribution and buying costs in the cost ledger. These retailers argue that such costs fall under the Accounting Research Bulletin (ARB) 43 definition of inventory costs as "the sum of the applicable expenditures and charges directly or indirectly incurred in bringing an article to its existing condition and location." The ARB 43 definition of "cost" requires the application of judgment. Only those costs incurred which actually add value to the merchandise may be capitalized.

It is impossible to provide an all-encompassing list of "approved" costs; however, several examples will demonstrate the general principles. Such costs would include the salaries of buyers (or a proportionate share of these salaries if buyers also perform other functions) and the costs incurred on buying trips. Another cost might be a distribution center's rent, utilities, and labor. In the case of retail chains using distribution centers, most of the costs incurred at the centers relate to physically moving the merchandise through to its ultimate saleable location. The distribution process also adds value by moving the goods from the point-of-sale to the consumer.

One requirement of the cost method is that physical inventories must be taken by SKU. While the retailer may want to know the retail value of its inventory, such information is not necessary in the initial valuation of ending inventory. However, if the value of certain inventory items are decreasing, due to over-stocks, obsolescence, or any other reason, the retail value of an item is important in insuring that ending inventory is valued at the lower of cost or market.

Cost of the physical inventory should be determined on the same basis as the book inventories. For example, if book cost includes only invoice cost plus transportation, reduced by applicable markdowns, physical inventory cost should include only these same costs.

The decision may be made to write down the inventory to reflect current market decisions (i.e., lower of cost or market). Such writedowns may be reflected as a direct writedown of a specific SKU or as a general inventory reserve.

COST OF SALES. Under the cost method, sales must be tracked by SKU and then the cost of the item sold must be determined. Here lies one of the major drawbacks of the cost method. Whatever costs are included in inventory costs (i.e., invoice cost, transportation, distribution) must be allocated, recorded, and controlled by SKU. This can be a very cumbersome process unless there are either very few SKUs or elaborate computer systems. Under the retail method sales need to be tracked only by selling price by department (although many retailers do track sales by SKU).

PRICE CHANGES. Price changes resulting from a diminution in value of the inventory should normally be reflected in the cost files. The book cost of a particular item is compared to the expected selling price (or "Market") less estimated costs to be incurred to sell that item (including carrying costs, labor, and so on). If the net market price is less than cost, failure to adjust the cost files will result in an overstatement of gross profit in the current period as the deterioration in value has not been reflected in the period in which it has occurred. Timely recognition of the reduction in market price preserves the normal gross margin percentage of the period in which the affected merchandise is sold.

For this reason, retailers often include an estimate of cost markdowns for interim reporting periods, adjusting these estimates to actual upon taking a physical inventory. These reserves are normally carried as general reserves since it would be impractical to allocate them to specific SKUs. The reserves are reversed at the beginning of the period and new reserves provided during the period, as applicable. This treatment more properly reflects income during interim periods as opposed to providing inventory adjustments at year-end only.

It should be noted that the above method properly reflects two types of markdowns in cost of sales during any period. The first is the markdown taken on individual items sold during the period as a result of lower of cost or market adjustments. The second is the general markdown reserve provided net of the reversal of previous general reserves or the specific writedowns taken against closing inventory, if a physical count has been taken.

Costing by Price Lines

The cost records may be subdivided into the price lines of each merchandise classification, with statistics as to the number of units handled in each price line. Given this data, average costs per unit within price lines are readily available. Cost of sales for a period may then be obtained by multiplying the number of units sold by the average cost per unit. This avoids the onerous chore of separately costing each individual sale.

Under this plan markdowns arise through transfer of units to a lower price line. Upon such transfer the cost of markdowns is readily computed since it represents the difference between cost values of units in the respective price lines multiplied by the number of units. Units of shrinkage are also costed by application of the average rates.

The taking and pricing of physical inventories is similarly facilitated since inventory counts are made by price lines and costed out using the respective average unit costs.

As noted, the biggest deterrent to the use of the cost method has been the need to keep detail cost files on an item-by-item basis. With only a few items, this can be done fairly easily. However, for retailers with thousands of SKUs, in the past such detail records have been cumbersome, and sometimes prohibitively expensive, to keep. Sales must be individually costed and certain costs such as transportation must be allocated.

However, today the record keeping burden has been eased by the availability of more sophisticated computer hardware and software. Yet item level costing may still be impractical for many retailers.

RETAIL METHOD

The retail method was developed in response to the difficulty of costing individual items. The retail method records purchases and sales at retail, recognizes price changes and then computes an estimated value for ending inventory at cost.

It is easier to control and summarize the values of physical inventories at marked retail prices than at cost. To do the latter requires either the use of cost figures in code on price tickets or a search in files for cost figures. There is always the possibility that a cost code may be decipherable by persons who are not entitled to have this information. For most retailers, it is impossible or impractical to obtain the actual cost of all goods on hand from the purchase files.

Advantages of the Retail Method

The retail method has the following advantages:

1. It permits periodic determination of inventories and profits without resorting to physical inventories.

2. It provides for a level of managerial control over gross margin by recording initial markon and changes in pricing through to maintained markon. Such changes include markdowns and stock shortages.

3. It renders feasible the taking of departmental inventories at various dates, other than the general fiscal closing, with appropriate adjustment of the related departmental book record.

4. It makes it possible to take physical inventories more easily since they require merely the summarization of marked retail prices which are readily available to counting personnel.

5. It obtains reductions in inventory values, evidenced by decreases in selling prices, as an automatic by-product of the method as soon as retail prices are remarked and processed by the retail accounting system.

6. It discloses the amount of stock shortages.

7. It facilitates the knowledgeable preparation of merchandise budgets.

8. It provides a basis for insurance coverage and settlements.

9. It tends to disclose, through apparently erroneous results, deficiencies in internal control systems and operating procedures.

The Retail Method as an Averaging Method

There is one major disadvantage: the retail method is basically an averaging technique. As such it is subject to distortion by the inclusion of extremes in the mix and can produce possible inaccuracies in the derivation of inventory values.

Under the retail method, the cost of merchandise on hand at any time is arrived at by deducting from retail the cumulative markon, generally representing the combined result of the markon of the opening inventory and the markon of purchases for the period to date. The cumulative markon is an average relation between the total cost of all merchandise (generally including opening inventory at cost) handled for the period and the total retail of the same merchandise. The cumulative markon is removed from ending inventory at retail by multiplying the cost multiplier percentage by the ending inventory at retail. The resulting amount is inventory at estimated cost. As noted in Chapter Three, the cost multiplier excludes the impact of markdowns and as a result, the retail method provides an inherently conservative estimate of the cost of inventory.

A simple example will illustrate this point. If a coat is marked down from $150 to $100 and the normal gross margin is 50 percent, the markdown period will reflect a markdown cost of $25 as the inventory is reduced from an original cost of $75 (.5 × $150) to $50 (.5 × $100). If the coat is subsequently sold for $100, the normal margin of 50 percent is preserved as the retailer realizes a gross profit of 50 percent ($100 – $50). The retail method allows markdowns to affect inventory costs in the period in which they occur rather than the period in which they are sold; obviously the more conservative and logical choice.

Cost multipliers are generally maintained by department and therefore represent an average of all goods in the department. Given the employment of this averaging principle, the merchandise cost of sales determined for a department under the retail method is not exact cost. Operation of the retail method and its underlying theory are discussed later in this chapter.

The retail method, like any other inventory method, must be tested periodically by comparison with physical inventories, and book figures should be adjusted to the physical count unless there is reason to doubt the accuracy of the physical count. Also like any other method of inventory control, its successful use is dependent upon the care with which all pertinent factors are recognized and reflected in the accounts. No method of control will give satisfactory results if accounting detail is compiled carelessly, inaccurately, or with the omission of material factors. Furthermore, as noted earlier, it is fundamentally a method of averages. Accordingly, its successful use depends upon its application to departments where average results, especially the use of an average cost multiplier percentage, do not distort the general picture. Any group of transactions where the extremes are frequently so great as to make average figures meaningless is not suited to the retail method. Usually, though, by subdivision a reasonably homogeneous inventory grouping can be achieved, making feasible the use of this method.

CHOICE OF METHOD

Over the years the retail method has been widely adopted. For department stores and for many other forms of retail operation, this method probably combines, more satisfactorily than any other, information and control at the lowest cost. It is, however, a serious mistake to disregard or ignore the advantages of the other methods for use under certain circumstances. In some large retail stores there will be departments where the cost control method serves the requirements of the business more adequately than the retail method, and other departments where the taking of frequent physical inventories without use of detailed control records may be preferable.

OPERATION OF THE RETAIL METHOD

Operation of the retail method requires merchandise statistics at retail as well as at cost, and summarization of transactions by each department or other appropriate merchandise classification rather than aggregate totals. With respect to inventories, "cost" figures are calculated using the retail method; some retailers use an alternative term, "mercantile," to refer to this estimated cost.

The merchandise statistics for each department or classification start with opening inventory at cost and at retail. Purchases are added at cost (plus other capitalizable costs) and at retail (equal to the marked selling price). There are also added markups at retail. Totals of these items represent merchandise handled during the period at cost and at retail. Utilizing these totals the cumulative markon is obtained. This is the difference between retail and cost of merchandise handled.

For purposes of valuing the year-end inventory, most retailers include the markon inherent in the opening inventory in computing the cumulative markon and the cost-multiplier. However, this is not a universal practice. Recognizing that they are increasingly subject to periods of changes in the mix of merchandise and changing markon percentage, some retailers have either exclusively used the markon on the current year's purchases or more heavily weighted this markon percentage in the year-end inventory valuation process. Such an approach, of course, is predicated on the assumption that the closing inventory is comprised primarily of merchandise purchased during the current year. The method selected to compute the cumulative markon percentage should be that which most appropriately reflects the retailer's circumstances and should be applied on a consistent basis.

To obtain closing inventory at retail, the total of retail deductions is subtracted from the total of merchandise handled at retail. Total retail deductions comprise the sum of net sales, markdowns, allowances, sales discounts, and shrinkage (estimated or actual). Closing inventory at retail is reduced to cost by deducting the cumulative markon inherent in the ending inventory at retail. The cost of ending inventory is calculated by multiplying the ending inventory at retail by the complement of the cumulative markon percentage, more commonly known as the "cost multiplier."

The ending inventory at cost, $6,775, represents 64.04 percent (complement of the cumulative markon percentage) of $10,580, the closing inventory at retail. (See Exhibit 20.1.)

EXHIBIT 20.1   Illustration

	Cost	Retail	Cumulative Markon Percentage
Opening inventory	$5,683	$ 8,795	
Purchases and transportation and other capitalizable costs, net	3,482	5,372	
Markups (less cancellations)		145	
Total merchandise handled	$9,165	$14,312	35.96
Net sales		$ 3,369	
Markdowns (less cancellations)		280	
Sales discounts		15	
Shrinkage (estimated or actual)		68	
Total retail deductions		$ 3,732	
Ending inventory	$6,775	$10,580	35.96

(A) Cumulative markon = $\dfrac{\text{Total retail of}}{\text{merchandise handled}} - \dfrac{\text{Total cost of}}{\text{merchandise handled}}$

$= \$14,312 - \$9,165 = \$5,147$

(B) Cumulative markon percentage = $\dfrac{\text{Cumulative markon}}{\text{Total retail of merchandise handled}}$

$= \dfrac{\$\ 5,147}{\$14,312} = .3596 \text{ or } 35.96\%$

(C) Cost-multiplier = $\dfrac{\text{Total cost of merchandise handled}}{\text{Total retail of merchandise handled}}$

$= \dfrac{\$\ 9,165}{\$14,312} = .6404 \text{ or } 64.04\%$

(D) Cost-multiplier percentage = 100 − Cumulative markon percentage

$= 64.04 = 100 - 35.96$

(E) Ending inventory at cost = Cost-multiplier × Ending inventory at retail

$= (.6404)\ (\$10,580) = \$6,775$

THE STOCK LEDGER

The principal record used in the retail method is a stock ledger which includes information for each department or departmental sub-division. Single-line specialty stores, as well as some other operations, may maintain stock ledgers by merchandise classifications (or price lines, styles, etc.) rather than by departments.

In other cases the stock ledger may be maintained by store or by departments within branch stores. It may be most useful, and least expensive, to maintain the ledger by store in cases where the merchandise classifications are limited and the product mix consistent from period to period.

Most retail chains find store ledgers impractical and although they track results of operations by store, the stock ledger is maintained by department. In many cases it is not sufficient to divide the stock ledger into broad department categories such as men's clothing or electronics. The diverse nature of the merchandise within such groupings may combine goods with an inappropriately extreme range of cost multipliers which could distort the calculation of inventory cost. Exhibit 20.6 provides a clear illustration of the danger in averaging unrelated items.

Retail operations are sometimes divided into two seasons with cumulative merchandise statistics kept on a seasonal rather than an annual or other periodic basis. For example, department stores on a January 31 fiscal year basis may record merchandise statistics for the spring season, from February 1 to July 31, and then start the records anew for the fall season, August 1 to January 31. However, this is not a universal practice; in the interests of simplicity and reduced recordkeeping requirements, the records are often kept on an annual basis and statistics are accumulated without regard to seasonal breakdowns. There is no loss of accuracy if merchandise purchases and the mix of ending inventory do not vary significantly on a seasonal basis.

The stock ledgers may be either abbreviated or detailed. With an abbreviated ledger a supplementary record is kept to accumulate purchase totals; where the ledger is detailed, the various purchase elements are entered directly. Exhibit 20.2 and 20.3 illustrate the abbreviated form of departmental stock ledger (a form used by most retail chains). Exhibit 20.2 illustrates the total page of such a stock ledger maintained on a year-to-date basis. Exhibit 20.3 is typical of the seasonal type of stock ledger and this case illustrates summary information by department. Exhibit 20.4 is prepared on the same seasonal basis as Exhibit 20.3; however, this ledger analyzes the same information on a store by store basis.

As illustrated in Exhibit 20.5 a detailed form of stock ledger consists of three principal parts: an upper section for accumulating cost of merchandise handled; a middle section for accumulating the corresponding retail, and a lower section for determining closing inventory at retail and cost, and gross margin.

EXHIBIT 20.2   Stock Ledger—Departmental Recap

	Current Month November	Year to Date November
Markon %		
Cost %		
Initial markon %		
Cost Additions:		
Opening inventory		
Opening freight		
Purchases		
Freight		
(Discounts)		
Total		
Retail Additions:		
Opening inventory		
Purchases		
Markups		
Total		
Retail Reductions:		
Sales		
Markdowns		
Shortage %		
Shortage		
Total		
Closing Inventory:		
Retail		
Cost		
Cost of Sales		
Gross profit dollars		
Gross profit % sales		

EXHIBIT 20.3 Seasonal Stock Ledger
Department Summary
Month of April 19XX

DEPT #		BEGINNING BALANCE	PURCHASES	MARKUPS	GOODS AVAILABLE	PHYS. INV. ADJ.	MARKDOWNS	RESERVE FOR SHRINK	SALES	ENDING BALANCE	GROSS PROFIT SEASON TO DATE	GROSS PROFIT CURRENT MONTH
01	R											
22	R											
	C											
28	R											
	C											
34	R											
	C											
45	R											
	C											
66	R											
	C											
ALL DEPTS.	R											
	C											

EXHIBIT 20.4 Seasonal Stock Ledger
Summary by Store
Month of April 19XX

STORE #		BEGINNING BALANCE	PURCHASES	MARKUPS	GOODS AVAILABLE	PHYS. INV. ADJ.	MARKDOWNS	RESERVE FOR SHRINK	SALES	ENDING BALANCE	GROSS PROFIT SEASON TO DATE	GROSS PROFIT CURRENT MONTH
2	R											
	C											
3	R											
	C											
5	R											
	C											
6	R											
	C											
7	R											
	C											
8	R											
	C											
9	R											
	C											
10	R											
	C											
12	R											
	C											
14	R											
	C											
16	R											
	C											
17	R											
	C											
18	R											
	C											
19	R											
	C											
20	R											
	C											
21	R											
	C											
ALL STORES	R											
	C											

EXHIBIT 20.5 Inventory Dollar Control

Merchandise Statement

Month of			Year to Date	
Amount	%		%	Amount
	1	Cost: Inventory—Beginning of period		
	2	Domestic purchases (Net)		
	3	Freight—in		
	4	Foreign purchases (Net)		
	5	Transfers (Net)		
	6			
	7	Cumulative cost (% = 7 / 14 for year)		
	8	Retail: Inventory—Beginning of period		
	9	Domestic purchases (Net)		
	10	Foreign purchases (Net)		
	11	Markups		
	12	Transfers (Net)		
	13			
	14	Cumulative retail (Markon % = 7 / 14 FR. 100)		
	15	Net sales: Store 1		
	16	Store 2		
	17	Store 3		
	18	Store 4		
	19	Store 5		
	20	Store 6		
	21			
	22			
	23	Total net sales		
	24	Markdowns (% = 24/23)		
	25	Allowances to customers (% = 25/23)		
	26	Discounts to employees (% = 26/23)		
	27	Shrink (% = 27/23)		
	28	Total retail stock ded. (23 to 27 incl.)		
	29	Inventory: Retail—End of period (14 − 28) (Ratio = 29 / 23)		
	30	Inventory cost—End of period (29 × %7 Yr. to date)		
	31	Workroom and other costs (% = 31/23)		
	32	Gross margin before discounts (23 + 30 − 7 − 31) (% = 32/23)		
	33	Cash discounts (____% of 28 for month) (% = 33/23)		
	34	Gross margin (32 + 33)		

_____ Dept no.   Dept no. _____

_____ 19____ Period   Period _____ 19____

Regardless of the form, the purpose of these stock ledgers is to record, on a summary basis for each department, all the transactions of the season or the year.

A variation on this theme is a method which uses a separate sheet for monthly records for each department and showing cumulative results for the season or year. This latter method has the advantage of summarizing on one page the key merchandise data of each month and of the period to date in addition to serving as the main record of transactions. Copies of the report can be supplied to buyers and executives as a monthly report of merchandising results, thereby avoiding the duplicate work of transcribing figures from the stock ledger of the monthly report of operations.

This type of form, as illustrated in Exhibit 20.5 reflects the accumulations of statistics on an annual rather than a seasonal basis, with the data for the departments of all stores combined in a single stock ledger and operating report. The theory underlying the pooled or common department concept is the universal applicability of a common departmental markon, with all retail deductions (markdowns, allowances, discounts, and shrinkage) shared in proportion to sales. Consequently, the same gross margin on the sales is "earned" by the department regardless of store location.

An abbreviated form of stock ledger is most likely to be used when the records are kept on a weekly basis and where the departmental figures are subdivided by such factors as merchandise classifications, price lines, or store locations. When the stock records are kept on a monthly basis, the abbreviated form is much more likely to be used as the more detailed version becomes cumbersome; too much information may obscure important merchandising trends.

The following discussion will use the stock ledger illustrated in Exhibit 20.6 on the following page to demonstrate how the stock ledger actually performs its recordkeeping function. Remember that the primary duties of the stock ledger are to measure merchandise, to estimate the cost of inventory at the end of the period (and therefore profit for the period) and to monitor the elements of gross margin.

Merchandise Handled

This term includes opening inventory and all elements of purchases that enter into the determination of cumulative markon. Purchases included consist of the following items:

1. Invoiced cost of domestic purchases, less merchandise returns, rebates, allowances and discounts.
2. Landed cost of imported merchandise; that is invoiced cost plus duty, freight, insurance, commissions, etc., less returns and allowances.

EXHIBIT 20.6 Departmental Stock Ledger
Month of July 19XX

Department _____ Dept. _____

| Period | Merchandise Handled | | Net Sales | Retail Deductions | | | | Closing Inventory at Retail | Alteration and workroom Costs | Mark-on % | Mark-down % | Sales Discount % | Shrinkage provision % | Alteration costs % | Gross Margin % |
	Cost	Retail		Mark-Downs	Sales Discounts	Shrinkage Provisions	Totals								
Inventory Feb. 1															
Month of February Season to Date															
Month of March Season to Date															
Month of April Season to Date															
Month of May Season to Date															
Month of June Season to Date															
Month of July Season to Date															

3. Inward transportation charges (at cost only).

4. Department transfers in, less transfers out.

5. Markups, less cancellations and other corrections of retail (at retail only).

6. Invoices in transit.

The retail and cost amounts of purchases (excluding invoices in transit) are detailed and accumulated by department in a subsidiary purchases ledger. In some retail companies, the cost of freight may be combined with the cost of the merchandise rather than identified separately.

Markups and corrections of retail must also be accumulated in a subsidiary price change ledger. The totals from these systems feed (after review for errors) into the stock ledger.

Smaller retailers may track those components manually and may even use a manually prepared stock ledger. Again, all components of purchases are accumulated departmentally in the equivalent of a purchase journal. Totals may be carried directly to the stock ledger or in some cases, the totals of the various components of purchases may be summarized in a supplemental report. The separate accumulation of purchase elements permits a review of the factors that enter into the computation of the cost multiplier. An example of such a summary is shown in Exhibit 20.7.

Invoices in Transit

In the determination of purchases for the stock ledger, a question arises as to whether merchandise handled should include all merchandise received or only merchandise which has cleared through the receiving and marking rooms and has been recorded on the equivalent of a purchase journal. In practice, certain merchandise is always "in transit"; that is, the invoices have not been recorded on the purchase journal although the merchandise has been received. The preferred method is to adjust the totals for these unrecorded purchases using the actual amount if known or an estimate if that is all that is available. The result is a more accurate description of operating results and more precise open-to-buy statistics.

As a practical matter, many retailers do not adjust purchases at month-end for invoices in transit because they are not a significant factor. For many retailers, the dollar amount of invoices relating to merchandise received but not yet recorded is only a small portion of the total dollar amount of invoices in transit; the majority normally represent those dated prior to month-end for which the related merchandise has not yet been received.

EXHIBIT 20.7 Purchase Record Summary

Month of April 19XX

Department _____

	Period ————		Period ————	
	Cost	Retail	Cost	Retail
1. Domestic invoices (net)	$2,466	$3,722		
2. Foreign invoices (net) at landed cost	850	1,500		
3. Freight-in charges	76	—		
4. Transfers-in	60	100		
5. Markups, etc.	—	145		
6. Invoices in transit, close of period (if any)	102	157		
	$3,554	$5,624		
7. Invoices in transit, beginning of period (if any)	85	135		
8. Transfers-out	30	50		
	$ 115	$ 185		
9. Total purchases	$3,439	$5,439		

When invoices in transit are not a significant factor the easiest procedure is to omit a purchase adjustment. An adjustment for invoices in transit would require the retailer to summarize the invoice cost of the related merchandise and then determine the retail amount for the same goods. The retail amount can generally be estimated, by department, using the known relationship between cost and retail for purchases recorded in the purchase journal or stock ledger. The retailer can then adjust purchases recorded for the month in the stock ledger using the summarized cost and estimated retail; this adjustment is reversed in the subsequent month and a new amount is accrued for that month-end.

Whether or not the adjustment is made most retailers do examine invoices in transit very carefully at year-end in order to verify that purchases include all invoices for which merchandise has been received or to determine that the amount of unrecorded goods is not significant. Retailers also scrutinize invoices in transit more carefully at the time of physical inventories in order to eliminate any record keeping errors and identify the "real" amount of merchandise shortage (shrink).

Cost-Multiplier

As defined earlier, the cumulative markon of a department is the difference between retail and cost of the total merchandise handled. The cumulative markon percentage is the cumulative markon as a percentage of total merchandise handled at retail. This percentage can be applied to ending inventory at retail to calculate the amount to be subtracted from this to reduce such inventory to an estimated cost.

It is mathematically simpler to use the complement of the markon percentage in computing inventory at cost, so generally it is the complement percentage (otherwise known as the "cost-multiplier") which is reflected in the stock ledger. The cost-multiplier is calculated by dividing the total cost of merchandise handled by the corresponding retail amount.

The cumulative markon and cost-multipliers should be reviewed carefully and compared with those prior accounting periods. This review serves two purposes: first to insure that the calculation of the cost-multiplier (and therefore ending inventory at cost) is correct and consistent with prior periods; and second, to note important trends in merchandising results which may influence future merchandising decisions.

Net Sales

Net sales represent sales net of all returns, allowances and discounts. Sales returns are deducted from gross sales because the merchandise has been restored to stock. When allowances are granted, no merchandise is returned to stock. To the extent that allowances are offset against sales they must be added to markdowns, so that there is a complete accounting for merchandise at retail.

Markdowns

Markdowns are entered as credits to inventory on the stock ledger in recognition of the reduction of the selling price from the retail originally recorded. Sales of marked down merchandise are credited to stock only at reduced prices.

Markdowns are frequently classified by causative factor, with a view to providing some insight into the effectiveness of buying and merchandising policies. The following classification of such factors is commonly used:

1. Promotional purchase remainders.
2. Slow-moving or inactive stocks.

3. Planned "event" or promotional markdowns.

4. Special sales from stock.

5. Price adjustments.

6. Broken assortments, remnants, discontinued lines, and damaged merchandise.

7. Allowances to customers.

Some retailers use the same price change form to record all types of price changes, including markdowns. Summarization of these price change forms will supply the necessary information regarding the amounts of markups and markup cancellations, markdowns and markdown cancellations, and corrections of retail. Exhibit 20.8 illustrates a typical form for recording price changes. More and more retailers are today recording markdowns at the point of sale, thus eliminating the need for these price change forms.

Sales Discounts

Sales discounts, primarily to employees, are deducted from the gross sales prices at the time of the sale. Charge account discounts are not deducted from sales prices at the time of sale, and inventory (at retail) is reduced for the full amount of the sale. Subsequently the sales price is reduced to reflect the discount at the time of payment of the charge account and the amount of these charge accounts discounts is allocated departmentally and deducted from departmental sales, with a corresponding addition to sales discounts.

EXHIBIT 20.8   Price Change Form

Department:	# 49		Store	# 22
Type of change:	Markdown—clearance		Price change form	# 001
Effective date:	01/15/XX		Authorization	# 245

SKU #	Merchandise Description	Old Retail Price	New Retail Price	Quantity Changed	Extended Value
5194	Boy's Coat	15.99	10.88	25	127.75

Buyer's Signature: M. Smith
Taken by: J. Doe
Date of price change: 01/17/XX

Shrinkage

The provision for shrinkage as entered in the stock ledger is accumulated throughout the year as an estimate of probable shrinkage based upon past experience. Book inventories have, therefore, already been reduced by an estimated amount of shrinkage before they are compared with physical inventories. If a difference exists between a physical inventory and a book inventory already reduced by an estimated shrinkage, the difference is equivalent to a correction of the estimated shrinkage. It indicates that the estimate of shrinkage was either too large or too small and an adjustment is in order, so that the stock ledger will reflect the actual inventory at the date of the physical inventory.

If the indicated adjustment is large enough to reduce shrinkage below a minimum deemed "normal" for the specific department, or, on the other hand, to increase it to an abnormally large figure, a study should be conducted to determine the cause. Usually no significant adjustments (especially reductions) to the provision for shrinkage are made until the book records and the summarization of the physical inventory have been reviewed for possible errors.

Ending Inventory

Ending inventory at retail is obtained by subtracting total retail deductions from the total of merchandise handled at retail and is subject to check by a physical inventory. Physical inventories are taken by some retailers on a cycle basis and by others seasonally (typically July and January), but all retailers should perform physical inventories at least once a year. The inventory amount shown by the stock ledger is adjusted to the amount of physical inventory through the shrinkage provision.

The cost of ending inventory, whether the unadjusted book balance or the amount of the physical inventory, results from the multiplication of the retail amount by the cost-multiplier.

Gross Margin

Gross margin equals the excess of net sales for the period over the total costs of merchandise sold. Total merchandise costs are the sum of opening inventory at cost, purchases at cost (net of discounts earned), less closing inventory at cost.

The examples of stock ledgers illustrated in this book do not include columns for the cost of sales (total merchandise costs). Although such columns could be included in stock ledgers the examples exclude them in recognition of industry practice and in order to focus attention on the more important statistic—gross margin. Gross margin is the foremost ratio in judging the results of departmental operations because it indicates how far the realized (or "maintained") markon percentage has fallen short of the cumulative markon percentage.

The stock ledger illustrated in Exhibit 20.6 provides a method of determining the percentage of gross margin through the use of certain other percentages. It is a short-cut method which avoids computation of inventory amounts at cost and total merchandise costs, and eliminates several mathematical steps. The various percentages used in this form generally are computed as desirable statistical information, and thus do not involve additional work. The procedure for utilizing this form in deriving the percentage of gross margin may be illustrated by assuming that the following data have been obtained from a stock ledger:

	Amounts	Percentages of Net Sales
Opening inventory at cost	$ 20,880*	
Purchase at cost	51,794*	
Merchandise handled at retail	126,518*	
Net sales	92,743	
Markdowns	5,653	6.10%
Sales discounts	1,079	1.16
Shrinkage provisions	368	0.40
Ending inventory at retail	26,675	

*From these totals the cumulative markon percentage of 42.56% is calculated:

$$\frac{126,518 - 20,880 - 51,794}{126,518}$$

From the foregoing percentages the percentage of gross margin is determined, as follows:

Percentage of cumulative markon		42.56%
Retail reduction percentages to be reduced to cost:		
Markdowns	6.10%	
Sales discounts	1.16	
Shrinkage provisions	0.40	
Total	7.66%	

Percentage of retail deductions reduced to cost, 7.66 × 57.44 (which is 100 − 42.56)	4.40
Percentage of gross margin	38.16%

PREPARING A GROSS MARGIN STATEMENT

As a proof of the percentage of gross margin derived under the above formula, a method of preparing a departmental statement of gross margin from
data in the stock ledger is illustrated below. As will be noted from the data
used in the preceding example, the elements of a complete gross margin
statement that are lacking are ending inventory at cost and the amount of
gross margin. Ending inventory and gross margin are derived while setting
up the statement.

	Amounts		Percentages of Net Sales	
Net sales	$92,743	$92,743	100.00%	100.00%
Markdowns	5,653		6.10	
Sales discounts	1,079		1.16	
Provision for shrinkage	368		.40	
Retail sales and reductions	$99,843		107.66%	
Merchandise costs:				
Inventory, beginning of period	$20,880			
Purchases	51,794			
Cost of merchandise handled	72,674			
Inventory, end of period	15,322			
Cost of merchandise sold	57,352	57,352		61.84
Gross margin		$35,391		38.16%

Net sales, opening inventory at cost, and purchases at cost, are available
and can be entered directly on the statement. Since the percentage of gross
margin is available, the corresponding amount is readily computed and
entered. Net sales less gross margin gives total merchandise costs which may
also be entered. The missing item, closing inventory at cost, is then calculated by deducting the cost of merchandise sold from the cost of merchandise handled. The amount of ending inventory at cost can be verified by
multiplying the ending inventory at retail, $26,675, by the cost-multiplier,
57.44 (complement of the markon percentage of 42.56).

CONTROLS OVER THE STOCK LEDGER

One of the most basic controls found in accounting is the reconciliation of
subsidiary ledger amounts to the corresponding general ledger or control

totals. The utilization of control totals plays an important role in the arena of retail accounting. The figures reflected in the stock ledgers determine both the end of period inventory balance and the results of operations for the period. These subsidiary ledger amounts must be compared to the corresponding control totals to insure that operating results are being calculated properly.

As was stated earlier in this chapter, the cost method is more practicable than the retail method for certain departments. Some retailers employ both methods at the same time, with the cost method used for only a comparatively small number of departments.

The stock ledgers used for the retail method may also be used for recording, in the appropriate columns only, the results of the operations of the departments controlled by the cost method. Where figures under both methods are included in a single stock record, the latter is controlled by accounts in the general ledger representing totals for all departments. Sometimes the figures for departments controlled by the retail method are controlled in the general ledger separately from cost department figures, with two distinct stock records being maintained.

The stock ledger (or ledgers) will include totals summarizing activity for all departments and/or all stores. These totals must be periodically reconciled (typically on a monthly basis) with amounts reflected in the general ledger. If there is a single stock ledger it will contain separate control totals for retail departments and cost departments, and a total of all departments. The control totals in the stock ledgers represent totals of the respective dollar columns of the individual departments. It should be noted that since the total inventory at cost for the retail departments is the sum of the amounts computed for each department, total inventory at cost cannot be computed from the control totals. Total ending inventory at cost can only be obtained by adding up the amounts calculated for each department.

Usually, the general ledger contains control accounts for net sales and cost of purchases, the latter including all the elements of purchases.

Two different procedures are followed with respect to the inventory account in the general ledger. Under one method the amount is not changed during a season or even during a fiscal year, whereas under the other the amount is changed each month to bring it into agreement with the stock ledger. Under the first method the general ledger is not in agreement, as to inventories or net profits, with the interim monthly balance sheets and income accounts. Under the other approach the books are always in agreement with financial statements. For this reason the latter method is most commonly employed.

It is not necessary to close out sales, purchases, expenses, discounts, and so on, to a monthly profit and loss account if an account is opened to reflect the change in inventory during the period. This makes it possible to obtain all the required elements of the income account directly from the general ledger, except closing inventory, which equals the opening inventory as adjusted by the account which reflects interim changes.

STOCK LEDGER ELEMENTS NOT SUBJECT TO CONTROL

There are two important component elements of the stock ledger without equivalent control totals on the general ledger. These are the retail amounts of purchases and price changes (most significantly markdowns). The retail of purchases as recorded in the stock ledger should represent the sum of the originally marked retail prices of merchandise placed in stock. Ordinarily, there is no mathematical proof of the accuracy of the retail of purchases. This means there may be errors in extensions or in tabulations, but they cannot be discovered by cross checking against a control account. This possible source of error in the operation of the retail method is important and merits particular attention.

Markdown calculations and tabulations represent another source of possible errors under the retail method. They cannot be controlled to the same degree as sales. In this respect also, it is important that sufficient attention be directed to obtaining accuracy in the figures. There should be an accountability for the numerical sequence of all price change reports, and calculations and summarizations should be verified. In addition, each price change form should be examined for authorized signatures which evidence that the price changes have actually been made on the merchandise. Many retailers employ an audit process (similar to sales audit) to check and verify that these retail amounts have been properly recorded.

The inability to reconcile purchases at retail and retail price changes with control totals on the general ledger also encourages retailers to use exception reports to detect errors. In the case of purchases, computerized systems can be programmed to detect unusual markons for specific purchases. For example, if the retail amount for a purchase is recorded below the item's cost or with an unusually low markon, the purchase can be detected and listed on an exception report. In the case of manual systems, the equivalent review would obviously be tedious. Similar exception reports can be generated for retail price changes.

When all transactions are properly recorded under the retail method, the shrinkage disclosed by the retailer's records should properly represent the results of thefts, price tampering, and damage to or loss of merchandise. However, in practice, paperwork errors inevitably occur and a portion of shrink reflects their impact.

RETAIL METHOD FORMULAS

Under the retail method there is an interrelation among cumulative markon, retail reductions and gross margin. The interrelation may be expressed by formulas applicable both to dollar amounts and to percentages. The percentages are expressed in terms of the common denominator, retail. Cumulative markon percentage is based upon the retail of merchandise handled during a period, but percentages of retail reductions, and gross margin are based upon the retail of merchandise sold during the period.

Illustrations of certain of these formulas follow. Dollar amounts and percentages are the same as those used in the illustration of the gross margin statement on page 229:

| | | Percentages on | |
| | | | Merchandise |
	Amounts	Net Sales	Handled
Net sales	$92,743	100.00%	
Markdowns	5,653	6.10	
Sales discounts	1,079	1.16	
Shrinkage provisions	368	0.40	
Total retail reductions	7,100	7.66	
Cost of merchandise sold	57,352	61.84	
Gross margin	35,391	38.16	
Cumulative markon			42.56%
Cost multiplier percentage			57.44

Cost of Merchandise Sold

Cost of merchandise sold equals the sum of net sales and total retail reductions, reduced to cost by application of the cost-multiplier percentage. The same formula is used to derive percentage of cost of merchandise sold. For example:

| | Dollars | | Percentages | |
	At Retail	Retail × 57.44%	At Retail	Retail × 57.44%
Net sales	$92,743	$53,272	100.00%	57.44%
Total retail reductions	7,100	4,078	7.66	4.40
Cost of merchandise sold	$99,843	$57,350	107.66%	61.84%

Gross Margin

Formulas for gross margin and percentage of gross margin may be stated as follows:

A. Gross margin equals net sales less the cost of merchandise sold. The cost of merchandise sold equals: (a) sales at retail × cost-multiplier *plus* (b) retail reductions (i.e., markdowns, provision for shrinkage, sales discounts) × cost-multiplier. Since the complement of the cost-multiplier is the cumulative markon, we can rearrange the terms above to achieve an alternate formula for gross margin:

B. Gross margin *also* equals: (a) net sales × the cumulative markon (b) less other retail reductions at cost.

C. Percentage of gross margin equals gross margin as a percentage of net sales. However, in light of the formula for gross margin expressed above this can alternatively be calculated as the percentage of cumulative markon minus the percentage of retail reductions at cost.

Illustration of these formulas, based upon the figures already used, is as follows:

	At Retail	At Cost
A. Net Sales	$92,743	
Cost of merchandise sold		$53,272(1)
Retail reductions	7,100	4,078(2)

Gross margin = Net sales − Cost of merchandise sold − Retail reductions at cost; in this case: 92,743 − 53,272 − 4,078 = 35,393.

(1) 92,743 × .5744
(2) 7,100 × .5744

Note: Cost-multiplier equal to 57.44%.

B. Alternate Calculation

Since in this case the cumulative markon = 100 − 57.44 = 42.56, gross margin also equals: (92,743)(42.56) − (7,100)(.5744) = 39,471 − 4,078 = 35,393. Note that each calculation produces the same result, a gross margin of 35,393.

C. Gross Margin Percentage equals:

35,393 ÷ 92,743 = 38.16% or as alternatively calculated, .4256 − 4,078/ 92,743 = .4256 − .044 = 38.16%.

The above example illustrates how gross margin is reduced from the margin that would have been earned on the basis of cumulative markon, by the adverse effect of markdowns, sales discounts, and shrinkage.

Cumulative Markon Percentage

Manipulation of the above equations produces an alternate formula for cumulative markon percentage. Since gross margin equals the cumulative markon *less* reductions at cost, we can realign the variables to prove that cumulative markon equals gross margin *plus* retail reductions at cost. Cumulative markon percentage can then be redefined as:

$$\frac{\text{Gross margin} + \text{Retail reductions}}{\text{Net sales} + \text{Retail reductions}}$$

Or using the data from the previous example:

$$\frac{35,393 + 7,100}{92,743 + 7,100} = \frac{42,493}{99,843} = 42.56\%$$

Note that retail reductions are restored at retail because cumulative markon was defined in Chapter Seven to exclude such reductions. Cumulative markon percentage can also be defined in terms of the applicable percentages of the other factors:

Cumulative markon percentage = Gross margin percentage + Retail
reductions as a percentage of sales

In this example: $38.16 + 4.4 = 42.56\%$.

Cost of Sales

Cost of sales is based upon the following factors:

Inventory, beginning of period	—
Purchases	—
Total = Gross cost of merchandise handled	—
Deduct: Inventory, end of period	—
Difference = Gross cost of merchandise sold	—
Deduct: Discounts earned	—
Difference = Total net merchandise costs	—

The factors stated are those which appear in a formal statement of cost of sales. However, other factors of cost-sales discounts, markdowns, and shrinkages—are not separately presented in a formal statement of cost of sales and gross margin.

Sales discounts are reflected in net sales, because the net sales are less than they would have been if the sales prices had not been reduced in the form of discounts to customers.

Markdowns are reflected partly in net sales and partly in inventories; that is, in sales for items which have been marked down and sold, and in inventory for markdowns taken on items which are unsold at the end of the period.

In the absence of errors in connection with recordkeeping or physical inventories, shrinkage represents losses caused by disappearance, destruction, or other unrecorded disposition (e.g., samples) of merchandise which might otherwise have been sold to produce gross margin. The effect of shrinkage on gross margin is reflected through inventories, since there is less merchandise to be carried forward to the new accounting period. Shrinkage increases the cost of sales although it has no direct relationship to sales.

Sales discounts, markdowns, and shrinkage are recorded in retail amounts, and percentages of these amounts are expressed in relationship to net sales. Net sales constitute a common denominator for expressing relationships, and the effect of these various elements upon gross margin can be determined from ratios based upon this common denominator. The amount of loss from sales discounts, markdowns, and shrinkages is not the retail at which they are recorded, but is the difference between retail and the cumulative markon contained in such retail. In other words, the amount lost is the amount required to purchase enough merchandise for sale on the basis of the cumulative markon, to realize the retail total of sales discounts, markdowns, and shrinkages. For this reason, the cost of these elements is determined by multiplying their retail amount by the cost-multiplier (100 minus percentage of cumulative markon).

DISPOSITION OF MARKON

The gross income of a retail operation arises principally from markons. As stated in preceding discussions, some part of initial markon is lost through shrink and markdowns. The remainder of markon is used to meet operating expenses and provide profit. It is critical to profitability that a sufficient initial markon is provided when setting prices and that subsequently this markon is safeguarded so that as little as possible is lost in reductions. It is informative to have a record of the portion of remaining markon used to meet operating expenses and the balance that is realized as operating profit.

The examples of reports on pages 237–239, Exhibits 20.9, 20.10, and 20.11 illustrate various forms of analyzing initial markon and its subsequent reductions.

In effect, these reports show how departmental statements for a designated period may be prepared to show markon originally provided, the portion carried forward to a future period in the closing inventory, and the disposition of the amount available, with the uses made of markons realized. By indicating the percentages of markon used for various purposes, as related to total markon provided, a clear picture of the disposition of markon is supplied. This serves to emphasize the importance of conserving for expenses and profit as large a portion of markon as possible, rather than losing it in reductions and unknown costs.

Different types of forms can be utilized to present these data for separate departments, for groups of departments, or for retail departments in total. The first form provides more detail than the second in order to make clearer the manner in which the figures are compiled. While the second form omits some figures, it does supply the pertinent data. Reports may be made monthly, for other intermediate periods, or for seasons or fiscal years.

The Tax Reform Act of 1986 ("the 1986 Act") significantly affected the way retailers must account for their inventory costs. The Internal Revenue Code now requires retailers to capitalize a portion of the costs of buying and warehousing merchandise. The primary impact of the 1986 Act is to decrease a retailer's allowable expenses for tax purposes and, therefore, under most conditions, increase the retailer's expense and liability. Prior to the 1986 Act, the costs of buying (defined broadly in include buyer's salaries and fringe benefits, the costs of buying trips and an allocated portion of the MIS, Human Resources, and Accounting department costs) were considered period costs for federal income tax purposes and eligible for deduction in the period in which they were incurred. Similarly, the costs of warehousing merchandise, including warehouse rent, depreciation, utilities, labor, and an allocated portion of general and administrative support, were also period costs.

A secondary impact of the 1986 Act was the administrative and accounting burden caused by the requirement to assemble or create the information necessary to comply with the 1986 Act. As an example, many retailers found that the Act required them to conduct a survey to determine what percentage of buyers' time was actually spent buying merchandise and by extension, what portion of their salaries would be capitalizable.

Many retailers had expensed such costs for both book and tax purposes prior to the 1986 Act. As a result, these retailers were faced with a dilemma; should they continue with their previous financial reporting practices and maintain separate inventory records for tax purposes or capitalize the required costs for both book and tax purposes? One benefit of capitalizing additional costs for book purposes is that earnings (already higher for tax purposes with the consequent tax implications noted above) would be increased. It should be noted, however, that not all costs capitalizable for tax purpose would be capitalizable for book purposes. Generally accepted accounting principles (GAAP) would preclude capitalization of general and administrative costs as well as the excess of accelerated (tax) depreciation over the straight-line calculations generally used for book purposes.

EXHIBIT 20.9 Report of Markon and Its Disposition
(Reconciliation Between Markon Provided and Total Operating Income)

	Markon	Markon Percentages	Dollar Amounts of Items	
			Cost	Retail
Provided:				
Markon in inventory, beginning of period	$175,000	35.00	$ 325,000	$ 500,000
Markon in current purchases	562,500	37.50	937,500	1,500,000
Markups less cancelations	10,000			10,000
Total provided	$747,500	37.19	$1,262,500	$2,010,000
Available for future:				
Markon in inventory, close of period	223,140	37.19	376,860	600,000
			$ 885,640	$1,410,000
		Percentage Used to Total Markon		
Total used	$524,360	70.15		

237

EXHIBIT 20.10 Report of Markon and Its Disposition
(Reconciliation Between Markon Provided and Total Operating Income)

		Percentages of Total Markon Used	Percentages on Sales
Total markon used	$524,360	100.00%	40.34
Lost:			
Markdowns, less cancelations	$ 70,000	13.25	5.39
Sales discounts	15,000	2.86	1.15
Shortages	30,000	5.72	2.31
Total reductions	$115,000	21.93	8.85
Earned:			
Gross margin before discounts	409,360	78.07	31.49
Discounts earned	40,000		3.08
Gross margin after discounts	$449,360		34.57
Expended: Operating expenses	400,000	76.28	30.77
Realized:			
Operating income:		1.79%	
From markon	9,360		.72
From discounts earned	40,000		3.08
	$ 49,360		3.80

Note: Deductions at retail amount to $1,415,000, of which retail reductions are $115,000, leaving $1,300,000 for sales.

EXHIBIT 20.11   Report of Markon and Its Disposition
(Reconciliation Between Markon Provided and Total Operating Income)

	Markon	Markon Percentages
Provided:		
Markon in inventory, beginning of period	$175,000	35.00
Markon in current purchases	562,500	37.50
Markups, less cancelations	10,000	
Total provided	$747,500	37.19
Available for future:		
Markon in inventory, end of period	223,140	37.19
		Percentages Used to Total Markon
Total used	$524,360	70.15
		Percentages Used to Total Markon
Total markon used	$524,360	100.00
Lost:		
Markdowns, less cancelations	70,000	13.35
Sales discounts	15,000	1.86
Shortages	30,000	5.72
Total reductions	$115,000	
	115,000	21.93
Earned: Gross margin before discounts	$409,360	78.07
Expended: Operating expenses	400,000	76.28
Realized: Operating income before discounts earned	9,360	1.79
Discounts earned	40,000	
Operating income	$ 49,360	

Another important factor influencing retailers' choices is industry practice. As more retailers choose to capitalize additional costs for book purposes, it becomes more likely that others will also change. Subsequent to the introduction of the 1986 Act, a number of retailers have chosen to change their method of inventory accounting for book purposes as well. This change is appropriate if it is judged to be a preferable accounting method, that is, a better matching of revenues and related expenses.

If the impact of the change in accounting for inventory is material, then the retailer's financial statements must comply with the disclosure requirements of Accounting Principles Board (APB) Opinion 20, Accounting Changes. These disclosure requirements include a description of the change in accounting principle, reflection of a cumulative effect of the change in the current period's income statement and pro forma disclosure of earnings (for all income statements presented) as if the change was applied retroactively.

CHAPTER TWENTY-ONE

LIFO

Retail and distribution companies have historically used a number of methods in valuing their inventories. These methods have included the gross profit, retail, and dollar value LIFO (last-in, first-out) methods.

During the 1970s and early 1980s, the dollar value LIFO methods became increasingly popular as a way to more closely match current costs with current revenues during periods of inflation, as well as reducing pretax income and corresponding taxes payable. These real economic benefits largely overshadow the perceived disadvantages to utilizing LIFO.

ADVANTAGES AND DISADVANTAGES OF LIFO

The single largest advantage to LIFO is the reduction in income taxes payable, resulting from matching last-in, first-out (current) costs to revenues when measuring a company's pretax earnings. This beneficial effect generally is created during periods of inflation and increasing inventory levels. For retailers utilizing the retail dollar value LIFO method, such effect can also be created depending on the amount of promotional activity and the nature of the business of a retailer.

Further advantages of the LIFO methods include improved cash flow and lower borrowings due to the decrease in income taxes payable, a heightened focus by management of the effect inflation can have on merchandise pricing and related merchandising decisions, state and local tax savings due to the lower LIFO inventory valuation, a more proper income statement, recognition of operating results based upon current merchandise costs, and comparability of financial results with other retailers in the industry.

The disadvantages of LIFO include the necessity of keeping a separate accounting system to calculate LIFO on an interim and year-end basis, this system will rarely be used to measure retail stock ledger profitability information (initial markon, maintained markon, gross profit); the requirement that inventory be stated at cost for tax reporting purposes compared to the lower of cost or market for financial reporting purposes, thereby creating differences in book and taxable income; increased difficulty in estimating interim and year-end operating results; and potential third party concerns (debtholders and shareholders), as a result of lower inventories and gross profit reported under the LIFO method.

Factors to Consider

In evaluating either the adoption or termination of LIFO, general economic factors, specific business factors, and tax factors need to be considered.

General economic factors to be evaluated are the expectation of inflation and the rate of inflation, interest rates and the expectation of industry expansion. Inflation increases in interest rates and increased expansion will support the need to seriously consider the LIFO inventory valuation method.

Specific business factors to be considered include a retailer's geographic expansion plans, especially as they relate to increasing levels of inventory; merchandising plans, including changes or broadening of the types of merchandise sold and changes in merchandising philosophy; and industry expansion, including specialty retailing, selling through catalogs, and any anticipated changes from current business operations. In addition, a retailer's working capital needs, including its borrowing requirements, as well as its financial reporting considerations, especially the potential depressing impact that LIFO will have on reported earnings must be weighed.

Tax factors to be evaluated include the requirement that companies utilizing the LIFO method for tax reporting must also use the LIFO method for financial reporting. In the year of adoption of LIFO, the prior year base layer for LIFO must be restated to adjust for LIFO cost. Such restatement may require amending the prior year's tax return and increasing the prior year's tax liability. Subsequent changes to LIFO, including termination of LIFO, require Internal Revenue Service approval prior to the change.

A company evaluating either the adoption or termination of LIFO must specifically weigh the above advantages and disadvantages.

DOLLAR VALUE LIFO

Dollar value LIFO is distinguished by the fact that all LIFO activity is recorded in dollars rather than in units. Dollar value LIFO calculations are performed based upon dollars in a defined LIFO pool.

The four methods used to calculate individual dollar value pools are the retail dollar value LIFO method, the double extension dollar value LIFO method, the index dollar value LIFO method and the link chain dollar value LIFO method.

The retail LIFO method measures inflation or deflation, as well as changes in inventory levels in retail dollars. Once retail dollar increments or decrements are determined, the LIFO cost is calculated using a cost multiple.

The double extension, index and link chain methods all measure inflation or deflation and inventory level changes at cost.

IMPLEMENTATION OF LIFO

A number of steps must be accomplished in implementing LIFO. These steps will vary depending upon whether the company previously valued its inventory utilizing the first-in, first-out (FIFO) methods or the retail method. The steps include:

- Determining what portion of inventory will be changed to LIFO.
- Determining the number of LIFO inventory pools.
- Determining the method of LIFO valuation.
- Determining which indices will be used in calculating LIFO, including which indices will be used to value current year's increments.
- Identifying the data requirements and sources utilized in the LIFO calculation.

WHAT PORTION OF INVENTORY WILL BE CHANGED TO LIFO

The decision to change to the LIFO method of valuation results from careful consideration of the advantages and disadvantages previously described in this chapter. If a retailer determines that it will change its inventory valuation method from FIFO to LIFO, there is an implicit presumption that the change will be for all its inventory, unless the retailer can demonstrate valid business reasons for not fully adopting LIFO.

The AICPA LIFO Issues Paper "Identification and Discussion of Certain Financial Accounting and Reporting Issues Concerning LIFO Inventories," File 317S, November 30, 1984, Accounting Standards Division, AICPA identified a number of business reasons, including the anticipation of significant price changes affecting only certain portions of the inventory, fluctuating inventory levels, impracticality due to cost or manpower considerations of total immediate adoption, or certain statutory reporting requirements for foreign subsidiaries for not fully adopting LIFO. In addition, certain divisions of a company or its inventory components may differ significantly, which dictate that different inventory methods be required.

For retailers, the decision to partially adopt LIFO may be based upon either the type of merchandise sold by the retailer or the type of retail operation. For department stores, the decision to adopt LIFO may be different for soft goods than for hard goods, depending on inventory levels or price fluctuations. For specialty retailers, certain divisions might adopt LIFO while other different divisions would more appropriately value their inventories utilizing FIFO or the retail method.

THE NUMBER OF LIFO POOLS

Once the determination has been made as to what portion of a retailer's inventory will adopt LIFO, the inventory must be grouped into pools for inventory valuation. In practice, factors used to establish pools include business divisions, economic activities, separate legal entities, substantially similar inventory items or classes of merchandise or selected types of classes of goods. The AICPA LIFO Issues Paper concluded that a valid business reason must exist for establishing inventory pools rather than just the existence of a separate legal entity or location.

The determination of how many LIFO pools will be utilized is closely linked with how the retailer monitors its inventory. As a general rule, most retailers monitor inventory at a much more detailed level (SKU, class, fine department) than the LIFO pool in which such inventory will be aggregated. As a result, a company must determine how and into what pools such detail inventory will be aggregated.

For department stores, discount department stores and specialty stores, a number of companies have utilized the 27 pools currently identified by the Bureau of Labor Statistics (BLS). The pools include a number of soft goods pools, durable goods pools, a composite soft goods pool, a composite durable goods pool, and a store total pool, as outlined in Exhibit 21.1. Other retailers, whose merchandise is not consistent with the BLS pool groupings, have developed their own pools. The consistent theme is to identify pools which will properly reflect similar groupings of merchandise for inventory valuation purposes.

LIFO VALUATION METHODS

As previously discussed, there are several valuation methods that can be utilized as part of the dollar-value LIFO method. Three of the methods—double extension, index, and link chain—are used by retailers whose accounting records record and monitor inventory movement at its cost. These methods will be described in greater detail later in this chapter.

The fourth method—retail LIFO—is used by retailers who monitor inventories at their retail values.

RETAIL LIFO

Development of Index

Companies which adopt the retail LIFO method of inventory valuation measure inflation or deflation at retail prices rather than costs of such merchandise.

EXHIBIT 21.1   Bureau of Labor Statistics Inventory Pools

1. Piece Goods
2. Domestics and Draperies
3. Women's and Children's Shoes
4. Men's Shoes
5. Infants' Wear
6. Women's Underwear
7. Women's and Girls' Hosiery
8. Women's and Girls' Accessories
9. Women's Outerwear and Girls' Wear
10. Men's Clothing
11. Men's Furnishings
12. Boys' Clothing and Furnishings
13. Jewelry
14. Notions
15. Toilet Articles and Drugs
16. Furniture and Bedding
17. Floor Coverings
18. Housewares
19. Major Appliances
20. Radio and Television
21. Recreation and Education
22. Home Improvements
23. Automotive Accessories

1–15: Soft Goods
16–20: Durable Goods
21–23: Miscellaneous Goods

Store Total

As a result, once the number of pools to be utilized has been identified, an index methodology must be developed to measure inflation or deflation within each pool.

For those retailers whose mix of merchandise matches the pools established by the Bureau of Labor Statistics, indices are published monthly which reflect the cumulative retail price index for the 27 BLS department store inventory pools. Use of such indexes, eliminates the time consuming need to sample merchandise items in each pool to internally calculate such an index.

Certain retailers may wish to utilize certain of the BLS pool indices for some of their pools of inventory and develop internal indices for those pools whose merchandise mix is not comparable.

In all cases, the retailer must be able to demonstrate that the internal or external index used is representative of the inflation or deflation experienced by its respective inventory pool.

Adjustments to Cost Multiple

The retail LIFO cost multiple, used to reduce LIFO layers expressed in retail dollars to cost, must include markdowns. For most retailers who value their inventory internally using the retail method, the retail method cost multiple must be recomputed to include markdowns.

The types of markdowns to be included are markdowns taken to reflect a permanent impairment in the value of the inventory. In practice, many retailers include markdowns taken related to items temporarily on sale in calculating the retail LIFO cost multiple. These markdowns, however, are not reflective of retail merchandise in ending inventory and are more properly excluded from the cost multiple calculation.

In the year that retail LIFO is adopted, the prior year cost multiple must be restated to include markdowns as part of the recalculation of the base year opening inventory. In subsequent years, the retail method cost multiple must be adjusted as part of the calculation of such years' retail LIFO layers.

Aggregation of Inventory into Pools

Once the number and types of pools have been identified, a company must determine if such pools will be separately applied on a location-by-location basis, or if locations will be aggregated on either a legal entity (corporation) basis or a corporate-wise basis.

In practice, a number of retailers have separate pools for each location and perform separate LIFO computations for each location. Other retailers aggregate inventory for a number of locations into separate pools for each legal entity. This practice has been historically followed in an attempt to conform the LIFO calculation for tax return purposes, which is performed on a corporation-by-corporation basis, with the LIFO calculation for financial reporting purposes.

The benefit in aggregating inventory by corporation is to mitigate the fluctuations in inventory levels and LIFO liquidations that are caused by the opening and closing of individual store locations.

Retail LIFO Computation

In the year a company changes or adopts the retail LIFO inventory valuation method, two separate calculations must be made. First, the base year LIFO layer must be established. Second, the current year computation must be performed.

In subsequent years, the current year computation is performed. This computation may result in an additional current year LIFO layer or may reduce prior year(s) and the base year's LIFO layer.

Establishing the Base Year Layer

In the case of a retailer previously valuing its inventory using FIFO, the retailer's previous year end inventory amount becomes the base year amount for subsequent dollar value LIFO calculations. If the retailer uses the retail method, the previous year-end inventory must be adjusted to cost. This is accomplished by recomputing the cost multiple used to reduce ending inventory at retail to cost. The recomputation, as outlined in Example 1, requires that beginning of the year inventory and retail markdowns taken on merchandise included in beginning inventory as well as merchandise purchased during the year, be included in deriving the recomputed cost multiple. The net effect of the recomputation will result in higher previous year-end inventory. The recomputed previous year inventory becomes the base year layer amount.

Current Year Computation

In years subsequent to the year retail LIFO is adopted, a separate computation is performed for each pool to determine if a current year increment layer is created or a liquidation of prior year layer(s) instead results.

The key data elements required to calculate the current year retail LIFO impact are the current year's cost multiple, inventory expressed in retail dollars and the internal or external index to be used to measure inflation or deflation.

Data Requirements

The current year's cost multiple, for retail LIFO purposes, must include markdowns. For retailers who value their inventory internally utilizing the retail method, certain adjustments to the retail method cost multiple must be made. In contrast with the year retail LIFO is adopted, only current year purchases and markdowns taken related to current year purchases are included in the current year LIFO cost multiple computation. The types of markdowns to be included are those taken on current year purchases due to a permanent impairment in the value of such purchases. Many retailers do not differentiate markdowns between those taken on beginning of the year inventory versus those taken on current year purchases. As a result, a proportional allocation is computed to determine what percentage of markdowns relate to current year purchases. Exhibit 21.2 demonstrates the recomputation of a retail method cost multiple to the retail LIFO cost multiple.

EXHIBIT 21.2   Recomputation of Previous Year-End Inventory When Implementing Retail LIFO for Pool X

Assumptions

1. Year ending 19X0 inventory in retail dollars	$200,000
2. 19X0 Markdowns	10,000

Calculation of Revised Cost Multiple for Pool X

	Retail Method			Retail LIFO		
	Cost	Retail	Cost Multiple	Cost	Retail	Cost Multiple
Beg. Inventory	$ 96,000	$160,000		$ 96,000	$160,000	
19X0 Purchases	302,500	500,000		302,500	500,000	
19X0 Markups		5,000			5,000	
19X0 Markdowns					(10,000)	
Total Available	$398,500	$665,000	59.92%	$398,500	$655,000	60.84%

Calculation of Revised Ending Inventory for Pool X

	Retail Method	Retail LIFO
Inventory in Retail Dollars	$200,000	$200,000
Cost Multiple	59.92%	60.84%
Ending Inventory	$119,840	$121,680

Difference, Increase in Ending Inventory = $1,840

Note: 19X1 = Current Year
19X0 = Previous Year

In computing the retail LIFO cost of inventory for each pool, costs multiples, retail inventory and indices must be pool specific. The retail LIFO cost multiple is calculated for a specific pool by aggregating the appropriate retail activity (purchases, markups, markdowns, discounts, freight, distribution costs, etc.) into the specific pool and computing the LIFO cost multiple as discussed in Exhibit 21.3.

In addition, inventory amounts, generally expressed at an SKU, class or fine department level must be aggregated into total inventory for each pool, depending upon the pools identified by the retailer, either those consistent with the BLS pool groupings or pool groupings internally developed.

Finally, a cumulative inflation index and an increment index must be computed. These indexes are used to determine whether or not a current year increment or decrement exists, and if an increment exists, to value the increment at current year retail amounts. The cumulative inflation index is computed by multiplying the prior year end cumulative index by the current year's annual inflation index. The cumulative increment index used in valuing the current year increment is computed by multiplying the prior year cumulative inflation index by the current year's increment inflation index, measured in either beginning of the year, average for the year or

EXHIBIT 21.3   Recomputation of Retail Method Cost Multiple to Retail LIFO Cost Multiple for Pool X

Assumptions

1. 19X1 Markdowns $15,000

Calculation of Retail LIFO Cost Multiple

	Retail Method			Retail LIFO		
	Cost	Retail	Cost Multiple	Cost	Retail	Cost Multiple
Beg. Inventory	$119,840	$200,000				
19X1 Purchases	310,000	515,000		$310,000	$515,000	
19X1 Markups		6,000			4,322*	
19X1 Markdowns					(10,804)*	
Total Available	$429,840	$721,000	59.62%	$310,000	$508,518	60.96%

The retail LIFO cost multiple is 60.96%, computed by dividing total available cost of $310,000 by total available retail of $508,518.

*The portion of 19X1 markups and markdowns included in the computation is based upon the ratio of 19X1 purchases to 19X1 purchases plus beginning inventory ($515,000 divided by ($200,000 + $515,000)) or 72%:

72% of $6,000 in Markups = $ 4,322
72% of $15,000 in Markdowns = $10,804

EXHIBIT 21.4   Computation of Cumulative Inflation Index and Increment Index

Assumptions

1. 19X0 Cumulative Inflation Index	100.00%
2. 19X1 Annual (Full Year) Inflation	3.20%
3. 19X1 Beginning of the Year (Earliest Purchases) Inflation	0.60%
4. 19X1 Average of the Year Inflation	1.60%

Calculation of Cumulative Inflation Index

The 19X1 cumulative inflation index is calculated as the 19X0 cumulative inflation index multiplied by the 19X1 annual inflation:

$$100.00\% \times 1.032 = 103.20\%$$

Calculation of Cumulative Increment Index

The 19X1 increment index is calculated as the 19X0 cumulative inflation index multiplied by either:

Beginning of Year Purchases: $100.00\% \times 1.006 = 100.60\%$
Average Purchases: $100.00\% \times 1.016 = 101.60\%$
End of Year Purchases: $100.00\% \times 1.032 = 103.20\%$

Note: 19X0 = Prior Year
19X1 = Current Year

end of the year prices. The current year's increment inflation index should be representative of the inflation in current year purchases of merchandise which are still on hand at year-end. In practice, most retailers use the annual inflation index as a proxy for inflation in current year purchases of merchandise. Exhibit 21.4 demonstrates the calculation of the cumulative inflation index and the differences that result in the increment index, depending upon how the current year inflation is measured.

LIFO Cost Calculation

Year-end retail LIFO inventory is computed in a series of four steps:

1. Eliminating the inflation in year-end retail inventory by dividing year-end retail inventory by the cumulative inflation index. This step converts current year retail inventory to its equivalent base year retail value.

2. Comparing the current year amount in base year retail value to the corresponding prior year amount also in base year retail value. If current year exceeds prior year, an increment exists; if prior year exceeds current year, a decrement exists.

3. Converting (in the case of an increment) the increment to its LIFO cost by restoring the increment to its current year value by multiplying by the increment index and then reducing the current year retail value to cost by multiplying the current year retail LIFO cost multiple.

4. Determining (in the case of a decrement) how many of the layers established in prior years have been liquidated. This is accomplished by comparing the amount of the decrement expressed in base year retail value to the amount of the most recent increment layer, also expressed in base retail value. If the most recent increment layer exceeds the amount of the decrement, the amount of the decrement is subtracted from the increment and a revised increment layer is recomputed as described in step 3. If the decrement exceeds the most recent increment layer, the entire most recent increment layer is eliminated by subtracting it from the decrement. The revised amount of the decrement is then compared to the next most recent increment layer to see how much further the layer(s) established in prior years must be liquidated as described as above in step 4.

Exhibits 21.5 and 21.6 demonstrate the calculation of a current year increment and decrement and resulting LIFO cost.

EXHIBIT 21.5   Calculation of Current Year LIFO Increment and Corresponding LIFO Cost for Pool X

Assumptions

1. Fiscal 19X0 base year:

Cumulative Inflation Index	100.00%
Cumulative Increment Index	100.00%
Retail Inventory Amount	$200,000
Retail LIFO Cost Multiple	60.84%

2. Fiscal 19X1:

Cumulative Inflation Index	103.20%
Cumulative Increment Index	103.20%
Retail Inventory Amount	250,000
Retail LIFO Cost Multiple	60.96%

EXHIBIT 21.5   *(Continued)*

Calculation of 19X1 Retail LIFO Inventory Cost

a. Reduce 19X1 retail inventory amount to equivalent base year retail value:

$$\$250,000 \text{ divided by } 103.20\% = \$242,248$$

b. Compare current year amount expressed in base year retail value to corresponding prior year in base year retail value:

19X1 retail inventory in base year retail value	$242,248
19X0 retail inventory in base year retail value	200,000
19X1 increment in base year retail value	$ 42,248

c. Convert the 19X1 increment to its LIFO cost by multiplying the 19X1 increment in base year retail value by the cumulative increment index and then by the 19X1 retail LIFO cost multiple.

$$\$42,248 \times 103.20\% \times 60.96\% = \$26,579$$

Recap of Year-End 19X1 Retail LIFO Inventory Cost

Layer	Retail Inventory	Cumulative Inflation Index	Retail Inventory in Base Year Value	Increment
19X0	$200,000	100.00%	$200,000	$200,000
19X1	250,000	103.20%	242,248	42,248

Cumulative Increment Index	Increment in Current Year Retail Value	LIFO Cost Multiple	LIFO Cost
100.00%	$200,000	60.84%	$121,680
103.20%	43,600	60.96%	26,579
Ending Retail LIFO Cost Inventory			$148,259

Note: 19X0 = Prior Year
  19X1 = Current Year

EXHIBIT 21.6   Calculation of Current Year LIFO Decrement and Corresponding LIFO Cost for Pool X

Assumptions

1. Fiscal 19X0 base year:

Cumulative Inflation Index	100.00%
Cumulative Increment Index	100.00%
Retail Inventory Amount	$200,000
Retail LIFO Cost Multiple	60.84%

2. Fiscal 19X1

Cumulative Inflation Index	103.20%
Cumulative Increment Index	103.20%
Retail Inventory Amount	202,000
Retail LIFO Cost Multiple	60.96%

Calculation of 19X1 Retail LIFO Cost

a. Reduce 19X1 retail inventory amount to equivalent base year retail value:

$$\$202,000 \text{ divided by } 103.20\% = \$195,736$$

b. Compare current year amount expressed in base year retail value to corresponding prior year in base year retail value:

19X1 retail inventory in base year retail value	$195,736
19X0 retail inventory in base year retail value	200,000
19X1 decrement in base year retail value	($ 4,264)

c. Subtract the amount of the 19X1 decrement from the most recent (19X0) increment layer:

19X0 increment in base year retail value	$200,000
19X1 decrement in base year retail value	(4,264)
Revised 19X0 increment in base year retail value	$195,736

d. Convert the revised 19X0 increment to its LIFO cost by multiplying the 19X0 increment in base year retail value by the cumulative 19X0 increment index and then by the 19X0 retail LIFO cost multiple:

$$195,736 \times 100.00\% \times 60.84\% = \$119,086$$

EXHIBIT 21.6 *(Continued)*

Recap of Year-End 19X1 Retail LIFO Inventory Cost

Layer	Retail Inventory	Cumulative Inflation Index	Retail Inventory in Base Year Value	Increment
19X0	$200,000	100.00%	$200,000	$195,736
19X1	202,000	103.20%	195,736	

Cumulative Increment Index	Increment in Current Year Retail Value	LIFO Cost Multiple	LIFO Cost
100.00%	$195,736	60.84%	$119,086

Ending Retail LIFO Cost Inventory	$119,086

Note: 19X0 = Prior Year
19X1 = Current Year

FINANCIAL REPORTING

Interim Reporting

As previously noted, for internal reporting purposes, most retailers monitor sales results, inventory levels and profitability using the retail method. The retail LIFO calculation is generally performed only at year-end. For companies subject to interim reporting requirements—to the SEC and shareholders for publicly owned companies or debtholders—special problems arise.

Inventory levels usually fluctuate during the year, depending upon the seasonal nature of the business. As a result, a retailer might experience a liquidation of LIFO layers on an interim basis due to sell off merchandise inventory. Oftentimes, the merchandise will be replenished and, in fact, result in an incremental current year LIFO layer at year-end. Conversely, a retailer might experience a build up of inventory on an interim basis, thereby creating an incremental current year LIFO layer. By year-end, if inventory levels decline sufficiently, a liquidation of LIFO layers would result.

Accounting Principles Board Opinion No. 28, *Interim Financial Reporting,* paragraph 14 (b) provides that "companies that use the LIFO method many encounter a liquidation of base period inventories at an interim date that is expected to be replaced by the end of the annual period. In such cases, the inventory at the interim reporting date should not give effect to the LIFO liquidation." Conversely, increments resulting at interim periods should not be recorded if liquidation of such layers are expected by year-end. In determining the interim LIFO charge or credit to be reflected in the financial statements, either a specific calculation may be performed on a year to date basis or an estimate of the full year LIFO effect may be calculated and prorated to the interim financial results. In practice, most retailers perform a calculation which estimates the annual LIFO charge or credit and prorate the amount to interim periods, usually based upon the relationship of interim sales to annual sales.

Interim Reporting in the Year of LIFO Adoption

The change to the LIFO method of valuing inventory is a change in accounting principle. In accordance with Accounting Principle Board Opinion No. 20, *Accounting Changes,* paragraph 20, the cumulative effect of the change in principle must be computed as of the beginning of the year. The effect, net of applicable income taxes, is reported as a separate item in the year to date income statement. Financial statements of the current and prior interim periods must be adjusted to reflect financial results utilizing the new method of valuing inventory.

Disclosure of the nature of the accounting change, the preferability of the new LIFO method and comparable FIFO financial data (the FIFO value of the applicable inventory and the effect on earnings and earnings per store of the change in accounting principle on the current and corresponding prior interim periods) is required in the footnotes to the financial statements.

Annual Reporting

Annual financial statements reflect year-end LIFO inventory based upon the full effect and calculation of ending LIFO inventory. The difference between (1) current year-end FIFO and LIFO inventory amounts (the current year-end cumulative LIFO reserve) and (2) prior year-end FIFO and LIFO inventory amounts (the prior year-end cumulative LIFO reserve) is the LIFO charge or credit to be recorded in the income statement.

For publicly held retailers, the full year LIFO charge or credit may be significantly different from the estimated effect recorded during the interim periods. This difference reflects a change in the estimate of the year's LIFO charge or credit which, if significant, must be disclosed as part of the quarterly financial results disclosed in the retailer's annual report.

The footnotes to the financial statements of publicly held retailers must include the excess of replacement cost of the inventories over their corresponding LIFO values. Management's Discussion and Analysis of Financial Condition and Results of Operations often will discuss the effect of LIFO and its results from operations, including the amount of LIFO charge or credit and its impact on net earnings and earnings per share. Such disclosures for publicly held retailers should also indicate the preferability of utilizing LIFO.

If the year of reporting is also the year in which the retailer changed to the LIFO method of valuing inventories, the footnotes must make comparable disclosures to those made in the interim footnotes during which the accounting change was made, including the nature of the accounting change, the preferability of the new LIFO method and the effect on earnings of the current and prior period(s) of the accounting change.

As a practical matter, retailers who adopt the retail LIFO method of valuing inventories net the adjustment to the base year layer opening inventory (resulting from adjusting inventory valued using the retail method to cost) with the amount of current year LIFO charge or credit. As a result, no cumulative effect of adopting retail LIFO is reflected in the financial statements.

Tax Reporting

Generally, the LIFO calculation performed for financial reporting purposes is the same calculation as that performed for tax reporting purposes. However, in certain special situations, as discussed later, the LIFO charge or credit may vary for tax reporting purposes.

Tax Reporting in the Initial Year

The change to the LIFO method is an accounting change for tax purposes. The election to change to LIFO does not have to be made during the year, but, rather is reported to the Internal Revenue Service as part of the retailer's filing of its year end tax return for the year in which the change is made.

The process of adopting LIFO for tax purposes closely parallels the process for financial reporting purposes. The retailer must decide the portion of inventory to be valued utilizing LIFO, the number of LIFO pools and the method of LIFO valuation.

The LIFO election process is performed on a corporation by corporation basis. However, if a retailer operates a number of corporations, Internal Revenue Code regulations require that the retailer value similar merchandise in all corporations using the same inventory method, unless a valid business purpose exists for the separate corporations.

In computing the base year opening inventory for tax purposes, IRS regulations require that the prior year-end inventory must be adjusted to cost. As a result, any obsolescence or other reserves that might have existed must be eliminated. The computation for tax purposes is the same as that described under "Establishing the Base Year Layer." The net effect of the recomputation will result in a higher prior year-end inventory, and, as a result, a requirement by the retailer to amend its corporate income tax returns for the prior year. The recomputed amount becomes that base year layer for tax reporting purposes.

Differences in Financial Reporting Versus Tax Reporting

In certain special situations, the annual LIFO charge or credit computed for financial reporting purposes may differ from that computed for tax reporting purposes. The difference may result from different historical base and prior year LIFO layers for financial reporting and tax reporting (Many retailers have acquired other retail businesses. Differences may exist between the fair value of the inventory acquired recorded for financial reporting purposes and the historical tax basis maintained for tax reporting purposes.) or differences in what inventory is valued utilizing LIFO, the number of LIFO pools or the method of LIFO calculation.

The nature of the difference, if significant, should be evaluated as to the need for disclosing the difference in the retailer's financial statements. In addition, the nature of the difference and its expected period of reversal must be evaluated in determining the effect on income tax expense in accordance with Statement of Financial Accounting Standards No. 96, *Accounting for Income Taxes.*

Valuation Reserves

The retail LIFO method is a cost method of valuing inventory. For financial reporting purposes, inventory must be valued at the lower of cost on market. The comparison is generally made on a pool by pool basis between the inventory result computed using the retail method and the inventory result computed using the retail LIFO method.

To the extent the retail method result is less than the retail LIFO result, a valuation reserve should be recorded for financial reporting purposes to reduce retail LIFO cost to market.

The reserve is not currently deductible for tax purposes and its period of reversal must also be evaluated in determining its effect on income tax expense and deferred income taxes reported in the financial statements.

Changes to LIFO

Subsequent to the adoption of LIFO, a retailer may decide to change its method of computing LIFO inventory. Changes retailers might make include the expansion/combination of existing pools, or the method of computation, or the elements comprising the LIFO cost multiple utilized in the computation. These changes must be evaluated for both financial reporting and tax reporting purposes.

For financial reporting purposes, the changes must be evaluated as their preferability, as well as whether or not the change reflects a change in accounting principle (generally the case with a change in pools, indices or cost multiples). If a change in accounting principle, the cumulative effect must be determined and reported in the financial statements just as in the case of when LIFO was first adopted.

For tax reporting purposes, a determination must be made as to whether or not a tax change in the method of valuing inventory has resulted. In the event of a change, the retailer must request permission from the Internal Revenue Service. Depending on the nature or amount of the change, the effect of the change will be ratably reported in taxable income.

Expansion/Combination of Existing Pools

Periodically, a retailer may add new departments or classes of merchandise to its inventory assortment. A determination must be made as to whether this merchandise constitutes a new pool or is similar to an existing pool. In the event of a new pool, the inventory on hand at year-end, converted to its retail LIFO cost becomes the base year layer for the new pool. If the merchandise is similar to an existing pool, the inventory on hand at year-end as well as the current year activity is aggregated with the merchandise and merchandise activity in the existing pool.

Expansion of the number of LIFO pools may be the result of the retailer refining its merchandise information system to separately monitor departments or classes of merchandise that previously had been aggregated with other departments or classes. Conversely, departments or classes that were previously considered as separate—because of changes in merchandise mix or philosophy—may now be more appropriately monitored and valued on a combined basis.

If components of one pool are to be expanded into two or more pools, the expansion is computed by developing a proportional relationship between the amount of inventory to be transferred into the new pool to the total amount of inventory in the existing pool. The percentage relationship is then utilized to split apart all historical layers of the existing pool into the new pools. The expansion of the existing pool into two or more new pools will have no net effect on inventory in total; it will only effect the component pools of inventory. Exhibit 21.7 demonstrates the expansion of one pool into two pools. If two or more separate pools are to be combined, the combination is computed on a layer by layer basis. For each layer, a weighted average cumulative and increment index is computed, as well as a weighted average LIFO cost multiple. Ending retail inventory is combined for each year's layer, and the retail LIFO cost for each year's layer is recomputed on a combined basis. As was the case with an expansion of pools, the combination of two or more pools into a single pool will have no net effect on inventory in total. Exhibit 21.8 demonstrates the combination of two pools into one.

EXHIBIT 21.7   Expansion of Pool X Merchandise into Revised Pool X and Y

Assumptions
1. Pool X historically has included merchandise departments A and B.
2. For the year ended January 31, 19X1, department A comprised 35% of the total inventory in pool X; department B comprised 65%.
3. Fiscal 19X0 and 19X1 inventory for pool X is:

Layer	Retail Inventory	Cumulative Inflation Index	Retail Inventory in Base Year Value	Increment in Base Year Value
19X0	$200,000	100.00%	$200,000	$200,000
19X1	250,000	103.20%	242,248	42,248

Cumulative Increment Index	Increment in Current Year Retail Value	LIFO Cost Multiple	LIFO Cost
100.00%	200,000	60.84%	$121,680
103.20%	43,600	60.96%	26,579
Ending Retail LIFO Cost Inventory			$148,259

Calculation of Expansion of Each Year's Layers

Each layer is apportioned 35% to the revised pool X, 65% to the new pool Y. The only amounts adjusted are the retail inventory amounts:

19X0 Layer
    Pool X retail inventory = 200,000 × 35% or $ 70,000
    Pool Y retail inventory = 200,000 × 65% or $130,000
19X1 Layer
    Pool X retail inventory = 250,000 × 35% or $ 87,500
    Pool Y retail inventory = 250,000 × 65% or $162,500

EXHIBIT 21.7 *(Continued)*

Each year's layer is then recomputed by converting retail inventory to its base year value, recomputing the increment and recalculating the LIFO cost of the layer. The recalculated pool X and Y inventory amounts are as follows:

Pool X

Layer	Retail Inventory	Cumulative Inflation Index	Retail Inventory in Base Year Value	Increment in Base Year Value
19X0	$70,000	100.00%	$70,000	$70,000
19X1	87,500	103.20%	84,787	14,787

Cumulative Increment Index	Increment in Current Year Retail Value	LIFO Cost Multiple	LIFO Cost
100.00%	$70,000	60.84%	$42,588
103.20%	15,260	60.96%	9,302
Ending Retail LIFO Cost Inventory			$51,890

Pool Y

Layer	Retail Inventory	Cumulative Inflation Index	Retail Inventory in Base Year Value	Increment in Base Year Value
19X0	130,000	100.00%	130,000	$130,000
19X1	162,500	103.20%	157,461	27,461

Cumulative Increment Index	Increment in Current Year Retail Value	LIFO Cost Multiple	LIFO Cost
100.00%	$130,00	60.84%	$79,092
103.20%	28,340	60.96%	17,276
Ending Retail LIFO Cost Inventory			$96,368

Note: 19X0 = Prior Year
19X1 = Current Year

EXHIBIT 21.8   Combination of Pool W and Y into Pool Z

Assumptions

1. Fiscal 19X0 and 19X1 inventory information for pool W is:

Layer	Retail Inventory	Cumulative Inflation Index	Retail Inventory in Base Year Value	Increment in Base Year Value
19X0	$150,000	100.00%	$150,000	$150,000
19X1	180,000	105.10%	171,265	21,265

Cumulative Increment Index	Increment in Current Year Retail Value	LIFO Cost Multiple	LIFO Cost
100.00%	$150,000	62.10%	$ 93,150
105.10%	22,350	63.00%	14,081
Ending Retail LIFO Cost Inventory			$107,231

2. Fiscal 19X0 and 19X1 inventory information for pool Y is:

Layer	Retail Inventory	Cumulative Inflation Index	Retail Inventory in Base Year Value	Increment in Base Year Value
19X0	$130,000	100.00%	$130,000	$130,000
19X1	162,500	103.20%	157,461	27,461

Cumulative Increment Index	Increment in Current Year Retail Value	LIFO Cost Multiple	LIFO Cost
100.00%	$130,000	60.84%	$ 79,092
103.20%	28,340	60.96%	17,276
Ending Retail LIFO Cost Inventory			$ 96,368

Calculation of Combination Indices and Cost Multiples

a. Recompute the combined cumulative inflation index for each year's layer by dividing the sum of the pools' retail inventory by the sum of the pools' retail inventory in base year value.

$$\frac{\text{19X0 Combined}}{\text{Cumulative Inflation Index}} = \frac{150,000 + 130,000}{150,000 + 130,000} \quad \text{or} \quad 100.00\%$$

$$\frac{\text{19X1 Combined}}{\text{Cumulative Inflation Index}} = \frac{180,000 + 162,500}{171,265 + 157,461} \quad \text{or} \quad 104.19\%$$

EXHIBIT 21.8 *(Continued)*

b. Recompute the combined cumulative increment index for each year's layer by dividing the sum of the pools' increment in current year retail value by the sum of the pools' increment in base year value.

$$\text{19X0 Combined Cumulative Increment Index} = \frac{150,000 + 130,000}{150,000 + 130,000} \quad \text{or} \quad 100.00\%$$

$$\text{19X1 Combined Cumulative Increment Index} = \frac{22,350 + 28,340}{21,265 + 27,461} \quad \text{or} \quad 104.03\%$$

c. Recompute the combined LIFO cost multiple for each year's layer by dividing the sum of the pools' LIFO cost by the sum of the pools' increment in current year retail value.

$$\text{19X0 Combined LIFO Cost Multiple} = \frac{93,150 + 79,092}{150,000 + 130,000} \quad \text{or} \quad 61.515\%$$

$$\text{19X1 Combined LIFO Cost Multiple} = \frac{14,080 + 17,276}{22,350 + 28,340} \quad \text{or} \quad 61.858\%$$

Each year's combined layer is then recomputed by taking the sum of the pools' ending retail inventory and, using the combined cumulative inflation index, combined cumulative increment index, and combined LIFO cost multiple; converting retail inventory to its base year value, recomputing the increment and recalculating the LIFO cost of the layer. The combined pool Z inventory amounts are as follows:

Layer	Retail Inventory	Cumulative Inflation Index*	Retail Inventory in Base Year Value	Increment in Base Year Value
19X0	$280,000	100.00%	$280,000	$280,000
19X1	342,500	104.19%	328,726	48,726

Cumulative Increment Index*	Increment in Current Year Retail Value	LIFO Cost Multiple*	LIFO Cost
100.00%	$280,000	61.515%	$172,242
104.03%	50,690	61.858%	31,356
Ending Retail LIFO Cost Inventory			$203,598

*As computed on a combined basis.

Note: 19X0 = Prior Year
19X1 = Current Year

Changes in Determination of Indices or Cost Multiple

If a change is made in the determination of the indices used to measure inflation or in the elements comprising the LIFO cost multiple, the change must be included in all LIFO layers and the LIFO cost of each layer. These types of changes will result in a change in the inventory from the inventory value prior to the change. Exhibit 21.9 demonstrates the effect of a change in the LIFO cost multiple on LIFO inventory.

EXHIBIT 21.9   Change in LIFO Cost Multiple

Assumptions

1. A change is made in the determination of the LIFO cost multiple by excluding promotional markdowns from the computation of the LIFO cost multiple. Previously, promotional markdowns were included in the computation. The effect on the LIFO cost multiple is:

LIFO Cost Multiple of Promotional Markdowns

	Included	Excluded
19X0	61.515%	60.50%
19X1	61.858%	60.80%

2. Assume the following inventory information from pool Z:

Layer	Retail Inventory	Cumulative Inflation Index	Retail Inventory in Base Year Value	Increment in Base Year Value
19X0	$280,000	100.00%	$280,000	$280,000
19X1	342,500	104.19%	328,726	48,276

Cumulative Increment Index	Increment in Current Year Retail Value	LIFO Cost Multiple	LIFO Cost
100.00%	$280,000	61.515%	$172,242
104.03%	50,690	61.858%	31,356
Ending Retail LIFO Cost Inventory			$203,598

EXHIBIT 21.9 *(Continued)*

Calculation

The LIFO cost for each year's layer is recomputed using the revised cost multiple:

19X0 LIFO Cost = 280,000 × 60.50% or 169,400
19X1 LIFO Cost = 50,690 × 60.80% or 30,820

Inventory for pool Z after the change in the determination of the cost multiple would be as follows:

Layer	Retail Inventory	Cumulative Inflation Index	Retail Inventory in Base Year Value	Increment in Base Year Value
19X0	$280,000	100.00%	$280,000	$280,000
19X1	342,500	104.19%	328,726	48,276

Cumulative Increment Index	Increment in Current Year Retail Value	LIFO Cost Multiple	LIFO Cost
100.00%	$280,000	60.50%	$169,400
104.03%	50,690	60.80%	30,820
Ending Retail LIFO Cost Inventory			$200,220

The net effect of the change is to reduce LIFO inventory by $3,378.

Note: 19X0 = Prior Year
19X1 = Current Year

Termination of LIFO

Occasionally, a retailer may decide to convert from the LIFO method of inventory valuation to the retail method or some other inventory method. As was the case in a change from some other method of valuing inventory to the LIFO method, the change back from the LIFO method to come other method must be evaluated for both financial and tax reporting purposes.

For financial reporting purposes, the reason for the change and its preferability for generally accepted accounting principles must be considered. If the change is made, Accounting Principles Board Opinion No. 20, *Accounting Changes,* paragraph 27, requires that prior years' financial statements be restated to reflect the change from LIFO to the new inventory valuation method. The nature of the change, its preferability and its impact on earnings and earnings per share for current and prior years must be disclosed in the footnotes to the financial statements.

For tax reporting purposes, the change is considered a change in accounting for inventory which requires permission from the Internal Revenue Service. The effect of the change will be ratably reported in taxable income. If a retailer elects to terminate its LIFO election, depending upon the amount of time the retailer had utilized LIFO, the retailer may be precluded from re-adopting LIFO for a period of years.

OTHER DOLLAR VALUE LIFO METHODS

The other non-retail dollar value LIFO methods used to value inventory are the double extension, index and link chain methods. The primary difference between the retail LIFO method and the other non-retail dollar value LIFO method is that the non-retail methods measure inflation or deflation and compute inventory layers at cost.

Historically, the double extension method was first developed as a means of computing LIFO inventories. The double extension method requires that, for each item within each pool of inventory, the unit cost be identified as of the beginning of the year LIFO is adopted, as well as for each succeeding year. The double extension method becomes increasingly cumbersome as time passes since for every item in the pool as of the end of each year that LIFO is calculated, the cost of each item must be known as of the most recent year-end and, as well as every previous year-end to enable the LIFO calculation to be performed.

Subsequent to the development of the double extension method, the index method was developed. This method eased the requirement of having to know the cost of each item in the pool as of each year-end by providing that only a representative sample of items in the pool be known. This method, however, still required that costs for a representative sample be known for each year since LIFO was adopted.

The link chain method was ultimately developed as a refinement of the index method. This method requires that the cost for a representative sample of items in the pool be known only for the current and most recent previous year-end. This refinement eased the burden of having to monitor the costs of each item in the inventory pool for each year LIFO had been in existence.

The majority of retailers who monitor their inventory at cost, utilize the link chain method to compute their LIFO cost.

Double Extension Method

The double extension method measures inflation or deflation from the first year LIFO was adopted up to the current year by reference to the entire current year pool of inventory (i.e., the number of units and their respective cost on hand at year-end for all items in that pool). The amount of cumulative inflation is computed as the ratio of the items on hand at the current year-end, extended by their current year-end cost, divided by the same items extended by their base year-end cost.

Incremental layers are computed by comparing the current year-end inventory value expressed in base year costs to the most recent prior year-end inventory value expressed in base year costs. If the current year-end exceeds the most previous prior year-end, an incremental current year LIFO layer is created by multiplying the excess by the cumulative inflation ratio. Exhibits 21.10 and 21.11 demonstrate the double extension method computation.

EXHIBIT 21.10 Computation of LIFO Inventory Utilizing the Double Extension Method for Pool X

Assumptions

1. LIFO is adopted as of February 1, 19X0. Pool X as of that date has a total cost value of $350 as follows:

Item	Units	Unit Cost	Total Cost
1	100	$2.00	$200
2	50	3.00	150
			$350

2. At January 31, 19X1, pool X has a total cost value of $600 as follows:

Item	Units	Unit Cost	Total Cost
1	120	$ 2.20	$264
2	60	3.10	186
3	10	15.00	150
			$600

3. The unit cost of item 3 as of February 1, 19X0 was $14.00.

EXHIBIT 21.10 *(Continued)*

Calculation of Year-End 19X1 LIFO Inventory Cost

a. January 31, 19X1 inventory cost must be converted to its base year
cost and compared to most recent prior year to determine if an
incremental 19X1 layer exists:

Item	Units	Base Year Unit Cost	Total Base Year Cost
1	120	$ 2.00	$240
2	60	3.00	180
3	10	14.00	140
January 31, 19X0 inventory at base year cost			$560

January 31, 19X1 inventory at base year cost	$560
February 1, 19X0 inventory at base year cost	350
19X1 increment at base year cost	$210

b. The 19X1 increment must be converted to its current year cost by
multiplying by the cumulative inflation for the pool X:

Item	Units	Base Year Unit Cost	Extended Base Cost	Current Year Unit Cost	Extended Current Cost
1	120	2.00	$240	$ 2.20	$264
2	60	3.00	180	3.10	186
3	10	14.00	140	15.00	150
			$560		$600

$$\frac{\text{Cumulative}}{\text{Inflation}} = \frac{\$600}{\$560} \quad \text{or} \quad 107.14\%$$

$$\frac{\text{19X1 increment}}{\text{at current cost}} = \$210 \times 107.14\% \quad \text{or} \quad \$225$$

Recap of Year-End 19X1 LIFO Inventory Cost

Layer	Base Year Cost	Cumulative Inflation	Current Year Cost
February 1, 19X0 Base	$350	100.00%	$350
January 31, 19X1 Increment	210	107.14	225
			$575

Note: 19X0 = Prior Year
19X1 = Current Year

**EXHIBIT 21.11 Computation of LIFO Inventory Utilizing the
Double Extension Method for Pool X**

Assumptions

1. LIFO is adopted as of February 1, 19X0. Pool X as of that date has a
total cost value of $350 as follows:

Item	Units	Unit Cost	Total Cost
1	100	$2.00	$200
2	50	3.00	150
			$350

2. At January 31, 19X1, pool X has a total cost value of $336 as follows:

Item	Units	Unit Cost	Total Cost
2	60	$ 3.10	$186
3	10	15.00	150
			$336

3. The unit cost of item 3 at February 1, 19X0 was $14.00

Calculation of Year-End 19X1 LIFO Inventory Cost

a. January 31, 19X1 inventory cost must be converted to its base year
cost and compared to the most recent prior year to determine if an
incremental 19X1 layer exists:

Item	Units	Base Unit Cost	Total Base Cost
2	60	$ 2.00	$120
3	10	14.00	140
January 31, 19X1 inventory at base year cost			$260
January 31, 19X1 inventory at base year cost			$260
February 1, 19X0 inventory at base year cost			350
19X1 decrement at base year cost			$(90)
February 1, 19X0 increment at base year cost			$350
19X1 decrement at base year cost			90
Revised February 1, 19X0 increment at base year cost			$260

EXHIBIT 21.11   *(Continued)*

c. The revised February 1, 19X0 increment is converted to its current
year cost by multiplying by the cumulative inflation through
February 1, 19X0 for pool X:

$$\frac{\text{Revised 19X0 increment}}{\text{in current cost}} = \$260 \times 100\% \quad \text{or } \$260$$

Recap of Year-End 19X1 LIFO Inventory Cost

Layer	Base Year Cost	Cumulative Inflation Index	Current Year Cost
February 1, 19X0 Base	$260	100.00%	$260
January 31, 19X1 Increment			
			$260

Note: 19X0 = Prior Year
19X1 = Current Year

Index Method

The index method measures inflation or deflation from the first year LIFO
was adopted up to the current year by reference to a representative sample
of items in the current year-end inventory. The amount of cumulative inflation is computed based upon the representative sample's ratio of items extended at their current year cost divided by the same items extended at their
base year cost.

Incremental layers are computed by comparing the current year-end inventory value expressed in base year costs to the most recent prior year-end
inventory also expressed in base year costs. If the current year-end amount
exceeds the most recent prior year-end amount, an incremental current year
layer is created by multiplying the excess by the cumulative inflation index.
Exhibits 21.12 and 21.13 demonstrate the index method computation.

Link Chain Method

The link chain method is a refinement of the index method. The link chain
method measures inflation or deflation from the first year LIFO was adopted
up to the current year by reference to a representative sample of items in

EXHIBIT 21.12

Assumptions

1. LIFO is adopted as of February 1, 19X0. Pool X as of that date has a total cost value of $400.
2. At January 31, 19X1, pool X has a total cost value of $750.
3. A representative sample of items included in the January 31, 19X1 inventory is:

Item	Units	Base Year Unit Cost	Current Year Unit Cost
4	70	$5.00	$5.50
5	60	5.50	$5.80

Calculation of Year-End 19X1 LIFO Inventory Cost

a. The cumulative inflation index must be computed:

Item	Units	Base Year Unit Cost	Extended Base Cost	Current Year Unit Cost	Extended Current Cost
4	70	$5.00	$350	$5.50	$385
5	60	5.50	330	5.80	348
			$680		$733

$$\frac{\text{Cumulative}}{\text{Inflation Index}} = \frac{\$733}{\$680} \quad \begin{array}{c}\text{or}\\ 107.79\%\end{array}$$

b. The January 31, 19X1 inventory must be converted to its base year cost and compared to the most recent prior year to determine if an incremental 19X1 layer exists:

$$\begin{array}{c}\text{January 31, 19X1 inventory}\\ \text{at base year cost}\end{array} = \frac{\$750}{107.79\%} \quad \text{or } \$696$$

January 31, 19X1 inventory at base year cost	$696
February 1, 19X0 inventory at base year cost	400
19X1 increment at base year cost	$296

c. The 19X1 increment must be converted to current year cost by multiplying by the cumulative inflation index for the pool X:

$$\begin{array}{c}\text{19X1 increment in}\\ \text{current year cost}\end{array} = \$296 \times 107.79\% \quad \begin{array}{c}\text{or}\\ \$319\end{array}$$

EXHIBIT 21.12   *(Continued)*

Recap of Year-End 19X1 LIFO Inventory Cost

Layer	Base Year Cost	Cumulative Inflation Index	Current Year Cost
February 1, 19X0 Base	$400	100.00%	$400
January 31, 19X1 Increment	296	107.79	319
			$719

Note: 19X0 = Prior Year
19X1 = Current Year

**EXHIBIT 21.13   Computation of LIFO Inventory
Utilizing the Index Method for Pool X**

Assumptions

1. LIFO is adopted as of February 1, 19X0. Pool X as of that date has a total cost value of $400.
2. At January 31, 19X1, pool X has a total cost value of $410.
3. The cumulative inflation index through January 31, 19X1, computed based upon a representative sample of items in January 31, 19X1 inventory, is 107.79%.

Calculation of Year-End 19X1 LIFO Inventory Cost

a. The January 31, 19X1 inventory must be converted to its base year cost and compared to the most recent prior year to determine if an incremental 19X1 layer exists:

$$\text{January 31, 19X1 inventory at base year cost} \quad \frac{\$410}{107.79\%} \quad \text{or} \quad \$380$$

January 31, 19X1 inventory at base year cost	380
February 1, 19X0 inventory at base year cost	400
19X1 decrement at base year cost	($ 20)

b. The 19X1 decrement at base year cost is subtracted from the prior year-end increment (i.e., base year layer) at base year cost to compute a revised prior year increment:

February 1, 19X0 increment at base year cost	$400
19X1 decrement at base year cost	20
Revised February 1, 19X0 increment at base year cost	$380

EXHIBIT 21.13 *(Continued)*

c. The revised February 1, 19X0 increment is converted to its current year cost by multiplying by the cumulative inflation index through February 1, 19X0 for pool X:

$$\frac{\text{Revised 19X0 increment}}{\text{in current year cost}} = \$380 \times 100\% \quad \begin{array}{c}\text{or}\\ \$380\end{array}$$

Recap of Year-End 19X1 LIFO Inventory Cost

Layer	Base Year Cost	Cumulative Inflation Index	Current Year Cost
February 1, 19X0 Base	$380	100.00%	$380
January 31, 19X1 Increment			
			$380

Note: 19X0 = Prior Year
19X1 = Current Year

current year-end inventory. The amount of cumulative inflation is computed, however, by multiplying the current year's inflation index by the prior year's cumulative inflation index.

The link chain method is the most advantageous of the three cost methods in that the costs of the representative sample of items in ending inventory need only be known as of the current year-end and immediately prior year-end. The annual inflation index computed as the measure of the current year's inflation is multiplied by the immediately prior year-end's cumulative inflation index to derive the current year's cumulative inflation index. The current year's cumulative inflation index is the measure of the amount of inflation from the time LIFO was adopted to the current year-end.

Incremental layers are computed by comparing the current year-end value expressed in base year costs to the most recent prior year-end inventory also expressed in base year costs. If the current year-end amount exceeds the most recent prior period amount, an incremental current year layer is created by multiplying the excess by the cumulative increment index.

The cumulative increment index is computed by multiplying the prior year's cumulative inflation index by the current year's increment index. The current year's increment index is determined based upon the inflation reflected in either earliest of the year purchases, average for the year purchases or end of year purchases. The type of current year increment index chosen to ultimately value incremental layers should be based upon the inflation inherent in the items on hand in ending inventory. Exhibit 21.14 demonstrates the link chain method computation.

EXHIBIT 21.14   LIFO Inventory
Utilizing the Link Chain Method for Pool X

Assumptions

1. LIFO is adopted as of February 1, 19X0. Pool X as of that date has a total cost value of $400.
2. At January 31, 19X1, inventory in pool X has a total cost value of $680.
3. A representative sample of January 31, 19X1 inventory items has the following costs:

Item	Quantity	January 31, 19X1 Cost	February 1, 19X0 Cost	Average Fiscal 19X1 Cost
1	40	4.40	4.00	4.15
2	30	5.60	5.25	5.40
3	55	2.05	2.00	2.02

4. The average fiscal year cost will be utilized to value any increments.
5. At January 31, 19X2 inventory in pool X has a total cost value of $700, the annual inflation from February 1, 19X0 to January 31, 19X2 was 5.30%, and inflation incurred for the average of fiscal 19X2 was 3.00%.

Calculation of Year-End 19X1 LIFO Inventory Cost

a. The annual inflation index and annual increment index must be computed:

Item	Quantity	January 31, 19X1 Unit Cost	January 31, 19X1 Extended Cost
1	40	$4.40	$176
2	30	5.60	168
3	55	2.05	113
			$457

February 1, 19X0 Unit Cost	February 1, 19X0 Extended Cost	Average 19X1 Unit Cost	Average Extended
4.00	$160	4.15	$166
5.25	158	5.40	162
2.00	110	2.02	111
	$428		$439

$$\text{Annual Inflation Index} = \frac{\text{January 31, 19X1 Extended Cost}}{\text{February 1, 19X0 Extended Cost}} = \frac{\$457}{\$428} \text{ or } 106.78\%$$

$$\text{Annual Increment Index} = \frac{\text{Average 19X1 Extended Cost}}{\text{February 1, 19X0 Extended Cost}} = \frac{\$439}{\$428} \text{ or } 102.57\%$$

EXHIBIT 21.14 *(Continued)*

b. The cumulative inflation index and cumulative increment index must be computed:

$$\frac{\text{Cumulative}}{\text{Inflation Index}} = \frac{\text{Prior Year Cumulative}}{\text{Inflation Index}} \times \frac{\text{Annual}}{\text{Inflation Index}} =$$

100.00 × 106.78% or 106.78%

$$\frac{\text{Cumulative}}{\text{Increment Index}} = \frac{\text{Prior Year Cumulative}}{\text{Inflation Index}} \times \frac{\text{Annual}}{\text{Increment Index}} =$$

100.00 × 102.57% or 102.57%

c. The January 31, 19X1 inventory must be converted to its base year cost and compared to the most recent prior year to determine if an incremetal layer exists:

$$\frac{\text{January 31, 19X1 inventory}}{\text{at base year cost}} = \frac{\$680}{106.78\%} \text{ or } \$637$$

January 31, 19X1 inventory at base year cost	$637
February 1, 19X0 inventory at base year cost	400
19X1 increment at base year cost	$237

d. The 19X1 increment must be converted to current year cost by multiplying by the cumulative increment index for pool X:

$$\frac{\text{19X1 increment in}}{\text{current year cost}} = \$237 \times 102.57\% \text{ or } \$243$$

Recap of Year-End 19X1 LIFO Inventory Cost

Layer	Base Year Cost	Cumulative Inflation Index	Current Year Cost
February 1, 19X0 Base	$300	100.00%	$400
January 31, 19X1 Increment	237	102.57%	243
			$643

Calculation of Year–End 19X2 LIFO Inventory Cost

a. The cumulative inflation index and cumulative increment index must be computed form the annual 19X2 inflation and annual 19X2 average inflation amounts given:

$$\frac{\text{Cumulative}}{\text{Inflation Index}} = \frac{\text{Prior Year Cumulative}}{\text{Inflation Index}} \times \frac{\text{Annual}}{\text{Inflation Index}} =$$

106.78 × 105.30% or 112.44%

EXHIBIT 21.14   *(Continued)*

$$\frac{\text{Cumulative}}{\text{Increment Index}} = \frac{\text{Prior Year Cumulative}}{\text{Inflation Index}} \times \frac{\text{Annual}}{\text{Increment Index}} =$$

106.78 × 103.00% or 109.98%

b. The January 31, 19X2 inventory must be converted to its base year cost and compared to the most recent prior year to determine if an increment exists:

$$\frac{\text{January 31, 19X2 inventory}}{\text{at base year cost}} = \frac{\$700}{112.44\%} \text{ or } \$623$$

January 31, 19X2 inventory at base year cost	$623
January 31, 19X1 inventory at base year cost	637
19X2 decrement at base year cost	$(14)

c. The 19X2 decrement at base year cost is subtracted from the prior year increment at base year cost to compute a revised prior year increment.

19X1 increment at base year cost	$237
19X2 decrement at base year cost	14
Revised January 31, 19X1 increment at base year cost	$223

d. The revised January 31, 19X1 increment is then converted to its current year cost by multiplying by the cumulative increment index through January 31, 19X1:

$$\frac{\text{Revised 19X1 increment}}{\text{in current year cost}} = \$223 \times 102.57\% \text{ or } \$229$$

Recap of Year-End 19X2 LIFO Inventory Cost

Layer	Base Year Cost	Cumulative Inflation Index	Current Year Cost
February 1, 19X0 Base	$400	100.00%	$400
January 31, 19X1 Increment	223	102.57%	229
January 31, 19X2 Increment			
			$629

Note: 19X0 = Prior Year
19X1 = Current Year
19X2 = Following Year

Treatment of New Items in the Pool

The three non-retail dollar value methods require that inflation or deflation be computed based upon changes in unit prices from base year to the current year-end. Depending upon the nature and mix of items in an inventory pool, over time, items will be eliminated from the pool and be replaced by new items.

To prevent distortion in the computation of the inflation and increment indices, if new items are included in the representative sample of current year-end inventory items, the comparable base year cost (or in the case of the link chain method, prior year-end cost) must be estimated or reconstructed.

Simplified LIFO

For tax reporting purposes, the internal revenue code provides that for certain corporations, (with average annual gross receipts over a three year period of less than $5 million) price indices published by the Bureau of Labor Statistics may be used in lieu of computing the inflation or deflation effect by measuring the change in the corporation's unit prices. Use of the government-published indices reduces the time and resources required when computing inflation based upon internal changes in unit prices.

The beneficial effect of using the government-published indices is reduced for corporations with gross receipts in excess of $5 million such that only 80% of change in the published indices may be used as a proxy for measuring inflation or deflation.

For corporations with receipts in excess of $5 million, use of only 80% of the change in the published indices, will probably not be appropriate for financial reporting purposes. As a practical matter, the corporation with gross receipts in excess of $5 million will compute the inflation or deflation effect using internal changes in unit prices due to the 80% of change limitation for tax purposes, as well as the inappropriateness of such limitation for financial reporting purposes.

CHAPTER TWENTY-TWO

Imports

In their search for more price competitive product sources, it's no secret that many retailers are increasing the amount of imported goods included in their merchandise mix.

However, the process of importing also results in the creation of a number of issues and risks, both financial and operational, that must be dealt with by the retailer.

For example, before deciding to import a particular product the retailer must be certain that there is enough supply available to justify the additional controls and personnel that will be required to import these goods successfully.

On the other hand, there may be such plentiful opportunities available for importing that the retailer might decide to open its own overseas importing department. Some retailers, pursuing this strategy, have gone so far as to establish their own importing company staffed by buyers, brokers, quality control personnel, and so on.

Still other retailers have gone even further to vertically integrate their businesses by owning and operating overseas manufacturing operations.

WORKING WITH COMMISSION MERCHANTS

Most companies either do not import enough merchandise to set up their own operations, whether manufacturing or overseas buying offices, or feel that their needs are better served by using commission merchants located in various countries.

Along with maintaining foreign vendor accounts, the functions carried out by these merchants include the following: local receiving of merchandise; assembling of merchandise for shipping; drawing up invoices; arranging payment; and shipping the merchandise to its desired destinations.

Beyond the carrying out of these functions the main advantage for retailers using these merchants is the ability to quickly call on local expertise in a country without having to commit major resources for the establishment of a permanent operation. The major disadvantage is the lack of control over the local broker who may be involved in juggling the demands of a large number of client companies.

Too, even if commission merchants are used, it is usually necessary for the retailers' own staff members to frequently travel overseas to make actual buying decisions.

U.S.-BASED BUYING GROUPS

A third choice used by a number of retailers is to join a U.S.-based buying group. These buying groups have full-staffed departments situated in various countries around the world. Staff members have expertise in local manufacturing, product selection, quality control, delivery, and so on. As a member of this buying group association, the retailer has the opportunity to receive advice on what and how to buy, how to insure the merchandise, and the most effective means of delivery.

LETTERS OF CREDIT AND TRANSPORTATION LIABILITIES

All retailers generally pay for merchandise, no matter how much volume is involved, through letters of credit, usually drawn on local banks.

Ownership of the merchandise generally passes to the buyer when it leaves the port of the manufacturer. This creates certain problems for the retailer. First, the merchandise must be insured from the shipping point since ownership has already passed.

Second, at any time the retailer probably has open, unissued letters of credit. Unless controlled, it is possible that funds could be released without authorization or credit availability could be needlessly tied up. Third, it is more difficult to negotiate with vendors regarding damages, shortages, and so on, once they have been paid.

SETTING UP ACCOUNTING CONTROLS

The importing of merchandise creates the need for different accounting controls than apply to retailers' domestic purchasing of goods. For example, while payment for the merchandise is made upon shipment, often the actual paperwork is received long after the shipment itself. This can create merchandise reporting problems as well as cut-off problems at the end of any period.

To keep such problems at a minimum it is important that buyers remain in close contact with the accounts payable department and assist this department in arriving at the cost of purchases.

In addition to the invoice cost and foreign charges that must be recorded for domestic purchases, import costs can include ocean freight, marine insurance, duties, foreign agents commissions, and broker fees. Also, when retailers have established a separate import department they add a percentage of import cost to cover some of the department's expenses.

Since all of these costs may not be known for some time retailers often estimate total landed costs that eventually must be reconciled and adjusted to actual. It is important that these estimates be as accurate as possible to ensure that the price savings is as real as estimated.

In addition, shipments from one vendor or buying agent often involve more than one merchandise department. At the same time, though, some of the above costs, notably freight, insurance, and commissions, are likely not to be broken down by product. Therefore, this requires the retailer to allocate them to the departments and/or SKUs. Although such allocations are usually done as a percentage of cost, the process can still be time consuming. This is especially true for retailers on the cost methods that specifically identify the cost of each SKU. There is also greater potential for misstatement of these costs.

OTHER IMPORTING DISADVANTAGES

Other potential problems involved with importing include the following:

- *Delivery Problems.* Lead times for imported merchandise are considerably longer than those for domestic goods. This means that merchandise for a specific season or event must be ordered and received early to ensure availability. In turn, this can result in increased handling and storage costs, as well as greater overall inventory risk. Companies may also miss out on "hot" items or find out that these cannot be reordered in time to meet current demand.

- *Quality Control.* Sometimes the quality of the goods manufactured abroad turns out to be below what is acceptable in the United States. If such problems occur, it is more difficult and costly to return merchandise overseas. It is also harder to exert quality control over foreign sources.

- *Quotas.* There is always the risk that the United States or the country of origin for the merchandise will decide to set quotas on imports/exports, whether for political or economic reasons.

- *Unstable Governments.* Many foreign countries have constant political unrest that increases the risk of doing business with them.

- *Foreign Currency.* Fluctuations in the value of the dollar, as well as in many foreign currencies, creates additional risks in dealing outside the United States.

- *Foreign Corrupt Practices Act.* This act established regulations for doing business in foreign countries and set stiff penalties for violations of the act meaning that these regulations must be strictly adhered to.

- *Tax Risks.* It is difficult to transfer funds in and out of certain countries. Also, some countries levy local and national taxes on merchandise to be exported.

SUMMARY

In summary, the decision to import must be carefully thought out and must involve merchandising, operational, and financial personnel. It may be necessary to import in order to be competitive or for product availability. If the proper controls are implemented, and all the risks considered, the benefits can be substantial.

CHAPTER TWENTY-THREE

Leased Departments

The term "leased department" describes a retail operation, involving merchandising or service activities, that is conducted within a specialty, department, or discount store by a company or individual independent of the one that operates the store itself. Such an arrangement is governed by an agreement between the store and the leased department operator setting forth particulars as to space allocated, methods of operation, responsibilities of the parties, allocation of expenses, and the portion of sales revenue that the store will receive as consideration for permitting the outside interest to conduct business in its establishment and perhaps to sell under its name. The nature of these arrangements is such that they may be looked upon as leases of store space and privileges, the basis for the term "leased department." The store confines itself to operations other than the department's merchandising or service activities and obtains, in lieu of ordinary mercantile profits, rental income of fixed amounts or percentages of the sales of the leased department.

The operators of leased departments are specialists in their lines of business. They provide the merchandise inventory, sometimes the fixtures, and incur specific operating liabilities. Their compensation is their net operating profit, which is largely dependent upon their merchandising ability.

Selection and buying of merchandise, pricing, inventory control, and sales promotion are the responsibility of the lessee, unless restrictions are imposed by agreement. The lessee likewise controls the sales force and most other employees in the department and pays their salaries. The store usually requires, however, that the lessee's employees be satisfactory to the store management, conform to the store rules, and recognize floor managers as representatives of the store.

ORGANIZATION AND THEORY OF DEPARTMENT LEASING

Under leasing arrangements the retailing operation is divided into two functional areas:

- The lessee provides the inventory, does the merchandise planning and purchasing, operates the selling department, sometimes provides the fixtures, and pays all salaries and direct expenses (in some cases directly to the store for services such as advertising).

- The lessor provides the store name and premises, establishes operating policies, makes deliveries, provides for supervision, housekeeping and other services, and does the required work on charge accounts (credit responsibility is usually assumed by the lessor).

Lessor-Lessee Relations

It is important for the retailer to check the background and stability of any potential lessee to ensure that the enterprise is sufficiently well capitalized to maintain an operation on a par with that of the rest of the store.

Some leased departments are operated on a more or less temporary basis, until the lessee can prove to the store that a department can be profitably operated. For example, a manufacturer may be willing to operate a leased department for a limited period only, with a view to demonstrating that its product lines can be profitably merchandised.

ADVANTAGES TO THE STORE

Invariably, the basic reason for leasing departments of a store to outside interests is that management believes that greater profit or better service to the public can be obtained this way, rather than by directly operating these departments. This conclusion may be based on one or all of the following factors:

- A store may hesitate to invest capital in new departments or additional lines of merchandise where, because of novelty or lack of experience in handling the particular merchandise, there cannot be definite assurance of success.

- It may be that, for certain departments, a store does not have purchasing facilities that enable it to maintain a stock that is sufficiently complete to satisfy its clientele or that can be purchased at prices which permit a fair rate of gross margin. A multistore leased department operator is likely to have the advantages of lower costs and retail prices, greater variety, and more exclusive styles. Lessees who are also manufacturers can offer a store greater leasing income than is likely to be earned by store operation of such departments, and at the same time assure the store of a more complete stock of merchandise and consequently better service to the public.

- There may be a desire to obtain the services of skilled merchandisers or specialists who can achieve strength and dominance in an area important to the overall store image. Successful and profitable departmental operation rests on a thorough knowledge of what to buy and how to sell. If the merchandising staff of a store cannot successfully merchandise certain departments, it is necessary either to engage qualified individuals at adequate compensation or to lease the departments to specialists. The latter approach has often been found to be more advantageous for such departments as optical, photographic, restaurant, and beauty parlor where specialized or even technical knowledge is required.

- A leased department can provide working capital since cash is available to a store that controls receipts but is not remitted until the end of specified accounting periods.

- Perhaps the chief factor that influences a store to lease some of its departments is the desire to achieve the maximum overall profit for the store. If contribution to profit per square foot is enhanced by utilizing selected leased departments in certain sections of the store, it is consequently in the best interests of the store to take advantage of leasing.

In essence, a successful lessee-lessor arrangement depends on the willingness of the store management to acknowledge that an outside merchandiser or operator can do a better overall job of running a particular department as compared to an internal operation directed by the store's own management.

Advantages to the Lessee

A lessee has certain advantages in leasing departments rather than opening independent locations, including the following:

- In most instances, the operator of a leased department is interested in obtaining a reasonable volume of business in a specialized line of merchandise or service where volume ordinarily might not be sufficient to warrant the expense of opening a separate store. Leasing a department may meet this requirement.

- The goodwill and prestige of a department store and the volume of business transacted on the premises present an unusually favorable background for the development of the leased department.

- An additional incentive in leasing departments is that, under leasing arrangements, a lessee is relieved of the extensive and intricate problems of store management. While a great deal of supervision is necessary in the operation of a store as a whole, the store premises represent a large unit which can be supervised and controlled without regard to departmental subdivisions. There is economy and efficiency in such a large-scale, specialized operation, just as there is in merchandising a particular line of goods in many places under lease arrangements.

Departments Usually Leased

Departments frequently leased involve those where personal service is a large factor. The principal element in the operation of such departments is competent, experienced management and skilled labor, rather than merchandise stock. For this reason, store management will turn to the trained organizations of lessees rather than attempt to acquire the knowledge necessary to operate and control such departments. Another factor influencing leases of service departments is that these departments may require installation of specialized equipment and fixtures. In many instances it is advisable for a store to avoid investment in such fixtures, especially where (for example, in beauty parlors) a heavy outlay is required in what may be more or less an experimental venture or untried field. If the store abandons its department the specialized equipment is practically a total loss. On the other hand, such equipment might have large value to a lessee who can move it to a new location.

The second type of area frequently leased includes merchandise departments. These include ladies' and children's footwear, furs, fine jewelry, electronics and appliances, health and beauty aids, cameras, records and tapes, books, stationery, and gourmet food departments.

Manufacturers will sometimes operate a chain of leased departments (or designer shops) in order to promote a distinctive product in outlets reasonably protected against the competition of rival manufacturers. In some cases, the operation of a leased department by the manufacturer may be only a temporary expedient until the store is convinced that the line can be profitably carried.

In instances where technical knowledge in sales and service is required, leasing departments to specialists has often proved more satisfactory than direct store operation. Miscellaneous departments such as candy and books have special problems unlike those of ordinary departments. These problems and the relatively small sales volumes are inducements to leasing.

The Lease Agreement

Relations between the store and the lessee are governed by a lease agreement. The agreement covers all matters pertaining to the term of lease, rental basis, merchandise, and customer relation policies, accounting and settlements, sales promotion, and the responsibilities and duties of the respective parties. It is also often advisable to insert a clause that provides, through arbitration or otherwise, a means for settlement of questions that may arise.

There are both ordinary problems to be considered and, in particular instances, special problems because of the kind of department leased. In the following outline of important lease provisions, no attempt is made to cover all of the subjects that may, from time to time, require attention; no lease can cover every facet of the operation or foresee all the problems.

TERM.   The contract may be for a long- or short-term. The longer term contract may be advisable where extensive outlays are made for special fixtures or equipment. Ordinarily, the term of a lease contract is rather short since it requires both the store and the lessee to constantly make efforts to improve if the operation is to succeed. In many cases the term is for one year and may include a provision for early termination.

LOCATION.   The agreement should clearly describe the space which is to be leased and its location in the store. It should specify whether the area may be increased or decreased, or the location changed; and if so, on what basis.

RENTAL.   Rental provisions vary. Usually, rental is a stated percentage of net sales; however, a minimum amount must be paid even though the percentage on sales falls below the guaranteed minimum. In some cases there may be a fixed monthly rental regardless of volume of sales, or a fixed monthly rental subject either to increase by a specified rate on excess, or to decrease by a specified rate on deficiency of sales as compared with a stated volume.

Minimum rentals at best are calculated to give stores a minimum return, and percentage clauses allow lessees to conduct their operation with less risk. Thus, the minimum-plus has become a way of life for many lessors and lessees. In addition, there may be charges for direct expenses and indirect expenses on a pro rata basis.

Various other bases may be agreed upon, as, for instance, a fixed percentage on gross or net sales up to a certain total, with either a larger or smaller percentage on sales in excess of that figure. Provisions of the latter kind are used where a store offers, as an inducement to the lessee, a lower ratio for large volume or where the lessee, in order to obtain a lease, offers extra rental in the event that the location exceeds the estimated business-producing possibilities. There may be special provisions for carrying forward deficiencies or excess of rentals from one season to another within the lease term with final settlement at specified intervals or at the end of the lease term. In some leases it may be provided that at the option of one or the other, or both parties, the lease may be terminated if sales fall below a certain minimum.

PAYMENT AND HIRING OF EMPLOYEES. It should be clearly stated which departmental employees or classes of employees are to be paid by the lessee and by the lessor, respectively, and which are to receive fringe benefits and be covered by pension plans. Ordinarily, the manager of the department and the sales and stock clerks are paid by the lessee. Cashiers, inspectors, and wrappers are usually paid by the store, as are employees of its housekeeping and service departments. Employees engaged in window display and in the receiving of merchandise are borderline situations, and the agreement should set forth clearly which party is to be responsible for the compensation of such employees. Leased department employees should be required to observe all store rules in order to avoid personality conflicts and to ensure that controls are uniformly enforced.

PAYMENT FOR DELIVERIES. Delivery should be specifically covered in the agreement. Sometimes the lessee is charged with deliveries at a specified rate per parcel. In other instances the lessor delivers without charge.

PAYMENT FOR ADVERTISING. Probably the more common procedure is for the lessee to be charged with advertising. This advertising is incorporated with the general store advertising, but is charged by the store to the lessee. In such cases it is important that the basis for the charges be clearly set forth—for example, whether the charge is to be on a lineage basis for the space devoted to the leased department, or whether any part of the general institutional advertising of the store is to be allocated, as well as whether charge is to be made for services of the advertising department of the store.

Another problem is whether the lessee is to receive credit for any reductions of advertising bills that the store may earn by reason of its aggregate lineage within a specified period. It is frequently provided that the leased department shall do a certain minimum amount of advertising.

The minimum may be a dollar or a lineage minimum, or an amount equal to a stated percentage of annual gross or net receipts as defined, or some similar basis, with the understanding that any deficiency is to be collected by the lessor after the close of the annual period as additional rent.

PREPARATION OF MONTHLY STATEMENTS. Ordinarily, the store controls the registers or the register tapes of the operator, collects the receipts, audits them, determines expenses and any other items chargeable, and renders detailed monthly statements to the lessee.

RESPONSIBILITY FOR CHARGE ACCOUNTS. In most instances, the store's credit department passes upon charge sales of leased departments and any resultant bad debt losses are assumed by the store. However, there may be exceptions to this procedure, particularly where a leased department is operated by a manufacturer or jobber interested in promoting sales and willing to assume responsibility for credits. In any event, the agreement should be specific.

INSURANCE COVERAGE. Presumably the lessee—that is, the owner of the merchandise of the leased department—is responsible for fire insurance coverage on such merchandise. Responsibility of the store, if any, for damage to merchandise through fire, water, theft, loss, or other cause should be clearly defined. Both parties to the agreement, particularly the store company, should be concerned with the adequacy of protection provided through compensation and public liability insurance policies. It is not unreasonable for the store to expect the lessee to carry adequate insurance to protect the store against any claims that might be lodged against the store by reason of the lessee's inability to satisfy such claims. The liabilities of the respective parties should be clearly defined and adequately covered by insurance.

OTHER PROVISIONS. Various other provisions should be included in the lease agreement, but it is not feasible to discuss many of them in this chapter. A few are touched upon in the remainder of this section.

Every agreement should set forth definitely which party has the right of employment, irrespective of which party pays the employees. It is usual to provide that the lessee may hire the employees paid by it, but that the store has the right to compel discharge of any employee who is objectionable or who does not comply with its rules. In some instances the store's personnel director may be entrusted with the hiring of certain employees of the lessee.

Other subjects of agreement deal with who shall provide and pay for supplies, utilities, and other services, the quality of the merchandise or service of the lessee, the general range of prices to be charged, the nature of display advertising, and appearance of the department. In some instances the lease agreement may contain definite provisions as to the basis on which and/or means by which, the contract may be canceled. In these cases, the agreement should include a noncompetition provision prohibiting the operation of a similar department in the market area of the store.

The agreement should be specific with respect to the time and manner of periodic settlements and whether interest is to be accrued upon either debit or credit balances outstanding subsequent to settlement dates.

CHAPTER TWENTY-FOUR

Special Accounting Issues

Thus far, this book has dealt with issues specific to the retail industry and especially those in the area of retail merchandise accounting. Retailers are faced with numerous other accounting issues, some of which are relevant primarily to their industry, some of which are more general in nature. The more important of these issues are discussed in this chapter, along with its relevance to, and impact on, the retail business.

PREOPENING COSTS

Planning for store openings involves personnel from all of a company's operational areas, including store operations, merchandising, financial, data processing, and so on. This planning often begins many months before the store actually opens for business. Most of the costs involved with such openings are considered to be period costs and are expenses as incurred, either because they are not incremental costs, cannot be specifically identified, or because of doubt as to whether or not the store will actually open. However, certain other costs are truly incremental, can be specifically identified as being applicable to a store that either has or is guaranteed to open and are incurred prior to the opening of the store. These costs may be deferred and amortized over a relatively short period of time after the store opens. Examples of the more common of these costs are:

1. Rent incurred in leasing a store for a period prior to its actual opening. For stores built by the retailer, the accounting rules relative to capitalization of interest cost should be followed.

2. Advertising the opening of a store.

3. Direct, incremental payroll costs related to a specific store, including costs to train store personnel, set up the store, and so on.

4. Travel costs incurred by company personnel to visit the location, plan the opening, and so on.

5. Data processing costs related specifically to a new store.

6. Security costs.

7. Utility costs.

There are additional costs that may also qualify for deferral depending on the specific circumstances of each company. Except in very rare situations, no corporate costs or allocations would be included as preopening costs. Additionally, any deferral of costs would end as soon as the store opens for business. Deferred costs must be both directly related to a specific store and incremental.

Each retailer needs to establish a corporate policy for the amortization of any deferred costs. This policy should be followed for all similar types of stores opened by the company. The policy should be established based on the justification for the deferral.

Several different amortization policies have been adopted by retailers and remain acceptable, depending on the specific facts and circumstances. The most widely followed policies are:

1. *Expense as Incurred.* Despite the common practice of deferring preopening costs, many retailers elect to expense all costs as incurred. This policy reflects both conservative accounting and the tenuous nature of success for any store.

2. *Amortize over the Remainder of the Fiscal Year.* This policy is most often applicable to retailers with accounting years ending in December or January. For most retail operations, the Christmas season

represents the major selling season. Certain retailers believe that preopening costs should be spread over at least one prime selling season to best match revenues and costs. Other retailers justify this policy as the best to spread costs over a short period of time after a store opens rather than burdening an interim period with unusually high costs. This is also a conservative accounting policy as all costs are fully expensed prior to the end of the fiscal year. The exception to this would be for costs related to a store not yet opened by the end of the year, thus applicable preopening costs would be deferred from one year to the next.

3. *Amortize over the 12 Months after a Store Opens.* This policy was more prevalent in the past than currently. The theory is that one entire 12-month selling season should bear the burden of these deferred costs. It is less conservative than the above policies as it results in deferred costs on the balance sheet at the end of any fiscal year in which stores were opened. For this reason, many retailers have switched to the policies noted in (1) and (2) above. However, it does remain an acceptable policy in most cases.

4. *Amortize over a Two- or Three-Year Period.* This policy has been adopted by relatively few retailers and is far less conservative than those described above. Certain retailers have argued that the life cycle for developing their business is more than one year. One example might be membership clubs where membership builds up slowly over a period of time. A second example might be a mail order business that needs to build up its customer lists. Those that feel this is an unacceptable policy argue that all new retail operations take a period of time to build up to "normal" volume.

In order to justify this policy, the retailer must provide strong proof of the longer life based on existing facts and circumstances, that is, a demonstrated pattern of slowly growing volume resulting, in part, from those costs incurred prior to the store opening. Additionally, there must be virtual certainty that the store will remain in operation for the period of amortization.

This policy brings with it a high degree of risk and is not widely accepted within the industry. Careful consideration is necessary before adopting an amortization period greater than one year.

Any amortization policy for preopening costs other than those noted above is considered unacceptable. For example, it would not be proper to amortize these costs over the term of the lease or over a period of time greater than two or three years. This is due to both the risk involved with any retail location and the difficulty in absolutely associating specific preopening costs with future benefits. For tax return purposes, preopening costs are generally expensed as incurred, thus giving rise to deferred taxes.

LEASE ACCOUNTING

One of the larger expenses for most retailers is the lease expense for store and warehouse facilities, as well as furniture, fixtures, and vehicles. While some retailers do own some or all of their locations, most have viewed leasing as a means of financing their operations. Leasing, as opposed to buying, ties up less capital and passes certain risks to the lessor. While leasing results in less control over the property itself, many retailers are willing to pass up this control to free additional funds for inventory, further expansion, and so on, or because they have weak credit ratings and could not finance a property. While leasing may free additional debt capacity, the major debt rating agencies, as well as most banks, do calculate a debt factor based on the existing operating leases. This factor may either be a present value calculation of future rental payments or a multiple of rent expense.

For many retailers, leases are one of their more valuable assets. A fair market value lease today may become a bargain lease in the future for a variety of reasons, including inflation, the maturing of a shopping center, a long fixed rent term and/or bargain renewal options, and so on. Some retailers, as a result of the size of their stores and/or their reputation, are able to obtain substantially below market lease terms from day one. Such stores are generally referred to as "anchor" stores because of their positioning in shopping centers.

Any lease must be classified as either operating or capital. This classification determines the method of accounting for that particular lease. Operating leases are those that do not create equity for the lessee, whether true or economic equity. Capital leases do create equity, whether legally or economically, as a result of the terms of the transaction. FAS 13, issued in November 1976, established four criteria for capital leases. A least that meets any one or more of these criteria is classified as capital:

1. The lease transfers ownership of the property to the lessor by the end of the lease term.

2. The lease contains a bargain purchase option.

3. The lease term . . . is equal to 75 percent or more of the estimated economic life of the leased property . . . .

4. The present value at the beginning of the lease term of the minimum lease payments . . . , excluding executory costs such as insurance, maintenance and taxes to be paid by the lessor, including any profit thereon, equals or exceeds 90 percent of the excess of the fair value of the leased property . . . to the lessor, at inception of the lease over any related investment tax credit retained by the lessor and expected to be realized by him.

In some circumstances, criteria 4 may be difficult to analyze because the fair market value of the leased property may not be objectively determinable. For example, many specialty retail operations lease a relatively small space in a large shopping mall. FAS 13, Paragraph 28 notes that, "if the fair value of the leased property is not objectively determinable, the lessee shall classify the lease . . ." using criteria 3 above only. This does not mean that all leases involving small stores in a larger center would qualify under these circumstances since the fair value is often determinable based on construction cost estimates, and so on. Rather, the specific circumstances surrounding any lease must be closely reviewed.

In order to determine the proper classification of capital versus operating lease, the lessee must know the basic terms of the lease plus:

1. The economic life of the leased property.

2. The executory costs, if any, included in the lease payments.

3. Their incremental borrowing rate or the lessor's implicit rate built into the lease if that rate is known and is less than the lessee's rate.

4. Any option periods included in the lease and any purchase options.

Disclosure

Operating leases, unlike capital leases, require income statement and footnote disclosure only, rather than balance sheet classification. Disclosure requirements are for all such leases with initial or remaining noncancellable lease terms greater than one year. These disclosures include:

1. The amount of net expense for each period for which an income statement is presented. Minimum rentals, contingent rentals, and sublease income should be disclosed.

2. Total future minimum rental payments and the minimum payments for each of the next five years.

3. Total minimum sublease income to be received in the future.

As noted previously, a capital lease is one that either legally or economically implies ownership. Therefore, the balance sheet must include an asset and obligation related to those leases. FAS 13, Paragraph 10, defines the amount of the asset and obligation as "an amount equal to the present value at the beginning of the lease term of the minimum lease payments during the lease term, excluding that portion of the payment representing executory costs such as insurance, maintenance and taxes to be paid by the lessor, together with any profit thereon." This amount cannot exceed the fair value of the property at lease inception.

During the lease period the asset is amortized as follows:

1. If classified as a capital lease since the lease transfers ownership to the lessee or the lease contains a bargain purchase option the amortization should match the lessee's normal depreciation policy for assets owned.

2. If classified as a capital lease for other than the reasons noted in (1) above, the amortization period should be the lease term.

The lease payment should be allocated to the lease obligation and interest to result in a constant rate of interest on the remaining obligation, that is, using the "interest" method.

The financial statement should separately identify the lease assets and obligations and related amortization. The footnotes should disclose:

1. The future minimum lease payments in total and for each of the succeeding five years.

2. For noncancellable leases, the minimum sublease rentals to be received.

3. Contingent rentals incurred for each period for which an income statement is presented.

For all leases there should be disclosure of the general nature of the leasing arrangements including the basis for determining contingent rentals, renewal or purchase options and restrictions imposed by the leases.

Step Function Leases

As a result of confusion concerning the accounting for operating leases with scheduled rent increases during the lease term, the FASB issued FTB 85-3 (FASB Technical Bulletin 85-3) in November 1985 and FTB 88-1 in December 1988. These bulletins cover all scheduled rent increases, whether as a result of normal increases over time, rent, holidays, to recognize the impact of inflation, and so on. The bulletins do not cover contingent rents, such as percentage rents. Contingent rents are accounted for as an expense as paid or incurred. The bulletins also do not cover capital leases, as scheduled rent increases for capital leases are an integral element of the calculation of the asset and related liability.

The bulletins state that rent expense must be recognized on a straight-line basis over the life of the lease, regardless of the timing of the actual payments. The following illustrations demonstrate application of this:

Case 1. A standard lease with a 20-year term and schedule lease payments of $50,000 per year plus 1 percent of gross revenue in excess of a stated amount.

In this example, the expense recognized each year would be the $50,000 scheduled rent plus any percentage rent based on the gross revenues.

Case 2. A 20-year lease with no rent in year 1 as an inducement to sign the lease, rent of $45,000 in years 2 through 5, $50,000 in years 6 through 15 and $64,000 in years 16 through 20.

In this example total scheduled lease payments over the 20-year term are $1,000,000, the same as the scheduled rent in Case 1. The expense recognized would be $50,000 each year ($1,000,000 divided by 20 years) even though no rent is paid in year one and only $45,000 per year in years 2 through 5.

It should be remembered that contingent rentals, such as the percentage rent in Case 1, are not included in this calculation. If you assume that the contingent rent in Case 1 is $10,000 in year 20, rent expense that year would be $60,000, versus $50,000 in year 20 for Case 2. Thus, the expense is lower that year for Case 2 although the actual cash paid is higher ($64,000 vs. $60,000).

The only exception to recognizing expense on a straight line basis would be in the relatively rare situation whereby this method does not truly represent the time pattern in which the leased property is physically utilized. Factors such as the time value of money, inflation, or future revenues do not relate to the time pattern of usage considered by the technical bulletin. Thus they do not provide exceptions to the straight-line method.

As noted, percentage rents are not included in the step function lease calculations. However, the period for determining the percentage rent often crosses over the company's fiscal year end. In such situations an accrual should be set up, both at year-end and on an interim basis, for the estimated percentage rent. This estimate should be based on past history, budgeted sales and any other relevant factors.

Landlord Concessions

Often a landlord will offer rent concessions to a prospective tenant to encourage them to move from one location to another. These concessions may include paying a tenant's moving costs, reimbursement for leasehold improvements in the current location, or assuming any remaining lease obligations.

Generally, payments by the landlord for moving costs or leasehold improvements should be recognized by the tenant as a reduction of rent expense in the new location on a straight-line basis over the term of the new lease. Additionally, if the tenant is not able to terminate the old lease or sublease their existing space, or must sublease the space at a loss, the expected loss should be recognized currently. In most instances, any nonreimbursed costs related to a move should be recognized currently rather than deferred. In fact, it is unlikely that the SEC would accept deferral of any such costs.

Tax Treatment

Both capital and operating leases can result in different expense recognition for books and tax returns, giving rise to deferred taxes. For tax returns, the expense is normally based on the terms of the lease, that is, the actual timing of payments contemplated. For a capital lease the combination of amortization expense and interest on the lease obligation generally exceeds the actual rent paid in the early years of the lease and is less in the later years as the obligation decreases. This gives rise to deferred tax debits in the early years of the lease, absent other factors affecting taxes outside the lease area. The debit eventually decreases to zero as the lease expires.

For operating leases with scheduled lease payments on a straight-line basis, generally the book and tax expense would be the same. However, for step function leases, the tax expense is based on actual rents paid or accrued under the lease term. In the previous example, the tax expense would be zero in year 1, $45,000 in year 2, and so on. The book expense would be $50,000 in both years. As with the capital lease example, above, book expense exceeds tax expense in the early years of this lease, resulting in deferred tax debits that again reduce to zero as the lease expires. In the unusual case of schedule rent decreases, deferred tax credits could result.

Sale-Leasebacks

Some retailers have tried to combine the best benefits of both owning and leasing by utilizing sale-leaseback arrangements. They actually provide the funds to build their locations and then sell the real estate to an investor. The selling price is based on market conditions and the terms the retailer sets for its leasing back of the property. Such an arrangement provides the retailer with control over the actual physical structure as well as lease terms that they determine. Normally the sale results in a gain recognized by the retailer, if a true sale occurs.

FASB 98 provides further guidance on when sale-leaseback accounting is applicable. Basically, the transaction must include a normal leaseback, must have payment terms that demonstrate the buyer-lessor's initial and continuing involvement in the property and must transfer all risks and rewards of ownership (demonstrated by the absence of any other continuing involvement, other than normal lease, by the seller-lessee).

With recent changes in the tax laws, the investors in such arrangements are generally more interested in the true economic value of the real estate, as measured by cash flow and/or potential appreciation, rather than in tax benefits. Institutional investors have become much more active in this market since a scarcity of quality real estate in which to invest has developed. Quality, in this case, is determined as much by the quality of the tenant itself as by the location of the property.

STORE CLOSING RESERVE

Frequently retailers make the decision to close one or a group of stores or operations within a store. Closings can be the result of:

1. Ongoing evaluation of the profitability of all stores.

2. Closing of all stores in a specific geographic location.

3. Closing of a group of stores or a specific, separate type of operation within a store.

4. Closing of a store to move to a new location in the same area.

The accounting treatment for and related disclosure of store closings depends on which of the above categories is applicable. Most closings are part of the normal operations of a retailer, thus the related changes are included with income from operations. If material, these changes might be included as a separate line item with footnote disclosure. Other closings may qualify as a discontinued segment. A more detailed explanation of the proper disclosures will be presented later in this chapter.

Costs to Be Accrued

Once the decision is made to close a store or stores or an operation within stores, the costs of these closings should be accrued. These should be costs directly related to the decision to close. The more frequent types of costs include:

INVENTORY MARKDOWNS.   Generally closings result in greater than normal markdowns in inventory when it is determined that the cost of these markdowns, whether in pure dollars, time and effort of people, and so on, is less than the cost of moving the merchandise to another store, remarking, and other related activities. If this is the case, then an estimate of the markdowns in excess of normal markdowns should be accrued when the decision is made, assuming that the markdowns will result in a loss from operations.

If a loss is also expected as a result of normal markdowns that amount should also be accrued. This could well be the situation as the store could be closing since it is in a poor location losing money. If the merchandise is to be moved to another location, the costs of moving, reticketing, and so on must be accrued since moving merchandise from store to store does not add value to the inventory.

OCCUPANCY COSTS. If the location is owned, the book value of the location plus an estimate of the costs to sell the space, including costs to maintain the location until it is sold, must be compared to an estimate of the selling price. If a loss is estimated, then that loss should be accrued. If a gain is estimated, the gain should not be recognized until realized. If the space is to be leased rather than sold, and if it is reasonably expected that the lease income will cover operating costs, the only accrual required is for operating *losses* estimated to be incurred until the property is leased.

If the property is leased, a calculation must be made of the present value of all future minimum rental costs, including base rent, common area costs, security, utilities, and so on throughout the base rental period. The amount calculated should be reduced by expected sublease income, if any. Again, if a loss results, it should be accrued. If a gain results, it would be recognized as earned over the life of the lease and sublease.

For an example of the above, assume a lease with 10 years remaining and a base rent of $50,000 per year. Additional costs include a 5 percent common area charge, or $2500 per year, plus insurance, maintenance, etc. costs of $5000 per year. Total payments over the remaining base lease term would be $57,500 per year. Using a 10 percent discount rate, the present value of these payments would be $363,000. Assume that the property can be sub-let for $45,000 per year, including all costs, and that it is estimated that it will take one year to sublease. The present value, again at a 10 percent rate, of $45,000 per year in years two through 10 is $247,000. The difference of $116,000 ($363,000–$247,000) should be accrued when the decision to close is made.

In most cases, sublease calculations require estimates, as no formal commitment exists. There may be situations whereby a formal sublease arrangement has been entered into, but for a period shorter than the base rental period. In the previous example assume the sublease was signed already, but only covering years one through five, with an option period for five more years. Judgment would need to be exercised to decide whether or not the base sublease period was enough of a commitment to establish value for the location. It may be argued that five years is a significant commitment and, therefore, it is very likely that either the lease will be extended or the property subleased again for the final five years at a rent of at least $45,000 per year. Thus, the sublease calculation would be for years two through ten at $45,000 per year, not just the five years committed.

As mentioned, this is a judgment area. A one-year lease is probably not a good measure of fair value for a sublease. However, an eight-year sublease on a ten-year base lease may create a different problem since it is likely to be difficult to sublease for only two years. It is important to ensure that sound business assumptions are used for the above calculations.

PAYROLL COSTS.   Payroll and payroll related costs should be accrued once the decision to close has been made. This includes direct payroll of those involved in actually closing the operations, preparing it for sublease, severance pay, vacation pay, additional pension costs, and so on. It may also include moving costs of a personnel to be kept by the company.

FIXTURES AND LEASEHOLDS.   The net book value of all fixtures and leaseholds in the store, reduced by the cash to be received upon selling these items (net of costs to dispose) should be accrued.

Depending upon the specific circumstances, there could be other costs that should be accrued. The above are the more prevalent ones, associated with most closings.

Disclosure

Most closings represent ongoing evaluations of various locations by management and normal business decisions to discontinue one or several stores. Any loss on such closings would be included with continuing operations. Depending on the materiality of the amount involved, it might be included as a separate line within the income statement or, more often, disclosed in the footnotes to the financial statements. Some retailers have adopted the policy of footnote disclosure of any such closing losses every year, regardless of the amount. They believe that these are recurring events that are important to the reader of the financial statements, thus warranting disclosure.

Occasionally a retailer will close an entire segment of the business. If material, the disclosure rules are different than noted above. APB 30 discusses discontinued operations and the accounting treatment for disposals of a segment as "A component of an enterprise whose activities represent a separate major line of business or class of customer." For a retail operation with several divisions, each in a different retail operation, that is, a department store division, a specialty clothing division, a supermarket division, and so on, identifying a segment might be fairly easy. However, for others this may not be the case. It is important to note that the following criteria must be met for the operation to qualify as a segment.

1. It must be a separate line of business, and

2. Its assets and results of operations must be readily distinguishable from the rest of the business.

Therefore, the closing of all stores in a specific geographic area is not likely to qualify as a discontinued operation.

Likewise, the closing of all the shoe departments within a department store chain is not likely to qualify as a discontinued operation. The retailer is remaining in the same general business, merely with less departments.

However, it might be argued that a department store chain closing all of its automotive service operations has discontinued a segment of the business. The service business may be separable from the merchandise sales operations (even if attached to the store) and cater to different customers. It is important, though, that the retailer considered this to be a separate business segment while it was in operation.

Disposals of segments should be disclosed in the statement of operations after income from continuing operations but before extraordinary items. Gain or loss on disposal should be broken out between operations and disposals and shown net of any applicable taxes. Any current and prior periods presented should also disclose the operations of the discontinued segment. The footnotes must disclose, at a minimum, additional information including the segment disposed of, how disposed and any assets or liabilities of the segment that remain.

INTERIM REPORTING

Many companies defer certain costs when incurred and spread them over the course of their fiscal year to better match revenues and related expenses. This is probably more relevant for the retail industry than any other due to the seasonality of most retail operations. Certain costs are incurred early in the fiscal year to benefit the peak selling seasons later in the year. By deferring costs, interim reporting is often more meaningful and comparable from year to year. The more seasonal the business, the more relevant the deferral. The costs that are the most likely to be deferred are those that fluctuate with the level of sales and can be separately identified. Still other costs need to be accrued during interim periods based on estimated results for the year.

The more common costs that are deferred or accrued during the year include:

1. *Occupancy Costs.* Normally rent and related costs are fairly constant during year. Therefore, such cost would be a much higher percentage

of sales during slow periods of the year versus the peak selling seasons, unless deferred. While some companies do defer such costs, this is not the common practice.

2. *Advertising.* Retailers often incur advertising expenses weeks or even months before realizing the benefits of the advertising. Thus, some of these costs may be deferred, during an interim period of a year, and expensed during the related selling season or as a percentage of sales.

3. *Warehousing and Freight.* Merchandise must be purchased well in advance of sales. Depending on buying decisions of the particular retailer, merchandise often is stored in warehouse or stores for a period of time. Warehousing costs tend to be higher during the slower seasons as the merchandise is delivered, sorted, labeled, and so forth in anticipation of peak seasons. The significance of the warehouse deferral is also dependent on whether or not the retailer capitalized some or all of the warehouse costs in inventory.

4. *Payroll.* Some payroll costs are variable as additional personnel are usually hired for peak seasons. For this reason store payroll costs are not usually deferred. However, certain payroll costs are fixed and specifically relate to inventory, such as merchandise buyer costs, warehouse personnel, etc. and may be deferred.

5. *Inventory Shortage.* An estimate of inventory shortage as a percentage of sales should be accrued during the course of the year, absent a complete physical inventory during the year.

6. *Insurance and Supplies.* These are generally less significant than the above costs, but often are absorbed based on a budgeted percentage of sales during the year.

7. *Bonuses.* Often bonuses are paid based on earnings for the company's fiscal year. If it is likely that such bonuses will be paid, the expense should be spread over the course of the year, either rateably or, more often, as a percentage of sales.

During the course of the year, these costs can be absorbed using several methods including:

- Based on budgeted sales, absorbed evenly each month.
- Based on the budgeted expenses for the year.
- Based on a percentage of actual sales, and so on.

The important point is that the method used should be the most applicable under the circumstances, and should be applied consistently.

It should be noted that such deferrals and accruals relate only to costs during the course of the year. These costs must be absorbed by year-end, as they are separate from normal prepaid expenses that may be deferred between years.

In addition to deferring expense, some retailers also defer gross profit during the year. Gross profit for many retailers is lower during the peak selling seasons than during the rest of the year. During the peak seasons competition is the greatest and promotional advertising increases. In an effort to maximize sales and gross profit dollars, the decision is often made to accept a lower gross profit percentage. For these reasons some retailers have justified the accrual of a constant gross profit percentage during the year, normally based on budgeted gross profit for the entire year. For retailers with fiscal year-ends shortly after peak selling seasons, such a policy would result in the deferral of income in the early periods of the year. To support the deferral, it is important that the reasonableness of the budgeted gross profit for the year be continually reviewed.

Depending on the type of retail operation and the cyclical nature of the business, certain deferrals are more applicable to some retailers than others. Due to the importance of proper reporting of income on an interim basis, deferrals should be reviewed annually to ensure that they remain proper and reasonable. Additionally, interim reports of most retailers should note that their business is seasonal and that the interim results may not be indicative of the full year. Certain retailers include a trailing 12-month statement with interim reports for just such reasons.

RIGHT OF RETURN

Most retailers accept merchandise returns from customers in the ordinary course of business. In some instances the right of return is a matter of written contract. In many other instances it is a matter of practice rather than formal policy, to enhance customer relations, promote business, and so on.

FAS 48, Paragraph 6, details the conditions that must be met in order for a sale to be recognized:

1. The price must be fixed or determinable.

2. Payment has either been made or obligated without further contingency.

3. The buyer's obligation remains even if the product is stolen or destroyed (risk passes to the buyer).

4. Buyer and seller are unrelated.

5. Seller does not have significant future performance obligations.

6. The amount, if any, of future returns can be estimated within reason.

Thus, to record a sale, an estimate needs to be made at the end of each accounting period of the amount of future returns. This requires an understanding of the customer return policies which vary widely from company to company. Some do not accept any returns other than for damages or exchanges, some accept returns within a certain amount of time, and still others accept returns at almost any time and for any reason. Normally past history is a good method of estimating. However, changes in circumstances, business, products, or other factors could make the calculation more complex. For example, a retailer could find it difficult to estimate returns due to:

1. Changes in technology.

2. Changes in demand.

3. Absence of many homogeneous transactions or the existence of a few very large transactions whereby one or a few returns could be significant.

Despite the existence of any of the above factors, in order to recognize a sale, some estimate of returns needs to be made. The nature of the estimate depends on the type of reason for the returns. For example:

1. If the return is due to damage, an accrual should be made for the costs to fix the products.

2. If the return will be for a cash refund or credit on future merchandise, the accrual should be for the gross profit realized on the sale. When the product is physically returned, the difference between the cash actually refunded and the accrual established is debited to inventory.

3. If returns are accepted only for an exchange for a similar item (i.e., a return due to color, size, etc.), retailers commonly do not establish a reserve. The belief is that the selling process is completed and there is no incremental costs due to the exchange and no accrual is necessary. This is acceptable if it can be clearly demonstrated, by past history and policy, that this is the case. If the merchandise being sold is unique and if cash is refunded if a like item is not available, this argument may not be valid.

The estimate of the reserve for merchandise returns must be continually reviewed for changes in policy or circumstances and in consideration of changes in the historical pattern of returns.

As a result of returned merchandise for which credit to buy other merchandise is issued, the retailer carries a liability on the books. It is normal that some of these credits are never redeemed. It is important for retailers to understand state and local escheat laws which usually provide guidance as to what should be done with these credits, as well as with abandoned gift certificates. In most cases, after a period of time (one to two years), if the customer cannot be located, the credited funds should be turned over to the state. Retailers that have adopted the policy of taking these credits into income are often in violation of these laws and face the possibility of fines and/or penalties.

PART FOUR

Financing

CHAPTER TWENTY-FIVE

Capital Budgeting

OVERVIEW

Traditionally, retailers have looked to sales volume as the key element to measure growth, performance, and for comparison with competitors. However, opening additional stores to achieve increased sales volume may not be the optimum focal point for many retailers. Rather, the focus should be on the maximization of return on resources available.

To achieve maximum returns on resources, retailers must have means of measuring performance before, during, and after an investment is made, whether that investment is in inventory, marketable securities, or fixed assets. This chapter will concentrate on the process of selecting the investment proposal that will generate the optimum return on investment for capital; this process is known as *capital budgeting*.

Capital budgeting is a mathematical approach to analyzing and controlling investments in capital assets by evaluating the profitability of each asset. The capital budgeting decision involves the planning of capital expenditures for projects that should benefit future periods. Due to the extended time frame, the capital budgeting process should incorporate accumulation of necessary data, evaluation and selection among alternatives, monitoring of the project, and reevaluation and adjustment of the initial plan.

The retailer typically applies capital budgeting to three types of capital investment scenarios:

1. Replacement of equipment either due to obsolescence or anticipated cost reductions resulting from technological improvements, such as the electronic point-of-sale terminal and supporting EDP systems.

2. Renovation or major repair to an existing location or locations.

3. Expansion either by building new facilities or through acquisition of existing retail chains.

The financing alternatives available to replace equipment or renovate an existing location are essentially the same. The organization can pay cash generated from operations, borrow funds from a lending institution, or lease the equipment. Store expansion presents several alternatives such as directly purchasing the site for the additional store, leasing the location, franchising its operations, or acquiring an existing chain of stores. The financial choice has an effect on the cash flow of the project that is critical to the final investment selection.

In most cases, capital budgeting decisions are based on cash flows rather than reported income for a given period. Because the emphasis is on cash flow, short (typically 1 year) and long-range capital expenditure plans are interrelated.

Long-range planning is strategic in nature, stating the organization's objectives and goals at a macro level. For example, the development of a new store prototype could change the basic management philosophy, or the development of a store cluster in a new geographical area could change management's merchandising strategy to accommodate the environment. Because the macro conditions and circumstances underlying the long-range strategic plan are subject to change, the long-range planning process needs to be fluid to meet the overall objectives of the organization.

Conversely, short-term capital spending is a function of long-term planning insofar as it is conceived within the framework of long-range capital spending decisions. Short-term budgeting encompasses current cash expenditures necessary to achieve the long-range objectives. This concept is apparent when considering that the capital budget decision is predicated upon annual cash flows associated with a particular project.

Generally, it is management's intention that investments in capital assets contribute to the organization's financial results. Management is also confronted with a number of investment proposals and ideas which are intended to benefit the company. A cost benefit analysis of each project is necessary to reject certain proposals and to limit the remaining choices to those proposals that, if selected, will benefit the company. The basic premise upon which the cost benefit analysis is performed is simply that the cost of the project minus the expected benefit equals a positive or negative cash flow. The expected benefits are measured in terms of annual cash flows. Projects with net positive cash flow are accepted while projects with net negative cash flow are rejected. The positive and negative cash flows are typically referred to as the return on investment (ROI).

The two methods most commonly used by retailers to calculate the ROI are the financial statements method and the discounted cash flow method.

Use of the financial statement method requires consideration of the impact of nonfund expenditures, such as depreciation, to determine the profitability of a project. To illustrate, assume that a company has $100,000 of equipment that is being depreciated using the straight-line method over 10 years ($10,000 per year), the company has $30,000 in earnings before depreciation and taxes, and is in the 40 percent tax bracket (Example 1).

Example 1.

Cash Flow for a Company

Earnings before depreciation and taxes (cash inflow)	$30,000
Depreciation (noncash expense)	(10,000)
Earnings before taxes	$20,000
Taxes (cash outflow)	(8,000)
Earnings after taxes	$12,000
Depreciation	10,000
Cash flow	$22,000

The company shows $12,000 in earnings after taxes, but it adds back the noncash deduction of $10,000 of depreciation to arrive at a cash flow figure of $22,000.

Now assume the company's net earnings before and after taxes are zero.

Revised Cash Flow for a Company

Earnings before depreciation and taxes	$10,000
Depreciation	10,000
Earnings before taxes	0
Taxes	0
Earnings after taxes	0
Depreciation	10,000
Cash flow	$10,000

Under this scenario the firm would have an undetermined ROI since the accounting income is zero while it has put $10,000 in the bank. In this case, a conclusion cannot be made whether or not to invest in the equipment, which indicates a significant weakness in the financial statement method. The emphasis must be on cash flow since it is the only common element with which to measure a project.

An alternative is the *discounted cash flow method.* Under the discounted cash flow method, the inflows of cash over the life of the investment are discounted back at the company's cost of capital to determine the present value of the cash flows. The present value of the cash flow is compared to the investment in the project, cash outflow, to arrive at the net present value (NPV). An investment with a positive net present value will usually be accepted, while a negative net present value indicates rejection. There are cases in which a positive NPV will be rejected. For example, if greater ROI will be generated by investing at better interest rates, investing in the company's own stock, or when comparing several projects, only some of which can be accepted, although all have positive NPVs. Cost of capital is defined as the organization's marginal cost of borrowing or conversely can be viewed in terms of lost opportunity to use funds elsewhere at a specified rate of return.

To illustrate the discounted cash flow, or net present value method, consider two investment opportunities, A and B. The investments are mutually exclusive of each other. For example, investment A is to add floor space to an existing store and investment B is to renovate the flagship store.

Since the organization has limited resources with which to operate, a decision must be made between investment A and investment B. Assume the following:

- Both investments require an initial cash outflow of $100,000 presently. The present value of the cash outflow is $100,000.

- The company's cost of capital is 10 percent.

- Investment A's estimated useful life is ten years. Net cash inflows are expected to be $15,000 annually for the first five years of the investment's estimated life and $20,000 annually over the remaining five years of the investment's useful life.

- Investment B's estimated useful life is five years. Net cash inflows are expected to be $20,000 annually for the first four years of the investment's estimated life and $30,000 in year five of the investments estimated useful life.

Investment A appears to be acceptable since the present value of the cash inflows is greater than the present value of outflows. Investment B is clearly unacceptable since the present value of the inflows is less than the initial investment.

The capital budgeting process does not stop when the investment decision is made. There are no assurances regarding the accuracy of the basic assumptions in the capital budgeting model. Likewise, without accounting controls over actual capital expenditures and project reporting, there is a risk that information provided to management will be misleading.

The basic assumptions in the capital budgeting model are anticipated useful lives of assets, projected cash flows, and cost of capital. Bearing in mind that the basic assumptions are estimates, the limitations inherent in the capital budgeting process become clear. For example, when a retail

	Investment A			Investment B	
1	15,000 × .909* =	13,635	22,000 × .909 =	19,998
2	15,000 × .826 =	12,390	22,000 × .826 =	18,172
3	15,000 × .751 =	11,265	22,000 × .751 =	16,522
4	15,000 × .683 =	10,245	22,000 × .683 =	15,026
5	15,000 × .621 =	9,315	30,000 × .621 =	18,630
6	20,000 × .564 =	11,280		$ 88,348
7	20,000 × .513 =	10,260		
8	20,000 × .467 =	9,340		
9	20,000 × .424 =	8,480		
10	20,000 × .386 =	7,720		
		$103,930		

	Investment A			Investment B	
	PV of Inflows	$103,930		PV of Inflows	$ 88,348
	PV of Outflows	100,000		PV of Outflows	100,000
	NPV	$ 3,930		NPV	$(11,652)

*Source is Standard Table, PV of $1.

organization enters a new geographical location, either through acquisition, franchising, or new store construction, there are numerous variables that may not have been considered in the planning model. These may include local customs and tastes, buying habits, competition, and underlying economic conditions, which may change. Periodic review of the assumptions utilized in initially accepting the project can provide useful information in determining whether to continue, modify, or terminate the investment. This is the case when considering that the longer the expected useful life of the asset, the greater the unpredictability of the actual return on investment.

When confronted with various investment alternatives, each dissimilar as to cash flow, expected life, and so on, a risk factor should be used in discounting the return on investment. The greater the risk associated with an investment the higher the required rate of return on the investment.

In order to facilitate meaningful analysis, controls should be established over actual capital expenditures. These controls need to be designed to preclude unauthorized expenditures, monitor cash flow requirements and provide accurate reporting of actual expenditures for comparison to the original estimates.

Significant unauthorized expenditures will distort the actual return on investment. This could cause the demise of a profitable project while allowing an unprofitable project to continue. Periodic cash flow requirements should be established and monitored to avoid unexpected use of operating cash and to enhance realization of the projected financial returns. Monitoring the cash flow requirement by itself is considered a control. Most importantly, comparing the actual expenditure to the original projected cash streams provides a basis upon which to make future decisions regarding the investment. The decision may be as dramatic as closing a store location or investing additional funds to expand a profitable operation. Analyzing actual to projected budget variances also provides a critical mechanism by which management can refine its assumptions in future capital budgeting models.

After completion of the project, it is a good idea to determine whether or not the investment decision was a success. This implies that all expenditures be accumulated and the progress of the project be tracked and, if the project is large enough, a postaudit should be performed. Tracking the projected expenditures requires separate accounting records for each project. A subsidiary ledger should be established to facilitate this process based on a unique project number. The number should appear on all invoices, vouchers, and so on associated with the project. Postauditing is certainly recommended for all construction jobs whether it is a new store or renovation of an existing store. After all of the data has been gathered, a final ROI calculation can be made to verify that the benefit derived exceeded the cost.

SUMMARY

Capital budgeting provides management with a means of evaluating investment alternatives, the success of which can be quantitatively measured. Historically, capital budgeting has been limited in that management uses the process to make the initial decision, infrequently monitoring its progress and re-evaluating the basic assumptions.

Capital budgeting is not without its limitations, since it is based upon assumptions and projections. However, if the process is monitored, it is a powerful tool with which retailers can analyze the impact on the financial results of any proposed investment. Since the process is limited, careful monitoring of actual versus budgeted results is required to ensure continued profitability to the retail organization.

CHAPTER TWENTY-SIX

Cash Management

Much like merchandise, cash represents a key asset and the retailer can significantly boost overall performance through effective management of the cash position. By increasing the amount of cash available, the retailer can build working capital, permit increases to merchandise and facilities, reduce borrowing requirements, or earn investment income by placing funds in interest-bearing accounts or securities.

The objective of a cash management program is to maximize available cash balances and to ensure that those balances are used as effectively as possible. To accomplish this objective, it is necessary to develop a system for collecting funds due as quickly as possible, rapidly converting those funds into earning assets, and delaying disbursements as long as possible.

POLICIES SUPPORTING EFFECTIVE CASH MANAGEMENT

While the objective of a cash management program is straightforward, developing an effective system is not simple. A retailer faced with a widespread geographic network, multiple payment options, diverse investment strategies, and varied disbursement requirements must address many issues. Policies are needed in the following areas:

- What forms of payment will be accepted? Among the options are cash, checks, own charge, third party credit cards, and debit cards.

- What banking relationships will be maintained for collection and concentration of receipts, investment of available balances, and disbursements?

- How will receipts be converted into useable funds? This involves policies for handling cash, settling debit and credit card transactions, and collecting accounts receivable?

- How will available cash balances be projected? This requires methods for estimating collections and disbursements to determine how much cash needs to be invested.

- How will available balances be invested to maximize investment income while maintaining liquidity to meet cash outflows?

- How will payments be disbursed to vendors?

COLLECTIONS

Collections policies and procedures are an area that has a major impact on the effective management of cash resources. In establishing collections practices, there are two principal criteria: the costs of collecting funds and the speed with which funds are collected.

Collections issues vary among alternative forms of payment; therefore, policies and procedures must be established for each type of payment accepted. These types are likely to include cash and checks, revolving credit, and third party credit and debit cards.

Cash Receipts

Cash is the most widely used form of payment, with virtually unlimited acceptance. Generally, three primary considerations must be addressed in determining practices for handling cash:

- Hold actual processing costs to a minimum. These processing costs will include the internal staff resources for processing cash receipts in preparation for deposit at the bank; they will also include the costs of vendors, generally the bank, who provide cash processing services. Costs of vendor services are likely to encompass fees for account maintenance, currency shipments, coin and currency verification, and check clearing. These external costs will be one factor influencing the selection of a bank with which to do business.

- Determine how much cash is needed to meet operating requirements. These requirements will be determined by the level of sales, as well as by the forms of payment that customers use to make purchases. Other services provided, such as check cashing, may raise cash requirements as well.

All efforts should be made to minimize the cash required on hand to meet operating requirements. Cash-on-hand represents funds that are not being used in other productive means, such as investment in interest-bearing accounts. In terms of foregone investment income, there is a very real cost to maintaining excess cash on the retailer's premises. On the other hand, shortages of cash also impose costs. These costs may take the form of inconvenience to customers or lost sales, or of monetary outlays to a currency supplier for emergency shipments. The costs of idle funds should be balanced against these costs of cash shortages in light of normal operating requirements to develop targets for cash levels.

- Minimize the time between receipt of cash and when funds become available for use. The first step in this process is to deposit funds in the bank as early as possible. To speed up this deposit, multiple deposits can be made during the day if cash levels warrant, one before the bank's daily cutoff, which may be as early as 2:00 P.M., and one at the end of the day. Goals need to be established for the stores' cashiers to have receipts prepared in time to meet these scheduled deposits.

Delivery of deposits to the bank will also need to be arranged. Depending on the proximity to the bank, staff availability, and the size of deposits, deposits can be delivered by a staff member, an outside messenger service, or armored carrier. While using an outside messenger or armored carrier may add significant costs, the earnings from earlier funds availability may outweigh these expenses.

It is important to ensure that the time between when funds are deposited and when funds become available for investment or other uses is as short as possible. This involves two components. First, the full amount of deposits is not always immediately available. Generally the bank will delay availability on a portion of checks in the deposit until the checks are cleared. This may be as long as three days for some checks, although the majority are likely to be collected within one day unless they are written on distant banks. In choosing a bank consider the schedule according to which the bank grants availability on the check portion of deposits. Generally, the bank should grant immediate availability if the checks are primarily drawn on local banks.

Second, it is necessary to move funds from the account of deposit to accounts from which funds will be used for investment or disbursements. This concentration of funds is described below.

Proprietary Credit Plans

A second form of payment is the proprietary credit plan, credit granted to the customer when the purchase is made. With this option, customers will be billed, usually monthly, for charges made during the billing period or carried over from prior periods. Retailers offering the proprietary credit option need to develop policies and procedures for accelerating the collection of funds once the billing cycle has closed. This involves two components: prompt billing and rapid receipt and processing of customer payments.

Once the billing cycle has closed, customer statements should be cut and mailed as soon as possible. Every day's delay in receiving payment represents foregone earnings since fewer funds are available for productive uses. The sooner customers receive their bills, the sooner the bills will be paid and the greater will be the funds available for investment or alternative uses.

Equally important is the time between when the customer mails a payment and the retailer receives available funds. This time period consists of three components: the days the payment is in the mail, the days the payment is being processed for deposit, and the days a check payment is being cleared before funds become available.

Operations that process payments internally want to cut this time period to a minimum. To achieve this goal, the payments processing unit should be organized to process payments as rapidly as possible and to deposit the bulk of payments on the day received. Each day's delay in depositing funds represents a foregone opportunity to use those funds. Similarly, the availability schedule offered on check deposits is a key criteria when choosing a bank, just as it is when choosing a bank at which to deposit daily store receipts.

The use of lockbox services may speed this collection process further. A lockbox service is an alternative to in-house processing of mail receipts. With a lockbox service, the retailer retains one or several banks to process payments. Payments are mailed to a post office box from which the bank picks up remittances several times a day. The bank then processes payments, a highly automated process since remittances are generally accompanied by machine-readable invoices. After processing, the bank deposits payments in the retailer's account and transmits payment information to the retailer. The bank may provide ancillary services such as microfilming remittance stubs and checks to facilitate recordkeeping and investigations.

The principal advantage of using lockbox services is that lockboxes are specifically designed to accelerate the collection process. Lockbox locations are selected based on nationwide studies of mail times and check clearing times. Payments sent to a well-located lockbox should be in the mail for a minimum period; the multiple pickups a day further cut mail time. Similarly, if the lockbox is well-situated, the time required to clear checks will be reduced and funds availability will be improved.

A second advantage to lockbox services is that they may cut processing costs. With a bank receiving and processing payments, the retailer reduces his internal processing costs. This is offset by the costs of the lockbox. However, since lockboxes are highly automated and designed to handle large volumes of payments, there may be economies of scale that enable the lockbox bank to offer prices below the retailer's own costs of processing payments in-house.

The use of lockboxes at multiple locations may cut the collections time further. By choosing lockbox locations around the country and having payments in each region mailed to a regional lockbox, mail float can be reduced. Since check payments are likely to be drawn on banks within the region as well, check float may also be cut. There are costs to using multiple lockboxes to reduce float, however. Establishing and managing multiple bank relationships may require additional resources. In addition, lockbox pricing may be volume-sensitive, and a relatively low payment volume may make the use of several lockbox locations uneconomical.

Third Party Credit and Debit Cards

Third party credit and debit cards have grown rapidly as accepted payments forms over the past several years. Credit cards, issued by banks as well as other providers of financial services, permit the customer to pay for merchandise with credit granted by the financial institution. The financial institution reimburses the retailer for the purchase. Debit cards are similar from the retailer's perspective. The key difference is that the financial institution involved does not grant credit to the customer but rather debits the customer's account for the amount of the purchase when the transaction occurs.

In addition to providing customer convenience and thereby promoting sales, credit and debit cards can be a valuable cash management tool. In evaluating cards against other payments forms and comparing the services of alternative providers of card services, the retailer needs to analyze the relative costs. These costs may involve several components.

First, providers of card services to the merchant may charge monthly account maintenance fees as well as per item fees for each transaction. The per item fees will include fees for authorizing transactions and settling transactions.

Second, the provider will charge a discount for merchant services. The discount is a percentage of the purchase amount which is shared between the bank, the bankcard organization, and the card issuer.

Third, delayed funds availability may be an implicit cost of merchant card services. Card transactions must be settled just as checks must be cleared. Consequently, the bank will not receive available funds immediately and may delay granting available funds to the retailer.

Providers of merchant card services vary considerably in their pricing approaches. Some will charge both per item fees and a discount and may delay funds availability by a day or two. Other providers will bundle all charges into the discount; the discount rate will be high but this will be offset by no per item fees and immediate funds availability.

The retailer can choose a number of methods for processing bankcard transactions. Originally bankcard transactions were paper-based. The retailer would complete paper tickets for each bankcard purchase and deposit these tickets at his bank. The bank would settle these tickets through one of the bankcard settlement arrangements and credit the retailer's account. This could be expensive because the retailer had to compensate the bank for the costs of processing the paper and for any delays in funds availability while the paper tickets were being processed.

Merchant banks are now offering electronic bankcard services to replace this paper-intensive method. These services can improve cash management effectiveness by lowering costs and improving availability. Generally, there are two options when considering electronic approaches to bankcard transactions:

1. Point-of-sale authorization. Under this scheme, each bankcard transaction is authorized electronically via point-of-sale terminals that transmit card and sale information to one of the national authorization systems. The principal advantage of this method is that both the cost for each authorization and the discount rate may be lower. Transactions continue to be settled based on paper tickets deposited at the bank.

2. Electronic draft capture services. Under this scheme, the retailer uses the point-of-sale terminal not only to authorize sales but also to capture the invoice information electronically. This electronic invoice rather than the paper ticket is used by the bank to settle transactions and to credit the retailer's account.

Electronic draft capture may offer significant benefits. Per transaction processing costs may be significantly lower because much of the paper processing by the bank has been eliminated and authorizations can be handled automatically. In addition, the electronic capture of information allows transactions to be settled more rapidly. This allows the retailer to receive available funds sooner, increasing balances available for investment or other uses. Finally, settlement arrangements for draft capture transactions may involve lower discounts, allowing the retailer to pay a smaller percentage of purchase amounts to the merchant bank.

CASH CONCENTRATION

Once steps have been taken to collect funds as rapidly as possible, by establishing procedures for early deposit of store receipts, building a lockbox network, or the like, policies and procedures must be developed to promote the rapid utilization of those funds. The use of widespread locations or multiple lockboxes can result in available funds in banks in several locations. Those funds must be transferred into productive uses as quickly as possible.

Typically, collected funds will initially move into interest-bearing accounts or securities. This investment function is normally controlled centrally through the treasury department. Consequently, collected funds must be transferred from multiple locations to a central account from which investments are made. This process is referred to as cash concentration.

For example, a retailer may have ten store locations spread throughout the Northeast. Each store maintains a local account to which it deposits receipts. These receipts must be transferred to the corporate account for investment by the treasury staff. Only when the funds are invested from the corporate account do they begin providing interest earnings to the company.

There are three main methods for performing this cash concentration function: Depository Transfer Checks (DTCs), electronic debits through the Automated Clearinghouse (ACH), and wire transfers. These methods differ in the speed with which funds can be transferred as well as in the costs of transferring funds.

A DTC is simply a preauthorized check drawn on the retailer's local bank accounts. With this system, the local store reports receipts daily to the treasury staff or to the company's concentration bank. The treasury staff or the concentration bank then issues the DTC and deposits it in the concentration account. The concentration bank clears the DTC through normal check clearing channels that evening. Funds become available one or two days later, depending on normal check clearing times.

An electronic debit through the Automated Clearinghouse, also referred to as an electronic DTC, works in much the same way. The local store reports receipts daily. Based on that report, the treasury staff or concentration bank will originate an ACH transaction to transfer the funds from the local bank to the concentration bank. The ACH transaction is really nothing more than an electronic check, which is cleared through the Federal Reserve and private sector automated clearinghouses. As with paper DTCs, funds become available one or two days later at the concentration bank.

With both paper and electronic DTCs, funds become available at the concentration bank one or two days after the stores report receipts to the treasury staff. Some treasury staffs are able to reduce this delay in availability by anticipating receipts and issuing the DTCs for anticipated amounts a day or two earlier. To use anticipatory DTCs, however, the treasury staff must be able to project daily receipts accurately and should make some arrangements to handle overdrafts in case actual receipts are below projections.

Wire transfers are a speedier method of moving funds from local accounts to the concentration account. With a wire transfer, either the local store or the treasury staff can transfer the funds virtually instantaneously from the local account to the concentration account. Thus, the funds will arrive at the concentration bank a day or two earlier than with DTCs and can be invested earlier.

The key disadvantage of wire transfers is that they are very expensive. Wire transfers are likely to cost between $10 and $20 dollars compared to $1 for a DTC. In choosing which concentration option to use, the retailer must weigh the greater cost of the wire transfer against the increased interest income from investing the funds a day or two earlier. The best option will depend on the size of the transfer and current interest rates. If a high dollar transfer is being made and interest rates are high, the increased interest income may exceed the additional cost of the wire transfer. For smaller payments, however, paper or electronic DTCs are likely to be the better option for the retailer.

DISBURSEMENTS

The goal in considering approaches to disbursements is to adopt disbursement policies and procedures that maximize the available funds for productive uses. On the disbursements side, this goal dictates a strategy of delaying payments as long as possible and minimizing the level of idle funds required to support the disbursements process. This allows cash balances to earn interest income for as long as possible.

In developing disbursement policies and procedures, three key questions must be addressed:

- When will payments to vendors be made?

- Who will have responsibility for handling disbursements?

- How will disbursements be made?

Timing of Disbursements

The timing of payments to vendors can have a major impact on how well cash resources are managed. Generally, delaying payments allows for use of the funds for additional time and earning additional investment income.

The advantages of longer use of funds, however, must be offset by two considerations. First, payment terms may vary by when payments are made. Early payment may entitle the retailer to cash discounts. If so, the benefits of longer use of funds will need to be weighed against the value of the cash discount. Whether it is decided to accept the discount or delay payment will depend on the size of the discount relative to the interest income that could be earned by holding the funds until a later payment date. Generally, it is advantageous to take the cash discount.

Second, consideration must be given as to how payment policies affect relationships with vendors as well as overall credit standings. Payment delays that increase available funds have the opposite effect on vendors: Slow payment delays the vendors' collections and reduces the vendors' available funds. Consequently, major delays in payments can lead to deterioration in vendor relations and service. Indeed, adopting extreme disbursement strategies can threaten overall credit standings.

While the payments should not be delayed at the expense of vendors, it is appropriate to negotiate advantageous payment terms that will postpone payment due dates and maximize offered discounts for early payment. The retailer may also be entitled to credits from vendors for returned goods. Available cash balances will be increased if it is permissible to deduct credits from vendor payments rather than waiting for direct payments from vendors.

Some inventory costs may be able to be shifted to vendors through dating. Under a dating arrangement, merchandise may be purchased before the normal selling period but payment withheld until the merchandise is sold. Such an arrangement can boost available funds considerably while significantly reducing the burden of financing inventory.

Responsibility for Disbursements

Responsibility for handling disbursements is a question of how centralized the control of disbursements should be. Practices vary considerably in this area. At one extreme, is a highly centralized disbursement process. A corporate treasury or controller unit handles all disbursements. This approach offers several advantages. With centralized responsibility there is better control over when payments are made. The disbursements process will be more closely tied to the collections and investments processes, permitting more efficient investments and better cash forecasting. With centralized responsibility, banking requirements may be streamlined, fewer disbursement accounts will be needed and a widespread network of decentralized disbursement accounts will not need to be funded.

On the other hand, centralization of disbursements may pose a significant administrative burden. Procedures must be established for transmitting accounts payable information from multiple store locations to the centralized unit and for verifying that invoices are valid and correct. Granting greater autonomy to each location to handle its own disbursements may reduce the administrative resources devoted to the disbursements process.

Disbursements Methods

The key issue in determining disbursement methods is what type of disbursement account to maintain. Generally there are three options: a regular demand deposit account, a zero balance account, or a controlled disbursement account. The selection of a preferred option depends on the costs of maintaining and funding the account versus the length of time during which funds can continue to be used supporting disbursements.

The least expensive account will be a regular demand deposit account. Account maintenance and transaction fees will be lower than for zero balance and controlled disbursement accounts. The principal disadvantage of this account is that the retailer must fund the account up front. When checks drawn on the account are presented to the bank, the account must contain sufficient funds to cover the checks; otherwise, the checks will be returned to the vendor's bank or an overdraft will be incurred and the retailer charged. To cover outstanding checks, balances will have to be maintained in the account. These balances represent idle funds on which interest income is being lost. While these balances may be reduced by estimating the lag between the time payments are sent to vendors and checks are presented to the bank, it will not be possible to eliminate these idle balances altogether and there will be the risk of incurring overdraft charges.

Zero balance and controlled disbursement accounts offer opportunities for reducing the idle balances required to support the disbursements process. With these accounts, the disbursement account need not be funded until checks are presented to the bank.

Under a zero balance account arrangement, the disbursement account will be tied to a second account which maintains balances. When checks are presented, the bank automatically transfers funds from this second account to the disbursement account. The advantages of this method are two-fold. First, if multiple disbursement accounts are maintained, for example, one for vendor payments and one for payroll, a common pool of balances can be maintained to fund both accounts by tying the vendor payments and payroll accounts to the same funding account. The balances in the combined funding account will generally be less than if separate balances had to be maintained for each disbursement account. Second, the bank may pay interest on balances in the funding account directly or by sweeping excess funds into an interest-bearing account.

A controlled disbursement arrangement allows even tighter control of idle balances. With controlled disbursement, the disbursements need not be funded at all until checks are presented to the bank. Each day the bank will report the checks that have been presented that morning. The exact amount of funds required can then be transferred to the bank that day. This permits keeping funds fully invested until checks are presented. Of course, there is a cost for this option. In addition to higher account charges, resources must be devoted to receiving balance information daily and for transferring funds to the disbursement account. If funds are invested outside the disbursement bank, they will have to be wired to the bank, and as noted previously, wire transfers can be quite costly.

In selecting which of these accounts to use for disbursements, the relative costs versus the value of reducing idle funds to support the disbursements process must be considered. If payments volume is relatively small, little investment income may be sacrificed by using a regular demand deposit account. This will be especially true if the amount of checks that will be presented on any given day can be closely predicted. On the other hand, if there is a large volume of payments, the increased investment income may outweigh the higher banking costs of zero balance and controlled disbursement accounts.

Some businesses have adopted remote disbursement procedures to further delay payments. By making disbursements from remote banks, these businesses can delay when checks will be presented on their accounts. This gives these businesses an additional day or two to use the funds. While remote disbursement may increase available funds and investment income, it generally is not a practice to be encouraged. Remote disbursement by the retailer will delay the vendors' collections, and may thereby affect vendor relationships and service. Since the result of the widespread use of remote disbursement is to increases the overall costs of the check clearing process, bank regulators strongly discourage this practice.

BANKING COSTS

An effective cash management program will require considerable use of banking services. Accordingly, the cost of those services will impact the benefits received from cash management program. In comparing alternative banks, it is appropriate to address not only how well a bank's services meet cash management objectives but also the costs of those services.

Evaluating relative banking costs is not simple. Three factors affect overall cost. First, is the explicit charges of the bank. These charges will include account maintenance fees, transaction fees, balance reporting fees, and overdraft fees and interest.

Second, is the availability a bank grants on deposits. As noted, banks will not grant immediate availability on check deposits because it may take the bank a number of days to receive funds itself. The slower the availability granted by the bank, the fewer funds will be available and the greater will be total banking costs.

Third, is the bank's compensating balance arrangements. Banks generally grant customers credits based on the level of balances in the customers' accounts. These credits are used to offset the explicit charges incurred for banking services. The credits earned for a given level of balances will depend on two things.

1. Credits depend on the proportion of balances which earn credits. This will be less than the full, or book, balance in the account. The bank will deduct uncollected balances, stemming from checks in the process of collection, before credits are calculated. The bank is also likely to deduct an additional portion of balances to compensate for reserve requirements, the proportion of balances which the bank must hold as idle funds itself, and for FDIC assessments for deposit insurance.

2. Credits depend on the rate used to compute credits. Most banks offer an earnings credit rate slightly below market rates as measured by an instrument such as Treasury bills. The rate offered will also affect whether to maintain balances to compensate the bank for services or to pay for services directly. Frequently, funds can be invested directly at a rate higher than the bank's earnings credit rate. If so, reducing compensating balances and paying for services explicitly is advantageous.

Most banks will provide customers with a monthly account analysis statement summarizing the banking relationship. The account analysis statement provides information on services used during the month and associated charges, average book and collected (available) balances, and earnings credits on compensating balances. This statement provides a good vehicle for monitoring banking costs and should be reviewed closely to ensure they are in line with services used.

CASH FORECASTING AND INVESTMENTS

Cash forecasting is a final critical component of the cash management process. The main objective of cash forecasting is to determine the level of funds available for investment.

Available balances should be forecasted daily. Several pieces of information will be needed to develop the cash forecast. The starting point will be the prior day's balances. The level of funds expected to be concentrated that day must be added to this balance. This amount will be estimated based on the reported receipts from individual locations as well as on experience in prior periods. The level of investments maturing that day should also be added, and, accordingly, requires a good system for tracking those maturities.

From this sum, subtract disbursements. If a controlled disbursement account is used, the bank will report disbursements daily. Otherwise disbursements should be estimated based on when bills were paid and historical check clearing times.

Based on this forecast, funds can be placed in various investments. This forecast should be developed as early in the day as possible since funds can generally be invested at higher rates earlier in the day.

Cash forecasts should also be developed for longer periods, for example, monthly or quarterly. These longer term forecasts will be valuable in developing a particular investment strategy. Generally, higher interest rates can be earned if investments are for longer periods. Knowing cash inflows and outflows for one or several months into the future will enable the undertaking of longer term investments while maintaining enough liquidity to meet anticipated cash outflows and unforeseen requirements.

Many banks offer treasury workstations that facilitate this cash forecasting and management process. These workstations offer online access to current collections and disbursement information. They may include modules for tracking investments and can generate a variety of reports concerning available cash and financial assets. They may also allow for online origination of electronic DTCs or wire transfers and online investment of available cash. The use of such workstations may improve financial information and thereby overall cash management while enabling a reduction of staff resources devoted to cash management activities.

CHAPTER TWENTY-SEVEN

Cash Forecasting

Cash forecasts serve as road maps pointing out periods during the fiscal year when excess funds may be available for investment or when cash deficiencies may occur. Thus, they are an important component of the overall cash management process. Facilitating planning actions with respect to potential investment opportunities and financing needs. This is a critical matter in many retail organizations, as cash receipt and disbursement levels can change dramatically during the course of the year, and advance information concerning the availability of funds or the need for additional funds facilitates effective management of cash resources.

CASH FORECAST PREPARATION GUIDELINES

Cash forecasts should generally be prepared with the following guidelines in mind:

- The amounts contained in the cash forecast should be based on the operating budget so that planning actions relative to cash management are consistent with the operating objectives.

- The key to the development of a cash forecast is the selection of underlying assumptions that reasonably set forth future cash receipt and disbursement patterns. The quality of the underlying assumptions is critical to the reliability of the forecast, while the forecast preparation procedures are of secondary importance.

- Although the selection of assumptions entails the exercise of judgment concerning future trends, historic data should be compiled and analyzed to serve as a guide in the selection of the cash forecast assumptions. This historic data should be compiled and analyzed with the following objective in mind: The identification of all the cash receipt sources and cash disbursement payment types and the establishment of the historic patterns concerning these matters. All receipt sources and payment types, that are unique as to their timing and which would be significant to a reasonably reliable estimate of future cash inflows and outflows, should be components of the forecast. Examples of typical cash receipt sources and cash disbursement payment types that would be encompassed by this process include the following:

1. *Typical Cash Receipt Sources*
   Cash sales, net of cash refunds.
   Customer accounts receivable collections.
   Third-party charge card collections.
   Layaway deposits and collections.
   Leased department receipts.
   Sub-tenant rental payments.
   Vendor rebates and reimbursements.
   Investment income receipts.
   Sales of property fixtures and equipment.
   Short- and long-term borrowings.
   Other revenue collections.

2. *Typical Cash Payment Types*
   Merchandise purchase payments.
   Payroll payments.
   Rental payments by type (base rent and percentage rent).
   Lease department settlement payments.
   Tax payments by type (real estate sales and use, income, and payroll).
   Insurance payments.
   Utility payments.
   Operating supply purchase payments.
   Transportation payments.
   Sales promotion and advertising payments.
   Professional service payments.
   Employee benefit plan payments.
   Bonus payments.

Capital expenditures.

Debt service payments.

Shareholder dividend payments.

Other operating expense payments.

These examples are not all inclusive. Many receipt sources and payment types have unique timing and should be provided for in the cash forecast.

All known and anticipated changes in business conditions should be considered when establishing the underlying forecast assumptions. Cash forecasts should be prepared for time periods that correspond with the retailer's cash planning needs. This often entails the preparation of both long- and short-term cash forecasts.

Long-term forecasts typically cover the entire fiscal year with subtotals which correspond to semiannual, quarterly, or monthly reporting periods. The short-term forecast, is in most cases for no more than a quarterly period with subtotals for monthly and weekly periods. Although the preparation of forecasts on a weekly basis is a cumbersome task, it is often necessary due to the significant variations in week-to-week cash receipt and disbursement volumes which many retailers experience.

Cash forecasting procedures should facilitate revision of the forecast so that changes in circumstances can be reflected in the forecasts for the remainder of the period. The ability to reflect changing circumstances enhances the usefulness of the forecasts and makes them a more effective management tool. Electronic data processing techniques are frequently utilized in connection with the preparation of cash forecasts.

Timing differences between the receipt of cash and the availability of such receipts for use as collected bank funds, as well as timing differences between the issuance of checks and their clearance by the bank, should be recognized in the forecast.

Revolving credit arrangements that set borrowing limits based on formulas that are tied to either accounts receivable balances, inventory balances or both are frequently established. In many situations, these arrangements also restrict the availability of the cash receipts. The effects of these matters should be recognized in the cash forecast.

SUMMARY

Cash forecasts are an important component of the overall cash management process, as they serve to point out periods during the fiscal year when additional funds may be needed or when funds may be available for investment. The key to the development of reliable cash forecasts is the selection of assumptions which reasonably set forth future cash receipt and disbursement patterns. Therefore, historic patterns should be carefully analyzed to provide guidance concerning future trends. In addition, all known and anticipated changes in business conditions should be considered when establishing the underlying forecast assumptions.

Cash forecasts should be prepared for time periods that correspond with cash planning needs. This often entails the preparation of both long- and short-term forecasts. Additionally, the cash forecasting procedures should facilitate expeditious revision of the forecasts to reflect changes in circumstances on a timely basis, thus enhancing their usefulness as a cash management tool.

CHAPTER TWENTY-EIGHT

Real Estate Financing

An increasing number of retailers have turned to leasing as a means of financing stores, warehouses, and furniture and fixtures. The ability to lease permits the acquiring of assets without having ever to raise funds equal to the purchase price. This attribute of leasing has made it a particularly attractive vehicle with which to finance expansion programs since it allows expansion and benefit from the new assets without actually owning them. Long-term leasing is similar to borrowing since it provides financial leverage and has other similar debt characteristics such as repayment schedules and interest rates. In the case of a lease, the interest rate is implicit. Since the adoption of Statement No. 13 on issues by the Financial Accounting Standards Board (FASB) in November 1976 the debt characteristics of certain types of long-term leases require disclosure in the financial statements. (See Chapter Twenty-Four.)

LEASING VERSUS OWNERSHIP

When planning the acquisition of a capital asset, there are numerous financing methods available, ranging from outright purchase to short-term rentals. The differences in these extremes, and the gradations between them, are primarily related to the degrees of ownership. When an asset is purchased outright for cash, the buyer has full rights of ownership. As soon as the buyer obtains outside financing, the degree of control begins to diminish. For example, in an installment purchase, the buyer will generally have full ownership rights with the exception of the ability to sell. The right of sale will be limited by the lien of the lender. If a potential buyer obtains full financing by using a long-term lease, he retains operating risks of obsolescence and maintenance, but relinquishes almost all risks of ownership. The lessor bears such risks, and the rental is priced accordingly.

The decision as to whether to lease or buy is one that can be made only after a careful analysis of the advantages and disadvantages, and the resultant cash flows, from the two basic options. The "analysis" cannot be made by the simplistic approach of comparing on the one hand one current (total) payment and full ownership with extended payments (which in the aggregate exceed the one payment) and no ownership on the other hand. Aside from being economically doubtful, this type of decision can no longer be made in the current era of low profit margins and high costs of money. Using the same logic, the retailer would pay a salesman ten years' salary when hired, as opposed to paying him on a weekly basis. If this seems ludicrous, why does it automatically make sense, for example, to buy outright a fixture with a 10-year life, instead of making monthly payments as the fixture, in effect, generates income? The example is obviously simplistic, but the point is still valid of consideration: "Turning capital investment" is becoming more and more a critical aspect of profitability, as "turning inventory" always has been.

While the examples given stress the advantages of leasing, there are equally impressive disadvantages. This chapter will highlight the pros and cons of leasing, detail the accounting and tax considerations, present methods for making a quantitative "buy or lease" decision, and offer some subjective points for consideration.

PROS AND CONS

For comparative purposes, the pros and cons from both the lessee's and the lessor's point of view are presented. To provide a framework for the subsequent technical discussions, the following list summarizes the advantages and disadvantages of leasing.

Lessee—Advantages

- One hundred percent financing of the cost of the property, on attractive terms.

- Financing of initial acquisitions costs is possible because these costs can be included in a lease. Such costs, including delivery charges, interest on advance payments, sales, and/or use taxes and installation costs, are not normally financed under other methods of equipment financing.

- Increased leverage at overall lower cost. Indirect financing via the use of leases effectively makes possible a larger amount of financing at an aggregate lower capital cost.

- Rental deductions generally allowable for tax purposes for the term of the lease without problems or disputes about depreciable life of the property.

- Possible improvement of net book income during the earlier years of the basic lease term. Rental payments in the earlier years of a lease are generally less than the combined interest expense and depreciation (even on the straight-line method) which a corporate property owner would otherwise have charged in the income statement.

- Potential reduction in state and city franchise and income taxes since the property factor, which is generally one of the three factors in the allocation formula, is reduced.

- Full deductibility for tax purposes of rent payment, notwithstanding that the rent is partially based on the cost of the land.

- The risk of obsolescence can be avoided by the lessee as compared with the risk he would assume on the purchase of such equipment.

Lessee—Disadvantages

- Loss of residual rights to the property at the end of the lease. If the lessee had full residual rights, the transaction would have been a financing instead of a true lease. The lessee may have purchase and/or renewal options, but the renewals result in payments to the lessor after the full cost of the property has been amortized.

- Rentals greater than comparable debt service. Since the lessor borrows funds with which to buy the asset to be leased, the rent is based on the lessor's debt service plus a profit factor. This amount may exceed the debt service that the lessee would have had to pay had such lessee purchased the property.

- Loss of operating and financing flexibility. If an asset was owned outright and a new, improved model became available, the owner could sell or exchange the old model for the new one. This flexibility may not be available under a lease. If interest rates decreased, lease payments would remain constant, whereas the owner of the asset could refinance the debt at a lower rate of interest.

- Loss of tax benefits from accelerated depreciation and high interest expense deductions in early years that would have produced a temporary cash savings assuming that equivalent financing had been obtained.

Lessor—Advantages

- Higher rate of return than on investment in straight debt. To compensate for risk and lack of marketability, the lessor can charge the lessee a higher effective rate, particularly after considering the lessor's tax benefits, than would be available directly to the lessee.

- Lessor's claim to a specific asset. Should the lessee have financial trouble, the lessor can look to a specific asset as opposed to being just a general creditor.

- Retention of residual value of the property at the end of the lease. The cost of the asset is amortized over the basic lease term. At that time, the lessee will abandon, renew, or purchase. In the first instance, the lessor can then sell the asset. In the latter alternatives, the lessor will receive payments that represent substantially all profit.

Lessor—Disadvantages

- Dependence on ability of lessee to pay rent on a timely basis.

- Potential detriment from unexpected changes in the tax law which could reduce tax benefits and related cash flow.

- Potential change in the depreciable life, thereby altering lessor's return. If the Internal Revenue Service significantly extends the depreciable life of the asset, the projected return upon which the lessor made the investment would diminish.

- Negative cash flow in later years. As the lease progresses, an increasing percentage of the rent goes toward nondeductible principal amortization. The interest and depreciation tax deductions both decline as the lease progresses.

- Potentially large tax on disposition resulting from depreciation recapture provisions of the Internal Revenue Code.

As the above comparisons indicate, there are many facets of leasing which must be considered before the decision is made. The pros and cons cited must be reviewed subjectively by the potential lessor and lessee to determine how the advantages and disadvantages apply to their respective financial and tax status. A critical advantage to one retailer may well have no bearing on the decision of another. For example, the benefit of not recording additional debt by leasing may be a great advantage to a heavily leveraged company, but may be insignificant to a firm with a small debt load.

EVALUATION TECHNIQUES

The quantitative analysis of the buy-versus-lease decision involves a cash flow comparison, and as such is essentially a capital budgeting type of question. The potential lessee must determine what the cash position would be under each alternative, and then compare the results using an approach which is believed to be the most appropriate for the particular company. Such comparison may be based on rate of return, present value of cash flows, or net cash position, to name a few currently used criteria.

The policies and criteria that a company uses in its capital budgeting procedures should carry over to the lease analysis so that the company's return on investment from a lease will be viewed against the same frame of reference. It is not, however, the purpose of this chapter to discuss and evaluate capital budgeting. Accordingly, the discussion here will center on the pertinent factors to be considered in a lease-or-buy comparison. The financial effects of an outright purchase will be examined first.

When a company purchases an asset, cash must be paid out to cover the purchase price. This cash is financed either by obtaining a new loan specifically for the purchase or from the company's funds made available by current borrowings. In either case, the interest cost associated with the funds should be recognized. For purposes of the lease-versus-buy analysis, the costs the company must carry, related to the asset, are the interest on the debt and the depreciation of the asset. Operating expenses such as insurance and maintenance are excluded since the lease would typically be a net lease with such expenses borne by the lessee whether owned or leased. Thus, at the time of purchase, the company receives a sum of money from some debt source which it disburses to purchase the asset. The company then pays a yearly debt service over the life of the asset; any salvage or residual value of the asset accrues to the company.

The cash outlays of the buyer consist of the initial purchase cost and the yearly interest and principal payments. The cash inflows are the loan, the tax benefits of the yearly interest and depreciation expense, and the salvage value.

Given the above facts and assuming that the company has sufficient taxable income that enables it to obtain the full benefit of the interest and depreciation deductions, the yearly and cumulative cash flow can be calculated.

In a lease, the cash flows are more easily defined. The lessee pays a yearly rental that is fully deductible. The rent is based on the debt service the lessor must pay, plus a profit return to the lessor. The interest on the debt is generally a function of the credit worthiness of the lessee, rather than the lessor, since the lender is basically looking to the financial viability of the lessee for the debt repayment. Thus, the cash flow analysis of the lessee consists of level annual outflows over the lease period, less the related tax benefit. Salvage or residual value considerations are inapplicable since the lessee has no rights of ownership in the asset leased.

At this point, the annual cash flows from an outright sale and from a lease have been developed. The next step is to compare the flows, by an accepted method such as the discounted present value, to determine which results in the greater cash benefit or yield.

In making the cash flow analysis, the potential lessee must consider the effects of changes in the assumptions used. For example, what will the resultant cash flow be if the Internal Revenue Service requires a longer depreciation period than originally calculated? How would a ½ percent change in interest rates affect the decision? Ideally, the result of the quantitative comparison should be a series of judgments which could then be assigned probabilities.

Thus, the results of the analysis could be similar to the following:

- With a 10-year life and an 8 percent borrowing, outright purchase is better by X dollars.

- A two-year increase in useful life reduces the benefit of outright purchase to $(X - Y)$ dollars.

- A ½ percent increase in interest reduces the benefit of outright purchase to $(X - Y)$ dollars.

- There is a 30 percent chance that the life will be increased two years.

- There is a 10 percent chance that interest rates will increase ½ percent.

Once hypotheses and computations similar to these have been made, a decision can be arrived at which would give the most realistic net dollar benefit.

QUALITATIVE CONSIDERATIONS

As part of the buy-versus-lease decision process, management should consider the qualitative factors of leasing or buying in addition to the quantitative calculations computed in the buy-versus-lease decision model.

Desire for operational flexibility can be impaired by leasing if the lease has restrictive clauses regarding subleasing. For example, the lease may require a comparable retail establishment as a subleasee, or contain clauses requiring the lessee to restore the building to its original condition. These could make the lease economically infeasible to get out of or to honor. In addition, the retailer's ability to close unprofitable stores due to poor performance can be restricted if the lease requires the store to remain open for a certain period of time.

Further, the lessor's financial condition and the lessor's reputation and relationship with other tenants should be assessed. A poor reputation may be a symptom of an uncooperative lessor. Finally, a significant estimated residual value could mean buying is cheaper than leasing.

ACCOUNTING AND TAX CONSIDERATIONS

Since the adoption of SFAS No. 13 in 1976 retailers are required to disclose their minimum lease payments over the next five years (see Chapter Twenty-Four). Operating leases on the other hand are not recognized on the balance sheet, rather the rental payments are treated as current operating expenses. The total rent expense for the accounting period is then disclosed in the footnotes to the financial statements.

In the field of leasing, there are two basic tax considerations: the treatment of gain or loss on the sale and leaseback, and the actual treatment of the lease as a true lease or as a financing.

The asset sold in a sale and leaseback is generally a "Section 1231 asset" —that is, a depreciable asset or land used in the taxpayer's trade or business. The Internal Revenue Code provides that the net gain on the sale of 1231 assets that are not subject to depreciation recapture should be treated as a capital gain, whereas net losses may be deducted from income as an ordinary loss. This treatment allows the future lessee great flexibility in timing a sale and leaseback to best fit the tax posture. For example, in a high-bracket year, the retailer could sell and lease back an asset that has a market value substantially below book and obtain a large ordinary deduction. The danger here is that the Internal Revenue Service (IRS) could declare the transaction a sham and disallow the loss deduction. The typical attack of the IRS has been that a sale has not really taken place. Rather, the corporation has retained control over the asset while obtaining financing with the asset as collateral. The IRS position has been the strongest in cases where the terms of the sale and the lease were not at fair market value and the lease was for an extended period. Accordingly, the taxpayer's strongest defense has been where arm's-length negotiations are apparent, the terms are clearly at fair market value, the buyer/lessor is not a related party, and the basic lease term is under 20 years. These defenses cannot be overemphasized. Case law has gone both ways, but the taxpayer has generally been successful where it has been possible to prove that the sale price and the rent were not less than fair market value.

Once the lease has been entered into, there are two ways it can be treated for tax purposes. If the IRS recognizes the lease as a true lease, the lessee is entitled to deduct, in the appropriate period, annual rent expenses for purposes of federal income taxes. Normally, the appropriate period is that in which liability for rent is incurred, in accordance with the terms of the lease, assuming the timing of such rent liability is not unreasonable. If, however, the IRS looks upon the lease as a financing, the lessee is deemed to be the equitable owner of the property and is permitted to deduct the depreciation and interest expense. As discussed earlier in the chapter, the former treatment allows a level deduction over the period of the lease with no disputes about depreciable life. The latter results in higher deductions in earlier years and lower deductions later, although the depreciable life may be contested by the IRS.

The test the IRS applies to determine whether a transaction is a financing is basically an analysis of the purchase options. If the lessee can purchase the property for an amount less than fair market value or for an amount approximately equal to what the debt balance would have been had the asset been bought outright, the transaction is viewed as a financing. If the lessee has a purchase option in an amount substantially in excess of probable fair market value or of the debt balance, the transaction receives lease status.

Comparing the accounting treatment to the tax treatment, there are many similarities. Generally accepted accounting principles are not necessarily in accord with the rules and regulations governing the determination of taxable income, and modification in financial reporting and tax reporting rules are made with the passage of time. It is entirely possible to view a lease agreement as a lease for financial reporting purposes, whereas it is deemed a financing for federal income taxes.

OTHER LEASING CONSIDERATIONS

Percentage Rental Arrangements

Percentage rental arrangements are made on the bases of the lessor's expecting to share in the earnings from the property.

Conversely the lessee is required to pay as rental a specific percentage of sales volume. The rates used to calculate the rent payment can be graduated as sales volume increases. The benefits from this type of arrangement are that the lessee is not burdened with a high cost for an unproductive location while the lessor is partially protected from the effects of inflation based on the concept that sales will increase over time. Likewise, the lessor is rewarded for locations that are high traffic and should command a premium rental rate.

Leases usually contain definitions of terms used (e.g., gross receipts) and state how the percentage rent is to be calculated. The bases upon which the rental is to be charged can vary from lease to lease.

Determining the accrual for percentage rents at the end of an accounting period can be difficult because tenants normally are not up to date in reporting their gross receipts and because sales reporting periods may be different from financial reporting periods. Therefore, a method of estimating the gross receipts expected by tenants for the period is needed. If the property has been in operation for a few years, historical data may be available to form a basis for an estimate. When actual data become available the real calculation is made and a settlement can then be determined.

As a practical matter, restatement of financial statements would not be necessary unless the difference between the actual rent and estimated rent was clearly material.

OTHER SOURCES OF FINANCING

Factoring of Accounts Receivable

Factoring is a financing arrangement whereby a third party, a factor, purchases receivables without recourse for nonpayment. Typically, the customer is notified of the transfer of the receivable and the factor assumes all credit and collection functions. The factor usually charges a commission fee, which is a small percentage of the face value of the accounts for the risk assumed with the possibility of uncollectible accounts. The selling company therefore receives the face amount of the receivables sold or factored less the commission fee.

Factoring of receivables can also be done on a non-notification basis. In this case the sellor retains the collection function, and its customers are unaware of the transfer of ownership of the receivable. Again, the factor purchases the receivables without recourse for uncollectible accounts. The benefits to selling or factoring receivables are fairly obvious:

- The company is usually relieved of the bookkeeping, billing, and collection functions.

- Immediate cash is available for business use.

- Losses from bad accounts are limited to the commission fee since the factor assumes all risk for uncollectible accounts.

- Financial planning and results can therefore be more accurately projected (including cash forecasts).

Drawbacks to selling or factoring the receivables are just as obvious:

- The commission fee charged may be greater than the actual uncollectible accounts.

- The company may lose interest income on those accounts sold.

- Agreements that are continuing whereby the factor assumes the credit function as well as the collection function the factor may establish the company's credit policies.

Factoring customer receivables is essentially early collection of receivables either in the form of cash or a receivable from the factor. The accounting treatment, therefore, is simply to record the cash collected and/or recognize a receivable from the factor for the balance not paid immediately in cash, expense the commission fee, and reduce receivables for those accounts which were sold. In this transaction accounts receivable have been liquidated and converted to cash, or to a receivable from the factor. As such, neither special disclosure nor a contingent liability account is required.

Franchising

Franchises are contracts for the exclusive right to perform certain functions or to sell certain products or services. These agreements involve the use, by the franchisee, of a trademark, trade name, patent, process, or know-how of the franchisor for the term of the franchise. Under the franchise agreement, the franchisee pays a fee to the franchisor as well as paying for other professional services incurred in obtaining the franchise. The franchisor may also require periodic payments based upon revenues or other factors in addition to the initial fee. The franchise agreement may also include certain restrictions on the franchisee such as capitalization of certain property improvements as part of property, plant, and equipment.

The concept of franchising has been with us for over 100 years. In that period three main forms of franchising have evolved—business format, product and trade name, and conversion franchising.

- Business format franchising involves business packages that include, along with access to a company's product, service, or trademark, a business format. This format usually includes a marketing strategy and plan, operating manuals and standards, quality controls, and an ongoing two-way communications network.

- Product and trademark franchising is the more traditional franchising arrangement in which the franchisee uses the franchisors trade name and sells the franchisor's products, but generally does not receive the total business package. Included in this group are automobile and truck dealers, gasoline service stations, and soft drink bottlers.

- Conversion franchising allows owners of established but nongrowth or even declining businesses to become a franchised outlet of a parent company.

The common thread throughout all three of these franchising arrangements is that the franchisee leverages off of the franchisors name, reputation, and industry expertise.

From a franchisor's perspective, franchising its operations provides a vehicle to expand operations without using internally generated funds; or, when funds are not readily available for expansion, allows for development and rapid expansion of a concept when the window of opportunity is short. Franchising can also add product quality in situations where the parent company feels that branch operations cannot adequately be motivated or controlled by headquarters. The rationale here is that the franchisee's sole livelihood depends upon the success of the franchise and will, therefore, be motivated to maintain the high level of quality in the product or service that the parent company has established.

Franchising is not without drawbacks. A certain degree of control over operations is relinquished, net income in excess of the franchise fee from profitable locations is lost, and there is the risk that the franchisee may not have the expertise or business skills to successfully operate the franchise. This could tarnish the reputation of the parent, the product or service.

Accounting Treatment

If the franchise agreement is for a specified period of time, the cost of the franchise should be written off systematically over that period. If the estimated economic life is less than the term of the agreement, the agreement should be amortized over that period. If the agreement is perpetual, the costs should be written off over a period not to exceed the estimated economic life or a period of time not to exceed 40 years (in accordance with APB 17). The economic life of the franchise should be evaluated periodically.

Franchises should be presented on the balance sheet at cost less accumulated amortization. The financial statements should also disclose the amortization method and term.

CAPTIVE INSURANCE COMPANY

Typically a captive insurance company is a foreign corporation wholly owned or controlled by a U.S. person or group of U.S. persons or corporations (associations) and used to insure risks that may not otherwise be insurable on an economic basis. In other words, the captive insurance company is a risk-financing vehicle.

Formation of a captive insurance company has the following advantages associated with it (beyond the other tax advantages associated with insurance companies and foreign corporations):

- Insuring uninsurable or difficult coverages—this can be important to a buyer with new or unusual coverage demands or to an insured rejected by the standard market, whether due to general market conditions or its own poor loss history.

- Lower underwriting costs—expenses, such as the insurance company's basic charges and brokers' insurance commissions, can be areas for savings.

- Investment income—substantial cash flows, which previously enriched the commercial insurer, will now instead benefit the captive. In addition, a foreign captive may enjoy investment choices offering higher yields than those available to a domestic regulated insurer.

- Easier placement of reinsurance—captives have direct access to many reinsurance markets. Moreover, association captives can have tremendous buying power, giving risk managers greater leverage in creating reinsurance capacity. Given a sufficient level of retention, the advantages may extend to previously uninsurable or difficult to place coverages.

- Insurance profit center—captives with adequate capital and capable staff may be able to generate profits on outside business, whether written on a direct or reinsurable basis.

- Loss control—captives can be formed incorporating certain claims defense and loss-prevention techniques tailored to the buyer's special needs. Commitment to a loss control program can enhance the effectiveness of a captive program by reducing losses and reinsurance expenses. Coverages can be tailored to fit requirements by a particular industry (e.g., steel, oil, banking) or to particular types of coverages for companies in a number of different industries (e.g., directors and officers coverage).

The tax considerations of the captive are the disadvantages of the captive. Two primary tax issues exist. The first is whether the captive will be recognized as a valid insurance company for tax purposes. If it is, then the captive can avail itself of certain favorable tax accounting rules presently permitted insurance companies. The second is whether a valid insurance arrangement exists between the captive and related policy holders. If so, premiums paid to the captive are currently deductible as ordinary and necessary business expenses.

Although the two issues are independent of each other, generally a positive answer to the second issue (whether insurance exists) results in a positive answer to the first issue. The following discussion covers the second issue in depth.

While the captive insurance company is not the sole answer to the capacity shortage and escalating premium environment it is clearly a risk-financing alternative that should be considered.

The various court decisions and other precedents to date indicate that from a tax standpoint it is preferable to either join in an association captive or, if a wholly owned captive is required for business reasons, to have the captive insure unrelated risks.

Careful planning must be done in organizing the captive and its operations. If properly structured the captive may produce certain tax advantages that might not otherwise be available.

OTHER FINANCING ALTERNATIVES

Use of a Captive Finance Company

One of the financing vehicles available to retailers that have their own installment credit account system is the captive finance company. This is a true asset-based financing vehicle that has the effect of shifting installment credit receivables, and the related borrowings against those receivables, to a separate wholly owned subsidiary. Under present generally accepted accounting principles, a captive finance company can be recorded by the parent under the equity method of accounting. This means the investment in the finance subsidiary can be recorded on one line in the parent's balance sheet. The income earned by the finance company is recorded on one line in the parent's income statement. Disclosure of the finance company's condensed balance sheet and income statement is required in the footnotes to the parent's financial statements.

The practical effect of this shifting is to remove the debt from the parent's financial statements and improve the parent's debt-to-equity ratio. Such a structure allows the finance company to borrow solely on the basis of the quality of the receivables. (Typically, lenders will allow borrowings of between 75 to 90 percent of the face value of the receivables.) Also, since borrowings are driven by the quality of the asset, lenders will accept debt-to-equity ratios of as high as 4:1 or 5:1 in the captive finance company. A retailer alone, without a captive, could never borrow with debt-to-equity ratios of 4:1 or 5:1. In fact, a retailer is considered heavily leveraged with a debt-to-equity ratio of 2:1.

Another consideration in using a captive finance company is the effect it has on the parent's current ratio. Depending on the debt structure before creating a captive, the shift of receivables and debt could have either a positive or negative effect on the current ratio. If vendors look to your current ratio before supplying you, this aspect must be considered.

The income generated by the captive finance company arises because the receivables are purchased at a discount from the parent. The discount is predetermined by contractual agreement with the parent. Normally, the discount is set to provide an earnings-to-fixed-charge coverage ratio of at least 1.5:1. Fixed charges are typically equal to the finance company's interest expense for a given accounting period, although fixed charges would be higher if the debt were being amortized.

The receivables are sold without recourse except that certain provisions are allowed for defaulted obligations and credits given for returned merchandise. Also, normally a percentage of the face value of the receivables is withheld upon sale by the parent. This percentage can vary, but most often is 10 percent.

All transactions are governed by an operating agreement between the parent and the finance company specifying the terms under which the receivables are sold. A settlement statement is typically prepared for each accounting period to determine:

- Amount of receivables purchased.
- Cash collections.

- Calculation of withholding account.

- Discount or income earned for the period.

- Ending balance in the intercompany account.

By incorporating and operating the captive finance company in a state that does not tax passive or interest income, some state tax savings could result.

There would be no effect for federal tax purposes since the finance company is a wholly owned subsidiary and the consolidated tax return rules apply.

Another financing vehicle is the revolving credit loan agreement or revolver. It is a common asset-based financing vehicle for accounts receivable. The benefit to a revolver is that a large portion of it can be classified as long term, which is beneficial to the current ratio. However, the term is still typically less than three years, and the long-term debt footnote in the retailer's financial statements shows a poor five-year payout schedule. Also, this particular financing method does nothing to improve the debt-to-equity ratio and can create certain restrictions on dividend distributions in particular.

The open line or demand loan is probably the least desirable choice from a financing perspective. Under this concept, the entire loan balance is shown as currently due within one year and restrictions can be quite extensive.

Sometimes retailers also seek to obtain financing based on inventories. Commercial finance companies typically loan up to 50–60 percent of the inventory value. However, vendors generally do not like to see inventory used as collateral, especially for another vendor or a lender. As a practical matter, inventory most often is financed from current working capital.

CHAPTER TWENTY-NINE

Insurance and Risk Management

Risk Management is the means by which companies protect their assets and personnel from loss. One method of risk management commonly used by business is the purchase of property and casualty insurance. However, the high cost of insurance and the more limited coverages available today are forcing managers to look for ways other than pure insurance to assume risk, transfer risk (liabilities), or prevent more complex types of losses. Since tremendous savings in insurance costs and self-insured or retained risks greatly impact the retailer's small margins and affect its ability to be competitive, risk management is an area which should attract the attention of retail financial manager.

Retail businesses have unique risks inherent to their operations. Retailers tend to have a high concentration of values (inventory) in stores and/or warehouses which vary by season and geographic location. In addition, exposure to crimes such as vandalism and shoplifting or employee theft is high. At risk are the company's financial assets in terms of property, inventory, profits and market share, as well as the company's human resources, including employees and owners.

In small stores or small retail chains, the controller customarily purchases the insurance, usually from a local independent insurance agency. Insurance costs for such small retailers are minimized through the purchase of special multiperil package policies. These combine several essential types of coverage into one simplified, easy to administer program.

In larger retail organizations, the insurance is purchased by the company's risk and insurance manager who usually reports to the chief financial officer. Insurance coverages are usually purchased through large insurance brokerage companies, who may offer claims and loss prevention support to their larger accounts. In addition, certain insurance programs are available providing cash flow benefits to large retailers and allowing them to self-insure certain coverages that are limited in size and are fairly predictable.

The basic principles of risk management apply to all retail operations, whether large or small. The tasks which comprise that process are:

Identification of the exposures to risk

Analysis of the alternative risk management programs

Selection of insurance or other alternative program

Implementation of the selected risk management program

Monitoring of the selected risk management program

IDENTIFICATION OF THE EXPOSURES TO RISK

Exhibit 29.1 lists the major categories of exposures that must be carefully assessed and weighed. Determination must be made as to which exposures are purely "the cost of doing business" and can therefore be safely absorbed by the company, and which exposures will need to be transferred to a third party, either contractually or through the purchase of insurance, to protect or limit the retailer's potential for loss.

These same risk exposures should also be considered when a company decides to start another retail business or acquire additional store locations.

The physical location of the retailer's operations will determine the kind of protection needed against fire and/or burglary losses. In turn, the location and type of protection needed impacts on the cost of fire and other property insurance coverages.

The hiring practices of a retailer, including conducting thorough reference checks on prospective employees, can help to prevent loss from employee theft and create a favorable impression with the fidelity bonding company. Careful screening of potential concessionaires (such as beauticians or opticians) also helps to limit exposure to malpractice claims which could damage the retailer's reputation. Such practices are viewed favorably by the insurers, translating into reduced insurance costs.

EXHIBIT 29.1   Potential Exposures to Loss

Exposures	Stores	Warehousing, Distribution Maintenance, and Other Support Operations
Construction and layout location:	X	X
1. Malls—key tenants, competition	X	
2. Inner city	X	X
3. Suburban stripcenters	X	X
Protection:		
1. Smoke and fire	X	X
2. Burglary and security	X	X
3. Shoplifting	X	X
4. Employee theft	X	X
Type of inventory (merchandise and supplies, such as bags and boxes):		
1. Location and method of storage— public or private (company owned or leased)		X
2. Location and method of display	X	
3. Flammables (fabrics & aerosols)	X	X
4. Values—replacement cost, actual cash value or book	X	X
5. Private label or name brand	X	X
6. Packaging	X	X
7. Seasonality/spoilage	X	X
Contingent exposures:		
1. Acts of God (flood, earthquake)	X	X
2. Surrounding occupancy	X	X
3. Power interruption	X	X
4. Sources of inventory (alternate supplies)	X	
Payroll:		
1. Review of classification to minimize workers' compensation cost (including minors, part-timers)	X	X
2. Hiring practices and training (checking references, apprehension of shoplifters)	X	X
3. Fidelity exposures (bonding) — employee theft, check alteration, or forgery	X	X

EXHIBIT 29.1   *(Continued)*

Exposures	Stores	Warehousing, Distribution Maintenance, and Other Support Operations
4. Worldwide travel	X	
5. Key man death	X	
Sales:		
1. Cash on hand	X	
2. Timing and method of bank deposits	X	
3. Accounts payable and receivable (files and records maintenance)	X	
4. Credit cards	X	
5. Layaways	X	
Methods of shipment:		
1. Ocean for overseas—C.I.F. F.O.B., Letters of Credit		X
2. Air for overseas or long distance	X	X
3. Trucking		
a) long haul (over 150 miles)		X
b) intermediate (over 50 miles)		X
c) short haul (under 50 miles)	X	
4. Small packages		
a) parcel post	X	X
b) U.P.S.	X	X
c) registered US mail	X	X
d) overnight mail	X	X
Ancillary Activities	Department and variety stores: pharmacy, food and alcohol service, furrier; concessions: beauticians, jewelers, etc.	Cut and sew rooms construction depts.
	Specialty stores: repair service, concessions	
	Advertising, catalogs, mail order, franchises (false ads, trademark infringement)	

In the area of merchandise distribution, trucking is generally accomplished either through an owned fleet, a private carrier, or a common carrier. Each means of conveyance has its own individualized risk exposure. Loss to shipments made under a store chain's own fleet cannot be transferred to a third party and must be absorbed by the store chain or insured. Loss to shipments delivered through private carriers can be contractually transferred to the carrier, that should be required to supply the store with a certificate of insurance. Shipments made via a common carrier can either be made on a reduced bill of lading or a straight bill of lading. A straight bill of lading fully insures a shipment, but is a more expensive method of shipment than a reduced bill of lading, which limits the shipper's liability.

Finally, there is a risk of losing merchandise on the premises of freight consolidators where cartons can be mixed with those of other companies or common carriers.

When shipping goods from overseas by sea, the terms of the bill of lading should also be carefully reviewed to determine when title for the goods is passed. The terms on the bill of lading may cover all insurance for the shipment (C.I.F.—cost, insurance, and freight) or may require that the retailer pick up the insurance exposure from the time the merchandise is loaded on board at the city of departure (F.O.B.—free on board).

It is very common for retailers who use United Parcel Service, Parcel Post, or other overnight carrier services to purchase insurance through that carrier. However, delays are often experienced in the settlement of claims through these insurance programs for loss of, or damage to merchandise. As an alternative, the retailer may wish to purchase a transit floater. This is usually less expensive and provides greater administrative ease in claims settlement.

All leases and contracts should be scrutinized not only for insurance requirements, but for language which holds the retailer liable for acts whether or not they are in its control. Wherever possible, liability should be shifted to another party, requesting that it be covered under the other party's insurance coverage. For example, if an independent contractor is brought in to do certain repair work in a store, the contractor should be required to provide evidence of insurance for its own employees, as well as comprehensive general liability insurance. The contractor's liability insurance policy should be endorsed to show, among other things, that the retailer and the landlord (if required by the lease agreement) are named as additional insureds.

Other parties entering into different agreements may provide insurance for all involved but will often charge a premium for such service. For example, the landlord in a mall may provide comprehensive property insurance for the premises, but will request reimbursement on a pro rata share from its tenants. Such insurance usually only covers the building itself; the contents (furniture, fixtures, and inventory) must be covered by the tenants' own policy.

The appropriate provisions of each of the following agreements should be considered in order to understand which party is really bearing the risk of loss:

Lease agreements for premises—stores and other buildings including:

- Construction allowances.
- Reimbursement of Landlord's insurance expense.
- Structural repairs.
- Waiver of subrogation.
- Fire legal liability.
- Rent abatement.
- Indemnifications or hold harmless clauses.

Lease agreements for vehicles and equipment including point of sale registers, telephones, electronic data processing equipment, material handling equipment (forklifts, etc.).

Mortgages, loan agreements, and security interest agreements.

Outside services—security, janitorial, and elevator and escalator maintenance.

Licensing, consignment, concession, and other related sales agreements.

Trucking employment and independent contractor agreements.

Railroad sidetrack agreements.

ANALYSIS OF ALTERNATIVE RISK MANAGEMENT PROGRAMS

Although insurance is not the only component of a risk management program, quite often it is the largest and most expensive. Insurance is categorized as either Property Insurance (including fire, lightning, flood, earthquake, boiler and machinery, business interruption) or Casualty Insurance (including workers' compensation, general liability, automobile liability) or Surety (including crime or fidelity, fiduciary liability, miscellaneous fuel tax or highway use bonds). The coverages usually found in a retailer's program are:

1. *Casualty Insurance*

   Workers' compensation

   Comprehensive general liability (includes coverage for false arrest of shoplifters)

   Automobile liability and physical damage (includes trucks, tractors, trailers and private passenger) vehicles

   Umbrella or excess liability

2. *Property Insurance*

Property damage on either a "named perils" basis (fire and extended coverages such as lightning, vandalism, etc.) or on an "all risk" basis (covers all risks with several exclusions)

Boiler and machinery

Business interruption

Electronic data processing

Ocean cargo (on a warehouse-to-warehouse basis)

Transit coverage (for cargo other than ocean cargo)

3. *Surety*

Comprehensive crime (includes employee fidelity, depositors' forgery and check alteration, and money and securities coverage for both inside and outside the premises)

General term bond

Miscellaneous bonds such as highway use and fuel tax bonds

Fiduciary liability (covers a breach of fiduciary liability as defined under the Employees' Retirement Income Security Act (ERISA))

The general liability and the umbrella or excess liability policies can be written on either an "occurrence" basis or a "claims made" basis. The claims made policy only provides coverage for claims which are reported during the policy period. The occurrence policy provides coverage for claims that occur during the policy period, no matter when they are reported. When available the occurrence form is preferable since it does not limit the reporting period for a claim. Whenever possible, the umbrella or excess liability policy should follow the same form and policy period as the underlying coverage so that there are no gaps in coverage or difference in terms or conditions.

A typical umbrella liability program is usually written in layers of limits of liability due to insurance market conditions. Often insurers within the layered program impose different exclusions or modifications to the exclusions found in the primary layer of coverage. As a result, coverage gaps may cause difficulty in claims settlement. Whenever possible, the umbrella layers should be written on a "following form" basis.

There are some special types of coverages that can be carried as protection against claims resulting from the operations of some of the ancillary services or concessions. For example, if alcohol is served in a restaurant on the retailer's premises, liquor law liability coverage should be purchased. Similarly, beautician's malpractice coverage, pharmacist's professional liability or incidental malpractice (for any nurse or physician who might treat an injured customer or employee) should be purchased to cover those exposures if applicable.

Often, retailers experiencing rapid growth maintain separate insurance programs for stores located in different cities but within the same chain, or for different chains owned by a common holding company. A misconception exists that separate corporations and separate policies protect the assets of the holding company from attachment in a liability claim award. From an insurance standpoint, the risk of maintaining separate insurance programs creates the possibility of potential gaps or duplications in coverage. These are often accompanied by administrative problems in the claims settlement process. Many of the property insurance policies can in fact be written on either a named locations only basis, or on a blanket basis where all locations are covered without listing them on the policy.

Property coverage is usually written with a "coinsurance" provision which dictates the minimum amount of insurance that must be maintained in order to receive full payment on a partial loss. Coinsurance should be regarded with caution since the insured could be liable for more of the loss than anticipated if property values have not been reported correctly to the insurer. Instead, the use of higher deductibles might accomplish the desired premium saving, without the uncertainty of being adequately insured.

The "peak season endorsement" should also be added to the property policies stating that the underwriter acknowledges that average inventory values will fluctuate dramatically during the year, based on the seasonality of the business.

Time element coverage (commonly known as business interruption coverage) provides insurance for loss of earnings or for extra expenses incurred during the period of time when a store is unable to operate due to a covered property loss. Many smaller retailers carry coverage called "loss of income," which provides a fixed amount of coverage for a fixed period of time. Larger retailers frequently purchase a form of business interruption called "gross earnings" coverage that is measured against the profit and loss statement of the retailer.

Another form available is extra expense coverage, which is particularly important for continuing operations during a period of renovation due to a covered property loss (such as pharmacies).

Retrospectively rated plans are used by those retailers with better than average loss experience. In order to qualify for a "retro" a retailer must have a certain premium level and enough loss experience to be rateable by the underwriters. In a retro arrangement, a deposit premium is determined at the beginning of the policy year and is paid throughout the year. Six months after the policy year ends, the loss experience which was actually incurred during that policy period is looked at through a formula which adds in the insurer's overhead and profit, claims handling charges, and premium taxes. The formula sets forth a minimum premium and a maximum premium, and adjustments continue to be made: (1) annually for three or five years (depending upon the insurance company filings), (2) until losses are all closed, or (3) until the insurer and the retailer mutually agree to make a final and binding adjustment, and future losses become the insurer's responsibility.

There are many variations to the basic retro arrangement that provide cash flow advantages to larger retailers. Some plans defer a portion of the deposit premium until the first retro adjustment is made. Others are written as "incurred loss retros" where all claims incurred, including outstanding reserves, go into the retro calculation. In other "paid loss retros," only claims' dollars actually paid out go into the retro calculation.

Under most retro arrangements, the insured takes a "self-insured retention" (SIR) which means that the insured is liable for the first $50,000 or $100,000 (or whatever amount is selected) of each and every loss. The maximum premium under the retro caps the retailer's exposure for the year, while the SIR caps it for the specific loss. Over and above the SIR and above the maximum premium is pure insurance.

In retro arrangements, the insurer generally continues to provide claims handling and loss prevention services.

In a true self-insurance plan, the retailer decides what level of loss it can absorb and buys pure insurance over that amount. A Third Party Administrator must then be contracted or a staff hired to handle the processing of claims.

Other alternatives available include the use of captive insurance companies or risk retention groups. A captive insurance company can be one that is owned solely by the retailer or by an association to write specific hard to place insurance. Excess insurance is purchased over and above the level of risk the captive is able to absorb. Captives are either located domestically in the United States or in certain offshore locations such as Bermuda, The Cayman Islands, Barbados, and so on, where there are favorable laws regarding their implementation.

The Risk Retention Act of 1986 was the U.S. Congress' response to the insurance industry crisis. This provided for the formation of purchasing groups or risk retention groups. These groups must have a membership that has similar interests, and coverage can only be written for certain liability exposures. The law provides for these risk retention groups to pool their coverage and form an insurance company domiciled in one of various receptive states. The usual requirements, separate filings with the Insurance Commissioners of each state in which coverage is afforded, are eliminated.

The formation of purchasing groups under the Risk Retention Act allows groups of smaller buyers with similar interests to purchase coverage at more favorable rates, taking advantage of the spread of risk and the group's larger premium volume. In order to work efficiently both captives and risk retention group alternatives require substantial premium volumes; they also require continuous, adequate funding to pay for all covered losses.

In addition to the more complex programs described above, premium can be deferred under certain arrangements with insurance carriers or can be financed and paid over time with certain other insurers. There is usually a cost associated with either arrangement for the use of the insurance carrier's money.

SELECTION OF INSURANCE OR OTHER ALTERNATIVE PROGRAMS

In the event that insurance is selected as the prime means of dealing with risk, retailers should be aware of the fact that the purchase of insurance involves the use of various service providers. The insurance carriers will either deal directly with its clients or through independent agents or brokers. Independent agents represent the insurance company and can collect premiums or in some cases underwrite on behalf of the insurers they represent. Brokers represent the insured's interests to the insurance companies, do not have premium collection ability or the binding authority of the insurers and are usually paid on a commission basis (a percentage of the premium) or with a fee negotiated with the insured.

Although the insurance carrier and the agent or broker often provide certain services as part of its premium, commission, or fee arrangement, some carriers work on an "unbundled basis." When services are unbundled, the retailer can pick and choose what services it requires and only pay for those that it selects.

Occasionally, insurers only provide the pure insurance coverage and the client must contract with "Third Party Administrators" for such services as loss prevention or claims handling, that are agreeable to, or are approved by the insurer.

Third Party Administrators can be truly independent or can be the agent or broker, depending on the expertise available. These special unbundled services are paid for through a separate fee, on either a flat fee, hourly rate, or per claim rate.

Many clients also make use of consultants for special projects where unique expertise is required. In addition, a retailer may use a consultant to supplement its own staff when necessary.

The cost of insurance will vary by line of coverage, the risk factors outlined in the first part of this chapter, and by the limit of liability and deductibles selected. Good loss prevention efforts and claims experience further impact the underwriters' judgment.

There are several categories of financial arrangements that can affect the insurance premiums ultimately paid. The most traditional insurance contracts have been written on a "guaranteed cost" basis where the underwriter estimates the expected claims, and adds a profit element and his overhead costs to determine a premium level. Once that level is set, the insured pays the guaranteed cost premium (which may either be flat or subject to audit based on such variables as sales, payroll, number of vehicles, and number of stores); there are no credits for good experience or additional premiums for poor experience.

IMPLEMENTATION OF THE SELECTED RISK MANAGEMENT PROGRAM

The criteria for decision making regarding the most cost effective program generally is determined by the following considerations:

- What is the size of company?
- The company's location—is it regionalized, national, or worldwide?
- What level of premium does the size of the company generate?
- What is management's philosophy—is it risk averse or a risk taker?
- Does the company have the cash flow to entertain self-insurance or other cash flow related insurance products? What are the other financial considerations which might make a cash flow product advantageous or an unacceptable risk?
- What are the company's future plans for growth through mergers or acquisitions?

MONITORING OF THE SELECTED RISK MANAGEMENT PROGRAM

Too many companies grow into small regional store chains, and then into large national chains without changing the type of insurance program originally carried, or giving thought to the necessity of implementing a formalized risk management program.

Periodic reviews of the cost effectiveness of the insurance program through competitive bidding is important for modifying the insurance program to meet the changing goals and objectives of the company. A review of the services provided by the insurance agent/broker or direct writer should be conducted to determine if those firms are continuing to maintain the capabilities of satisfying the company's needs. However, competitive bidding generally should not be done within a three year period unless absolutely necessary to avoid a reputation of merely "shopping the market."

Experience has demonstrated that a structured loss prevention program can significantly reduce claims and related loss costs if strictly adhered to by individual store and warehouse management. Many large store chains have developed written manuals discussing company policy addressing employee safety, property conservation, public liability, and security arrangements.

Smaller retail chains often rely on the inspection reports provided by their insurance carriers. Larger chains sometimes supplement their insurers reports with that of a private contractor. Both smaller and larger chains, however, can benefit in assigning an "in-house" individual to periodically inspect store or warehouse facilities for safety violations.

It is also beneficial to have an individual review claims data supplied by the insurance company to detect trends and patterns in the frequency and severity of claims. Most insurance agencies or brokerage firms perform this activity without charge if requested to do so.

All retail companies, large or small, must establish a rigid procedure for claims reporting. Penalties can be assessed for not filing an employee's workers' compensation accident report to the appropriate state workers' compensation board on a timely basis. O.S.H.A. (Occupational Safety and Health Act) logs must be maintained and posted prominently on bulletin boards. Certain types of accidents require notifying the Department of Transportation or Environmental Protection Agency. More importantly, delayed notice of a general liability claim could lead to a denial of coverage by the company's insurance carrier. It is, therefore, strongly recommended that all retail companies install an incident reporting system for potential general liability claims, regardless of how serious store management perceives an accident to be.

While most retailers depend on their insurance company to investigate reported claims, many larger companies, some of which may be self-insured, will have their own internal claims investigation unit. Regardless of who investigates the accident, it is important for management to instruct all store personnel to fully cooperate with individuals who have the proper authorization to investigate accidents.

Claim investigators sometimes pinpoint an otherwise unforeseen hazard within one store that might exist throughout the store chain. Correcting this hazard in stores where no accident has occurred is a good example of what is termed "loss reduction techniques."

Another example of loss reduction is the ability to provide emergency medical care. Store managers should be encouraged to learn CPR and other emergency first aid applications.

Once a claim has occurred, there are other techniques to control costs which are termed "post loss reduction techniques." In property claim situations, protection of undamaged property from further loss can be accomplished by hiring special security, restoring alarm and sprinkler systems, making temporary repairs, ventilating smoke, disposal of damaged merchandise, and providing emergency power. In the casualty area, post loss reduction techniques can include rehabilitation services for disabling injuries, subrogation against other responsible parties, withdrawal from the market of damaged or defective products, and so on.

A retailer's claims experience ultimately affects its insurance premiums, either prospectively or retrospectively. Claim reserves, which are the best estimate of the future monetary value of a claim, are normally set by the insurer or the third party administrator. Therefore, it is good practice to schedule periodic meetings with either the insurance agent or broker and/or the claims department of the insurance carrier to review outstanding claims in order to verify that claim reserves are not overstated and that claims are being settled in the retailer's best interests. The review allows the retailer to provide input as to whether a claim might be precedent setting or should be denied based on mitigating circumstances of which the insurer may not be aware. Other methods commonly used to control expenses include:

1. Employee training.

2. Pre-hire physicals for employees.

3. Contracting with medical providers for employee physicals and emergency treatment.

4. Reference checks.

5. Participation in selection of defense attorneys.

6. Monitoring claims investigation and defense costs.

7. Coordination with other coverages (such as Workers' Compensation with disability benefits, etc.).

8. Subrogation and/or impleading of third party defendants (liens, etc.).

9. Control of salvage (brands and labels).

10. Review of tax deductibility of certain uninsured claims.

11. Rental of temporary premises or equipment, hiring of temporary personnel in order to resume normal business activity as soon as possible.

12. Research federal loans carrying low interest rates during declared state of emergency situations.

PART FIVE

Financial Analysis

CHAPTER THIRTY

The Retailer's Income Statement Analysis

Financial statements are the most widely used media for disseminating information about a company. While complying with accounting standards and governmental reporting requirements, they can function as an excellent public relations tool.

Financial statements are one resource for analyzing a company. Financial statements provide historical information and should be used to supplement the financial statement user's understanding of the business. The numbers need to be correlated with what is going on in the business.

There are no operating problems that do not have financial reporting overtones. For example, poor merchandising leads to slow moving inventory and the possible need for a reserve for future markdowns. Conversely, there are no financial reporting problems that do not have operating implications. For example, customer accounts receivable collection problems (with proprietary or "house" accounts), which must be evaluated to determine the adequacy of the allowance for doubtful accounts, do not arise in a vacuum. They could arise from the faulty assignment of customer credit limits, or from sporadic and/or ineffective collection policies.

Certain operating and accounting issues are unique or of more significance to retailers. This chapter discusses financial reporting disclosures and issues of importance to retailers.

THE RETAILER'S INCOME STATEMENT

Net Sales

Net sales of a store are defined as "gross sales less returns and allowances (except policy adjustments) and less discounts to employees and others."

In some stores the service departments such as restaurants and salons represent an important part of store operations. For this reason, their sales and results of operations may be reported separately from the conventional retail departments that sell merchandise at normal markons. Under these circumstances, frequent consolidation of the retail and service departments results in distorted relationships which are not comparable with figures of other retailers.

Gross sales do not include receipts from customers for *alterations* which are applied as reductions of workroom and alteration costs. For the sake of simplicity, workroom and alteration costs would be included in other costs of sales in the condensed income statement.

Sales taxes collected on merchandise sold and installment carrying charges should be excluded from sales. *Installment carrying charges* are an element of other income, net, and are shown as finance charge income in the accompanying statement.

In the event *contract and wholesale* operations are a significant factor, the related sales, costs and expenses should be segregated from the more conventional retail operations. Contract or wholesale volume is typically obtained at lower profit margins than realized by the regular retail business. Consequently, consolidation of such diverse elements results in abnormal relationships in the total all-store combined figures. If the combination of wholesale and retail operations produces operating results deemed distortive, the store's income account should be broken down into two or more separate sections.

Cost of Goods Sold

Income statements for retailers are frequently more condensed than those seen in other businesses. Retailers have adopted a format for the income statement that reflects the cost of acquiring merchandise and preparing it for sale, such as special packaging, as part of cost of goods sold. Retailers believe that this format more realistically presents the real costs incurred in making merchandise available to consumers at retail. This format also indirectly responds to criticisms directed toward the large spread between retail prices and merchandise costs as reflected in published statements.

Traditionally, the special format of income statement published by publicly owned companies, and responsive to financial reporting rules of the Securities and Exchange Commission, classifies "occupancy and buying costs" as part of cost of goods sold. Since there is not precise uniformity in the identification of these elements of expenses, there can be differences in interpretation and grouping among retailers, thereby reducing the degree of comparability.

For example, one discount department store lists "cost of goods sold, transportation, and buying expenses" as the captioned amount of cost of sales. Grocery stores are not as descriptive and merely state the captioned cost of sales as "cost of goods sold." It is not clear whether they are including buying and occupancy costs in this captioned amount.

Given the lack of uniformity in grouping costs and expenses, as well as a certain unwillingness to disclose data deemed competitively disadvantageous, some major retail companies have adopted a different format for external reporting purposes. This format groups all costs and expenses together, exclusive of certain designated items (normally, maintenance and repairs, depreciation, taxes other than income taxes, rentals, retirement expense, and interest expense).

Some companies, while grouping all costs and expenses together, have chosen to show cost of goods sold as a separately captioned amount. In effect, there are three general schools of thought in presenting costs and expenses for a company engaged in retailing:

1. *Traditional Method*

   Cost of goods sold, including occupancy and buying costs.

   Selling, general and administrative expenses.

   Depreciation.

   Interest expense.

2. *"Exclusive of" Method*

   Cost of goods sold and expenses, exclusive of the following items:

   Maintenance and repairs.

   Depreciation.

   Taxes other than those based on income.

   Rentals.

   Retirement expense.

   Interest expense.

3. *Combination Method*

   Cost and expenses of retail operations:

   Cost of goods sold.

   Selling, general and administrative expenses.

   Maintenance and repairs.

   Depreciation.

   Taxes, other than those based on income.

   Rentals.

   Retirement expenses.

   Interest expense.

   Total costs and expenses.

There can be many variations to meet specific situations. From an accounting standpoint it may be preferable to see occupancy and buying costs classified as part of cost of goods sold, however the other forms of presentation also have merit. Whatever format is chosen, it should be used consistently, period to period, to enable the readers to make appropriate comparisons.

It is apparent that the special formats of the income statement were designed largely as vehicles for the public presentation of operating statistics. Practically speaking, these formats do not provide the detailed insights necessary to effectively monitor and control the ongoing operations of a retail enterprise. In effect, the special formats would be used only when preparing formal statements for public dissemination.

Leased Department Operations

Retailers often have leased department operations (see Chapter Twenty-Three). Financial statement presentations of these operations vary from company to company. Since the retailer receives only a commission from the leased department operator, based generally on gross sales, the cost of the merchandise handled and operating expenses of the lessee are not known. Some retailers report the amount of commissions from leased departments as an element of other income, not to be included in gross margin. However, the National Retail Federation (NRF) Retail Accounting Manual considers such commissions as an element of gross margin. When using this format, the company should indicate that sales do include leased department sales. In these instances, the difference between the leased department sales and the commissions from leased departments is reflected as a charge to cost of goods sold.

In offering merchandise for sale to the general public, the retailer is not distinguishing between owned department and leased department merchandise. Including leased department sales in the retailer's net sales reflects the total sales of the retail company. Proponents of this alternative agree that the use of the leased department, rather than a company-operated department, is a merchandising decision, often made because of the special nature and/or highly specialized merchandising requirements of leased operations. The company can operate these departments if it so chooses; therefore, a true reflection of its selling capacity is *all sales.*

Although this argument may have some merit, it is preferable to show total net sales, including leased department sales, from which leased department sales are deducted to arrive at owned department sales. Commissions from leased departments are then shown separately. This alternative handles the problem of reflecting total selling capacity, while not distorting owned-sales/cost-of-sales relationships.

The sample income statement in Exhibit 30.1 reflects separate disclosure to leased department sales and leased department income and combines

EXHIBIT 30.1   Sample Income Statement Format

	Fiscal Year Ended January 26, 19X1
Total Sales	$XXX XXX
Less: Leased department sales	X XXX
Net sales	$XXX XXX
Leased department income	XXX
Interest and other income	XXX
Total income	$XXX XXX
Costs and expenses:	
Cost of goods sold, transportation, and buying expenses	XXX XXX
Store operating, administrative, and general expenses, including leased department expenses	XX XXX
Depreciation and amortization	XXX
Interest and debt expense	XXX
Total costs and expenses	$XXX XXX
Income before state and federal taxes on income	X XXX
Taxes on income	XXX
Net income	$ XXX
Earnings per common share	$ X.XX

leased department expenses with store operating, administrative, and general expenses.

Operating Expenses

Operating expenses should be planned by functional groups and actual performance should be measured against plan on a periodic basis. Separate statistical statements showing the details of operating expenses are normally prepared in conjunction with the income statement. The amount of detail any one company may wish to report will vary depending upon the size of the operation, the organizational structure, and the level to which responsibility can be reasonably assigned.

A considerable portion of Book 1 of the NRMA Retail Accounting Manual is devoted to the area of expense accounting and reporting. It should be consulted for specific details. This chapter will consider only the basic concepts of expense reporting.

In preparing their Retail Accounting Manual, the NRMA was confronted with certain practical problems. A chart of accounts had to be provided for expense accumulation, summarization, and reporting that could be used by most retailers regardless of size or type of operation. At the same time, some degree of uniformity in reporting practices had to be maintained in order to make figure exchange feasible.

As a solution, the NRMA breaks down the various functions or centers of activity into 10 expense summaries, with 44 expense centers within these summaries, which can be used by even the smallest of retail operations:

010	Property and equipment
100	Company management
200	Accounting and management information
300	Credit and accounts receivable
400	Sales promotion
500	Services and operations
600	Personnel
700	Merchandise receiving, storage, and distribution
800	Selling and supporting services
900	Merchandising

Companies that wish to show more detail can utilize the 44 expense centers provided within these expense summaries. For example, expense summary 400, sales promotion, has the following expense centers:

400	Sales promotion	
	410	Sales promotion management
	420	Advertising
	430	Shows, special events, and exhibits
	440	Display

A company may use any or all of these expense centers, depending on its needs. However, if all the expense centers within a specific summary are not used, the expense elements pertaining to the unused centers should be included in the management expense center of each summary. In the

400 summary example cited above, if a company did not wish to use the expense center 430—shows, special events, and exhibits—any expenses incurred for these types of activities would be included in 410, sales promotion management.

For companies desiring an even finer breakdown of expenses, the NRMA provides 22 subexpense centers. Each company can decide which, if any, of these subexpense centers to use. Sales promotion would cover the following if all of the expense areas of activity were used:

400   Sales promotion

    410   Sales promotion management

    420   Advertising

    421   Newspaper

    425   Radio

    426   TV

    427   Direct mail

    428   Other

    430   Shows, special events, and exhibits

    431   Public relations

    432   Merchandise shows

    434   Special events and exhibits

    440   Display

    441   Display production

    444   Sign shop

In addition to capturing expense by areas of activity, the NRMA Retail Accounting Manual also classifies expenses by natural division, describing the type of expense. There are 17 basic natural divisions of expense as follows:

01   Payroll

03   Media costs

04   Taxes

06   Supplies

07   Services purchased

08   Unclassified

09   Travel

10   Communications

11   Pensions

12   Insurance

13   Depreciation

14   Professional services

16   Bad debts

17   Equipment rentals

18   Outside maintenance

20   Real property rentals

92   Credits and outside revenues

Provision is also made for three transfer accounts. Although not comprising basic natural divisions, they are used in addition to the natural divisions:

02   Allocated fringe benefits

90   Expense transfers-in

91   Expense transfers-out

A great deal of attention and emphasis has been brought to bear in planning and controlling expense by area of responsibility. As an integral segment of the monthly or period financial reporting package, management should receive a statement similar to the one shown in Exhibit 30.2. This statement displays expense by expense summary compared to budget, and to last year, and additionally shows variances from budget. These amounts are shown both for the current month or period (or four- or five-week) and season or year-to-date. The statement as presented shows only the 10 expense summaries, companies that use expense centers and/or subcenters may wish to display those as well.

Management should also be provided with a monthly (or four- or five-week period) statement of operating expenses by natural division. (Exhibit 30.3). Each supervisor assigned responsibility for a work center should be provided periodically with a natural expense breakdown of their work center. This is done by displaying the natural divisions of expense applicable to

EXHIBIT 30.2 Comparative Statement of Operating Expenses by Expense Summary

Period _____

Classification and Name of Expense	Month				Season to Date			
	This Year	Budget	Budget Ver.	Last Year	This Year	Budget	Budget Ver.	Last Year
	Amount %	Amount %	Amount %	Amount %	Amount %	Amount %	Amount %	Amount %
010 Property and Equipment								
100 Company Management								
200 Accounting and Management Info.								
300 Credit and Accounts Receivable								
400 Sales Promotion								
500 Services and Operations								
600 Personnel								
700 Merchandise Receiving, Storage, and Distribution								
800 Selling and Supporting Services								
900 Merchandising								
Total Expenses								

Source: Retail Accounting Manual, NRF.

EXHIBIT 30.3 Summary of Natural Divisions by Expense Center

Expense Center	01 Payroll	02 Allocated fringe benefits Dr./Cr.	03 Media costs	04 Taxes	06 Supplies	07 Services purchased	08 Unclassified	09 Travel	10 Communications	11 Pensions	12 Insurance	13 Depreciation	14 Professional services	16 Bad debts	17 Equipment rentals	18 Outside maintenance and equipment service contracts	20 Real property rentals	90 Expense transfers in (Dr.)	91 Expense transfers out (Cr.)	92 Credits and outside revenues (Cr.)
010 Property and equipment																				
020 Real estate, buildings, and building equipment				x							x	x			x		x			x
030 Furniture, fixtures, and non building equipment				x							x	x			x	x				x
100 Company management																				
110 Executive office	x	x			x	x	x	x									x			
130 Branch management	x	x			x	x	x	x												
140 Internal audit	x	x			x	x	x	x					x							
150 Legal and consumer activities	x	x			x	x	x	x					x							
200 Accounting and management information																				
210 Control management, general accounting, and statistical	x	x			x	x	x	x	x				x					x		
220 Sales audit	x	x			x	x	x	x										x		
230 Accounts payable	x	x			x	x	x											x		
240 Payroll and timekeeping department	x	x			x	x	x		x									x		
280 Data processing	x	x			x	x	x	x							x	x				x
300 Credit and accounts receivable																				
310 Credit management	x	x			x	x	x	x					x					x		
330 Collection	x	x			x	x	x	x										x		
340 Accounts receivable and bill adjustment	x	x			x	x	x							x						x
350 Cash office	x	x			x	x	x													
360 Branch/store selling location offices	x	x			x	x	x		x										x	
400 Sales promotion																				
410 Sales promotion management	x	x			x	x	x	x												x
420 Advertising	x	x	x		x	x	x	x	x											x
430 Shows, special events, and exhibits	x	x			x	x	x	x												x
440 Display	x	x			x	x	x	x										x		
500 Service and operations																				
510 Service and operations management	x	x			x	x	x	x					x							
530 Security	x	x			x	x	x						x							
550 Telephones and communications	x	x			x	x	x		x						x					
560 Utilities	x	x			x	x					x	x				x				x
570 Housekeeping	x	x			x	x	x												x	x
580 Maintenance and repairs	x	x			x	x	x					x				x			x	
600 Personnel																				
610 Personnel management	x	x			x	x	x	x					x							
620 Employment	x	x			x	x	x	x												
640 Training	x	x			x	x	x	x					x							
660 Medical and other employee services	x	x			x	x	x	x			x									
670 Supplementary benefits	x	x			x	x	x			x										
700 Merchandise receiving, storage and distribution																				
710 Management of merchandise receiving, storage & distribution	x	x			x	x	x	x										x		x
720 Receiving and marking	x	x			x	x	x	x												x
730 Reserve stock storage	x	x			x	x	x								x	x		x		
750 Shuttle services	x	x			x	x	x								x	x		x		
800 Selling and supporting services																				
810 Selling supervision	x	x			x	x	x	x										x		x
820 Direct selling	x	x			x	x	x	x												x
830 Customer services	x	x			x	x	x		x											x
840 Selling support services	x	x			x	x	x													x
860 Central wrapping and packing	x	x			x	x	x								x					x
880 Delivery	x	x			x	x	x	x											x	
900 Merchandising																				
910 Merchandising management	x	x			x	x	x	x												
920 Buying	x	x			x	x	x	x					x							
930 Merchandise control	x	x			x	x	x								x					

each center for the current month versus budget, and season or year-to-date actual versus budget.

THE RETAILER'S BALANCE SHEET

Components of the typical retailer's balance sheet have fairly standard captions and format; however, the content of the particular accounts can have some unique qualities. This section addresses the contents of balance sheet captions.

Cash

Cash may include cash on hand and cash in the bank; payroll, disbursements, concentration accounts, as well as individual store deposit accounts. Concentration accounts are used by retailers to move funds from all the individual store bank accounts. The retailer's cash account would also include the deposit amounts for bankcards such as MasterCard and Visa, where the retailer's account is credited with the funds the same day the credit card documentation is provided to the bank. Cash accounts may also be established for foreign purchases under letters of credit.

Accounts Receivable

Accounts receivable would normally include regular customer accounts, revolving charge, installment, layaway and deferred billing accounts, and amounts due from third party charge companies such as American Express. Accounts receivable may in some instances also include the other bank card receivables, net of service fee charges, if they are not reflected in cash. The inclusion of bank card receivables in accounts receivable or cash generally depends on the processing time for the bank card deposits and availability of the funds to the retailer.

Other Receivables

Other receivables may include leased department receivables, loans and advances to officers and employees, amounts due from cosmetics and other demonstrators, debit balances in accounts payable including amounts due from vendors for merchandise returns, advertising rebates, volume allowances and freight claims. Offsetting amounts due from a vendor against the liability to that vendor is permissible in accordance with FASB Technical Bulletin No. 88-2.

Bad Debt Reserves or Allowances

Reserves or allowances for bad debts are recorded by retailers for both customer receivables and other receivables. In addition to the bad debt losses relating to customer accounts, a retailer frequently incurs losses for uncollectible freight claims and vendor debit balances. As with customer accounts, other receivables require ongoing, constant collection efforts if writeoffs are to be avoided.

Given the large number of individual customer accounts, it is impossible to determine the adequacy of bad debt reserves by reference to each customer account. Retailers must rely on historical aging and bad debt writeoff statistics and trends. In addition, retailers must consider changes in the economies in which stores are located, as well as policy changes instituted. For example, a liberalization of the retailer's credit policy will affect the retailer's aging and will have to be taken into account when analyzing and estimating the bad debt reserve requirements. For interim reporting purposes, retailers frequently record an estimated or budgeted amount, often a percentage of net sales based on prior year actual.

At year-end, the appropriate bad debt reserves must be determined using various formula approaches. One approach is based on the accounts receivable aging. The aggregate reserve is developed by applying specific percentages to the various aging categories, with increasingly higher percentages utilized for older age categories. The percentages utilized should be based on a historical analysis which correlates bad debt experience with aging; tempered for current business developments and policies.

An alternative, but less desirable, approach is to relate historical bad debt losses to net sales over several years and record the reserve based on that percentage relationship. This approach should recognize that, to a certain extent, bad debts recognized in the current year will relate to sales recorded in the prior year. Accordingly, a knowledgeable correlation will have to be made between the timing of sales and the corollary bad debt reserve requirement.

Inventory

Merchandise inventories are normally the most significant asset on the retailer's balance sheet. The inventory category normally includes inventory that has been received as well as inventory that is in transit. Inventory costs include inward freight, express, and cartage. Foreign purchased inventory costs include all shipping cost, insurance costs, and duties paid—commonly called "landed costs." Landed cost may include outside buying office expenses or commission fees. All inventory costs should be recorded net of trade discounts.

Inventory reserves may be required because, at any point in time, a diminution in the value and saleability of inventory may have occurred but has not yet been reflected in currently marked retail prices. Inventory reserves are an offset to retail merchandise inventory, and may include reserves for future markdowns, as well as for shortages, discounts and allowances.

Markdowns taken subsequent to the end of the period should be reviewed to determine whether unrecorded markdowns were inherent in such inventory.

At least three opinions exist as to when a reserve for subsequent markdowns should be established. Only two approaches have been accepted in practice. The most conservative could be termed the balance sheet approach. Under this approach, the reserve would include any markdowns taken in the month subsequent to year end on the theory that such markdowns were inherent in the year-end inventory.

A second method, the income statement approach, states that February, normally the month after year-end, should have a normal level of markdowns to reflect the customary presidents' birthdays sales and other sales. Therefore, the reserve only includes markdowns which are deemed abnormal. For example, a decline in turnover or significant deterioration in merchandise aging may necessitate significant markdowns which should be rolled back and for which a reserve should be established at year-end. Either of these two methods is appropriate as long as the method is used consistently. The last method which is not recommended is that the reserve should only contain markdowns authorized prior to year end. This philosophy ignores the fact that the merchandise . . . .

The establishment of the reserve is highly judgmental and requires discussions with merchandise managers and buyers in addition to the chief financial officer in order to identify and quantify required future markdowns. The reserves should be calculated based on actual experience for the period immediately following balance sheet dates. The reserves may be estimated on an overall basis, but should be corroborated by reference to merchandise categories within the various departments.

Various methods can be used to estimate a reserve. One approach would be to establish a reserve by applying designated percentages, by aging category of inventory, reserving higher percentages for out-of-season stock than for current season stock. Alternatively, differing percentages can be applied to the excess inventory within each aging category, with such excess estimated by reference to planned sales. It is important to remember that no formula replaces judgment and knowledge about the specific problem areas in each department.

Prepaid Expenses

Prepaid expenses may include prepaid rent, supplies (including bags, boxes and other wrapping supplies), and prepaid advertising, and catalog expenses. Also included in this caption are prepaid maintenance contracts and store preopening expenses (for new stores expected to be opened in the following year). Business licenses may be another component of prepaid expenses for a retailer. Only advance payments should be included in prepaid expenses.

Property and Equipment

In addition to owned land and buildings, categories of assets included as property and equipment that are significant to retailing include leasehold improvements, point-of-sale and computer equipment, and store fixtures.

Beneficial Leaseholds

The asset beneficial leaseholds normally will be recorded in connection with the acquisition of a retail enterprise. Beneficial leaseholds are the values assigned to the benefits derived from acquiring unexpired leases containing more favorable rates than would be obtained if the leases were negotiated currently. Generally determined by an outside appraisal firm, these intangible assets are recorded at fair market values, net of related income taxes. Beneficial leaseholds are generally amortized on a straight-line basis over the related remaining lease terms. Since stores are leased over different periods and at varying rents, beneficial leaseholds should be recorded and amortized on a store-by-store basis. Separate records, by store, are also necessary in the event of a store closing since the related intangible asset will have to be written off. If the total amount is insignificant, however, it may be more efficient to amortize the entire amount over the average remaining lease term for all leases.

Accounts Payable

Accounts payable are frequently segregated into accounts payable for retail merchandise which would include the liability for merchandise in transit and freight, and accounts payable for store operating and home office expenses.

Accrued Expenses

Probably the most significant accrued expense for retailers is accrued rent, common area maintenance due landlords, and accrued minimum rent liability. The latter is the most controversial, arising from the promulgation of FASB Technical Bulletin 85-3, Accounting for Operating Leases with Scheduled Rent Increases which requires scheduled rent increases covered under escalation clauses to be recognized on a straight-line basis over the lease term. For example, assume a five-year lease with the following rent schedule:

Year(s)	Annual Rent	Total Payments
1 and 2	$15,000	$ 30,000
3 and 4	20,000	40,000
5	30,000	30,000
Total rent payable over five years.		$100,000

Under generally accepted accounting principles, the rent expense charged against income would be $20,000 each year ($100,000 ÷ 5-year term). The FASB has taken the position that a lease is similar to owning a building in that it is being used for the same time and purpose each year. Therefore, each year should be charged with a pro-rata share of the rent. Others argue that in circumstances where the rent was negotiated at a lower rate in the early years of the lease, in anticipation of sales increases in the future, a proper matching of revenues and expenses occurs when the rent is expensed as incurred (i.e., based on the rent schedule). For all practical purposes, this latter argument is not acceptable under generally accepted accounting principles.

Other accrued expense items which are normally significant for retailers include:

- Accrued advertising.

- Accrued payroll and incentive bonuses, particularly selling commissions.

- Accrued vacation pay.

- Accrued personal property and real estate taxes.

- Accrued sales and use taxes.

There may also be a liability for future returns of merchandise sold included in accrued expenses. Typically, retailers do not establish a reserve for future returns since it is normally deemed immaterial to the balance sheet as well as to the income statement.

Customer Liabilities

Customer liabilities include customer-related items such as gift certificates outstanding, customers' advance deposit payments and mail order deposits.

Reserve for Store Closings

A reserve for store closings should be established when a decision to close a store is made by management. Major factors to be considered in determining the reserve amount include:

- Severance pay and related employee benefits and employer's share of taxes.
- Beneficial leasehold unamortized balance.
- Net book value of furniture and fixturings, less any salvage value.
- Lease buyout payment or present value of minimum lease payments net of any sublease rental income which can be realistically anticipated.
- Losses on disposal of inventory.
- Handling and shipping costs to transfer the merchandise to other stores.
- Settlements with leased department operators.
- Impact on collectibility of customer accounts.
- Operating losses from the decision date to the actual store closing.

The impact of each of these items should be quantified for inclusion in the reserve for store closings.

Deferred Taxes

Deferred taxes which are typical for retailers arise from the use of accelerated depreciation methods solely for tax reporting purposes:

- Differences in the timing of the recognition of pension and deferred compensation expense,
- Differences between book and tax inventory costing, and
- Deferred taxes applicable to the allowance for doubtful accounts.

Other Liabilities

Income taxes payable and other liabilities, both current and noncurrent, are similar in their content to those found in nonretailers' balance sheets. For a sample retail income statement and balance sheet, see Exhibit 30.4. Other statements such as the statement of cash flow and the statement of shareholders' equity are similar in presentation and format to those of nonretail companies.

EXHIBIT 30.4   Sample Balance Sheet Format

ASSETS	January 26, 19X1
Current Assets:	
Cash	$ XXX
Marketable securities, at cost which approximates market	XXX
Receivables:	X XXX
Trade	XX
Other	XX
Total Receivables	X XXX
Merchandise inventories	XX XXX
Prepaid expenses and other current assets	XXX
Total Current Assets	XX XXX
Property and Equipment:	
Land and buildings	X XXX
Property under capital leases	XXX
Fixtures and equipment	X XXX
Leasehold improvements	XXX
Beneficial leasehold interests	XXX
	XX XXX
Less: Accumulated depreciation and amortization	X XXX
Net Fixed Assets	XX XXX
Other Assets and Deferred Charges	XXX
Excess of Purchase Price over Acquired Net Assets ("Goodwill"), Net	XXX
	$XXX.XXX

EXHIBIT 30.4   *(Continued)*

LIABILITIES AND STOCKHOLDERS' EQUITY	January 26, 19X1
Current Liabilities:	
Accounts payable:	
Trade	$ X XXX
Leased department concessionaires and other	XXX
Total Accounts Payable	X XXX
Current maturities of long-term debt and capital	
lease obligations	XXX
Accrued payroll	XXX
Accrued expenses	X XXX
Other liabilities	XXX
Dividends payable	XXX
Taxes on income	
Total Current Liabilities	XX XXX
Deferred income taxes, noncurrent portion	XXX
Deferred compensation	XXX
Capital lease obligations	XXX
Long-term debt	X XXX
Other long-term liabilities	XXX
Stockholders' Equity:	
Common stock $.XX par value per share:	
Authorized XX XXX shares	
Issued and outstanding XX,XXX shares	X XXX
Additional paid-in capital	X XXX
Retained earnings	XX XXX
Less: Common stock in treasury, XX shares at cost	XX
Total Stockholders' Equity	XX XXX
	$XXX XXX

NOTES TO THE RETAILER'S FINANCIAL STATEMENTS

Certain footnote disclosures are unique to retailers. Key information regarding a retailer's financial reporting can be obtained by reviewing the accounting policies and other notes to the financial statements.

Accounting Policy Footnote Disclosures

FISCAL YEAR. In general merchandise retailing, the fiscal year is typically the last Saturday of a month, often January. For grocery stores, it is frequently the last Saturday in December. The natural yearly cycle of business activity, particularly focusing on seasonality of the business, should be persuasive when selecting a year-end. It is preferable to select a fiscal year-end at the time business activities are at their lowest level, rather than during a peak season. Considerations include:

- When inventories are at, or near, a minimum level to facilitate the taking, summarization, and valuation of physical inventories.

- When the working capital ratio is highest (typically after peak selling season when inventories have been converted into cash and/or receivables, and payables should be at low levels).

- Availability of employees to complete year-end closing within required reporting deadlines (90 days as mandated by SEC and loan covenant requirements) and without conflicting with peak season selling activities or normal employee vacation practices.

In addition, the tax consequences of selecting a particular year-end date should be considered (federal, state and property) with a view to minimizing the overall corporate tax burden.

Other internal considerations include the impact on:

- Budgeting requirements and comparability of data.

- Internal reporting and comparability of data.

- Contractual, incentive and bonus plan arrangements.

BASIS OF PRESENTATION. Of particular significance is the treatment of leased department sales, for example, whether such sales are included or excluded from net sales.

MERCHANDISE INVENTORIES.   Inventories should be indicated as being stated at the lower of cost or market, with the specific cost method indicated, normally the retail method, LIFO method or specific identification.

PROPERTY AND EQUIPMENT.   There should be an indication that these assets are reflected at cost with information regarding the depreciation methodology used and the average lives used for depreciation purposes by category of asset.

STORE PREOPENING COSTS.   This policy note should address whether store preopening costs are charged to operations in the year a new store is opened, or capitalized and amortized over a period of time generally not longer than 12 to 18 months. Preopening costs include those related to employee training, preopening rent and advertising, and new credit card promotions. Indirect general and administrative costs should be expensed as incurred.

DEFERRED REVENUES.   Appliance, electronics or furniture stores may sell service contracts beyond the period covered by the manufacturer's warranty. The policy regarding recognition of revenue arising from the sale of these contracts should be stated. For example, a statement may be included that revenue from the sales of these contracts is recognized over the life of the contract, in a manner that matches revenues to direct expenses and projected product service costs.

REVENUE RECOGNITION.   Layaways and other customer deposit/sales can be recognized when the deposit is received, with appropriate consideration for sales cancellation experience, or when final payment is made and the customer takes the merchandise. The policy for revenue recognition on these transactions should be stated.

Finance charge income must be recognized when earned, assuming it is deemed to be fully collectible. Otherwise, an appropriate allowance for uncollectible amounts should be established. The method utilized for recognizing finance charge income should be included in the policy statement. Retailers are required by the SEC to disclose the amount of their finance charge income and where it is included in the income statement. Some retailers have chosen to show finance charge income as "other income," others have chosen to reflect it as "revenue before cost of goods sold." The most prevalent treatment, however, is to treat finance charge income as a reduction of selling, general and administrative expense. The rationale is that this income represents a recovery of a portion of the costs incurred to realize credit sales and to process and maintain customer accounts receivable.

Inventories

For inventory valuation purposes, retailers need to comply with the general rule that inventory must be stated at the lower of cost or market.

In complying with this requirement, retailers will use the retail method, the LIFO method which effectively is superimposed on the retail method, or one of the cost methods (normally specific identification on average cost).

The market value of inventory is the estimated sales price of merchandise less the normal departmental markon. Application of the retail method will automatically provide an inventory value which is the lower of cost or market assuming the sales price affixed to the merchandise is realistic. This occurs because the cost multiplier used (normally on a departmental basis) to convert the retail of merchandise to cost results in an inventory value which "ensures" the realization of a normal gross margin upon sale of the merchandise. This result is achieved notwithstanding the dollar amount of markdowns taken on merchandise.

The cost method is utilized by retailers with a limited number of SKU items and price lines such as furniture chains, and by specialty retailers with high ticket items such as furs and jewelry. Detailed inventory records must be maintained, normally on a SKU basis or by merchandise classifications. Historically, the cost method is burdensome because the individual sales must be costed out which requires the maintenance of detailed item or classification cost records, making it practical only for retailers with a limited number of items or styles of merchandise. This is changing with the increased capabilities of computers to maintain cost on an item basis, and some retailers have begun to question the need to use the retail method.

The gross profit method, which is an estimating method, is used primarily by drugstore and convenience store chains. In this method, beginning inventory and purchases are reported at cost, and cost of goods sold is calculated using a gross profit percentage. The gross profit percentage is estimated. Physical inventories, costed at actual, are then required in order to adjust the records to actual cost. The estimated gross profit resulting from the use of this method may be suspect because there is never any assurance that the gross profit for any period has not been affected by the mix of merchandise sold. Moreover, gross profits can be manipulated to distort the results of operations by changing the estimated gross profit percentage, a distortion that will not surface pending the taking of a physical inventory. Other problems with the gross profit method are as follows:

- The company does not know, with reasonable accuracy, the amount of inventory on hand at any date in time, particularly in connection with the taking of a physical inventory. Consequently, they are unable to ascertain or quantify the shortage experienced for a period.

- Management has no assurance that its monthly gross profit reporting is accurate. Bearing in mind the absence of any departmental data regarding purchases at cost and retail, and the related impact on gross profit of any significant changes in the mix of merchandise sold. Additionally, the absence of data on departmental markdowns can further distort inventories, particularly when taken in conjunction with the discretion exercised by store managers in establishing and/or revising retail prices.

The retail method is used most often in modern retailing. Under this methodology, which is a form of perpetual inventory maintained at retail prices, effectively, merchandise is controlled by the retail price instead of the cost. Accountability for all changes in the marked selling prices of merchandise is an absolute requirement. In this averaging method, cost multipliers are used to convert inventory from retail to cost at the end of any period. This method provides an excellent control over the retailer's major asset, as well as critical merchandising data (e.g., data regarding initial markon, markdowns, and shortages). Certain definite advantages that are inherent in its use are as follows:

- It permits periodic determination of inventories and profits without resorting to physical inventories.

- It allows the taking of departmental inventories at various dates, other than the general fiscal closing, with appropriate adjustment of the related departmental book record.

- Physical inventories can be taken more expeditiously since they represent compilations of marked retail prices which are readily available to counting personnel.

- Depreciation of inventory values, evidenced by a reduction in selling prices, is obtained as an automatic by-product of the method as soon as retail prices are reduced.

- It discloses the initial markon of purchases, the effect of markdowns on profits, and the amount of stock shortages.

- It facilitates the knowledgeable preparation of merchandise budgets.

- It provides a basis for insurance coverage and settlements.

- And lastly, it tends to disclose, through apparently erroneous results, deficiencies in operational and internal control systems and procedures or in their implementation. (See Chapter Twenty for more on the Retail Method.)

Debt

The footnote disclosure relating to debt includes, in addition to the amounts outstanding, the interest rates, maturity dates, and the most restrictive covenants of the underlying loan agreements, available lines of credit, and collateral for the indebtedness. For retailers, the collateral frequently includes receivables, inventory and tangible fixed assets.

Lease Commitments

Retailers are heavy users of leased physical facilities and to a lesser extent, of leased fixtures and leased equipment. These leases must be classified as operating or capital leases in accordance with State of Financial Accounting Standards No. 13, "Accounting for Leases." This pronouncement, and its subsequent interpretations and amendments, presents numerous problems. Store leases are typically required to be capitalized, but each lease must be evaluated to determine whether it meets the criteria for a capital lease.

With capital leases, an asset and an offsetting liability are recorded. Under operating leases, all costs are reflected as rent expense and no asset or liability recorded. In determining the applicability of FASB No. 13 capitalization criteria, certain factors are unique to retailing, and require the use of judgment as there are few clear-cut answers. For example, in evaluating the economic life of the property being leased, the economic life of the mall or strip center must be considered as well. In addition, leases frequently include options which must be evaluated to determine whether there are bargain renewal options within the definition of FASB No. 13. Given the required level of judgment in applying the criteria of FASB No. 13, two retailers with identical leases in the same mall may reach differing conclusions on the appropriate accounting treatment. The issue of whether a lease is a capital versus an operating lease should be addressed on a store-by-store basis.

The disclosures required by FASB No. 13 for leases include the future minimum lease payments, as of the date of the latest balance sheet, in the aggregate and for each of the five succeeding years. These amounts should be present valued. It is important to note that minimum rents do not include percentage rents, which are very common in retailing.

The total rental expense for each period for which an income statement is presented must also be disclosed, with separate amounts for minimum rents, percentage or contingent rents, and sublease rentals. A brief description of the basis on which percentage rents are computed should be included, as should the fact that options to renew and escalation clauses exist.

In situations where a retail company has closed stores with remaining lease obligations, these obligations must be included in full in the above disclosures.

Other Off-Balance Sheet Financing

Any off-balance sheet financing, in addition to operating lease arrangements, must be disclosed in the notes to the financial statements. These may include disclosures related to guarantees of indebtedness of other companies or individuals.

Exhibit 30.5 reflects an example of the disclosures for notes unique to a retailer's financial statements. Other notes such as disclosures for income taxes, pension and employee benefits, accrued expenses, postretirement benefits, capital stock and option plans are all similar to the disclosures seen in the footnotes to the financial statements of nonretailers.

EXHIBIT 30.5   Sample Notes to Financial Statements

A. Summary of Accounting Policies:

1. *Fiscal Year.*   The Company's fiscal year ends on the last Saturday in January.

2. *Inventory Valuation.*   Merchandise inventories are stated at lower than cost, using the retail last-in, first-out (LIFO) costing method, or market.

3. *Preopening Costs.*   In 19X1 the Company began charging preopening costs to operations in the month a new store opens. Previously, costs associated with opening stores were amortized on a straight-line basis following the opening of each new store over a two year period.

4. *Finance Charge Revenues.*   Finance charges on customer credit accounts are recognized in the period in which they are earned. Unearned finance charges on installment sales contracts are recognized over the contract life.

5. *Closed Facilities under Lease.*   Estimated net future costs related to facilities closed prior to the termination of the related lease agreement are expensed at the time the final decision is made to close the facility. Such costs are recorded at their present value and include future anticipated expenditures required by the lease agreement and other related occupancy costs. Additional costs expensed are those associated with the reduction of fixed assets to realizable values and other costs related to the closings.

6. *Deferred Revenues.*   The Company sells service contracts beyond the manufacturer's warranty period. Revenue from the sale of these contracts is recognized over the life of the contract in a manner which matches revenues to direct selling expenses and projected product service costs. Selling expenses and product service costs

EXHIBIT 30.5 *(Continued)*

relating to the service contracts are charged to operations as incurred.

7. *Property and Equipment.*   Land, buildings, fixtures, and equipment and leasehold improvements are recorded at cost. Property under capital leases is recorded at the lower of the net present value of lease payments or fair market value. Major replacements and betterments are capitalized. Maintenance and repairs are charged to earnings as incurred. Cost of assets sold or retired and the related amounts of accumulated depreciation are eliminated from the accounts in the year of disposal, with the resulting gain or loss included in earnings.

8. *Depreciation and Amortization.*   For financial statement purposes, depreciation and amortization of fixtures and equipment and leasehold improvements are provided on the straight-line method principally over a 10-year period. Depreciation of buildings is provided on a straight-line method principally over a 25-year period. Property under capital leases is amortized on a straight-line basis over the lease terms.

9. *Beneficial Leasehold Interests.*   Beneficial leaseholds are recorded at fair market value net of related tax effect and relate to the unexpired leases of the ABC stores acquired in the ABC merger. Amortization is provided on a straight-line basis over the remaining life of the store leases. Amortization of beneficial leaseholds was approximately $XXX in 19X1 and accumulated amortization at January 26, 19X1 was $XXX.

B. Inventories:

The Company values substantially all of its inventories utilizing the retail last-in, first-out (LIFO) method for stores and the LIFO method for wholesale and warehouse operations. If the first-in, first-out (FIFO) cost method had been used, inventories would have been increased by $XX,XXX at January 26, 19X1.

C. Lease Commitments:

The Company's retail operations are conducted primarily in leased properties. Initial lease terms normally range from 15 to 25 years with renewal options generally available. In most cases, management expects that, in the normal course of business, leases will be renewed or replaced by other leases. The leases are either gross leases, which provide for annual rentals that include executory expenses such as real estate taxes, insurance, common areas and other operating costs paid by the lessor; or

EXHIBIT 30.5 *(Continued)*

net leases which provide that the Company pay the above-mentioned expenses. In addition, the Company subleases portions of certain stores and nearby facilities to subtenants whose operations are intended to complement the Company's marketing strategy.

Contingent rent expense, which is based on sales, includes $XXX incurred on capital leases for 19X1.

Certain leases have provisions which could require restoration of leased premises at the termination of the lease. The accounting for capital leases includes estimates for significant restoration obligations, while restoration costs related to operating leases are accrued at the time they are reasonably determinable and it is considered probable that the Company will incur such costs.

Future minimum lease activity as of January 26, 19X1 is as follows (000s omitted):

Fiscal Year Ending	Lease Payments		Sublease Income	
	Capital Leases	Operating Leases	Capital Leases	Operating Leases
19X2	$	$	$	$
19X3				
19X4				
19X5				
19X6				
Thereafter	———	———	———	———
Total minimum lease payments	XX XXX	X XXX	(XXX)	(XXX)
Less amount representing estimated executory costs	XXX			
Net minimum lease payments	XX XXX			
Less amount representing interest	X XXX			
Present value of net minimum lease payments	XX XXX			
Less currently payable	XXX			
Long-term capital lease obligation	$XX XXX			

EXHIBIT 30.5   *(Continued)*

Amortization of capital leases was approximately $X in 19X1.
Accumulated amortization of capital leases at January 26, 19X1 was $X.
Rent expense was as follows (000s omitted):

	Fiscal Year Ended January 26, 19X1
Minimum rent on operating leases	$XX XXX
Contingent rentals	XXX
Sublease rentals	(XXX)

SUMMARY

The Financial Executives' Division of the National Retail Merchants Association has developed and promoted the adoption of standard content and format for retailers' financial statements. The key reference for the preparation of a retailer's financial statements is their Retail Accounting Manual, Books I & II. These manuals place emphasis on merchandise accounting and management reporting, and contain a detailed explanation of expense center accounting.

Book I also discusses merchandise accounting, with particular emphasis on the determination of gross margin. It details the accounting for nonretail operations such as cost departments, workrooms and other costs associated with sales. Another area discussed in Book I is management reporting for retailers. This section details various types of reports which may be helpful in management's analysis of the company and its performance.

Book II includes a chart of accounts for the balance sheet with detailed explanations of what is typically included in each. It discusses cash management, with particular emphasis on forecasting, and items to be considered in maximizing cash flow. There is also a section dealing with the issues facing a retailer considering a change to the LIFO inventory costing method, including a detailed explanation of the various LIFO calculations required.

Other sections cover warehousing and distribution, fixed asset accounting, budgeting, and financial reporting as it relates to the impact of changing prices and current cost. The final section of Book II provides guidelines for records retention.

CHAPTER THIRTY-ONE

Financial Statement Analysis

This chapter addresses the review of financial statements and nonfinancial factors used by financial analysts to gather key information about a retailer's operating performance. This can be a very difficult task due to differences in accounting policies and disclosures. Included in the group of financial analysts are creditors, investment bankers, stockholders, and prospective purchasers. Each type of analyst has his own methodology for evaluation of the financial statements, and will take into consideration a variety of nonfinancial factors in evaluating the retail company.

One of the first issues that the analyst encounters is whether the accounting income can be relied upon as a fair presentation of earnings, compared with prior performance. In a period of high inflation, the impact of inflation must be taken into consideration. Real growth statistics are expressed with the impact of inflation removed.

Analysts are also alert to possible income manipulation which can be accomplished and disguised in a variety of ways, including adjusting cost estimates, shifting costs and revenues between periods, and changing accounting policies. Due to the numerous alternative accounting policies available, it is frequently difficult to compare one retailer to the next. Studies have shown that the accounting method selected by a company did not influence the judgment of analysts as long as sufficient information was provided, in the notes to the financial statements, to make comparisons with other companies in the same retail segment. For example, most analysts are familiar enough with LIFO to be able to adjust the accounting income reported with income reported utilizing the retail method for valuing inventories.

The valuation of the assets is another difficult task for the analyst. Asset valuation frequently cannot be performed simply by analyzing the financial statements since the methodology for writing down asset values, namely, depreciation, is only a method for allocating cost over a period of years. Visiting the stores, with a view to noting whether they are attractive and appear to be well maintained is preferable. It is also important for an analyst to obtain an understanding of the retailer's store renovation and merchandising policies that can be the keys to future capital requirements and inventory valuation issues. Also of interest are hidden asset values, particularly in owned real estate and in valuable leaseholds.

Financial analysts can make various judgments from a scrutiny of financial statements and from physical inspection of the retailer's physical facilities. However, in the final analysis, it is often the quality of management that determines the failure or success of a retail company.

A comprehensive analysis of a retailer can be made by focusing upon five major areas—merchandising, store operations, management team, real estate, and information systems. These areas are interdependent and a weakness in any one can limit the success of the retailer.

MERCHANDISING

A successful retailer must have a merchandising strategy and a focused customer base. To effectively evaluate the company, a financial analyst must have a thorough understanding of the retailer's pricing strategy and identified target customer.

One of the most important factors in the merchandising analysis is market niche. The analyst must determine how well entrenched the retailer is in the identified market niche, the competition, and the demographics within the identified niche.

During interviews with key members of management, significant information should be obtained to evaluate how effectively the retailer is reacting to the dynamics of the marketplace and the needs of customers. Items of interest include status of vendor relations, the availability of normal industry trade credit, and the payment terms being experienced by the retailer.

In addition, information should be obtained regarding the increases or decreases in the number of customer transactions, changes in the average sale amount, the calibre and strength of the competition, how the company is reacting to competition, and future growth anticipated and how it will be funded.

Advertising and sales promotion are an integral part of merchandising. The analyst needs an appreciation of the retailer's strategy, including the nature and cost of media utilized and the overall merchandising objectives of the promotional program.

STORE OPERATIONS

Store operations can best be evaluated by visiting the stores for first hand review of merchandise presentations and the condition and quality of store fixturing. Discussions with operations personnel should address the way management monitors individual store operations, including visits by members of management and buyers, reviews of store operating performance against budget and last year, how store managers are compensated, and how store managers interface with area or district managers and headquarters merchandising personnel, particularly with regard to merchandise replenishment. In addition, operations personnel should be asked to disclose the number of marginally profitable and/or loss stores and the company's plans for either turning around or disposing of these stores.

Customer relationships and credit policies also affect retail operations. An understanding of how credit programs are used to attract and retain customers is beneficial. Analysts should be aware of, and understand, other programs offered such as layaways and personal shopping.

MANAGEMENT TEAM

Some analysts feel so strongly about the importance of good management that they believe they can identify a successful retailer by following good, experienced management from retailer to retailer. Key questions for evaluating management are:

- How knowledgeable and committed are they?
- Do they have an ownership interest?
- How have they programmed the company to grow?
- What is the quality of the people with which they have surrounded themselves?
- Does management maintain tight control over the company?

A key factor in analyzing management is whether there is a definitive strategic direction for the company, complete with in-depth planning for the future.

Analysts need to obtain information on management, particularly their experience with the company and any prior employment experience. An organization chart should be obtained with a view to determining the lines of responsibility, accountability, and to identify the key decision makers. It is important to have depth of experience and quality key personnel in merchandising, advertising and sales promotion, operations, finance and control, management information systems, and warehousing and distribution. A weakness in any one of these areas can cause significant problems for the retailer.

Analysts should ascertain the degree of top management's involvement with the individual stores. Management training programs, and other training programs across the board, can be quite important to the success of the retailer.

The best management is usually the most motivated. The analyst should obtain a thorough understanding of the management incentive/bonus programs and other employment agreements. Employee benefit plans should be reviewed for all levels of employees. Sales force incentive programs directly impact customer service, and must be evaluated for effectiveness.

REAL ESTATE

It is important for retail financial analysts to tour a company's stores on a recurring basis. In addition to evaluating store locations, this permits a determination of the quality of the stores, whether they have been regularly renovated or if significant capital expenditures will be required in the near future. Analysts want to know if there are problem stores that should be closed, and what the costs associated with the store closings will be. Moreover, they will be interested in determining the impact of store closing on sales and bottom-line results.

After payroll, rent is one of the major expenses for retailers. The terms of the leases, including escalation clauses, the remaining renewal options, and the amount of percent of sales rent and common area maintenance charges above base rent must be evaluated. A well-negotiated lease that maintains a stable level of rent expense well into the future can result in a significant benefit to the bottom line.

INFORMATION SYSTEMS

Automated Information Systems play a vital role in merchandising, monitoring, and controlling all facets of operations at management levels. Analysts should ascertain how up-to-date the management information and business support systems are and whether they provide accurate information on a timely basis. They should also determine how effectively management uses these tools.

FINANCIAL RATIOS AND OTHER CONSIDERATIONS

See Chapter Nineteen. Typical financial ratios monitored by analysts are:

- Comparable store sales and operating profit.
- Sales per square foot.
- Gross margins in total and by merchandising category.
- Operating expense ratios.
- Pretax and net income as a percent of sales (return on sales).
- Return on assets.
- Return on capital.
- Interest coverage ratios.
- Total debt as a percent of capital.

SUMMARY

Analysts perform historical trend analyses of sales, gross margin and other income statement amounts, and attempt to project into the future based on the trends. They monitor closely the real growth of sales after eliminating the impact of inflation.

Analysts look for a consistent pattern of growth in sales and net income. Other financial information analyzed includes the size of debt and how well it can be managed with current cash flow.

There are different concerns for department stores, specialty stores, and discounters. Department stores normally need less cash flow and can afford extra leverage. On the other hand, specialty stores must be more flexible and need to expand in order to increase their sales volume. There is a greater risk associated with specialty stores since theirs is more of a "rifle-shot" approach to the various markets. However, there is normally a bigger payback in a specialty store market because higher gross margins can be maintained.

Discounters have a lower gross margin and, therefore, must maintain lower operating expense percentages. An indication of a troubled retail situation and one of potential store/company failure is a decline in comparative store sales. In addition, one can often predict a store's failure by visiting the store and noting whether there is poor housekeeping, a lack of discipline, particularly as reflected in minimal service to customers, and a poorly presented and inadequate stock position. Another indication would be a decline in the gross margin realized by the retailer when compared with others in the same industry segment.

While a retailer's financial statements provide key financial information, a more thorough and in-depth knowledge of the company is necessary to properly evaluate current and prospective viability. Analysts must visit the stores, talk to members of management, and become familiar with the retailer's market niche. Only then will the picture be complete.

Index